Betty Jerman

Kids' Britain

PICCOLO

First published 1986 by Pan Books Limited
This revised edition published 1992 by
PAN MACMILLAN CHILDREN'S BOOKS
a division of Pan Macmillan Limited
Cavaye Place, London SW10 9PG

9 8 7 6 5 4 3 2

ISBN 0 330 32030 0

Designed by Gavin Dodds
Typeset by Pan Macmillan Production
Printed and bound in Great Britain by
Clays Limited, St Ives plc

Contents

Dedicated to my children
and your children

Foreword

Education? Yes, this book is about education if you define it as being about the whole child, expanding horizons, offering challenges, laying the foundations for adult life through an appreciation of beauty in paintings, music, wildlife, an understanding of the past so as to have an informed understanding of the present, an introduction to the magic of theatre, discovering the excitement of reading for pleasure that can bring such joy in childhood and in adult life, opportunities for friendship through mingling with others, developing physical skills through exercise or through sports so that the body is also in tune.

After all, if you had a Good Fairy at the christening you would hope she would grant a child happiness, not riches but enrichment, a good life not confined to a narrow, discontented perspective but brimming with contentment. Childhood nurture of potential intellectual and physical talents is a powerful influence on children's well-being. So that is what this book is about. It is about having fun too.

Part one: Family outings

Here you will find information about where to take the children for a quite extraordinary range of experiences, discoveries, adventures.

Palaces, castles, stately homes that were once fortresses (who was feuding against whom?), and their furniture, silver, porcelain, weaponry, family portraits, memorabilia, domestic quarters, are all a wonderful source of social, historical and cultural education.

There are museums on every conceivable subject, hundreds of years of history, political, social, natural, of wars, forms of transport, industry, about maritime life human and fishy, about costume, childhood, and some even re-creating life and work in times past. You could be pleasantly surprised by their new ways of presentation and interpretation to help understanding, especially in those devoted to science and technology.

You will find farms with domestic animals, safari parks with wild ones, any amount of country landscape, woods and lakes to explore.

I hope you will be astonished, intrigued by the sheer variety of what there is nationally to delight all ages.

Schools and playgroups should also find some fresh ideas for visits here.

Part two: Children in mind

Exciting opportunities offered to children – sometimes parent-accompanied (say to museums, art galleries, theatres) and sometimes just delivered and collected. Think of preparing foods from different periods, making, devising and/or constructing any number of objects from any number of materials (I touch only briefly on these when I mention ornaments, toys and embroideries on the craft side). They could be trying out how people lived, dressing up, re-enacting the past. Or discovering the joys of reading for pleasure. Or learning theatrical skills, clowning, make-up, acting, filming. Or listening to music and/or playing instruments themselves. Or looking at paintings and sculptures, or any number of historic objects with some enlightenment about what they are seeing. Or trying, tasting, a variety of sports. This section is about **for**, as well as **by**, children. It also covers activities for the highly gifted and for the handicapped.

> Working parents who always have children in mind, especially in out-of-school hours, will find some clues here on organizing child care.

Part three: Going it alone

This section is about children going to day camps or to residential camps to live with people other than the family, mostly other children, and cared for by other adults.

Betty Jerman 1992

Against all odds

The Queen, as a girl, went to museums, the London Zoo, generally with her grandmother Queen Mary. I imagined that today, with photographers behind every bush hoping to cash in by catching the Royals off guard, the Princes William and Harry would not be able to go on such outings like children not in the limelight. I held forth indignantly about this injustice, 'Poor little Princes', to Captain Barry Newman, managing director of the Beckonscot Model Village, Beaconsfield, which is proud to have been visited by the Princess Elizabeth and her grandmother.

I was wrong. The Princes too went to Beckonscot. First there was a phone-call from the Prince of Wales's office. When they arrived their detective checked with their nanny if Harry was young enough, under 3, to get in free before otherwise paying for admission like anyone else. All were in casual clothes including their nanny who would have drawn attention in uniform. Barry Newman commented that if other visitors did recognize them, they had the courtesy to let them enjoy themselves unimpeded by public attention.

Around the same time, probably by chance, a passing professional photographer recognized them in the children's playground at London's Coram's Fields. *Today* newspaper followed this up and drew from Buckingham Palace: 'The Princes are taken to lots of different parks and places every day but for security reasons no arrangements are made in advance.'

Intrigued by the possibility that their parents might cleverly manage to give them the kind of childhood experiences and memories our children take for granted, even against the odds and the public attention, I have since followed their adventures, now in the school holidays.

Harry with nanny chatted to an angler by the Serpentine and went on the *Belfast* in the Thames. With detective and nanny they both went to the London Zoo, saw jousting knights at Littlecote, travelled on London Underground. Both boys went to Slimbridge Wildfowl and Wetlands Centre with their father but he took only Harry round SS *Great Britain* in Bristol. They met Santa Claus at

Selfridges with their mother and went to a Disney film. With the Princess they drove on the dodgems at a Cotswold fair and another time, at Alton Towers, got wet on the water chute. They learned about maritime life with their maternal grandmother at Oban's Sea Life Centre. They have also visited the London Toy Museum, dropped into the Natural History Museum like other Londoners and regularly attended what Ann Rachlin calls her 'Musical United Nations' where she narrates her own stories to music.

I know all this from newspaper reports, maybe a gossip column item after the event, sometimes a picture with a story that it was a while before they were recognized, since they paid, where necessary queued, and were as casually clothed as any other group.

It is understandable that some tourist attractions would notify a national newspaper *after* Royals visit to promote their appeal, but it is too far-fetched to suggest that professional photographers stake out the country's theme parks during the school holidays in case they pick on the right one. It is a reasonable assumption that the Princess is first recognized in the throng and, since a camera is often carried on days outdoors, it is the amateurs who swing into action and produce the photographs that have appeared in newspapers.

Several national tabloids carried pictures of the Princess and her sons at Thorpe Park during the 1991 Easter bank holiday. Out of interest I checked with the management. Informed beforehand that the party was coming they had told no one, had not tipped off any newspapers.

So it does look as though this family's determination that their children should be discovering, exploring, trying things out for themselves in the extraordinary variety of delights for the young in this country today, like any children, is bedevilled by amateur as well as professional picture-takers. I still suspect that they have successfully managed visits to a number of the other attractions I have mentioned here with no one intruding on their private lives, even if other visitors have recognized them.

Official near future Royal Engagements are listed in the *Daily Telegraph* and the day's engagements in *The Times* and the *Independent.*

A plea

Windsor Castle closes for Garter Day in June, Holyrood also in June for the Queen's annual visit to Scotland, Sandringham when the Royal Family is in residence and now even at Christmas with building work going on at Windsor, the Crown Jewels for their annual clean-up. Many museums and art galleries close Good Friday, Christmas and New Year's Day; some close Mondays. But then Sandringham can be closed one weekend for a royal party, the Museum of Costume in Bath was closed for some time to put right structural defects, Osborne House opened late one season because of repairs and London's Monument closed for around a week for building work. I was in York once and found a new attraction closed for the day, earlier than set out in the printed leaflet in my hand. We would have been there earlier but had been warned that the Minster would be closing earlier than usual that day and entirely the next for a royal-attended occasion, so had gone there first.

If regular or temporary closures occur at that level then they can surely happen with small, maybe family-run enterprises. Soon after the first edition of *Kids' Britain* was published I heard that one centre I had mentioned had burned down, another had closed because of a death in the family, yet another had changed hands and become a totally different kind of business.

None of this, if you think about it, is extraordinary or a matter of astonishment. Yet I also heard from several readers who had filled a car or a minibus with children, set off for a considerable journey and were annoyed with me when pleasurable anticipation turned into grumpy frustration because the chosen goal was closed. My sympathies. I can imagine the disappointment, especially for the children.

So *please, please*, do not take anything for granted when planning an expedition. Balance the cost of a checking phone-call against such a let-down.

Part one:
Family outings

Introduction

We were studying the diagram outside Nottingham Castle. Alongside a man, with a baby in a back sling, lifted up his son, who did not look as if he had yet celebrated his fifth birthday, and pointed out on the plan how the castle 'used to be'. Later I saw them again by Mortimer's Hole, where he was explaining about the 'noblemen' who entered the castle that way to sort out the medieval royal power problems.

I shall never know whether his children, by junior-school days, will be groaning, 'Oh, Dad, not another museum' (or stately home or ruin) when he proposes a family outing. They will certainly have unconsciously absorbed not only educationally useful amounts of historical information but also quantities of impressions, slants, memories and tastes.

I know about that since my husband also spread his interests and considerable knowledge before our children, which is how I came to be going round Hatfield House, for the first time, with toddler son slung round my neck like a scarf. Could not risk lurchings towards Queen Elizabeth I's stockings! Still have happy memories of a return visit with school-age daughter and friends and sitting in the sun in period-style fragrant gardens.

But same son, in another stately home, on his own feet (though we were as usual far behind rest of family) was deeply shocked when a floor-to-ceiling door suddenly opened beside him and a female guide hissed, 'You don't come this way.' It put him off ancient monuments and stately homes for years.

Fortunately there is now, among those in the family outings business, a great deal more sensible thinking about all ages and their requirements.

Outings can be from your temporary holiday home, hotel, motel, caravan or cottage.

A family on holiday can include individuals who enjoy

sandcastles, pool dipping, playing beach games and those bored by that and wanting to play golf or visit a tiny church. Recognize that the party *can* divide, and that parents can influence choices. A mother and son can well mutually enjoy art collections, theatre, while father and daughter go riding, or father and son can explore churches while mother and daughters beachcomb. Or vice versa!

It's the same at home. You could have down the road (well, relatively near) a medieval hunting lodge, an ancient battle site, a wildlife park and/or a major sports complex.

Outings can be for an afternoon, a whole day, at weekends, on bank holidays, in half-terms, or during the school holidays.

This is not always about spending money, paying entry. Childhood memories are made of feeding the ducks in the park, a wander along a river bank and maybe spotting a kingfisher, squelching toes in wet sand and dancing away from the waves.

So what are you seeing?

I once read in a newspaper gossip column about the Queen inviting a guest to look at the 'OOmas', meaning, 'OO, Ma, this is a Rubens'. I've done it myself (silently) faced with the original of a painting seen so often in reproduction. Telling a child that 'This is a famous painting' is not enough. Why is it?

What I am getting at is that you can drift around stunning exhibits, pictures, settings (indoors/outdoors), missing most of what they are about. So I recommend buying the printed guides, or joining up with guided groups, even for fees. Sometimes you will find child-based material (or adult-based needing interpretation) about what's what, what to look for, in both newer museums and galleries and the long-established. I do wish that more of the type of attractions I have listed would provide the kind of material (worksheets, quizzes) that they produce for schools and make such visits so valuable. It is always worth asking to make a need known. But you could be astonished at what you dig out from long-forgotten school lessons, surprised how centuries-old marriages, political goings-on, have relevance worldwide today, as will your children in time. So it's fascination for all ages.

And I mean *all* ages. The retired usually get discounts on entry charges. I've met them taking grandchildren around in the many short and long school holidays, as well as in family parties. They are a special bonus, particularly in places now showing what life was like for ordinary folk, rural or town-dwelling. They can explain from personal memories strange things like mangles, that black stuff called coal, the 'blue bag', not for dyeing everything blue but for making things whiter than white before detergents (also a remedy for insect stings), and about those jugs and bowls in the bedroom for washing or about carrying a bath into the kitchen, to be filled from kettles, since hot water did not come out of the tap. It could be about working with a horse or hankering for the exotic cars now gleaming in museums and borrowed, or copied, for films.

I have mentioned buying printed materials, taking it that you inspect first to see if it is what you want, because otherwise you can miss so much of what to see indoors and outdoors. If you do buy, then file them away ready to lend or swap with other families, especially in the south-east for those who gravitate to London for outings. Special cheers for those who put up plentiful information, to read on site or as audio-visuals.

What's new? Well, 'Talking Heads', seeming to move, express, speak (through modern technology), are a lively way of bringing a display, an exhibition, to life. Personally, I find the taped commentary (either in a cassette linked to earphones, or hand-held) – to use a cliché – the 'greatest thing since sliced bread'. You can pause, take a longer look, savour single treasures. With printed information I seem to spend more time reading than looking. Admittedly an illustrated guide can always be looked at again.

Costs

Writing my *Guardian* 'What's on in the school holidays' I am constantly shocked by what a family treat will cost. All praise to parents who feel such expenditure is worthwhile. Luckily the majority of our museums and galleries charge no entry fees so you can balance between one charging and one free. But I do wish those charging would still let children in free. After all, they are the future.

Noticeably the shop, on the way out, is now almost inevitably there to tempt us. The pocket money items can be much the same pens nationwide with the appropriate name printed or, in some places, a carefully chosen selection worthwhile buying as a souvenir.

I am not assuming everyone travels by car, though many road numbers are given. It's certainly worth writing or phoning to get leaflets or information on exactly where, and what's on when, and how you can get there. Look for public transport discounts like British Rail's Family Railcard.

Under-5s (even under-6s) generally get free entry but you can meet the 'No pushchairs' notice, or find them unmanoeuvrable over steep stairs; baby under arm, buggy slung over other, eyes swivelling towards other child innocently marking stately walls. Solved by baby sling and/or division of family into 'You go first, then I'll go' accompanied by different ages. Parents do take very young children to places they will barely comprehend. But that is what it is all about. In a year or so you want to go back, to fire your growing children with the fascination.

At what age children should be taken into historic houses is a moot point. Children come in 57 varieties of personality. You will know your own child. But a youngster, through its parents, absorbs that here is something worthwhile, something to relish, of interest, grows accustomed to such an experience. Think of the dad at Nottingham Castle. On the other hand, think too that most stately homes lie in acres of open land with possibly lakes, wildlife, maybe deer, even if they do not provide playgrounds or pets' corners where younger ones can see young animals, and living chickens pecking round are often as extraordinary a sight for today's children as a tiger in a safari park or an elephant in a zoo. The 'grounds' are often a separate entry charge.

Take especial note that the admission charges given will only give you a rough idea of expenditure; they *do* increase. Sometimes too there are extras besides refreshments or parking.

Schools

The majority of the attractions I have mentioned cater for
school groups. I would hope that teachers will find something
they did not know about, worth exploring as a possible
class/classes visit. Parents too appreciate that school excursions
are an integral part of the learning process. Museums and art
galleries have their own Education Departments; more historic
houses, safari parks, even theme parks, have them too. Some
stately homes provide special accommodation for school
groups; sometimes they will be greeted by people dressed in
costumes of earlier periods, so as to give atmosphere. Packs,
with quizzes, guides, illustrations and information, are generally
available. May I mention that from a number of many different
projects, I heard the recommendation that, for the best service,
school groups should always be booked beforehand.

Geographical

For clarity, I hope, I have assembled **Family Outings** according to
the **Tourist Board** areas and arranged this section geographically.

The map on the following spread shows the whole of the
United Kingdom divided into **Tourist Board** areas. There is also
a map showing the boundaries of each individual area at the
beginning of each section. But remember that an attraction in
one Tourist Board area can be only a mile or so from one in an
adjoining board's area. Most boards produce useful leisure
maps marking and lifting from the usual geographical detail
those places which could interest families. They also produce
solid booklets. Look, too, for signs to **Tourist Information
Centres** where you will find useful leaflets and information.

This is really about being a tourist in your own country and,
with such a wealth of things to see and do, it seems ungrateful to
stay at home!

Symbols used in the book

Under many entries you will find one or more symbols. These are designed to give extra information about the places mentioned in an economical and easy-to-refer-to way.

Means that **admission is free**: but, in some museums and galleries, if a *special* exhibition has been mounted you may have to pay to see that. It's always worth checking on entry fees – they do change.

This means that **groups are welcome** and are offered special rates, guided tours, etc., *if booked in advance*. A group may be an extended family, church group, playgroup, Brownie troop, etc. It may be mostly children with adults in charge, or all adults. Always double-check special terms and/or preferred times for group visits.

This refers **specifically to school groups**, for which special rates and visiting times can be arranged. A school party will consist of several children under adult supervision.

Means that children (especially the very young) are welcome to visit or take part if **accompanied by an adult**. Occasionally an adult may attend *only* if accompanied by a child member (i.e. National Film Theatre).

Means children are welcomed **unaccompanied by an adult** to visit (museums/galleries) or to theatre or film performances. It often means, too, that children are welcome to *take part* in specially organized regular activities throughout the year or during holiday times (i.e. theatre, film-making, orchestras, sports, etc.), or to stay for a residential holiday without parents as in **Section 3**.

This means that there are **facilities for people with disabilities** which may include special facilities for the deaf and partially sighted. See also the special section on the handicapped.

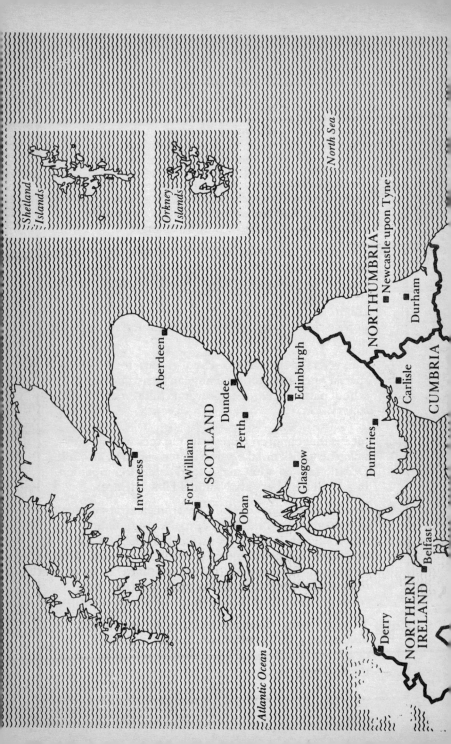

West
Country

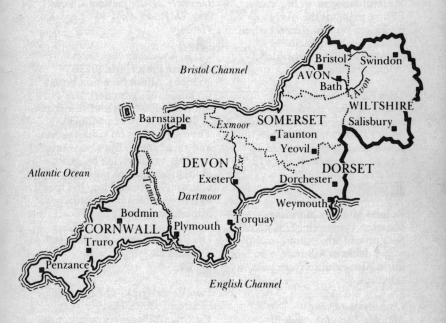

Cornwall

Geevor Tin Mines Pendeen, nr Penzance. A30 [0736 788662]. One of the few tin mines in Cornwall still producing tin so you can see the big machinery and the mill separating the tin from the rock at surface level. Underground tours also (10-year-olds upwards). Mining and Mineral Museum in the Visitor Centre explains the history, including pre-war disaster when the sea broke in, includes working models, maps, also a video presentation.

Open Easter–September Sunday–Friday, also Saturday in school holidays, museum and video, adult £1.90, OAP/child £1.25, family ticket, surface tours £3.25 and £2, underground tours £12.50 and £10.
🏛 🚻 🔳

Roland Morris's Maritime Museum Penzance [0736 63890]. Section of 18th-century man-o'-war, 4 decks of full-scale men and guns. Also exhibits from sunken warships.

Open April–October, Monday–Saturday, adult £1, OAP/child 75p.

Chysauster Ancient Village Newmill, nr Penzance. 1³/₄ miles from Badgers Cross on B3311 [0736 61889]. Some 2000 years old, late Iron Age, mostly Roman-British. Residents were cattle herders and tin workers. 9 houses, most of them intact with the original height of the walls. Single stony track around 400 yards from car park up to village. Superb views, land and sea. Children's activity books on Celts and Romans available. Occasional theme plays, story-telling in summer.

Open daily Easter–September, otherwise closed Monday and December 24–26, January 1, adult 85p, OAP 65p, child 40p. English Heritage.
🏛 🚻

Paradise Park Hayle [0736 753365]. About breeding birds in danger of extinction. You can see some 400 birds and animals in 100 aviaries and paddocks. The emphasis is on conservation and rare breeds. But also young animals – rabbits, lambs, goats, chinchillas, guinea pigs – for children to see and touch. Otter sanctuary. Falconry centre. Miniature railway.

Open daily all year, adult £4, OAP £3, child £2.
🏛 🚻

Flambards Triple Theme Park Helston [0326 574549]. Victorian Village: reconstruction with 40 shops, cobbled streets, figures, fashions and the 'Chemist Shop Time Capsule', the entire contents of the sealed-over-100-years Somerset chemist

> **Admission charges:** don't assume these are static. In many cases I found that increases were envisaged for the next season.

shop, discovered in 1987, except drugs now considered dangerous but once readily for sale like morphine and arsenic. Britain in the Blitz: life-size re-creation of a wartime street with the whine of bombs, shelters, sandbags, and the heart-pulling evacuation of children. Cornwall Aero Park: aeroplanes, helicopters, many with accessible flight decks to explore. Splendid gardens. You pay extra for boats, rides, dry swimming in a ball pool, bouncing on a cushion of air, supercinema. Exploratorium: hands-on science, beamed voices, bouncing a ball on air, making bubble pictures, shaking hands with your reflection. Free 'Route Guide for the Disabled' and wheelchairs available if booked.

Open daily Easter–October, adult £6.99, OAP £3.50, child £5.99.

Cornish Seal Sanctuary Gweek, nr Helston [032622 3611]. 10 pools, one for sick or injured whales and dolphins, seal hospital, aquarium, nature trail, exhibition hall, donkey paddock.

Open daily all year, adult £3.75, OAP £3, child £1.80, winter (limited facilities) £2, £1.50 and £1.

Poldark Mine Wendron, Helston [0326 573173]. 18th-century Cornish tin mine with choice of 3 underground routes. You wear protective helmets. You can post a letter in Britain's deepest post-

box. Cornish Heritage Museum and Poldark Village, 14 chambers with collections from the past including the domestic side. Museum quiz with cash prize. Also indoor and outdoor amusements, bikes, boats, inflatables, dry swimming.

Open daily mid March–October, adult £4.25, OAP £3, child £2.50, smaller charges some days after 6 p.m. and Saturday, with museum and mine tour extra.

Shire Horse Farm and Carriage Museum Treskillard, Redruth [0209 713606]. Shire horses, of course, with wagon rides included in admission charge. Display of horse-drawn vehicles. Old farming implements. Working blacksmith's shop and wheelwright's.

Open Easter–June and September–October Sunday–Friday, July 1–August 31 daily, adult £2.50, child £1.50.

Where no admission price information included this **does not mean that admission is free**, only that details not available at time of writing. Telephone or write if you wish to know details in advance. Free admission is shown by

St Agnes Leisure Park St Agnes [087255 2793]. Cornwall in miniature, dinosaurs, fairyland, Haunted House, Grand Animated Circus, Super X Simulator, etc. in large landscaped gardens.

Open daily March–October, adult £3.80, OAP £3.20, child £2.50.
▦ 🚌 ▨

World in Miniature Bodmin Road, Goonhavern. B3285 [087257 2828]. Large scale models (Buckingham Palace and the White House each 24 ft long), Mount Rushmore with presidents' faces 30 ft high, the Parthenon as it was 20 ft long and 8 ft high, also the Leaning Tower of Pisa, Statue of Liberty, Stonehenge, etc. Various materials are used, some natural wood and stone, some fibreglass. Also a life-size reconstruction of a Western town called Tombstone. You walk around, see the animated figures in the saloon, jail, barber shop, livery stable, bank, etc. You can sit in or on the stagecoach, prairie wagon, or fibreglass horses to have a picture taken. Cinema. Adventuredome with thrills.

Open daily mid March–October, adult £3.80, OAP £3.20, child £2.50.
▦ 🚌 ▨

Dairyland Farm Park and Country Life Museum Trefillian, Barton, Summercourt, nr Newquay. A3058 [087251 246]. Working farm of some 550 acres

where a herd of 160 cows can be seen from a viewing gallery being milked daily around 3.15 p.m. Also Country Life Museum with old farm implements including tractors. Also Farm Park with pigs, cows, goats, rabbits, game birds, guinea pigs, ducks, donkeys, etc. which can be fed and/or touched, as appropriate.

Open daily April–October, adult £3.80, OAP £3.50, child £2.20.
▦ 🚌

Dobwalls Theme Park Dobwalls, nr Liskeard [0579 20325, Info line 0579 20578]. Miniature railway steam or diesel with 2 miles of scenery based on American Rio Grande and Union Pacific railroads. Mr Thorburn's Edwardian Countryside, series of small galleries where you can see, smell and touch re-creations of the wildlife Thorburn painted, and see the pictures. Life-size models, soundtracks of birdsong and animal cries. Braille pad introductions. Viewing holes at wheelchair height. 5 adventure play areas, aerial cableways, 2 enclosed slides.

Open daily all year but limited winter train facilities. Admission adult £5.99, OAP/child £3.99, reduced after 2.30 p.m. and excluding train rides.

Goonhilly Satellite Earth Station Goonhilly Downs, Helston TR12 6LQ [0872 78551]. Watch world events first-hand as data is beamed to the giant aerials via orbiting satellites. Operate a TV dish aerial. Visitor Centre with museum, audio-visual show. Conducted bus trip tours the station. The Downs are a nature reserve with wild plants, animals and birds.

Station open daily Easter–end October, adult £2.50, OAP/child £1.50.

Land's End Sennen, TR19 7AA [0736 871501]. The First and Last House. Famous signpost. Dollar Cove Suspension Bridge. 'Man Against the Sea' exhibition. 'Spirit of Cornwall' exhibition, traditions, mining, fishing. Greeb Cottage, typical smallholder's home with sheep, pigs, poultry, craftsmen now in residence. Little Cornwall, miniature settings. 'The Last Labyrinth' (not for very young), dramatic legends through medium of electronic theatre. Playgrounds. Tours by Landtrain or Horse-drawn bus. School holiday events like Easter egg hunt, October teddy bear month, owners given free entry.

Open daily except Christmas Day, single charge adult £4.95, child £2.50, less out of July–September.

St Michael's Mount Mount's Bay [0736 710507]. Reached by foot at low tide or by boat (charges around 60p each way, child half fare). 14th-century castle with narrow passages so numbers restricted at any one time. Fine views towards Land's End.

Open daily Easter–October, Monday–Friday, otherwise conducted tours only. Educational tours (booked) April–May. Adult £2.80, child £1.40. National Trust.

World of Model Railways Meadow Street, Mevagissey [0726 842457]. Watch the trains going round, some 2000 models from old-fashioned locomotives to modern equipment, probably the largest collection in the world. Automatic functioning over around half a mile of track, all indoors.

Open Easter and daily spring bank holiday–October, winter Sunday afternoons, adult £1.75, OAP/child £1.25.

Wheal Martyn Museum St Austell [0726 850362]. 19th-century clay works restored with working water wheels. Also ancient vehicles, locomotives. Nature trail, children's adventure trail.

Open daily April–October, adult £3.20, child £1.60.

Charlestown Shipwreck and Heritage Centre nr St Austell [0726 69897]. Audio-visual display on history of Charlestown with working models of blacksmiths, coopers. There is a display of shipwreck material, which you will also come across elsewhere in this county.

Open daily April–October, entry charges.

Land of Legend and Model Village Polperro [0503 72378]. Outdoor, knee-high replica of this fishing village. Booklet explains about the 'House on Props' built over river, the Shell House, covered in shells, the smugglers' cottage. Indoors, in what was the old forge, 'Land of Legend', audio-visual with large puppets. Merlin puppet tells the stories of King Arthur; the 3 witches of Cornwall; legend of white hare (seen by tin miners as portent of disaster); Helston's annual dance; stories about wreckers, china clay, etc.

Open daily March–October, adult £1.20, OAP/child 60p.

The Monkey Sanctuary nr Looe (signposted) [05036 2532]. Breeding colony of woolly monkeys who come out into the grounds, trees, among visitors.

Open 2 weeks at Easter and May–mid September, Sunday–Thursday, adult £3.50, child £2.50.

Lanreath Farm and Folk Museum Churchtown, Lanreath, nr Looe [0503 20321]. All kinds of engines, farm implements, also cider press, working mill, old-style kitchen. Demonstrations of what did what.

Open Easter–October Sunday–Friday, adult £1.75, child £1.

Carnglaze Slate Caverns St Neot, nr Liskeard. Off A38 [0579 20251]. 500-year-old slate caverns, cathedral size. On the surface a natural setting of cliffs and gardens, where visitors, having bought their tour ticket, have been known to sit around, enjoy and wait for the next tour. But no picnicking is allowed because some people leave tins/cans which damage the wild creatures who come out at night. 40-minute tour includes the history of the mine, how it was worked and a demonstration of tools used. Entry down flight of stairs, so pushchairs need to be parked. Children of **all age groups** visit, but wrap up warm, the caverns are chilly. Tour includes lakes – a little one and a stunning big one, brilliantly turquoise blue (rousing Oohs and Aahs).

Open daily Easter–September, adult £2.50, OAP/child £2.

Tropical Bird and Butterfly Gardens Padstow [0841 532262]. You can walk among the birds in the Tropical House (many endangered species bred here), or sit by the lake and watch the ducks and flamingos. You don't actually walk among the butterflies but between two separate glasshouses in what is like a large greenhouse. One is for British butterflies with the appropriate kinds of plants and temperature, the other for tropical ones. You can see the life cycle: eggs, hatching stages and sizes. The chrysalis is put on to boards so you can see it hatching. In Butterfly World, a butterfly museum, they are in big show-cases and displayed in their own natural habitats, around the world. One case includes the predators too, bats, small weasels. Another shows the massed migration, butterflies hanging on trees, in just one place in Central America. Worksheets available for children.

Open daily all year except Christmas Day, adult £2.75, OAP £2, child £1.50.

Bodmin Farm Park Fletcher's Bridge, nr Bodmin. Off A38 [0208 72074]. Cattle, sheep, pigs, goats, chickens, ducks, shire horses, rabbits and guinea pigs. You can walk into the paddocks among the animals; a lot can be touched and this is a special experience. Small museum of old farm tools, horse-drawn equipment. Also donkey and pony rides.

Open May–September, Sunday–Friday, adult £2, child £1.

A World of Nature 15 Lansdown Road, Bude [0288 352423]. Wet and dry. Wet: aquaria with what you might find thrown up on the tide line, seashore, like crabs, mermaid's purses, seaweed. Dry: woodland scene with badgers, foxes, owls, cliff scene with stuffed sea-birds. Guided tour explains about nature in Bude, sea and land marine biology,

land flora and fauna, the history and what is happening.

Open normal shop hours, adult 40p, child 10p.

Devon

Gnome Reserve West Putford, nr Holsworthy [040924 1435]. Believe it or not, over 1000 gnomes and pixies in a woodland garden. More to be seen being made in the pottery studio.

Open March–October, Sunday–Friday and bank holiday Saturday, adult £1.50, OAP £1.25, child £1, half price March, April and October.

Watermouth Castle Berrynarbor, nr Ilfracombe [0271 863879]. Not your normal castle with pictures, furniture, armour; rather, an entertainment. It includes: mechanical instruments like organs, barrel organs, pianolas, singing birds, many more; a model railway with lots of trains going round in a 20-by 40-ft room; 'Smuggler's Dungeon', where smugglers lived, drank, some of the figures being animated; a Gnome Village outdoors.

Open Easter–spring bank holiday and in October Sunday–Thursday, spring bank holiday–September Sunday–Friday, entry charges.

Cliff Railway Lynton. Earlier technology, 700-gallon water tank on each car is filled up at the top and descending hauls up the next one from below. Goes back to 1890. 900-ft railway with 30-degree gradient.

Exmoor Brass Rubbing Centre Lynton [05985 2529]. Brass rubbing on replicas, fascinating pastime for all ages. Materials, guidance, provided. New Hobbycraft section.

Open March–October, Monday–Friday, daily in school holidays, free admission but charges for rubbings.
🏛️ 🚌

Exmoor Bird Gardens Bratton Fleming, nr Barnstaple [05983 352]. Landscaped gardens with exotic birds, waterfowl, penguins, children's zoo. 12 acres.

Open daily all year, adult £3, OAP £2.75, child £2.

Cobbaton Combat Vehicles Museum Chittlehampton, nr Umberleigh [07694 414]. Private collection of World War II British/Canadian equipment, tanks, trucks, armoured cars, etc.

Open daily Easter–October, adult £2.50, OAP £2, child £1.25.

Morwellham Quay Open Air Museum nr Tavistock. A390 [0822 832766]. Historic port restored as it was mid-19th century, staff dressed mid-Victorian costume. Cooper, blacksmith in their workshops

talk to visitors, explain what life was like. Dukes of Bedford had a country carriage-way to get about, part of it is restored and shire horses and carriages take you on a trip, the coachman appropriately dressed. You can travel on a little train, some 500 ft underground into an old copper mine with a sound and light show telling of mining techniques since medieval times. Also a mid-Victorian farm, 9 shire horses, traditional farm animals, 2 19th-century cottages with different lifestyles, one a miner's, one lower middle class, a Victorian games area, an Assayer's laboratory, the ketch *Garlandstone* being restored, the Limeburner's Cottage, at certain times a gypsy, with caravan. Try on replica Victorian costume over your own. Map/guide provided. Best to start with the introductory slide show. 32-page *Young Explorer's Activity Guide* obtainable. Lots of steps and cobbles.

Open daily except Christmas Eve–January 1, adult £5.45, OAP £4.95, child £3.95.
🏛️ 🚌 🎁

Dartmoor Wild Life Park and West Country Falconry Centre Sparkwell, nr Plymouth. Off A38 [075537 209]. Various animals to be seen like tigers, deer, wolf packs, tethered birds of prey, pheasants, waterfowl. But also: falconry displays with talks, explanation of purpose, Easter–September, actual times need to be checked; 'Encounters of the Animal Kind' in a large barn when staff bring in small hand-reared creatures, wolf cubs, snakes, birds of prey, tigers, raccoons, etc., theme being listen to talk, maybe touch, learn. Additionally worksheets, spotter sheets, for families.

Open all year, adult £3.50, OAP £3.50, child £2.50.

National Shire Horse Centre Yealmpton, Plymouth [0752 880268]. 40 shire horses, with parades at 11.30 a.m., 2.30 p.m. and 4.15 p.m. in summer. Falconry Centre, eagles, hawks, buzzards, owls, and flying displays noon and 3.30 p.m. daily July–September, April–June and October Sunday–Thursday. Butterfly House, free-flying. Stables, pets' area and Petting Paddocks, horse-drawn cart rides. Events like bank holiday entertainment for children. Pushchairs/ wheelchairs for hire.

Open daily except December 24–26, adult £4.25, OAP £3.75, child £2.95, nominal entry fee mid November–mid March since no parades, shows.

Brixham Aquarium The Quayside, Brixham [08045 2204]. Collection of all specimens found in UK waters – sharks, octopus, conger eel, etc.

Open daily Easter–September, adult 75p, OAP/child 50p.

Model Village Babbacombe, Torquay [0803 38669]. Even children will tower over the hundreds of models and figures in this long-standing, opened early sixties, representation of English life, including a railway chugging round the countryside, cricket pitch, churches, hamlets, farms, villages, pubs, golf course, sports stadium, modern towns with trading estates, Hall with assembled hunt, much more, made from a variety of materials, music where appropriate, suitably lit up at dusk, and all set in 4 acres of gardens.

Open daily all year, adult £2.80, OAP £2.30, child £1.70.

Paignton and Dartmouth Steam Railway Paignton [0803 555872]. Steam train trip Paignton to Kingswear, for ferry to Dartmouth. Country-coastal scenery.

Open daily June–September, March, Easter and November Sunday, Tuesday, Thursday and bank holidays April, May and October, Santa Specials, return adult £4.80, OAP £4.40, child £3.30.

River Dart Country Park Ashburton [0364 52511]. Nature trails including tree trails, children's adventure playgrounds, picnic meadow, fly fishing.

Open daily Easter–September, adult £3, OAP/child £2.30.

Gorse Blossom Miniature Railway Park and Gardens Liverton, nr Newton Abbot [0626 1821 361]. Travel on a steam-powered miniature railway through some 8 acres of gardens, park. Walk the labelled woodland paths. Assault course. Model railway.

Open daily Easter–September and December for Father Christmas Grotto, adult £2.95, OAP £2.50, child £1.95.

Parke Bovey Tracey. B3344 [0626 832093]. 200 acres of National Trust parkland, walks through woodlands and beside River Bovey.

Open daily all year.

Parke Rare Breeds Farm Bovey Tracey. B3344 [0626 833909]. Some 27 varieties of rare animals: ponies, sheep, cattle – long horn, white, belted (meaning with black band around tum) – peacocks, ducks, geese, pigs, in paddocks labelled with who's who. Guidebook available telling history. You don't go into paddocks but you do find some, such as pigs, stand by fences waiting for a scratch. Also pets' corner.

Open daily April–October, adult £2.75, OAP £2.50, child £1.50.

Wonderful World of Miniature Exmouth [0395 278383]. Grand model railway layout with 40 trains functioning over 7500 ft of track, over 200 scale miles.

Open daily April–October, otherwise weekends, adult £1.50, OAP £1, child 75p.

World of Country Life Sandy Bay, Exmouth [0395 274533]. An assortment of animals to pick up and pat, rabbits, goats, etc. Also a shire horse and tractors, steam engines to sit on are among the 2000 exhibits in the museum to do with country life both outside and domestic. Victorian cottage. Deer park, llamas, shire horses.

Open daily Easter–October, adult £2.75, OAP/child £1.65.

World of Boats at Exeter Maritime Museum The Quay, Exeter. A30, A38, A377 [0392 58075]. Over 100 boats from all over the world: Brunel's steam dredger, rather later Atlantic rowing boats (meaning those rowed single-handed), a steam tug, Arab dhows, a Hong Kong junk, and all sorts of strange and historic craft to climb aboard, explore. Also indoor museum in 19th-century warehouses. Being ferried to the boats adds to the fun.

Open daily except December 25–26, adult £3.25, OAP £2.50, child £1.90.

Rougemont House Museum of Costume and Lace Castle Street,

Exeter [0392 265858]. Regency house in parkland. Costumes in newly restored period rooms, lace exhibitions, demonstrations.

Open all year Monday–Saturday and July–August Sunday afternoons, adult £1.50, OAP/child 75p.

Royal Albert Memorial Museum Queen Street, Exeter [0392 265858]. Butterfly displays, stuffed giraffe, tiger, hippo, crocodile (model of elephant), mummy cases, guns, swords, an American gallery all about Eskimos and Red Indians and their customs, clothes.

Open all year Tuesday–Saturday.

Underground Passages Princess Hay, Exeter [0392 265858]. Exeter's medieval system of water supply, now under a shopping precinct. Some steps so park the pushchair. 20-minute guided tour through a maze of tunnels. Hear how cathedral and town in 12th century created this facility; people used to drop a bucket on rope to gather water. Mostly dry but can be flooded in winter so ring to check.

Open all year Tuesday–Saturday, 2–5.30 p.m., adult £1, child 50p.

Killerton House Broadclyst, nr Exeter [0392 881345]. 18th-century house, Acland family. Now cleverly a combination of furnishings, pictures, and a costume museum. The rooms

are brought to life with figures of all ages, different roles, dressed in their appropriate period clothes. Hillside garden, 15 acres.

House open Easter–October Wednesday–Monday, garden daily all year. House and garden £3.60, garden only £2.20, winter, garden only, £1, children half price.

Bickleigh Castle Bickleigh, nr Tiverton [08845 363]. Great Hall, guard room, armoury including figures in armour, an 11th-century chapel (the oldest complete building in Devon). Also: a Stuart period farmhouse, a *Mary Rose* exhibition (an earlier resident, Sir George Carew, was vice-admiral on the Tudor ship) and a display of World War II prisoner-of-war escape equipment. Museum of 18th–20th-century domestic objects and toys.

Open Easter–May, Wednesday, Sunday and bank holidays, late May–September daily 2–5 p.m. except Saturday, adult £2.50, child £1.25.

Devonshire's Centre, Bickleigh Mill Bickleigh, nr Tiverton [08845 419]. Craftsmen to be seen working. Also 19th-century-style farm with rare breeds of animals and shire horses. Bird gardens. Motor Museum.

Open January–mid March weekends, otherwise daily, except December 25–January 4, adult £3.50, child £2.50.
🎦 🚋 🏛

Grand Western Horseboat Company Tiverton [0884 253345]. A 2¹/₂-hour trip by horse-drawn boats along the Grand Western Canal, opened 1814 (now part of the Grand Western Canal Country Park) and travelling through pleasing Devon villages.

Open daily Easter–October, adult £5, child £3.35.
🎦 🚋 🏛

Vintage Toy and Train Museum Sidmouth [0395 515124, ext 34]. 50 years of toys, Hornby railways, Dinky toys, Meccano, etc. May be nostalgic for parents, inspiring explanations to children.

Open Easter–October, Monday–Saturday, except bank holidays, adult £1, child 50p.

Farway Countryside Park Farway, nr Colyton [040487 224]. Traditional farm animals, nature trails. Covered barn for rainy days. Adventure playgrounds. Grass ski centre. 100 acres.

Open daily Easter–October, entry charges.
🎦 🚋

Pecorama Pleasure Gardens Beer, nr Seaton [0297 21542]. A miniature passenger-carrying railway. A ride round the grounds which includes a tunnel takes around 20 minutes. Outdoor attractions: gardens, putting and croquet lawns. Indoors an exhibition of 12 working model railways, layouts, landscaped, could give ideas to model railway addicts.

Exhibition open all year except Sunday. Outdoors, Easter two weeks, May bank holiday, daily spring bank holiday–August, September–October, Monday–Saturday, combined ticket adult £2.35, OAP £2.10, child 95p, garden only £1.10, £1.10, 55p, exhibition only £2.10, £1.10, 75p.
🎦 🚋 🏛

The Mayflower Stone Sutton Harbour, Plymouth. From here the Pilgrim Fathers set sail to the New World in 1620.
The Aquarium The Hoe, Plymouth [0752 222772]. Part of research laboratory of the Marine Biological Assoc of the UK. Temperate marine fish locally caught, conger eels, starfish, octopi and other invertebrates.

Open all year Monday–Saturday, Sunday in summer, adult £1.50, OAP £1, child 75p.
🎦 🚋 🏛

Plym Valley Railway Centre Coypool Road, Marsh Mills,

Plymouth [0752 330478]. Largest steam engine in Northern hemisphere. Five others being restored. Diesel cranes.

Open daily all year.

Merchant's House Museum 33 St Andrew Street, Plymouth [0752 66800 ext 4383]. Fine 16th-century town house. Plymouth's history including complete Victorian pharmacy.

Open Easter–September, Tuesday–Sunday, otherwise Tuesday–Saturday, bank holidays, adult 75p, child 20p.

Plymouth Dome The Hoe, Plymouth [0752 600608]. Visitor Centre with interpretation of Plymouth's history and people from Stone Age beginnings to satellite technology. Audio-visual shows. Hands-on computers.

Open daily all year, adult £2.35, OAP £2.05, child £1.60.

Smeaton's Tower The Hoe, Plymouth. Dismantled from Eddystone Rock and rebuilt here 1882.

Open Easter, daily spring bank holiday–September, adult 65p, OAP 50p, child 35p.

Prysten House Plymouth [0752 661414]. Immediately behind St Andrews Church, Royal Parade. Late 15th-century priest's house with well. Historical tapestry in making almost twice the size of the Bayeux tapestry, depicting the colonization of the New World.

Open April–October Monday–Saturday, adult 50p, OAP/child 25p.

Paignton Zoo Totnes Road, Paignton [0803 527936]. More than 1300 animals covering 300 species including elephants, lions, chimps, fruit bats, friendly farm animals. 75 acres of Botanical Gardens. Jungle Express, miniature railway around Gibbon Island. Nature trails. The Ark, family activity centre, where you can look, touch, listen, learn, like finding out about animal skills and abilities. Can you race a cheetah, see as well as an owl? Does a crocodile actually shed crocodile tears? Sponsor an animal from £15 a year.

Open daily except Christmas Day, adult £4.90, OAP £4.20, child £3.

Tapeley Park and British Jousting Centre Instow, nr Bideford EX39 4NT [0271 860528]. Jousting, school visits [0271 861200]. Home of the Christie family so Glyndebourne Costume Display in house, also William Morris Collection. Italian gardens with Tool House, Shell House. Woods with lake.

Medieval jousting (riding the tilt, spearing the heads, lancing the rings, foot combat) bank holiday Sunday/Monday, displays, demonstrations, Easter–September, Wednesday–Friday and Sunday.

Open Easter–October, Sunday–Friday and bank holiday Saturdays, jousting tournament days, adult £4.50, OAP £3.50, child £2, non-jousting days, £1.90, £1.50, £1. Extra for house.

Bicton Park East Budleigh, East Devon EX9 7DP [0395 68465]. 60 acres of gardens with pinetum and glasshouses. Countryside Museum, early agricultural tools, artefacts of rural life and estate history. Shell House, collection of shells and fossils. Also woodland railway, ghost train, Bicton buggies, brass rubbing centre. Admission price covers entry, all static exhibitions and play areas. Extra for other attractions.

Open daily March–October, adult £3.85, OAP £3.60, child £2.80, family ticket.

Somerset

Cricket St Thomas Wildlife Park nr Chard. A30 [046030 755]. Elephants, monkeys, sea-lions, penguins, jaguars, etc., in paddocks, pens. Museum of bygone rural life/crafts, like a milking parlour, brass, wool and wood work. Heavy horse centre in the stables with occasional rides. Also pigs, rabbits, goats. May be familiar since location for BBC TV series *To the Manor Born*.

Open daily all year, adult £5, OAP £4, child £3 (summer rates).

Fleet Air Arm Museum RNAS, Yeovilton, nr Ilchester [0935 840565]. Over 50 historic aircraft with equipment, Concorde prototype, also exhibition on Falklands campaign. Wrens exhibition.

Open daily all year, adult £4, OAP £3, child £2.

East Somerset Railway Cranmore, nr Shepton Mallet [074988 417]. Old-style country station with around 10 steam locomotives in the loco shed. Museum, art gallery.

Open March, November and December weekends, daily April–October, steam days adult £3, child £1.20, non-steam days £1.50 and 60p.

Tropical Bird Gardens Rode, nr Bath [0373 830326]. In 17 acres of woodland, flower gardens, lakes, hundreds of exotic birds, many flying free, others in labelled cages. Breeding penguins, flamingos, parrots, waterfowl, cranes. Also aquarium, reptile house. Pets' corner open in summer includes calf, sheep, rabbits, ducks, donkey, etc. The tree trail aids identification of rare samples.

Open daily except December 25, adult £3.10, OAP £2.60, child £1.60.

Wookey Hole Caves Wookey Hole, Wells. Off M5 [0749 72243]. Spectacular caves, stalagmites, stalactites, tunnels blasted out of solid rock, also underground river, catwalks across deep ravines. Take woollies even in summer when sun shining outside. Park prams, carry baby buggies for use later in circular tour. It includes: the museum covering history of caves; giant water wheel; Victorian-style making paper by hand in mill building (most days craftsmen working); Lady Bangor's fairground collection, around 70 elaborately shaped and painted fairground creatures with memorabilia and a working fairground organ crashing out tunes; Madame Tussaud's Attics, literally storage space for some 200 heads of the famous, instead of in London, including accessories like Princess of Wales's dresses, Ringo's drum kit; vintage slot-machines; Magical Mirror Maze.

Open daily except week before Christmas, adult £4.50, OAP £3.95, child £2.95.

🏛 🚌 🌐 *except cave tour*

Cheddar Showcaves Cheddar [0934 742343]. Showcaves with stalactites, stalagmites, in massive chambers, some quarter of a mile underground, at foot of Cheddar Gorge. So concrete pathways, steps, guides to answer questions, also audio system. Also museum with archaeological exhibits, diorama about life in Mendips from Roman times. Fantasy grotto, high-tech light display with holograms and flickering plasma globe. Jacob's Ladder, 322 concrete steps to the top of the gorge, view of 5 counties. Adventure caving: for newcomers, 12 upwards, 1½ hours, 4 times a day, safety equipment provided and leader. Adventure Day: Junior Orienteering Course, allow 4 hours, compass lent. Book these extras. Extra charge.

Open daily except December 24–25, adult £4, OAP/child £2.50.

🏛 🚌 🌐

Coombe Sydenham Country Park Monksilver, Taunton. B3188 [0984 56284]. Sir Francis Drake married Lady Elizabeth Sydenham whose father built the Hall in 1585 on site of earlier monastic settlement and substantial remains of the medieval house are incorporated in the Elizabethan building. Present owners have embarked on an extensive restoration scheme so visitors return to see progress. In the restored Court Room you can touch the cannon-ball and learn its legend, including the Drake connection. Elizabethan-style gardens, corn mill dating to Domesday Book. Trout farm, deer park, 500-acre country park. Magic Story Trails through the country park to see nature at work through the eyes of authors such as Lewis Carroll. Also worksheets for children.

Open early April–October, Sunday–Friday, Court Room and gardens Monday–Friday, adult £2.80, child £2, family ticket.

The County Museum Taunton Castle, Taunton [0823 255507]. Antiquities (including the Low Ham mosaic), the Somerset Military Museum, industrial history, geology, costume, dolls, coins, medals, in and around the Great Hall of the castle where Judge Jeffreys held the 'Bloody Assize' in 1685. Summer school holiday activities for children: making wattle and daub panels, making a bonfire kiln, drama, Eskimo games and sledge-building, for 7s upwards.

Open Monday–Saturday, adult 70p, OAP/child 20p. Friday free.

West Somerset Railway Minehead [0643 704496]. Travel by steam railway between Minehead and Bishops Lydeard, some 20 miles.

Open daily June–mid September, also December 26–January 1, otherwise weekends, from adult £1.10, OAP 88p, child 60p.

New Road Farm New Road, East Huntspill TA9 3PZ [0278 783250]. 300-year-old farm demonstrating modern and traditional methods. Over 60 different breeds of animals. Study milking and maybe try your hand. Bee demonstrations, feeding routines, haymaking, sheep-shearing, a blacksmith at work. Observation badger sett, barn owl release scheme and foxes to see. 'I Spy' farm trail, about an hour. Somerset County Council's Levels Visitor Centre with audio-visual effects and hands-on experiences.

Open April–September Tuesday–Sunday and bank holidays, otherwise weekends, adult £2.25, OAP £1.75, child £1.25.

Fleet Air Arm Museum Royal Naval Air Station, Yeovilton. Off A303 [0935 840565]. Aircraft, weaponry, uniforms, illustrating history of flight from bi-planes to modern jump jets. Audio-visuals, dioramas, re-creation of scenes from two World Wars. Simulator of going up in helicopter or microlite. Climb into cockpits. Observe from Observation Galleries take-offs/landings on adjacent Royal Naval Air Station.

Open daily except December 24–26, adult £4.10, OAP £3.10, child £2.10.

Avon

Woodspring Museum Burlington Street, Weston-super-Mare [0934 621028]. Edwardian Gaslight

Company's workshop for mending things, with the showrooms, gas fires, other domestic appurtenances of those days. An attractive setting in a courtyard with museum displays of a Punch and Judy stand, dairy, chemist's shop, penny-farthing bikes, toys and other kinds of nostalgia. The indoor nature trail is popular with children, including the deaf. It shows different landscapes in the county – sea, sand dunes, cliffs, gardens, moorland, woodland, etc. Stuffed animals and birds are labelled. Press buttons (always an attraction) and get answers for your trail on where they can be found.

Open all year Monday–Saturday except Good Friday, Christmas and New Year.

Avon Valley Railway, Bitton Railway Centre Bitton Station, Willsbridge, Bristol [0272 327296]. Steam locomotives and rolling stock including Stanier Black Five to operate steam railway.

Steam open days are the first Sunday in the month and bank holidays Easter–October. Open all year Saturday and Sunday, Santa Specials, return £2, OAP/child £1.20, family ticket.

Blaise Castle House Museum Blaise Castle Estate, Henbury, Bristol BS10 7QS [0272 506789]. Museum of past rural and domestic life in 18th-century

house. Blaise Castle open some summer Sundays, marvellous views. Estate, acres to explore. Events: farm days with farm animals, butter-making; guided walks; discovering the hillfort, or wildflowers. Children's school holiday activities: exploring the woods, trails, games, quizzes, arts and crafts.

Museum open all year Saturday–Wednesday.

Ashton Court Estate Long Ashton, Bristol. A370 [0272 639174]. Bristol's largest park, 825 acres with 250 acres of natural woodland, formal gardens where open-air plays are performed in summer, a deer park, 2 approach and putt courses, miniature steam railway, a grass ski slope, also a printed nature trail and an orienteering course obtainable for small sums. You pay, of course, for specific facilities. Ashton Court Mansion, with guided tours on certain dates. Ashton Court Visitor Centre (in stable block) with exhibition, opens for events. Events: vintage car rallies, festivals, balloon fiesta, kite festival, walks, talks, beetle safari or feeding the deer. Children's workshops and activities, i.e. finding out about badgers.

Open daily all year.

The Exploratory The Old Station, Temple Meads, Bristol BS1 6QU [0272 252008]. Hands-on science. Some 150 'plores' grouped into 10 specific scientific areas. Try to touch a bulb and your hand goes through, a ball hovers in mid-air, play an elliptical snooker table, illusions, gyroscopes, lasers, bubbles, to fascinate all ages, say 5s upwards. Shop, 'not a souvenir tea-strainer in sight', rather a real fossil, an Exploratory kit, informative book.

Open daily except Christmas week, adult £3.25, OAP/child £2.25.

Bristol Industrial Museum
Princes Wharf, Prince Street, Bristol [0272 251470]. The industrial history of the Bristol region told in extensive exhibits with water, land and air vehicles, including a mock-up of the cockpit of Concorde, and a very large Fairbairn steam crane. Working model railway layout.

Open all year Saturday–Wednesday.

Bristol Zoological Gardens
Clifton, Bristol [0272 738951]. More than 400 species of mammal from small ones in a pets' corner to big ones like elephants and tigers. Also breeds endangered species. Aviaries, aquarium, reptiles, new monkey houses and a house where you can see night-time creatures like bush babies and fennec foxes. Feeding times between 11.45 a.m. and 3.30 p.m. Gardens, lake.

Open daily except Christmas Day, adult £4.50, child £2.20.

City of Bristol Museum and Art Gallery Queens Road, Bristol [0272 223571]. About ancient history, natural sciences, fine and applied arts, Egyptology, ethnography and, of course, shipping. Stuffed animals from the zoo among other exhibits appealing to children. Enquire here about the Magnet Club's imaginative programme for school-age children, mostly but not entirely in Bristol's museums. Membership free. Programme examples: discovering trees, paintings, sculpture, medieval, Tudor, Victorian Christmas times, fossils, dinosaurs, life for a Georgian servant, lots more, year round.

Open daily all year.

National Lifeboat Museum
Princes Wharf (adjoining Industrial Museum), Wapping Road, Bristol [0272 213389]. Only one of its kind. Lifeboats back to 1909, including first *Blue Peter* programme fund-raised lifeboat. Pictures, models, etc.

Open daily.

SS Great Britain Great Western Dock, Gasferry Road, Bristol [0272 260680]. Isambard Kingdom Brunel's massive (over 300 ft long) first ocean-going propeller-driven ship in history, launched in 1843. Hull salvaged and brought back from the Falkland Islands in 1970, now being restored to original appearance in the docks where it was built. Look up at the prow towering above you, with its symbols representing industry, agriculture, etc. This ornamental strip was known as the 'Gingerbread'. It was gilded – hence the saying 'Taking the gilt off the gingerbread'. Look, too, for the methods of letting light down into the ship. Stand holding the wheel and looking down the length of the deck, imagine taking out to the New World what was the Concorde of the times. Revisiting probable to see progress of the extraordinary restoration. Walkway for visitors, some ladders, notices explain, guidebooks available. Dockside museum.

Open daily except December 24–25, adult £2.50, OAP/child £1.70.

Daupnines Theatrical and Historical Costume Collection 77–83 West Street, Old Market, Bristol BS2 0HB [0272 551700]. Original costumes from shows like *My Fair Lady, Mikado*. History of hairstyles from medieval times to the present. Changing designs of wedding dresses. Uniforms. Reconstruction of Victorian period dressing-room and of a Victorian street scene. On models plus accessories. School groups dress up as Victorian children.

Open all year Monday–Saturday, closed bank holidays, adult £2, OAP £1.50, child £1.

Museum of Costume Bennetts Street, Bath [0225 46111]. Housed in the Assembly Rooms which you will surely go and have a look at anyway in this visually stunning city. Fashions for adults and children from around 1618 (some even before) to present day, presented on figures. Some are in room settings, some in cases. Also toys and dolls. Guided tours available.

Open daily all year, adult £2.20, child £1.30, under 8s free.

Roman Baths Museum Pump Room, Stall Street, Bath BA1 1LZ [0225 46111]. It's such a pity the baths are no longer open, even once a year; I had the privilege of swimming in the Great Bath once, then sitting around on the shallow steps talking of this and that; sheer relaxation. To a modern child this looks like an open-air swimming pool now viewable from the Terrace housed in a museum where you can see the source of the water, another pool, impressive hot springs, the 'Sacred Spring' into which coins are thrown, and an extraordinary amount of Roman remains – including the imposing Minerva's Head. I expect you will also visit the Pump Room in the same building, once Bath's social centre, and taste the waters.

Open daily all year, adult £3.50, child £1.70, under 8s free.

Arnolfini Gallery 16 Narrow Quay, Bristol BS1 4QA [0272 299191]. Up to 16 major exhibitions of contemporary art every year. Also 200-seat auditorium for live programme of theatre and dance which doubles as a cinema showing foreign language, independent and first-run films. After school workshops Tuesday and a Saturday club for 8s–15s, practical workshops taken by local artists and based on the current exhibition. School holiday activities: open summer workshops, all-day practical art workshops for 8s–15s (charge).

Open Monday–Saturday 10 a.m.– 7 p.m., Sunday noon–7 p.m. Free entry, charges for cinema, live performances.
🏛 🎪 🚃 ⊗

American Museum in Britain Claverton Manor, nr Bath [0225 460503]. 200 years, from the 17th to the 19th century, of American history shown in 18 rooms filled with furniture, pictures and other valuables. It is the only museum on American domestic arts in Europe. Over 50 patchwork quilts are on display at any time as well as coverlets and hooked rugs. The 18th-century 'Conkey's Tavern' will especially attract if gingerbread is being baked. Life-size tableaux of pioneers' camps, cowboys round a chuck wagon, Indians in ceremonial dress. Souvenirs in appealing reconstruction of 19th-century American country store (ironmonger, haberdasher,

chemist). Outdoors: a Conestoga Wagon, an observation platform of a railroad car and a replica of a tepee to explore. Events: American Civil War camps, drills, skirmishes re-enacted.

Open Easter–October, Tuesday–Sunday 2–5 p.m., adult £4, OAP £3.25, child £2.50.
🎪

Sally Lunn's Refreshment House and Museum 4 North Parade Passage, Bath BA1 1NX [0225 61634]. Where famous brioche bun is baked and sold. Museum down some suitably creepy stairs. Ancient ecclesiastical kitchen with faggot oven, Tudor kitchen tools and utensils. Displays of human litter through the centuries. Excavations reveal the Roman, Saxon, onwards levels. Odd addition is a small tunnel, running under modern road, containing stalactites and stalagmites.

Open all year Monday–Saturday entry 30p adult, otherwise free.
🎪 🚃

Bath Postal Museum 8 Broad Street, Bath [0225 60333]. Once Bath's main Post Office from which first-known posting of world's first postage stamp, Penny Black, sent prematurely by an over-enthusiastic employee in 1840. Life-size model of a Post Office of those days. Otherwise with colourful memorabilia tells story of 4000 years of communication, clay tablets to computers, pigeons to space ships. Try writing with a quill pen.

Open daily April–October, otherwise Monday–Saturday, except Good Friday, December 25–26, January 1, adult £1.50, child 50p.

Bath Industrial Heritage Centre
Camden Works, Julian Road, Bath [0225 318348]. Wonderful conglomeration. In what was 18th-century Real Tennis Court, a Victorian ironmonger's shop, an amazing clutter since nothing was thrown away in case it was needed, including the paperwork, in a period when you could buy one screw or have it made for you; also the same man's mineral water business – the pump that put in the fizz, the labels his daughters pasted on by hand, returned empties. His 'Horehound beer' was said to cure all ailments. Find out the secret of marbles as bottle stoppers, try your hand at mixing 'pop'.

Open only weekends, adult £2.50, OAP/child £1.50, family ticket £7.

Wiltshire

Great Western Railway Museum
Farringdon Road, Swindon [0793 526161 ext 3131]. Static, no steaming. 5 full-size, real thing, locomotives, lots of smaller stuff like timetables, signals, prints, maps, photos. Also models of locos, room devoted to Brunel including his drawings. Also a foreman's house in the original Great Western Railway village, furnished in Victorian style including gas lights.

Open daily all year except Sunday mornings, adult £1.65, OAP/child 80p.

Great Barn Avebury, nr Marlborough. A361 [06723 555]. Wiltshire Rural Life Museum with bays you can browse round, touch things, concerned with the saddler, blacksmith, dairy, shepherding, laundry, wagons, 18th-century kitchen with rushlight holders. Sunday afternoons craftsmen function, spinner, weaver, pipe-maker, blacksmith, sheep-shearer, woodturner, carver, hurdle-maker, taxidermist, stained-glass window-maker, etc. Also life-size facsimile to be seen of the Avebury giant, Fred Kempster, 8 ft 4 in, 27 stone, village inhabitant early 20th century.

Open daily mid March–mid November, otherwise weekends, discount family ticket, entry charges.

Stonehenge West of Amesbury on A344 [0980 623108]. Massive stones set on Salisbury Plain, going back 5000 years, purpose still unknown, probably best known for midsummer celebrations in connection with the Druids. Stone circle now cordoned off for erosion reasons so you view it from a path or from the grass, having emerged from entrance gate and subway.

Guidebooks available at entrance.

Open daily except over Christmas, New Year. Times may change. Adult £1.90, OAP £1.50, child 95p.

> Groups should always book beforehand. It's difficult to believe, but I have heard of classes of schoolchildren just turning up. When a place is already busy they are unlikely to get full attention or full pleasure from the visit.

Wilton House nr Salisbury. A30 [0722 743115]. Home of Earl of Pembroke. State rooms, art collection, gardens, exhibition of 7000 model soldiers. 'Pembroke Palace', family's doll's house including miniaturized copies of some of the paintings, working miniature model railway. Might be combined with visit to Stonehenge?

Open Easter–October, Tuesday–Saturday, Sunday afternoon and bank holidays, adult £4.20, OAP £3.50, child £3.

Longleat House and Safari Park Warminster. A362 [house 09853 551, safari 09853 328]. Elizabethan house, home of Marquis of Bath, pictures, china, furniture, robes, astonishing ceilings, park by Capability Brown. A miniature railway to ride, 'the world's largest maze', the Dr Who exhibition, a Victorian working kitchen, Butterfly Garden in a

tropical greenhouse, Safari Boats, Lord Bath's Bygones. Then the safari park, probably best known for the lions of Longleat, but add in giraffes, zebras, hippos, gorillas, tigers, camels.

House open daily except Christmas Day. The rest open early March–early Nov, discount ticket for all attractions adult £9.50, OAP/child £7.50, single ticket like house £3.50, safari park £4.50, grounds/gardens £1, reduced for OAP/child.

> Remember locations can be closed for a one-day event or for renovations. Have you read 'A Plea' to check before you set off? See page 11.

West Dorset

Bredy Farm Old Farming Collection Burton Bradstock, nr Bridport. Off B3157 [0308 897229]. Nice combination on this modern dairy and arable farm attractively situated on River Bride. Watch the modern milking methods through glass panels, afternoons. Collection includes the implements, tools a Victorian farm would have had, dairy, cultivation, harvesting, cider-making. 18th-century sawmill sometimes working, water wheel.

Open spring bank holiday–September Monday–Saturday, adult £1, OAP 75p, child 50p.

Abbotsbury Swannery and Sub-Tropical Gardens Abbotsbury. B3157. The 16th-century village has many attractions, coastal footpath, beach, craft industries. Swannery [0305 871684] and gardens [0305 871387] are over a mile apart. Swannery, unique colony of some 400 mute swans, going back to 14th century, naturalists' walk. Gardens, exotic species growing outdoors, peacocks, aviary.

Swannery open daily April–mid October, adult £2.30, OAP £2, child 80p. Gardens daily March–October, otherwise Tuesday–Sunday, adult £2.50, OAP £2, child 60p.
▦ ▭ ▨

Sea Life Centre Lodmore Country Park, Greenhill, Weymouth [0305 788255]. You walk over, around, under or between massive tanks containing different fish from sharks to mackerel. Also 'Splash Pool', 'Touch Tanks', fish farming, walks, displays, more.

Open daily all year except Christmas Day, adult £3.95, child £2.95.
▦ ▭

Nothe Fort The Harbour, Weymouth [0305 787243]. Opened 1872 when feared that French might invade. Prams, pushchairs, can be parked since steps have to be negotiated. Take cameras for coastal views from the ramparts. Furnished rooms, uniforms on figures, guns, models of guns and warships. Dioramas of military life showing how soldiers lived in the barrack room, cook house. Guided tours.

Open daily June–September, otherwise Sunday afternoons, adult £1.50, OAP £1, accompanied under-13s free.
▦ ▭

Deep Sea Adventure 9 Custom House Quay, The Old Harbour, Weymouth [0305 760690]. Diving equipment, machines used to explore the ocean from 17th to 20th centuries, like Halley's Diving Bell, 1690 (air in barrels) to the bomb room in the HMS *Edinburgh* wreck. Lots of items from famous shipwrecks and about '*Titanic*, the Unsinkable Legend'. Computer games and play-submarine. Treasure hunt with metal detector. Live diving displays in high season.

Open daily all year, adult £2.95, OAP and 15s–16s £2.50, child 4–14 £1.95, family ticket: 2 adults, 2 children £8.50, 2 extra children free.
▦ ▭ ▨

Weymouth Tropical Jungle Lodmore Country Park, Greenhill, Weymouth [0305 783311]. Giant greenhouse with free-flying butterflies from all over the world. You move among them, also round a layout set in Purbeck stone like the miniature lake, streams and among not only jungle plants but also British ones (dock leaves 10 ft high!). Separate section includes caterpillars since some never spot them in main building, small moth house, an insect house behind glass holding tarantula, stick insects, scorpions, giant wood lice, hundreds of locusts and the bright green frog beetle. Audio-visual, also wildflower meadow in front to attract British butterflies. Guided tours if booked in advance.

Open daily Easter–October, adult £4.25, OAP/child £3.25.

The Dinosaur Museum Icen Way, Dorchester DT1 1EW [0305 269880]. Claims to be 'Britain's only museum devoted to dinosaurs and their relatives'. Displays have information to reach everyone from 5 years and include actual fossil material as well as life-size and skeletal models, graphics, dioramas, audio-visual and interactive exhibits, computerized, electronic, mechanical. Discovering is built in, like the 'feely' experience. Was a dinosaur's skin hot, cold, hard, soft, furry? Or try working out the skin colour so as to melt into the landscape, escape predators. Gallery video programmes on dinosaurs, fossils, fossil hunting. The museum suggests other attractions, like Thomas Hardy's reconstructed study in Dorchester's County Museum, nearby Weymouth's splendid sandy beaches, or a drive through the Isle of Purbeck where the museum's set of dinosaur footprints were found,

or a visit to Lyme Regis where, it says, 'remains of prehistoric creatures are still to be found on the beach today'. Modern display techniques make this museum suitable for the non-sighted and for wheelchair visitors (except for the video presentation).

Open daily except December 24–26, adult £2.30, OAP £2, child £1.65.

Tutankhamun, The Exhibition High West Street, Dorchester [0305 269571]. The tomb reconstructed. Walk through the ante-chamber filled with treasure, witness the raising of the golden coffins. In the Hall of Treasure the facsimiles of golden treasures including the famous golden mask. With sounds and smells.

Open daily all year, adult £2.75, OAP £2.25, child £1.65.

Old Crown Court Dorchester [0305 251010]. As it appeared for trial of Tolpuddle Martyrs in 1834. Cells and stocks below.

Open all year Monday–Friday, except bank holidays.

Maumbury Rings Dorchester. Stone Age sacred circle, Roman coliseum where gladiators fought, and in medieval times there was bull, bear, cock fighting here.

Open daily all year.

Worldwide Butterflies and Lullingstone Silk Farm Compton House, Sherborne. Off A30 [0935 74608]. Look at butterflies, moths, alive, flying, breeding, hatching, in a stately home, or in its grounds. Learn about conservation. Eggs/caterpillars available for rearing. Activity sheets obtainable to give greater understanding, enjoyment, for the young. Then something different, the Lullingstone Silk Farm, originally in Kent, about rearing English silk, from ancient processes, and used as material in gowns for 2 coronations and other royal occasions including Princess of Wales's wedding dress. Vintage tractors and even a fire engine to explore.

Open daily April–October, Easter if earlier, adult £3.75, OAP £2.95, child £2, family ticket.

Dinosaurland Coombe Street, Lyme Regis [02974 3541, information line 0839 222008]. Museum, with life-size dinosaurs in natural habitat, covering birth of this planet to their extinction. Geological Timescale explains that where you stand was a seabed which is why fossils can be found if you look. Video explains how museum exhibits are collected. Fossil exhibition. Fossil Shop sells locally collected fossils. Aquaria, children's corner with live birds and reptiles. Children's worksheets. Rare: 'Children's Rock Pooling', not a matter of collecting crabs to stew in a beach bucket but comparable with inland supervised pond-dipping. Children 5 upwards have the wonderful opportunity of being guided by an experienced teacher for about 2 hours at low tide to discover the living world in the rock pools, studying live creatures but putting them back. Plastic or old shoes. *£3 per child.*

'The Fossil Beach Walk' (under 10s must be accompanied), also guided and at low tide, shows you how to fossil hunt safely and correctly with the chance to discover one. Around 1½ hours. Uneven ground, not for pushchairs.

Adult £2.70, child £1.50, tickets for both obtainable at least 15 minutes before commencement, times needing to be checked by phone.

Then 'Dinosaurland Nature Trails', 3-hour walks into the undercliff, a nature reserve teeming with wildlife and rare plants. Need booking at least 4 days in advance.

£7.50, £4 accompanying children. Sundays 11 a.m.
These 3 events Easter–August. Open daily Easter–October 9 a.m.–5 p.m., November–March 11 a.m.–3 p.m., except December 18–27, adult £1.95, OAP £1.50, child 95p.

Personal apology. Charges say adult, OAP, as though an old age pensioner is not an adult! Well it was a question of 'the retired', 'senior citizen' and sundry other euphemisms, so for clarity and brevity I chose OAP. I have met you, all over the country, talking to your grandchildren, explaining what there is to see that is interesting; informed but often in a personal (remembering) way. So if you also get discounts on entry charges, like children, good luck. I reckon it's fun.

South of England
Southern Tourist Board

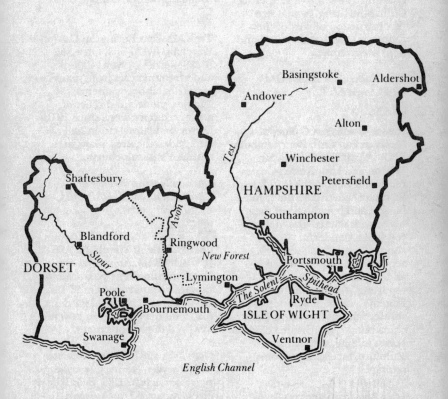

Basingstoke

Aldershot

Andover

Alton

Test

Winchester

Shaftesbury

Petersfield

HAMPSHIRE

Southampton

Blandford

Ringwood

Avon

New Forest

DORSET

Stour

Portsmouth

Lymington

Spithead

Poole

The Solent

Ryde

Bournemouth

ISLE OF WIGHT

Swanage

Ventnor

English Channel

East Dorset

Terracotta Warriors from China
Bournemouth Exhibition
Centre, Old Christchurch Lane
(off Old Christchurch Road),
Bournemouth [0202 293544].
Life-size pottery figures of
generals, bowmen, foot soldiers,
cavalry men, discovered in 1975
guarding the tomb of Emperor
Ch'in Shi Huang. Actual size
reconstruction of part of the
Emperor's tomb with sound and
light programmes.

*Open daily, adult £2.85, OAP
£2.35, child £1.70.*
🏛️🚻

**Russell-Coates Art Gallery and
Museum** East Cliff, Bournemouth
BH1 3AA [0202 299644]. Sir
Merton and Lady Russell-Coates
relished travelling the world, late
Victorian/Edwardian time, and
bought and bought. So in their
house with stained-glass dome,
you find a wonderful
conglomeration of their
acquisitions. Napoleon's table
and wine cooler, newspapers
reporting Waterloo, Empress
Eugénie's cabinet, a Buddhist
shrine, Samurai armour, a Delft
china puzzle jug, diorama of New
Forest wildlife, and pictures,
sculpture, furnishings, room
settings.

*Open Monday–Saturday all year,
except Good Friday and Christmas
Day, adult 50p, child 10p, less
December–March, Saturday free.*
🏛️🚻🅿️

Kids Free Fun Festival Details:
Dept of Tourism, Westover Road,
Bournemouth [0202 291715].
Punch and Judy, clowns, story
time, parachuting teddies, beach
club, *3 weeks in August. Hotel
discounts.*
End August, Festival of Lights
including thousands of flickering
candles, lit by children, and
'Dancing Waters' display.
🏛️

Tank Museum Bovington Camp,
Wareham BH20 6JG. Off A352
[0929 462721]. Over 140 tanks
and armoured cars from many
countries, also armaments,
engines, models and relics of
armoured operations since 1916.
Driver simulators, cut-in-half
tank, video theatres, play tanks,
children's assault course.

*Open daily except 10 days at
Christmas, adult £3, OAP/child
£1.50, family ticket.*
🏛️🚻🅿️

Corfe Castle nr Wareham. A351
[0929 480921]. An impressive
Norman ruin where Saxon King
Edward was murdered in 978.
On a hill, with plentiful gardens.
Also a model village tells how life
was lived in previous times.

*Open daily mid February–November,
mid November–February weekends
from noon, adult £1.80, child 90p.
Free to National Trust members.*
🏛️🚻

Durlston Country Park Durlston,
nr Swanage [0929 424443]. 261
acres of downlands, meadows,

cliffs, farmland, with natural wildlife like 400 species of plants, 200 species of birds, 13 species of butterflies, 30 of animals like badgers, foxes, deer. Visit the Information Centre first. Guided walks in summer, a couple of days a week, can tell you about herbal folklore or butterflies, or printed self-guide trails tell you what to look for. Also Great Stone Globe of the World, 40 tons in weight, 10 ft in diameter, built in Victorian times, Tilly Whim Caves and Durlston Castle, a Victorian folly, now a restaurant.

Open daily April–October.

Brownsea Island Poole Harbour [Warden: 0202 707744]. 500 acres, beaches, glades, nature trails. Includes a nature reserve, sanctuary for ducks, geese, heron, gulls, common tern, run by Dorset Naturalists' Trust, guided afternoon 1½-hour tours. Open April–June and September Tuesday–Thursday, weekends and bank holidays, morning self-guided tours, guided tours daily July–August. Small fee. Refreshments by landing quay.

Landing fee £1.20, child 60p, National Trust members free. No dogs. Open mid March–September. Frequent boats from Poole Quay [0202 666226].

Natural World The Quay, Poole [0202 686712]. Aquarium and Serpentarium: sharks, piranhas, alligators, venomous snakes, bird-eating spiders, coral reefs. Check feeding times at entrance. Have your picture taken with a large snake?

Open daily except Christmas Day, adult £2.95, OAP £2.25, child £2.

Waterfront Museum The Quay, Poole [0202 683138]. The Poole story. A Victorian street scene (pharmacy), traditional crafts, smugglers plotting illicit deeds, underwater archaeology (film shows of divers at work and finds from the Studland Bay wreck), full-size replica of an Iron Age log boat. Audio-visual shows.

Open all year Monday–Saturday, Sunday morning except Good Friday, December 25–26, adult £2.95, OAP £2.25, child £1.50, family ticket.

Hampshire

Beaulieu John Montagu Building, Beaulieu SO42 7ZN [0590 612123]. A lot, Palace House (home of Lord Montagu), abbey ruins, National Motor Museum with lots of carefully polished vehicles, an overhead monorail, 'Transporama', a sound/visual about transport, veteran bus rides around the premises, a miniature railway layout, and a year-long series of events like car rallies, steam festivals, a crafts fair. 'Wheels', mobile pods take you through 20 displays illustrating the development of motoring from the pioneers and on to and beyond the year 2000. Children's mini-car and bikes circuit. Certainly add in Buckler's Hard, 2¹/₂ miles away, once a thriving 18th-century shipbuilding village, now with Maritime Museum (you might see models being made) and original cottages brought to life with furnishings, figures, of the people who once lived there, labourers, shipwrights, inn patrons.

Open daily all year except Christmas Day, adult £6.50, OAP/child £4.50, family ticket £20.

New Forest Wagons Balmer Lawn Road, Brockenhurst SO42 7TS. A337 [0590 23633]. Horse-drawn wagon rides, a way of seeing parts of the New Forest otherwise accessible only on foot or on horseback. You can take time to appreciate the changing landscape, maybe sight elusive species, deer, fox, badger. Protected against showers or strong sun. Ask the drivers questions, very experienced. Book in advance, after all, a wagon load has to be worked out. Advisable to take packed lunch or tea. Rides, about an hour.

Open daily April–September, adult £3.50, child £1.60, under-5s £1, dogs (quiet, on lead) 50p.

New Forest Butterfly Farm Longdown, Ashurst, nr Southampton SO4 4UH. Off A35 [0703 293367]. Step into a tropical garden and view exotic butterflies and moths from round the world flying freely. Take cameras, look carefully for those barely distinguishable among the foliage. Also (behind glass) scorpions, tarantulas, praying mantis, etc. Outside there are dragonfly ponds. Learn about butterfly behaviour and which plants encourage butterflies in your garden. (New Forest walks adjacent.) 20-minute woodland tours in horse-drawn traditional wagons, May–September, school holidays and bank holidays April–October.

Open daily April–October, adult £3, OAP £2.80, child £2.

Breamore House Fordingbridge, off A338 [0725 22468]. Elizabethan manor house, Carriage Museum, including fire-fighting equipment and last stagecoach to run between London and Southampton, Countryside Museum with agricultural machinery and replicas of dairy, wheelwright's, blacksmith's, saddler's, etc. Also ancient and modern mazes. Annual events include such as assemblies of vintage vehicles, agricultural steam engines, a craft fair. Medieval tournaments some days in May, then Tuesday–Thursday, Saturday, Sunday to early September and daily August. Separate admission charges.

*Open April Tuesday–Wednesday,
Sunday, Easter holiday, May–July
and September Tuesday–Thursday,
weekends and holidays, daily
August, from 1 p.m, adult £3.50,
OAP £3, child £2.*

The Roman Villa Rockbourne,
Fordingbridge. Off B3078 [072
53 541]. Probably largest in
England, 73 rooms uncovered,
excavation continues. Mosaics,
bath complex, the finds are in
the museum.

*Open April–October, weekday
afternoons, weekends and July–August
all day, adult 80p, child 40p.*

Paultons Country Park Ower,
Romsey. A36/A31 [0703
814442]. Small walks, gardens,
aviaries, or large walks, round 10-
acre lake to see wildfowl, some
100 species, including flamingos.
Also animals in large paddocks,
wallabies, deer, pets' corner. The
19th-century water wheel works
and village life museum
illustrates the rural past with
machinery, wagons, tools.
Romany Museum. Go-Kart track,
adventure playground.

*Open daily March–November, adult
£5.25, OAP £4, child £5.25.*

Broadlands Romsey. A31 [0794
516878]. Splendid home of Lord
Mountbatten, previously
Palmerston's. Exhibition in
William and Mary stables with
audio-visual illuminates Lord and
Lady Mountbatten's public lives.
Look for Japanese Instrument of
Surrender and swords (also tomb
in Romsey Abbey).

*Open mid April–September,
Saturday–Thursday, Good Friday,
daily from August 1, adult £4.50,
OAP £3.60, child £3.*

Finkley Down Farm Andover. Off
A303, east of Andover [0264
52195]. Ponies, horses, cattle,
sheep, pigs, goats, poultry, some
rare, farm animals. Pets' corners
where children can handle, feed,
rabbits, lambs, kids, chicks. Also
barn with rural bygones,
children's adventure playground.

*Farm and country park open daily
Easter–September, adult £2,
OAP/child £1.*

Museum of the Iron Age
6 Church Close, Andover,
SP10 1DP [0264 66283]. The
story of the Iron Age hillfort and
its changing fortunes, but also
what life was like for prehistoric
ancestors, fighting men,
weapons, defences, and the
domestic side, houses, crops,
food storage, farming, farmyard
animals, crafts, death and burial.
Illustrated work packs available.
Children's holiday activities
Easter and summer – say 5s
upwards: making Woolly
Mammoths, cave paintings,
papier-mâché figures,
discovering about explorers,
smugglers, pirates, fossils, Celtic
feasts.

Open all year Tuesday–Saturday and April–October Sunday, 2–5 p.m., adult £1, OAP/child 50p.

The Hawk Conservancy Weyhill, nr Andover. Off A303, west of Andover [0264 772252]. See and photograph hawks, falcons, owls, eagles, vultures, etc. Birds flown at intervals, weather permitting.

Open daily Easter–October, adult £2.75, OAP £2.50, child £1.60.

Intech Hampshire Technology Centre, Romsey Road, Winchester SO22 5PJ [0962 63791]. Stimulates greater understanding of technology, science, design and engineering, entertainingly, through exhibits to take apart, test, such as: making a bridge that stays up; keeping balls in the air with air jets; making someone else's reflection appear in a mirror; working out someone's weight through a balancing act. 'Psst!' inside information brochure available.

Open daily except Christmas and New Year.

Winchester Cathedral
Winchester. Look for the 12th-century font where royalty have been baptized, still used today. Decorations around the black stone tell about St Nicholas, patron saint of children, with such tales as when there was famine and disaster and a man

salted down his three dead sons in a barrel for winter sustenance. St N. came along and brought them back to life. Look too for well-ornamented mortuary chests containing ancient bones, including Canute's. Then here too look for the shrine to St Swithun, who asked to be buried outside so he was in the sun and the rain, but when the cathedral was rebuilt yet again he was brought inside and there was rain for 40 days. It still does from July 15 and is connected with him. I heard that this 9th-century bishop, doing walkabout, performed only one miracle in his lifetime when a woman knelt before him, spilling the eggs she carried, and when he picked them up they were whole. Look for Jane Austen's grave, marked by floor-level stone and beside it a commemorative brass and a window. Look too for a small statue on a plinth commemorating William Walker, the diver. Apparently a large section of the cathedral was sinking because of no proper foundation. He worked under the floor, in water, in 1906–12 to put things right. Cathedral free but maintenance contributions welcome.

Great Hall Winchester. Look for Round Table, no legs, on the wall, thought to date from Edward III, then repainted for visit of Henry VIII, and so face in the centre is his, with knights' names around it. Look too on wall opposite with names of knights since, and the stained-glass windows, so lots of nostalgia back to Arthur. Look also for tall stainless-steel gates commemorating a modern royal couple, the Prince and Princess of Wales.

Closed Good Friday, Christmas Day and Boxing Day, free.

Marwell Zoological Park Colden Common, nr Winchester. A333 [096274 406]. Walk or drive over 2 miles round park to see numbers of animals in paddocks, zebras, giraffes, tigers, including rare animals, which the charity breeds, so young animals to see. Train rides through park. Children's farmyard. Free camera loan service.

Open daily all year, adult £4.85, OAP £3.35, child £3.85.

Mid-Hants Railway Alresford Station, Alresford [0962 733810, talking timetable 0962 734866]. Better known as the 'Watercress Line', because it used to transport watercress to market. Steam trains, of course, between Alresford (charming town to explore) via Ropley with engine shed and yard where locos are restored, and Medstead, where the Working Omnibus Museum Project is based: exhibition and short vintage bus rides, May–September Sunday, bank holidays. It now runs through to Alton (burial place of Sweet Fanny Adams) and connects with British Rail. Picnic area at Ropley

Station from which to watch the trains. Events: Father's Day Specials, Teddy Bears' Day, steam trains to Santaland.

Open most of June, July, August, otherwise most Sundays, bank holidays, 'Return', unlimited travel on purchase day, adult £5.10, OAP £3.80, child £3.30, family ticket, single £3.60, £2.35, £2.15.

Hampshire Farm Museum Manor Farm, Brook Lane, Botley, nr Southampton [04892 87055]. Farm life as it used to be between 1850 and 1950. Sheep, goats, Wessex Saddleback pigs. Ducks, chickens roaming freely. Restored machinery regularly demonstrated. In Upper Hamble Country Park containing upper reaches River Hamble. Park always open.

Farm open daily April–December except Christmas Day, January–February weekends, school holidays, park: charge for vehicles except in winter, farm: park charge plus adult 75p, OAP/child 40p.

Portsmouth's Naval Heritage Centre HM Naval Base, Portsmouth [0705 839766]. Story of the Royal Navy, set in old Royal Dockyard.

The Mary Rose [0705 750521], flagship of Henry VIII's fleet, sank off Portsmouth in 1545. Raised in 1982. Giant hulk, like cutaway model, an awesome sight viewed from a gallery in a special dry dock. Archaeologists and shipwrights are preserving it (by constant spraying) and refitting sections. Some 18,000 artefacts in the *Mary Rose* exhibition give a remarkable view of 16th-century life at sea: a syringe for injections, purses, guns, longbows, games, musical instruments, combs, manicure sets, clothes, cooking equipment.

Adult, £3.90, OAP £3, child £2.50.

special dry dock. Archaeologists

HMS Victory [0705 819604]. Nelson's flagship, the world's only surviving ship of the line. Restoration to way she looked in Battle of Trafalgar. Royal Navy and Royal Marines guides illuminate the past.

Adult £3.90, OAP £3, child £2.50, and includes entry to Royal Naval Museum (see below).

HMS Warrior 1860 [0705 291379]. World's first iron-clad warship now restored to original style. See how the officers and men lived, sit at a mess deck table, climb in a hammock, examine a cat-o'-nine-tails, put questions to Quartermasters in period costume. 4 decks to explore.

Adult £3.70, OAP £3, child £2.20.

Royal Naval Museum [0705 733060]. From Tudor times and continuing the story up to Falklands campaign 1982. Uniforms, medals, personal

effects, with dioramas illustrating specific actions.

Centre open daily, except Christmas Day, adult £1.80, OAP/child £1.30.

D-Day Museum and Overlord Embroidery Clarence Esplanade, Southsea [0705 827261]. Centrepiece Overlord Embroidery, 34 panels telling story with 50 different materials including gold braid for the King's uniform. Otherwise reconstructed scenes, an air-raid shelter, a factory, 1940 dining-room, with figures, gas masks, outdoors Sherman tank among military vehicles, tell the human story behind the 1944 invasion of Normandy. Personal tape commentary included in admission.

Open daily except December 24–26, adult £3, OAP £2.25, child £1.80, less off-peak season October–March, family ticket.

Southsea Castle Clarence Esplanade, Southsea [0705 827261]. Built by Henry VIII. Exhibition, audio-visual on life in castle. Keep, gun platforms, panoramic views, underground tunnels.

Open daily except December 24–26, adult £1, OAP 75p, child 60p, less off-peak season, family ticket.

Natural History Museum Cumberland House, Eastern Parade, Southsea [0705 827261].

Wildlife dioramas, full-size reconstruction of a dinosaur. Ice Age audio-visuals. Freshwater aquarium and free-flying butterflies.

Open daily except December 24–26, Butterfly House open May–October, adult £1, OAP 75p, child 60p, less off-peak season, family ticket.

Aldershot Military Museum Queens Avenue, Aldershot [0252 314598]. Open 1984 telling the story of the British Army since 1854, starting in the 19th century with camps for troops returning from the Crimean War, a royal pavilion built for Queen Victoria when she visited, expanding into schools, hospitals, making Aldershot the only complete military camp built in the kingdom since the Romans. Victorian Barrack Room, models of early aircraft, camps, uniform and other memorabilia about the military base for other wars.

Open daily except Christmas, adult £1.40, OAP 80p, child 40p.

Hall of Aviation Albert Road South, Southampton [0703 635830]. History of aviation in the area. Story of some 26 aircraft works including where Mitchell, Spitfire designer, worked. Largest of displayed aircraft, Sandringham Flying Boat (boardable), of time when the roast was carved at your table and you stopped off on the way;

no jet lag. Staff, airline ex-personnel, talk about what life was like.

Open all year Tuesday–Sunday, daily in school holidays, adult £1.50, child 75p.

Royal Marines Museum Eastney, Southsea PO4 9PX [0705 819385]. Medals, including one to a dog, audio-visual of Falklands campaign, live insects infesting food on 18th-century ships, objects from HMS *Invincible* which sank in 1758 (including a wooden plate, source of 'a square meal a day'), story of Hannah Snell who posed as a man in the Marines. Walk through a refrigerated Arctic display to experience conditions there. Junior commando assault course.

Open daily except December 24–26, adult £2, OAP/child £1.

Southampton Art Gallery Civic Centre, Southampton [0703 223855]. Fine collection of paintings from 14th century to contemporary including Van Dyck, Reynolds, Renoir, Monet. Special children's gallery. School holiday activities, mostly 8s upwards, could be to do with the port, ships, shipbuilding, bridges (the Floating Bridge), or making things (papermaking, tapestries, wonderful hats). There are quizzes too. Can be in other city locations like Bargate Museum.

*Open all year Tuesday–Friday,
Sunday afternoon.*

Medieval Merchant's House
58 French Street, Southampton
[0703 221503]. Restored,
furnished as for Fortin family in
13th century, earth floors,
replicas of pottery, wall hangings
decorated with jousting knights,
staff in period costume.

*Open daily Good Friday–September,
October–Maundy Thursday
Tuesday–Sunday, adult £1.40, OAP
£1.05, child 70p, includes personal
stereo guided tour.*

Isle of Wight

Just 23 miles long and 13 miles
across, reached by short sea trip
from Portsmouth, Southampton,
Southsea or longer by car ferry
from Portsmouth, Southampton,
Lymington. A gentle pace,
regular bus services, sandy
beaches or rock pools for the
bucket-and-spade brigade, good
walking country and quiet
villages are part of the charm.
Even a floating bridge, hauled by
chains, which takes vehicles and
pedestrians to Cowes. Magazine-
size guide from the Tourist
Office, see page 244.

Needles Pleasure Park, Alum Bay
[0983 752401]. You can still
reach the multi-coloured beach
by over 200 steps. Otherwise a
splendid seascape view and an

exciting experience swinging out
for the descent by chair-lift.
Worth considering whether very
small children should try this.
You can still collect the coloured
sands yourself or visit the DIY
Sand Shops, select and fill a
phial. Also amusements and
adventure playground on the
headland.

Open April 13–October 31 daily.

Osborne House, East Cowes
[0983 200022]. Pomp (The
Durbar Room) and domesticity
in what was Queen Victoria and
her family's country retreat. Her
rooms are left as they were so
look for the marble replicas of
the children's limbs, Albert's
walking sticks, their desks, their
bathrooms, (loos now
concealed), the children's chairs.
Otherwise the Queen's bathing
machine, Swiss Cottage with a
child-size kitchen and their
gardening tools marked with
initials. The Prince encouraged
the youngsters to collect things.
They went on doing so when
older and from world-wide. The
museum displays a weird and
wonderful collection. New: a
restored Royal Nursery.

*Open daily April 1–October 31,
adult £3.20, OAP £2.40, child
£1.60.*

Carisbrooke Castle, near
Newport [0983 522107]. Moated
Norman castle ruins where
Charles I was imprisoned prior

to execution. In spacious grounds donkeys work the 16th-century donkey wheel to raise water from the 161-foot well. Splendid views from the top of the keep reached by steps, not for pushchairs.

Open all year, adult £2.30, OAP £1.70, child £1.15.

Wax Museum, Brading [0983 407286]. In ancient Rectory Mansion with courtyard, priest hole, Henry VIII, Charles I, Queen Victoria, and such as a chimney sweep, a dying maiden, old hag in the stocks and a chapel where a spooky figure plays the organ and a coffin lifts to reveal a hand. The Chamber of Horrors depicts in gory detail man's inhumanity to man and woman.

Open daily, adult £3, child £2.10.

Animal World, Brading [0983 407498]. Animals, birds and reptiles from all over the world in colourful dioramas, looking lifelike. Also Professor Copperthwaite's Fabulous Exhibition of Weird and Freaky Mutations.

Open daily, adult £1.90, child £1.40.

Lilliput Museum of Antique Dolls and Toys, Brading. Over 1000 items in this comprehensive collection of dolls many with historic connections like the Russian doll sent to the daughter of the owning family by Mr Khrushchev in 1960. Also enticing old-fashioned toy shop offering everything for the Victorian doll's house.

Open January 15–March 15. Museum entry adult 90p, OAP/child 60p.

Maritime Museum, Bembridge [0983 87223]. A shipwreck centre with treasures from the deep and stories of how the ships were lost. Pirate gold, early and modern diving equipment, ships' models, underwater photographs. Worksheets and spotter packs for children.

Open daily April 1–October 31, adult £1.50, OAP £1, child 90p.

Model Village, Godshill [0983 840270]. Big-scale stone models, many with real straw thatch and all with tiny flower gardens. Also detailed model of Godshill's own church and cottages.

Open daily April 1–October 27, adult £1.30, OAP 95p, child 55p.

IOW Rare Breeds and Waterfowl Park, Undercliffe Drive, St Lawrence, Nr Ventnor [0983 852582]. Over 40 rare breeds of cattle, deer, goats, pigs, poultry in 30 acres and 100 species of waterfowl. Special areas for children to meet the animals.

Open daily April 13–October 31,
adult £1.60, OAP £1, child £1.

**Blackgang Chine Fantasy Theme
Park**, Blackgang [0983 730330].
30 acres of cliff-top gardens,
Smugglerland (climb aboard a
Smugglers' Lugger),
Adventureland (Drive a tank,
launch a rocket), Frontierland
(gold mine, Wild West Loco),
Dinosaurland (giant models),
Nurseryland (characters from
nursery rhymes, giant maze),
among attractions which include
a giant-size Snakes and Ladders
for family play.

Open April 2–October 28, adult
£2.99, child £1.99.

**Blackgang Sawmill and St
Catherine's Quay**, Blackgang
[0983 730330]. Story of timber,
waterwheel, sawpit, steamsaw,
with realistic models in
workshops. In the owner's little
cottage, see Granny's bedroom
around 1880 and in the period
kitchen watch out for a mouse
popping out of a big crock. The
Quay tells of wreckers,
smugglers, fishermen, the
lifeboat service. Queen Mary's
hat caught on the 87-ft skeleton
of a whale.

Open daily April 2–October 28.
Adult £1.65, child £1.20.

South East England

West Sussex

Fishbourne Roman Palace and Museum Salthill Road, Fishbourne, nr Chichester. A27 [0243 785859]. Remains of largest Roman residence excavated in Britain. Mostly now under cover, probably a local royal palace. Also Roman-style garden, museum of 'finds', model and audio-visual programme. Free taped guided tours available for pre-booked blind and partially sighted visitors.

Open December–February Sunday only, otherwise daily, adult £2, OAP £1.60, child £1. Wheelchair pusher free.

Weald and Downland Open Air Museum Singleton, Chichester. A286 [0243 63 348]. Re-erected, restored, historic buildings, houses, barns, market hall, working water mill, blacksmith's, carpenter's, plumber's workshops. You can explore the insides as well as enjoying the attractive exteriors. Charcoal made in woods, woodland trail. In a country park.

Open daily April–October, November–March Wednesday, Sunday, bank holidays, adult £2.80, OAP £2.20, child £1.25, family ticket.

Rainbow's End Family Adventure Park Hotham Park, Bognor Regis [0243 825255]. Waterless swimming, fully clothed, in thousands of semi-pressurized balls, animated scenes – Treasure Island, Beatrix Potter's stories, etc., mini farm and bird haven.

Open daily March–October, adult £2, OAP/child £1.75.

Amberley Chalk Pits Museum Houghton Bridge, Amberley, West Arundel. B2139 [0798 831370]. Industrial history in 36 acres of former chalk quarry and limeworks. The working life of our forebears but not gleaming pieces of tidy machinery as in indoor museums. Spread around: stationary engines, a forge, a village garage, tools, industrial relics. Working potter, blacksmith, printer, pumping and brick-making exhibits. Add an ancient omnibus and a narrow-gauge steam railway to travel on, plus a nature trail and Visitor Centre.

Open March–July and September–October Wednesday–Sunday, daily July–September, adult £3.70, OAP £2.70, child £1.50.

The Wildfowl and Wetlands Centre Mill Road, Arundel [0903 883355]. Wide variety of tame swans, ducks, geese, other birds in pens, lakes, paddocks, with observatory and hides, Visitor Centre with viewing gallery, film theatre. Feed the birds, Children's activities like bird brass rubbing, jigsaws, mask-making in school holidays.

Open daily all year, adult £2.70, OAP £1.70, child £1.40.

Arundel Castle Arundel. A27 [0903 883136]. Ancestral home of Dukes of Norfolk, large, extensive, impressive, pictures, furniture, treasures, in a long history entwined especially with Henry VIII. Also exhibition of ceremonial garments like coronation robes, state uniforms and Mary Queen of Scots' personal possessions.

Open April–October Sunday–Friday afternoons, adult £3.55, OAP £3, child £2.55.

Coombes Farm Tours, Church Farm Coombes, nr Lancing [0273 452028]. Around 1½-hour trip by tractor/trailer, around a 1000-acre farm with cows/calves, sheep/lambs, wheat/barley, wildlife carefully conserved, a dew pond you can see working. An unusual experience which means wellies and warm clothes (can be chilly on higher levels), keeping your eyes open and certainly listening to the farmer's daughter who tells you just what is going on. In wet weather a film show of the farming year in the barn, also corn-dolly-making, spinning. Worth a SAE to Jenny Passmore for information.

Open March–October, the tour is by parties of various numbers so a family needs to book itself into one: adult £2, OAP £1.75, child £1.25.

East Sussex

Royal Pavilion Old Steine, Brighton [0273 603005]. How a palace is expected to look according to pantomime and fairy stories. Outside stunning enough, domes, minarets, inside matches it in ornate Chinese-style magnificence. Created by Prince Regent. Many original fittings. Real swans, ducks, a rat, stuffed, in Great Kitchen.

Open daily except December 25–26, adult £2.80, OAP £2, child £1.40.

Brighton Museum and Art Gallery Church Street, Brighton [0273 603005]. Near Pavilion. Development of Brighton, the people, transport, penny slot-machines, seaside souvenirs, costume (caveman's furs to court dresses), curiosities like mummified cat and mermaid. Parents with pre-schoolers events. School holidays: brass rubbing, drama. Family activities: example Saturday workshops making sculptures from rubbish, castes, hand-made paper.

Open daily except Monday, Sunday mornings, Good Friday, December 25–26, January 1.

Booth Museum of Natural History 194 Dyke Road, Brighton [0273 552586]. British birds mounted in natural settings, butterflies, animal skeletons, geology including bones of local dinosaur and 'Unnatural History' display about the environment. Children's school holiday activities like making animal costumes, collages, nest-building, egg-decorating at Easter.

Open Monday–Wednesday, Friday–Saturday, and Sunday afternoons.

The Brighton Sea Life Centre Marine Parade, Brighton [0273 604 233]. Tropical, freshwater fish, sea-lions, turtles, sharks, rescued seals nursed back to health, a living coral reef, reptiles.

Open daily except Christmas Day, adult £3.75, OAP/child £2.75.

Preston Manor Preston Park, Brighton [0273 603005]. Old manor house furnished and illustrating the life of a rich Edwardian family. Servants' quarters, hall, butler's pantry, maids' rooms. Walled garden and family pets' graveyard. Have had families' summer hols taster of life as an Edwardian servant.

Open all year Tuesday–Sunday and Monday bank holidays except Good Friday, December 25–26, adult £2, OAP £1.60, child £1, family ticket.

British Engineerium off Nevill Road, Hove BN3 7QA [0273 559583]. In Victorian pumping station in wooded grounds overlooking Hove Park. More than 2000 models and full-size exhibits restored as working examples, road, locomotive and marine steam engines, hot air and internal combustion, early electric motors. Original workshop. Museum In Steam Sunday/bank holidays, but termly special 'School Steam Day'. Children's worksheets.

Open daily except December 18–26, adult £2, OAP/child £1.50.

Planet Earth Garden Paradise, Avis Road, Newhaven [0273 512123]. Miniature railway (rides), audio-visual of solar system, life-size moving Triceratops, fossil museum. Experience an earthquake, discover Neanderthal Man, walk through a simulated tropical rain-forest.

Open daily all year, adult £3.25, OAP £2.85, child £2.25.

The Living World Seven Sisters Country Park, Exceat, Seaford. A259 [0323 870100]. Natural history across the world, meaning living native and foreign insects, and other invertebrate life, displayed in 2 Sussex barns: butterflies, moths, ants, snails, termites, bees, scorpions, spiders, stick insects, much more telling you about countryside and seashore. Friston Forest adjacent with signposted walks. Pathway to the sea.

Open daily Easter–November 1, weekends, half-terms, school holidays in winter, adult £2, OAP/child £1.20.

Drusillas Park Alfriston BN26 5QS [0323 870234]. Off A27. Designed as a learning experience for children so low viewing windows at child's level, and wheelchairs. Monkey Walk, Meerkat Mound (designed with help from local children so you pop your head up in the middle), Monkey Mountain Sanctuary, Penguin Bay, Beaver Country, World of Owls, the Rain-Forest Story (the consequences). Adventure playground graded in ages and indoor play barn. Plans for play equipment for disabled children. Lots of inter-active games. Extensive material for schools also available for families. For 3s–11s, from simple I Spy-type quizzes to Zoolympics, 16 activities including physical feats animals can do. 'Make and Paint' workshops in school holidays and events like Indian Pow Wow, Family Barbecues, Circus Carnival (learn circus skills).

Open daily except Christmas Day though some features closed in winter, adult £3.75, OAP £2.50, child £3.50.

Bluebell Railway Sheffield Park Station, nr Uckfield [082 572 2370]. Largest collection of veteran locos, carriages in the south, 1865 to 1958. Trains steaming through 5 miles of Sussex countryside from Sheffield Park to Horsted Keynes, with period atmosphere recreated in stations, which may seem familiar from TV features and films. Special events like August children's fun day and Christmas Santa Claus Special.

Open daily June–September, otherwise bank holidays, weekends, some other days, tickets including museum, loco sheds, travel, adult £3.50, child £1.75, family ticket.

Bentley Wildfowl Reserve and Motor Museum Halland, nr Uckfield. A22 [0825 84 573]. Lakes/ponds, over 1000 waterfowl, geese, ducks, swans. Also flamingos, cranes, etc., plus collection of roadworthy vintage veteran cars and motorcycles. Small animal section. Gardens, woodland walk, natural history display.

Open daily mid March–October and winter weekends, closed January, adult £3.10, OAP £2.40, child £1.50, family ticket.

Butterfly Centre Royal Parade, Eastbourne [0323 645522]. A butterfly safari park, so you wander around tropical level glasshouses, among free-flying butterflies from all over the world. Keep your eyes open, and camera poised, for elaborate courtship rituals, apart from other stages of rearing.

Open daily March–November, adult £2, OAP/child £1, family ticket.

Bodiam Castle nr Robertsbridge. Off A229/B2165 [0580 830436]. Probably among last to be built before gunpowder changed the battle style, so a fairy-tale castle. Floor replacement now gives access to the interior and circular stairs to the battlements. Audio-visual tells what life was like, knights jousting, invaders, banquets, etc. Annual National Trust Activity Days for schoolchildren, dressing up and trying bygone life. May, long-bow competition with some participants in chain-mail and armour.

Open daily April–October, November–March Monday–Saturday except Christmas, adult £1.70, child 90p.

Children's Farm Great Knelle Farm, Beckley, Rye TN3 6UB. Off A28 [079 726 321]. Working mixed farm (help feed the animals), arable, hops, dairy and beef herds, sheep, pigs, rare breeds. Also goats (watch out for your ice-cream), rabbit village, miniature ponies, donkeys, working blacksmith's shop, Puppet Theatre – *The Naughty Nellie Show*. The Tractor Train gives a wider view of farming. Join the Wild West Wagon Trail,

dressing up as cowboy or girl, ring for details of that. Free buses meet some Kent and East Sussex steam trains from Tenterden at Northiam Station, mostly summer school holidays.

Open Easter Sunday–October 31, Sunday–Friday, Saturday in August, adult £3, OAP/child £2.50.

Rye Town Model Strand Quay, Rye. Foot of Mermaid Street [0797 226696]. Scaled indoor model of this ancient town, polystyrene buildings even a foot high, streets cobbled with tapioca, trees from horsehair and green cork, each building faithfully reproduced. Story told with music, voices, light (and darkness), sound effects (some rather noisy): Elizabeth I's visit, attacks by the French, chasing of smugglers, plus murders, legends. Then you go into the town and see where it all happened.

Open daily April–October and winter weekends, adult £1.50, OAP/child £1.

Rye Harbour Nature Reserve Rye. Warden Dr Barry J. Yates, 2 Watch Cottages, Nook Beach, Winchelsea, E Sussex TN36 4LU [0797 223862]. Well over 1000 acres between Camber Beach and Winchelsea Beach. Carpets of plants like yellow horned poppy, sea kale, sea pea, over 260 species of bird, many rare and breeding, and a host of other animals such as brown hares, bats, marsh frogs.

Three bird-watching hides, open all the time, one accessible to wheelchairs. Study pack for primary schools £5. Booking only necessary for groups of 10 or more.

Open all year through respected footpaths.

Hastings Sea Life Centre Rock-a-Nore Road, Hastings TN34 3DW [0424 718776]. Ocean Tunnel gives views of sea creatures through glass, sharks, etc. Also big tanks with other marine life and a 'Touch Pool' rather like an indoor beach.

Open daily except Christmas Day, adult £3.60, child £2.50.

Shipwreck Heritage Centre Rock-a-Nore Road, Hastings [0424 437452]. 'Medieval Shipwreck Adventure', sound and light show telling story of a 500-year-old shipwreck in the setting of a ship in simulated dock. Exhibition 'Roman and Later Treasures from Shipwrecks'.

Open April–October weekends and bank holiday Mondays, daily June–mid September, adult £1.50, OAP £1, child 75p, family ticket.

Smugglers' Adventure at St Clement's Caves West Hill, Hastings TN34 3HY [0424 422964]. In a labyrinth of caverns over 50 life-size figures help tell story of 18th–19th-century smuggling along this coast. Dramatic sound and light, push buttons, video theatre, museum. Also 'The 1066 Story' (same phone number for details) in nearby ruins of Norman castle, within a medieval siege tent, projected images, lighting, narration, paintings reconstructing original castle. Separate charges. Also West Hill Cliff Railway, enquiries same number. Separate charges.

Open daily March–October, Smugglers' also open in winter except Mondays, adult £3, OAP/child £2.

Kent

Kent and East Sussex Railway Tenterden Town Station, Tenterden TN30 6HE [05806 5155, recorded message 05806 2943]. Steam travel, 13-mile trip round Rother Valley from Tenterden's Edwardian station to Northiam, operated by volunteer enthusiasts. Railway's history in Video Theatre and Exhibition Room. Special annual events including Santa Specials.

Open April–January weekends, bank holidays, daily in summer, adult £4, child £2.40.

Romney, Hythe and Dymchurch Railway New Romney N28 8PL [0679 62353]. Steam, main line in miniature, locos $1/8$ normal size hauling 14 miles across historic Romney Marshes.

Indoor railway exhibition at New Romney, yards, engine shed, etc.

Open March and October weekends, daily April–September, Hythe–Dungeness return £6, child half fare.

Port Lympne Zoo Park Mansion and Gardens, Lympne, nr Hythe CT21 4PD [0303 264646]. Mansion's spectacular interiors include a Moorish patio, tent room, mural room. 300-acre park home to part of John Aspinall's collection of rare and endangered animals, rhinos, chimps, tigers, largest herd of elephants in the UK, wolves, bison, buffalo, etc. to be studied on foot or by Safari Trailer £1.80 and £1.30 (booked beforehand). Worksheets for children.

Open daily except Christmas Day, summer adult £5, OAP/child £3, reduced winter.

Bleak House Fort Road, Broadstairs [0843 62224]. Charles Dickens's clifftop holiday home, where he wrote or planned novels. Victorian furnishings, personal possessions. Also Maritime Centre with exhibition of major Channel wrecks and 'The Golden Age of Smuggling' in cellars has surprises like some smugglers survived to a ripe old age.

Open daily Easter–November, adult £1.50, OAP £1.30, child 85p.

The Shell Grotto Grotto Hill, Margate [0843 20008]. A shell temple of ancient origin, discovered underground in 1835. Having visited, *as a child*, I still recall the experience and the subtle colour effects.

Open April–October weekdays, also weekends in summer, adult 80p, OAP 60p, child 40p.

Seasalter Heritage Centre Blue Anchor Corner, Seasalter, Whitstable. Contact: John Patterson, 19 Macdonald Parade, Seasalter [0227 277191]. Unusual kind of beach fun for children based in a Portakabin containing: a beautifully painted diorama illustrating the history of flint stone; history of bullet development with display of historic bullets found on beach; old photos; fossils; odd stones brought in by children, charts of shells, seaweed, marsh flowers; microscope (viewing sections of a cockroach proves a sickly favourite). Children's quizzes with prizes.

Open daily end May–mid September.

Howletts Zoo Park
Bekesbourne, nr Canterbury CT21 4PD [0227 72186, or recorded information 0303 264646]. 70-acre rare wildlife park with gorillas, elephants, tigers, small cats, monkeys, leopards, herds of Indian deer and antelope. John Aspinall and his family may be seen with the animals. Worksheets for children.

Open daily except Christmas Day, adult £5, OAP/child £3, less in winter.

Brambles English Wildlife and Rare Breeds Wealdon Forest Park, Herne Common CT6 7LQ [0227 712379]. 26 acres of natural woodland. Farm animals can be fed. Rabbit World, walk-in rabbit pen, large duck pond, nature trail to see fallow and sika deer, owls and red foxes. Under-5s playground with playhouses and small bikes. Wellies advisable if wet.

Open daily Easter–October, adult £1.80, child £1.

Canterbury Heritage – Time Walk Museum Stour Street, Canterbury [0227 452747]. 14th-century hospice. Now tells the story of Canterbury from the Romans to present day, including banners, coats of arms, paintings, domestic arrangements, massive indoor chimney, a loom, the original engine that drew the very first passenger steam railway in 1830, a wedding dress of 1804, trying to show that there is more in Canterbury to see than the cathedral and the Chaucer connection. But does contain a reconstruction of Thomas à Becket's tomb (destroyed by Henry VIII, possibly because of costly jewels) from archaeological evidence including pilgrims' badges. Who said badges are new?

Open daily except Sunday mornings in winter, adult £1.20, OAP 90p, child 60p.

Canterbury Cathedral
Canterbury. Royal tombs, knightly effigies, but most head for the place where Thomas à Becket was murdered in 1170. Now includes floor plate marking where Pope John Paul II and Robert Runcie, Archbishop of Canterbury, knelt together in 1982. But look around, there is still a service for Huguenot descendants. And there's always Nellie Cook, who poisoned her master and his new love with a pie, and was bricked up in the walls. During excavations a skeleton and the remains of a pie were found. Her ghost is supposed to walk Friday evenings. Cathedral guides even point out an impression of her shape (a bit blurred) on the wall

in an archway. Tape guide and cassette player for the blind, free.

Open daily, free, but contributions to maintenance welcome.

🏛 🎪 🚌 ⊞

The Canterbury Tales St Margaret's Street, Canterbury CT1 2TG [0227 454888]. In 14th-century church. Join the pilgrims walking from Southwark to Becket's tomb. Life-size figures, animals, settings, sights. Hear the tales of the Courtly Knight, the Bawdy Miller, the Wife of Bath, the Nun's Priest and the Pardoner, chivalry, romance, jealousy, pride, through personal head-sets with adult and child versions included in admission price.

Open daily all year, adult £2.50, child £1.50.

🎪 🚌

Ethnic Doll and Toy Museum 34 St Margaret's Street, Canterbury [0227 471032]. Thought to be the only one in the country. Displays of authentic ethnic dolls from all over the world, dolls' houses, miniature rooms, model cars, etc.

Open daily except December 25 and January 1, adult £1.20, OAP £1, child 60p.

Eurotunnel Exhibition Centre St Martin's Plain, Cherlton High Street, Folkestone, CT19 4QD [0303 270111]. Discover how the tunnel is being built, and how the environment is being

protected. Large model railway layout of terminals and tunnels, full-size mock-up of section of a shuttle train, inter-active map of Europe, viewing tower.

Open all year, Tuesday–Sunday, Monday bank holidays, adult £2.50, OAP/child £1.50.

🎪 🚌

Sittingbourne and Kemsley Steam Railway The Wall, Milton Regis, nr Sittingbourne [0795 424899]. Steam: 2 miles narrow-gauge track, originally serving paper mills, 7 locos, display of rolling stock.

Open April–mid October, Sunday/bank holidays, August mid-week, return trip, adult £1.80, OAP £1.30, child 90p.

The Historic Dockyard Chatham [0634 812551]. Ships built here since Tudors. Georgian and Victorian buildings, 8 museums, various weaponry, in 80 acres. A lot of walking and little likelihood of seeing it all in one visit. Start at Visitor Centre to check day's events like the making of rope by traditional methods in the 1128-ft-long Ropewalk, and guessing its breaking point. Among highlights, Wooden Walls exhibition, the fascinating story with life-size figures and settings, voices, seen through the eyes of an apprentice shipwright, of the building of a wooden warship, timbers, crafts, fitting out, into war. Also: large collection of boats, midget submarines, steam engines; sloop *Gannet* (1878) being restored; Heavy Horse Stables (wagon rides in summer); try knot-tying or breaking out a flag; watch flags being made. Tours. Events like steam rally, tug-o'-war, boat jumbles.

Open October–March Wednesday, Saturday, Sunday, late March–late October Wednesday–Sunday and bank holidays, adult £4.50, OAP £4, child £2.50, family ticket.

Charles Dickens Centre Eastgate House, Eastgate, High Street, Rochester [0634 844176]. Tableaux, settings, with sound/light, life-size models of Mr Pickwick, Miss Haversham, Nancy, Fagin, Oliver, in reconstructions of scenes from the books. Events include annual Dickens Festival, late May/early June with people, all ages, turning up in Victorian costume.

Open daily except Good Friday, Christmas, adult £1.70, OAP/child £1.10.

Leeds Castle Maidstone ME17 1PL [0898 800680]. Fairy-tale, built on two islands in a lake. Centuries of history, royal owners, furniture, pictures, gardens, greenhouses, vineyard replanted on Domesday-listed site, unusual waterfowl, aviary and duckery, new maze with underground grotto (caves and tumbling water) in centre.

Medieval Dog Collar Museum. Worth getting the special events list, like an Easter egg hunt, hot-air ballooning.

Open daily mid March–October, November–March weekends, daily post Christmas week. Can be closed for special events, castle/park adult £6.20, OAP £5.20, child £4.20, less for park and attractions only.

Maidstone Museum and Art Gallery St Faith's Street, Maidstone ME14 1LH [0622 754497]. Archaeology, natural and social history of Kent, weapons, armour, musical instruments, ethnographical material from the Pacific, extensive costume collection. Children's school holiday activities like kite-making, pond-dipping, carving birds from soap, Tudor life.

Open all year Monday–Saturday, Sunday afternoon.

Tyrwhitt–Drake Museum of Carriages Archbishop's Stables, Mill Street, Maidstone [0622 754497]. Around 50 vehicles from 1675, mostly 19th century, state (Queen Victoria and Oliver Cromwell), but also a goat carriage, sledges, a hearse, sedan chair, costermonger's barrow, more.

Open all year Monday–Saturday, April–September Sunday afternoons.

Finchcocks Goudhurst, off A262 [0580 211702]. Living Museum of Music. Georgian, housing around 70 historical keyboard instruments, organs, harpsichords, clavichords, spinets, early pianos, which are played on open days in a light-hearted entertainment, even hilarious, one includes drums and bells in its effects. Festival September/October, music by professionals and children. See also **Music** page 271.

Open days Easter–September Sunday, also Monday bank holidays, August Wednesday–Sunday, adult £3.50, child £2.

A Day at the Wells The Corn Exchange, The Pantiles, Tunbridge Wells [0892 546545]. 18th-century 'society' took the medicinal waters here. Life re-created with full-size appropriately garbed characters: settings – a London inn, Wells coffee house, at the springs ('Dippers' dispensed), visiting the fashionable Pantiles of course, and finally a ball in the Assembly Rooms with gambling going on in a corner. Taped personal commentaries, adult and child version, included in admission.

Open daily except Christmas Day, adult £2.75, OAP £2.25, child £1.75.

Bewl Water Lamberhurst, Tunbridge Wells, A21 [0892 890661]. Best to start in the Visitor Centre: here there are trails, footpaths, and bridleways for the devoted walkers/riders, trout fishing, various watersports, an adventure playground, annual events summer weekends. Definitely a case of getting the leaflet to find out more about your particular interest.

Penshurst Place Penshurst, Tonbridge. B2027/2176 [0892 870307]. Home of Viscounts De L'Isle, massive Great Hall, pictures, furniture, tapestries. Also 10-acre walled garden, lake, nature trail, toy museum, playground with tuck shop, and display of agricultural bygones.

Open March–September Tuesday–Sunday afternoons, Monday bank holidays, adult £3.50, OAP £3, child £1.75, less for grounds plus toy museum.

Whitbread Hop Farm Beltring, Paddock Wood [0622 872068]. Shire horses, foals, the Hop Museum with memorabilia from hopping families, farm animals like ducks, goats, sheep, rabbits, nature trail, craft demon-strations. Annual Hop Festival.

Open daily mid April–November, adult £2.50, OAP/child £1.50.

Dover Castle Dover CT16 1HU [0304 201628]. Medieval fortress, great keep 21-ft-thick walls (not accessible for wheelchairs), Constable's Tower, Georgian/Victorian earthworks. Long-time defence role including Napoleonic Wars. Battle of Waterloo model with thousands of lead soldiers. History of 'The Queen's Regiment' with sights, sounds, smells. Guided tours of 'Hellfire Corner', World War II HQ, in Napoleonic-time tunnels, including ops room, newsreel, film, view across Channel from a balcony (extra £1.75, 50p).

Open daily except December 24–26, January 1, adult £3, OAP £2, child £1.50, English Heritage members free.

Chislehurst Caves Old Hill, Chislehurst [081 476 3264]. 20 miles of caverns and passages hewn out of chalk over 8000 years. Guides take you on a 45-minute lamplit tour and tell about Flint Knappers, Cavaliers, the Druid Altar, Haunted Pool, Children's Caves, those who sheltered there from bombing during World War II. Additionally, Sunday and bank holidays, 1½-hour adventurous tour.

Open daily Easter–September, otherwise weekends, during school holidays and for parties, adult £2, child £1, extra for the long tour.

White Cliffs Experience Market Square, Dover CT16 1PB [0304 214566]. Historium, press a button and hear what it was like having a baby in Roman Britain, join the Romans facing the Cantiaci Tribe at Walmer, row a real Roman galley or clamber up the rigging of an old ferry, step into a living cartoon in the Time and Tide Show, pick your way over the rubble of a 1944 Dover street. Museum, real objects, models, set pieces, tell the town's story.

Open daily April–October, historium adult £4, OAP £3.50, child £2.50, museum 95p and 50p.

Surrey

Chessington World of Adventure Leatherhead Road, Chessington KT9 2NE [0372 727227]. Theme park. Rides that take you up, over, down and around. Zoological Gardens with hippos, gorillas, etc. Circus World and the Tamara Coco Circus. Safari skyway, high-level train.

Open, theme park, circus and zoo March–October, zoo only closed December 23–January 1, adult £9.50, child £8.50.

Thorpe Park Staines Road, Chertsey [0932 562633]. Over 70 attractions, rides, lots of children's rides, 1930s working farm reached by train or boat trip, with sheep, pigs, cattle, goats, theatre, paddling beach, nature trails.

Open daily Easter–October, one price covers attractions, adult £9.50, OAP/child £8, less in low season.

Rural Life Centre Old Kiln Museum, Reeds Road, Tilford, Farnham [025 125 2300]. Private collection, over 10 acres, of the tools, crafts, including domestic, over 100 years of farming. Narrow-gauge railway, diesel and steam, Sundays, with children's rides. Rustic Sunday, last Sunday in July, craftspeople demonstrate, plus shows for children.

Open April–September, Wednesday–Sunday plus bank holidays, adult £2, OAP £1.50, child £1.

Birdworld and Underwaterworld Holt Pound, Farnham. A325 [0420 22668]. Divide into 2: 1000 birds from tiny hanging parrot to ostrich; then the underwater part, massive aquaria with the kind of coral, colours seen in tropics and inhabitants like blind cave fish, the dangerous piranha, lots of pretty things. Outdoors too, add wildlife, foxes, squirrels, butterflies, in Alice Holt Forest, 2000 acres. Visitor Centre nearby [0420 23666].

Open daily almost throughout the year, Birdworld, adult £2.60, child £1.40, Underwaterworld 80p/40p.

London

I am a Londoner but I am still constantly astonished by the sheer size of the capital. So first a word of caution. Planning is essential for sightseeing, especially with children. To think light-heartedly, 'While we're in London anyway, let's pop over to . . .' could have you running out of daytime. It takes longer to get around than you might imagine!

Sightseers divide into two groups, those from a long distance who may concentrate on such as the Tower, Buckingham Palace, Tussaud's, and those from shortish distances like the suburbs,

Home Counties, who will advisedly pick on 'clusters' for any single expedition, like Kew Gardens and the Kew Bridge Steam Museum, or Tower Bridge, the Tower and HMS *Belfast*, or Kensington Palace, Kensington Gardens and the London Toy and Model Museum, and who will find travelling and sightseeing pleasanter if they avoid the major attractions during the summer main tourist season and explore those at half-terms, Christmas or weekends. Save Tussaud's for New Year's Day.

Visitors should avoid travelling in the discomfort of commuters' rush hour and always check that their goals are open.

Car travel is only feasible if you are sure of parking places. The Underground and buses are more practical with the Travelcard covering both and the Docklands Light Railway. To travel on a bus is a treat in itself for modern children anyway and younger ones on the upstairs front seats will pretend to 'drive'. Free Underground and bus maps are available at Travel Information Centres (page 75) and *Travelling in London*, also free, explains about all the tickets as well as about buying from automatic machines and using the ticket gates. Consider too a sightseeing tour by bus with a commentary or a river trip (page 74).

Travel, even with reduced fares for children, is a big item in the cost. I checked costs for a couple of short journey visits from the suburbs. A birthday treat with 2 adults and 6 girls who went into the Tower, took a short Thames boat trip, looked at Westminster Abbey, Big Ben and Parliament, had refreshments, cost around £100. A similar birthday treat of 2 adults, 3 boys going to London Dungeon and HMS *Belfast* came to over £10 each. Both parties also went to Trafalgar Square and bought packs of bird food. A mother in the first party concluded drily: 'They'd have been happy just with that.' The second party stayed feeding pigeons an hour, buying half a dozen packs each.

So remember Trafalgar Square and cameras. And that many museums and art galleries are still free, parks are free, and open spaces like around the Tower, possibly consuming your own home-made picnic while watching the river traffic.

Resources

Travelcards Obtainable at Underground stations and London Tourist Information Centres (TICs) offering virtually unlimited travel on the Underground and bus networks. Valid for 1 or 7 days. For 7-day Travelcards a passport-sized photograph is required, and those nearing their 16th birthday who still get reduced fares require a child-rate photocard (from London Post Offices or from the TICs); proof of age will be required.

Overseas visitors can buy Visitor Travelcards with the same benefits from their local travel agencies before departure. The ticket comes with a set of discount vouchers to attractions.

London Tourist Board Telephone Information Services
General London Information 071 730 3488 (automatic queuing system). *Open Monday–Friday 9 a.m.–6 p.m.* Ask the multilingual staff about where to go, what to see, what's on, about travel routes, catering facilities.

Credit Card Booking Line 071 824 8844. *Open Monday–Friday 9 a.m.–6 p.m.* This one for booking accommodation and tours, and for guidebooks, maps, etc. Booking charge. Riverboat Information 071 730 4812. For tours or for booking parties.

London Tourist Board enquiries by post Correspondence Assistant, Distribution Dept, London Tourist Board and Convention Bureau, 26 Grosvenor Gardens, London SW1W 0DU.

LTB Tourist Information Centres These give information and advice on accommodation, sightseeing and travel. Tourists can reserve rooms, book travel, theatre and sightseeing tour tickets, purchase guidebooks and phone cards.

Victoria Station Forecourt, SW1 *Open daily April 9–Nov 4 8 a.m.–8 p.m., Monday–Saturday 8 a.m.–7.30 p.m., Sunday 8 a.m.–5.30 p.m., reduced winter opening hours.*

Harrods, Knightsbridge, SW1 *Open during store hours.*

Heathrow Terminals 1, 2, 3, Underground Station Concourse Heathrow Airport *Open daily 8 a.m.–6.30 p.m.*

Selfridges, Oxford Street, W1 (Basement Services Arcade) *Open during store hours.*

HM Tower of London, West Gate, EC3 *Open April 9–November 4, Monday–Saturday 9.30 a.m.–6 p.m., Sunday 10 a.m.–6 p.m.*

Liverpool Street Station *Open Monday–Friday 9.30 a.m.–6.30 p.m., Saturday 8.30 a.m.–6.30 p.m., Sunday 8.30 a.m.–3.30 p.m.*

Other Tourist Information Centres British Travel Centre, 12 Regent Street, Piccadilly Circus, SW1Y 4PQ 071 730 3400 (not Sundays). *Open Monday–Friday 9 a.m.–6.30 p.m., Saturday and Sunday 10 a.m.–4 p.m., June–September, Saturday 9 a.m.–5 p.m.*

Locations of other TICs include Croydon, Greenwich, Harrow, Hillingdon, Ilford, Kingston-upon-Thames, Lewisham, Richmond, Twickenham.

Major bus tour companies Evan Evans [071 930 2377], Frames Rickards [071 837 3111], Golden Tours [081 743 3300], London Buses [071 227 3272].

Online Leisure Information Computerized terminals in public places fed by the Online database tell you what's on at cinemas, theatres, about exhibitions, pools, parks and sports centres, museums and tourist attractions. Free 'Get on and go' maps, sponsored by the Countryside Commission, Nature Conservancy Council, etc. (information from Online), a guide to London's outdoor activities, listing sports centres, city farms, country parks, walks, nature trails, are available from local libraries, sports centres, TICs or by mail from London Buses (A&P) FREEPOST, London SW1H 0YH or ring 071 371 0247.

Public information terminals: Barbican Arts Centre, City Information Centre, near St Paul's Cathedral, TICs in Croydon, Greenwich, Luton, Tower Hamlets, libraries in Bromley, Ealing, Enfield, Greenwich, Kensington, Lewisham, Epsom, Sutton, Tower Hamlets, also Allders Department Store, Sutton, and some sports centres.

Sportsline Ring 071 222 8000 for person-to-person information on all sports for all sorts, how to get started, where to go and how much it will cost. At home with a toddler and feeling far from fit? Beginners' badminton with a crèche alongside may be near you. Your children are showing interest in a sport, ask about holidaytime 'taster' courses. *Open Monday–Friday 10 a.m.–6 p.m.*

Kidsline Ring 071 222 8070 for person-to-person information. The service is quite accustomed to children making their own enquiries. So ask about what's happening, what's on, in theatres, museums, galleries, parks, sports, youth centres, films, special events, where a child can pursue a hobby, ideas for cheap and free London family outings or countryside trips. *Open Monday–Friday 4 p.m.–6 p.m. termtime, 9 a.m.–4 p.m. school holidays.*

Countryside Hotline Ring 071 222 8000 for person-to-person information on around 3000 places in London's countryside. Open farms, country parks, canals, narrow boats, wildlife, cycleways, pick your own fruit and vegetables, guided walks, trails, nature reserves, rivers, lakes, woods.

Hampton Court Palace East Molesey, Surrey, KT8 9AU [081 977 8441]. Five centuries of royal history starting with Tudors, Henry VIII and his Queens, the next builders being William and Mary using Wren, so courtyards, cloisters, pictures, state apartments, the eye-dazzling Chapel Royal, Great Kitchen, Great Hall, and, after the 1986 fire, an exhibition showing ancient builders', workmen's graffiti and primitive insulation. Splendid free gardens (also maze, Royal Tennis Court, Great Vine) give lots of space for young children. The palace needs interpretation. Older children may find it in the personal taped commentary for hire. Free Palace Trails for families available in school holidays. A new family pack on the maze and gardens can be bought from palace shops. Tudor kitchens re-created: a real wood fire beneath a cauldron and a spit turning, preparations for a banquet for over 1000 guests in 1542, peacocks, venison and boar, reproduction cookery vessels around, fanciful marchpanes – and individual audio guides. School holiday activities: Family Treasure Hunts, 10 upwards (chocolate eggs prizes at Easter), or trails and quizzes looking for heraldry, royal initials (remember Henry's wives), badges, also party games, story-telling, craftwork like designing a palace, a coat of arms. 50p each charge.

Open daily except December 23–26, January 1, adult £4, OAP £3, child £2.50, family ticket, BR Hampton Court.

Kensington Palace The Broad Walk, Kensington Gardens W8 [071 937 9561]. Not the front part where the Prince and Princess of Wales, Princess Margaret and other Royals have apartments but the Court Dress Collection in the State Apartments. Queen Victoria's childhood home, where she learned she was Queen, so her bedroom, some of her clothes, possessions. Court state occasions required special clothing. Dresses and uniforms spanning 12 reigns in period room settings. Princess of Wales's wedding dress on display. School holiday activities: family treasure hunts, say 10s upwards (eggs for prizes at Easter), story-telling, trying on court dress. 50p each charge.

Open daily except Good Friday, December 24–26, January 1, adult £3.50, OAP £2.60, child £2.50, family ticket, Tube High Street Kensington.

Kew Palace Kew Gardens, Kew, Surrey [081 940 3321]. Smallest of royal palaces, 17th century, used as a family retreat by George III and Queen Charlotte. Now decorated and furnished as during their habitation. School holiday activities: family treasure hunts, free palace trails for families, say 10s upwards.

Open daily April–September, adult £1, OAP 75p, child 50p, Tube Kew, BR Kew Bridge.

Banqueting House Whitehall SW1 [071 930 4179]. Built for James I, for banquets, dances, plays. Vast hall with Rubens ceiling. Where Charles I executed. *Seventeenth-Century London, a young person's history trail* (say 9s upwards), £1.20 including postage, with suggestions for full or half-day trail of 17th-century London.

Open all year Monday–Saturday, Sunday afternoons, except Good Friday, December 24–26, January 1, adult £1.90, OAP £1.45, child £1.25, Tube Embankment.

HM Tower of London Tower Hill, EC3N 4AB [071 709 0765]. Royal palace and fortress since William the Conqueror, 1078. Houses the Crown Jewels (check not having annual clean early in year), Royal Armouries, a collection including suits worn by monarchs. Has housed such as Elizabeth I (when a princess)

and many who were executed, Lady Jane Grey, Anne Boleyn. Block and axe can be seen. Generations of children have savoured being unchided referring to the Bloody Tower. Yeoman Warders in Tudor uniform (Beefeaters) give free guided tours at adult level so parents may prefer to request beforehand suitable worksheets which are available to teachers taking school groups from the Tower's Education Centre. The Royal Armouries sell a booklet *Family Trail* (around 20p) about the White Tower collections. Under-10s must be adult-accompanied. Look for the ravens; legend has it that without them the Tower and the Kingdom falls. Changing of the Guard, Tower Green 11.30 a.m. daily in summer, alternate days in winter. Given the Tower's age only certain buildings are easily accessible by wheelchair, not the Crown Jewels.

Open all year Monday–Saturday from 9.30 a.m., March–October Sunday from 2 p.m., except Good Friday, December 24–26, January 1, adult £5.90, OAP £4.50, child £3.70, family ticket, Tube Tower Hill, BR Fenchurch Street.

Tower Bridge SE1 2UP [071 409 0922]. One of the 2 original Victorian steam pumping engines kept working though no longer providing the power to raise the bridge. Panoramic views from the fully glazed overhead walkways. Take cameras.

*Open daily 10 a.m.–4.45 p.m.,
except Good Friday, December 24–26,
January 1, adult £2.50, child £1,
Tube Tower Hill, BR London Bridge.*

HMS Belfast Morgans Lane,
Tooley Street SE1 1JH [071 407
6434]. Last survivor of Royal
Navy's big gun ships, in wartime
action up to Korean War. Now a
museum. All 7 decks to be
explored (lots of steps) with
marked route to discover how
sailors lived and worked at sea,
including punishment cells.
Allow 2 hours.

*Open daily except December 24–26,
January 1, adult £3, OAP/child
£1.50, Tube Tower Hill, BR London
Bridge.*

London Dungeon 34 Tooley
Street SE1 [071 403 0606].
Medieval horrors, the cruel
suffering humans inflicted on
humans. Not for under-8s or the
sensitive.

*Open daily all year, adult £5, child
£3, Tube/BR London Bridge.*

Tower Hill Pageant Tower Hill
Vaults. A 'dark ride' in
automated vehicles transports
visitors past tableaux depicting
2000 years of London's history,
Romans, Viking hordes, the
Blitz, with sounds, smells, and a
unique not seen before display
of archaeological evidence from
Roman, Saxon and medieval
finds, incorporating the research
of Museum of London

archaeologists and historians.
Inspiration, of course, the style
and techniques used at the
Jorvik Viking Centre, York. On
the floor above the Museum of
London display includes unique
waterfront finds recovered
during archaeological
investigation over the past 20
years including reconstruction of
part of a Roman ship found
embedded in the Thames.

*Open daily all year, adult £4.50,
OAP/child £2.50, Tube Tower Hill.*

Docklands A frontier town, a
building site, a theme park
without the hotdog stands and
loos, viewed from mostly
overhead in the toytown
Docklands Light Railway (closed
weekends for maintenance, bus
replacement, and to be avoided
in the rush hour) and starting
from Tower Gateway, near the
Tower, and from Stratford and
travelling to Island Gardens
where you can walk the Foot
Tunnel to Greenwich.
Travelcards cover DLR. St
Katherine Docks, by Tower
Bridge, waterside attractions,
boats and yachts; other docks
with architecturally unusual new
offices or homes with yachts
moored alongside; Canary
Wharf tower, tallest in London;
water sports (water skiing,
windsurfing, wetbikes,
canoeing), 7s–18s, Victoria Dock
[071 511 2326], Shadwell Basin
[071 481 4210]; City Farms,
Surrey Docks, Rotherhithe [071
231 1010], Mudchute, Isle of

Dogs [071 515 5901], Newham, Beckton [071 476 1170].

London Docklands Development Corporation (LDDC) Visitor Centre, 3 Limeharbour E14 9TJ [071 515 3000]: *A Visitor's Guide to Docklands*, free, provides map, history, details of attractions; *London Docklands and East London: What to See and Do* lists museums, theatres, sports facilities, restaurants, street markets.

Alexandra Palace and Park
Wood Green N22 4AY [Information line 0898 400 338]. Redeveloped after 1980s fire, palace now an exhibition centre (Model Engineer and Modelling exhibition Christmas holidays). New, at palace's east end, regional-size ice-rink: family sessions, junior disco (under-14s only), tuition for mothers and toddlers, juniors. Group and school group discounts. In 196-acre park: pitch and putt golf course, boating lake, children's playground, animals, Play Centre (playgroup, after school club, holiday play schemes [081 348 1358]), ski slope [081 888 2284], Grove Community workshop for all ages and disabled or able [081 883 7173]. Bank holiday funfairs. Park entry free, charges for events, ice-rink, etc.

Park open all year; children's play area closes sundown, BR Alexandra Palace.

Bethnal Green Museum of Childhood Cambridge Heath Road E2 9PA [081 980 2415]. Largest toy collection on public view in the world, 46 dolls' houses from mansion to cottage, dolls, trains, bears, puppets and toy theatres, folk toys, a mass of games. Child-orientated, local children could probably give you a guided tour, particularly of their favourite exhibits, having been visiting since pre-school days. Saturday Art Workshops 11 a.m.–1 p.m. and 2–4 p.m. for 3s upwards, accompanying adults welcome. Painting corner for the very young, for older children a theme – puppets, paper printing, games, kites, jigsaw puzzles, hats, windmills, dolls' houses, optical toys. Christmas and Easter holiday activities like making a museum case, pop-up books, shadow puppets, summer holidays 'Summer Games', playing board games from across the world, or inventing your own, again with games, stories for under-5s. Annual 'Spirit of Christmas' exhibition.

Open daily except Fridays, Sunday mornings, Tube Bethnal Green.

Whitechapel Art Gallery
Whitechapel High Street E1 7QZ [071 377 0107]. Exhibitions of paintings and sculptures national and international. 'Family Days', children 6 upwards, in school holidays: could be drawings, collage, working with a magic lantern, in workshops allied to current exhibitions.

*Open daily except Monday, Tube
Aldgate East.*

▣ ▦ ▤ ▨

Geffrye Museum Kingsland Road
E2 8EA [071 739 8543]. Tells the
story of popular furniture and
furnishing in Britain through a
series of period rooms from
Elizabethan times to setting up
home in the 1950s. Workshops,
demonstrations, talks, Saturdays,
half-terms, Easter/summer
school holidays, all ages (under-
7s adult-accompanied), have
included festive cooking
internationally, bringing still-life
paintings to life, making mosaics,
a giant map, local walks. Quizzes.
Winter: 'Toddlers' Specials!',
activities for toddlers and their
parents.

*Open all year Tuesday–Saturday,
Sunday afternoons, Monday bank
holidays, Tube/BR Liverpool Street.*

▣ ▦ ▨

Bank of England Museum
Threadneedle Street EC2R 8AH
[071 601 5545]. Entrance
Bartholomew Lane. About
money (soft, from 17th-century
handwritten receipts to today's
technologically sophisticated,
hard, gold bars from Romans to
modern) and the human dealers
from a re-creation of 18th-
century quill pen users to the
modern computer users. Pick up
a phone to hear about the work
of a modern dealer, touching the
illuminated green screen for
appropriate sections, foreign, gilt
or money markets. An inter-
active video explains the Bank's

work; tap the screen to test your
knowledge. No free samples,
only a badge for children, but
gold bars (chocolate) on sale.

*Open all year Monday–Friday
10 a.m.–5 p.m. Easter–end September,
Sunday and Lord Mayor's show day
11 a.m.–5 p.m. Tube, Bank.*

▣ ▦ ▤ ▨

Museum of London London
Wall EC2Y 5HN [071 600 3699].
Story of London and Londoners
told with vehicles (Lord Mayor's
dazzling coach), costume,
artefacts, jewellery, furniture,
from prehistoric to World War II
memorabilia and lifestyle,
including Romans, the medieval
period, Tudors, Stuarts,
Georgians, Victorians. Children's
holiday activities: like making a
mini-museum, a miniature
garden, film props, participating
in dance, mime, dressing up,
walks, talks. Annual Christmas
young people's lecture.

*Open daily except Monday, Sunday
mornings, adult £3, OAP/child
£1.50, family ticket £7.50, free
4.30–6 p.m., Tube Barbican.*

▦ ▤ ▨

Covent Garden Market WC2
[Information 071 836 9136].
Once London's fruit, veg, flower
market. Since 1980 a shopping
centre plus entertainment, in
attractive 1830s listed buildings
and on Inigo Jones's Piazza.
Apart from regular street
entertainment events can
include: February Chinese New
Year, 3 days of celebrations and

entertainment and an annual pancake race; Easter celebration with family events; April Magic Festival, 3 days of magic and spectacle; June Dance Festival, 3-day event of dance, mime, movement; August Kids' Festival, Bank Holiday event; October Punch and Judy Festival, Hallowe'en Festival; December Sunday Children's Christmas markets. Places of interest: Puffin Bookshop, Unit 1, specialist children's book and toy shop; The Doll's House, Unit 29, hand-made dolls' houses and miniature furniture; Eric Snook, Unit 32, high-standard toy shop; Cabinet Mechanical Theatre, Unit 33/34, exhibition of over 60 amusing push-button mechanical models and a shop; Benjamin Pollock Toy Shop, Unit 44, traditional toy theatres and puppets; Light Fantastic Gallery, Unit 48, a gallery holography; and two museums (see below).

Tube Covent Garden.

London Transport Museum
Piazza, Covent Garden WC2E 7BB [071 379 6344]. Story of London's transport system since 1829 told with buses since the horse-drawn, railway locos, memorabilia, working models, video displays, posters. 'Drive' a London bus or a Circle Line train, climb into other exhibits. Very much a 'touch things' museum. Children's holiday activities like modelling, painting, competitions, functioning model railway layouts or model steam railways with rides.

Open daily except December 24–26, adult £2.60, OAP/child £1.20, family ticket, Tube Covent Garden.

Theatre Museum Russell Street, Covent Garden WC2E 7PA [071 836 7891]. Theatre, ballet, dance, opera, musical theatre, circus, magic, rock and pop, illustrated by over 2 million objects, including costumes, photographs, playbills, prompt books, props and puppets. Box office [071 836 2330] sells tickets for West End shows and its own Studio Theatre (productions, workshops, talks, films). Exhibitions like 'Slap!', the secrets of stage make-up. Holiday activities have included panto events, competitions, workshops. Family trail sheets.

Open daily except Monday, adult £2.50, OAP/child £1.25, family ticket, Tube Covent Garden.

Spitting Image Rubberworks
Cubitts Yard, James Street, Covent Garden WC2E 8PA [071 240 0393]. From the TV satire: Royals (the Queen in a tiara, at breakfast), politicians, personalities from sport and show business. Traditional puppeteer-operated and new computer-controlled puppets. Behind the scenes workshop tour. Have your picture taken with a puppet.

Open daily all year from 11 a.m., adult £2.90, child £1.90, Tube Covent Garden.

Royal National Theatre South Bank SE1 [071 928 2252]. Christmastime shows for children and families: *Pied Piper, The Magic Olympical Games, Whale,* the story of the international rescue of 3 whales trapped by ice, *The Wind in the Willows.* Supporting events like, with the last-named, children's workshops on turning humans into badgers, rats, through make-up, or learning the weasel walk, toad trot, mole march. Also *Platforms* with talks, readings by Adrian Mole's creator Sue Townsend, Alan Bennett, etc., and puppets, Punch and Judy, clowns.

Foyer open Monday–Saturday, 10 a.m.–10 p.m., free, Tube/BR Waterloo.

Museum of the Moving Image South Bank SE1 8XT [071 401 2636]. About cinema and TV, so hundreds of clips from silent days films and from black and white TV. Actor-guides from the Magic Lanternist to 1940s cinema usherette. Have a go at making your own animations with Zoetrope strips, read the *News at Ten,* be interviewed by Barry Norman, audition for a part on the replica Western set. See Marilyn Monroe's dress, or 'Charlene's' wedding dress from *Neighbours,* a large model of Frankenstein's monster, a Dalek, step aboard a Russian train, press any number of buttons.

Open all year Tuesday–Sunday, Monday bank holidays June– September except December 24–26, adult £3.95, OAP/child £2.75, family ticket, Tube/BR Waterloo.

National Film Theatre South Bank SE1. See under **Films**, page 265.

South Bank Centre South Bank SE1 8XX [071 928 8800]. 3 concert halls, Royal Festival Hall, Queen Elizabeth Hall and Purcell Room, and the Hayward Gallery. Events in RFH like ballet *The Nutcracker, Swan Lake,* children's concerts (see Ernest Read, **Music** page 269), story-telling, reading workshops, performances by the National Children's Orchestra (**Music** page 273). Events in Purcell Room like story-telling to music. 'Saturday Splash', Arts Workshops for 7s–10s, singing, dancing, games, making a video film, more. 'Saturday Centre', Arts Workshops for 11s–14s, older level of same plus creating animation, shadow and light shows, learning performing skills. Register for both with Education Dept [071 921 0848].

Foyer open daily, 10 a.m.–10 p.m., free, Tube/BR Waterloo.

Commonwealth Institute
Kensington High Street W8 6NQ
[071 603 4535]. Promotes the
over 50 Commonwealth countries
through permanent and
temporary exhibitions reflecting
their people and issues. All kinds
of colourful happenings and not
only in major school holidays; age
range/interest say from 5
upwards but depends on what's
going on. Could be story-telling
with masks, audio-visuals, dance,
mime, comedy about India, with
lots of child participation such as
wearing a sari like a Hindu bride
or marching with Hanuman's
army; or watching puppet
performances, say, from Canada,
Nigeria; or Black Australia
multimedia presentation, stories,
slides, dances, songs; an 'African
Music Village', hearing African
music, hearing talks about it,
making instruments, from bits
and pieces, in workshops, trying
them, also trying African food.
Free family Sunday entertainment
2.30–4.30 p.m.: could be dancing,
singing, mime, and workshops
like learning the Maori alphabet
or Caribbean carols.

Open daily except bank holidays,
Tube High Street Kensington.

🏛️ 🚇 ♿ 🅿️ 🧸

Geological Museum Exhibition
Road, South Kensington SW7
2DE [071 589 3444]. Displays of
minerals, rocks, fossils, gold,
diamonds. 'Treasures of the
Earth' exhibition: press buttons
to learn more about copper,
zinc, clay, etc. 'Britain's Offshore
Oil and Gas' designed like an oil
platform, has computer games,
video show filmed from
helicopters. Old favourite: stand
on a platform and get an
earthquake experience. School
holidaytime activities for
children, say 8- to 12-year-olds,
and parents. Could be an
introduction to the museum or
talks like 'Fossils for Fun', or
looking at the minerals in the
museum, lots of films, also lots of
family walks with magnifying
glass and umbrella as
recommended equipment.
Decorative tunnel to Natural
History Museum and one
admission charge covers both.

Open daily, free entry Monday–Friday
4.30–6 p.m., weekends and bank
holidays 5–6 p.m., otherwise adult
£3, OAP/child £1.50, family ticket,
Tube South Kensington.

🏛️ 🚇 ♿ 🅿️

Natural History Museum
Cromwell Road SW7 5BD [071
938 9388, Information line 042
692 7654]. Full of opportunities
for finding out by pushing
buttons, turning handles,
listening, watching, smelling,
touching, about how our bodies
work, about mammals (the life-
size model of the Blue Whale still
suspended), dinosaurs
(Diplodocus still dominating the
main hall), 'Creepy-Crawlies' (a
life-size termite mound and
Crawly House showing how
arthropods share our lives).
Large basement school assembly
area (seats and tables for over
300) and Discovery Centre,
opened by Princess of Wales in

1989 and familiar to Princes William and Harry in school visits, is open to public at weekends and during school holidays. In the Discovery Centre children, say 7–11, can find out why the tortoise did not win the race, how fishes float, what a python skin feels like, and try beachcombing. Also in the holidays: 'Focus Points' special trolleys around with specimens for handling and staff to answer questions and the 'Art Cart' with drawing materials. 'Ecology', world's first permanent exhibition on global ecology. Within a towering greenhouse, a moonlit rain-forest, the largest video wall in the world with a 20-metre diameter globe tracing the water cycle from ocean to mountaintop and back, a volcano erupts and a community, plants, animals, begins again from scratch, the heart of a leaf to be explored. Decorative tunnel to Geological Museum and one admission charge covers both.

Open daily, free entry Monday–Friday 4.30–6 p.m., weekends and bank holidays 5–6 p.m., otherwise adult £3, OAP/child £1.50, family ticket, Tube South Kensington.

🏛 🚃 ⊞

Science Museum Exhibition Road SW7 2DD [071 938 8181]. History of transport (locomotives, carriages, cars, aircraft), of science, of medicine. First museum in the world with push-button approach, back in the thirties. 'Launch Pad', the country's first 'hands-on' centre means having fun while finding out about science and technology, by beaming voices, making a bubble sheet, building an arched bridge, shaking hands with yourself, generating electricity by pedalling a bike. Flight Lab, 24 hands-on exhibits that test the principles of flight. 'Food for Thought' exhibition includes Food Pyramid to be assembled according to a healthy diet. Holiday activities: films, 'Professor Pepper's' Victorian science lectures, children's drama activities, actors playing historic roles (like Crapper of flush loo fame, Amy Johnson, the flyer), quizzes.

Open daily except Sunday mornings, adult £2.50, OAP £1.50, child £1, season tickets, Tube South Kensington.

🏛 🚃 ⊞

> **Remember:** most museums and art galleries close over Good Friday, Christmas and New Year's Day.

Victoria and Albert Museum
Cromwell Road SW7 2RL [071
938 8500]. Furniture, jewellery,
ceramics, costume, sculpture,
paintings, medieval to present
day. Children's holiday activities
include trails and 'Introductory
Tours' for 7s–13s, a taste of the
treasures.

*Open daily except Sunday mornings,
voluntary contributions, Tube South
Kensington.*
🏛️🎪🚌🔲

National Army Museum Royal
Hospital Road SW3 4HT [071
730 0717]. About the
circumstance rather than the
pomp of Army life since the 15th
century. Example: an historical
re-enactment not about a battle
but 18th-century soldiers
cooking, mending, playing with
their children. War-gamers will
head for the Battle of Waterloo
model including over 70,000
figures. Children's school
holiday events include films, war-
gaming, model-making, the
chance to handle weapons and
uniforms, mystery competitions
and trails which will lead you to
the skeleton of Napoleon's horse
Marengo.

*Open daily except Sunday mornings,
Tube Sloane Square.*
🏛️🎪🚌🔲

Tate Gallery Millbank SW1P 4RG
[071 821 1313]. Paintings and
sculptures from Pre-Raphaelites
to pop, also the Turner
Collection. Holiday events:
informal gallery tours with a

theme, indoor/outdoor, animals,
as a useful introduction, followed
by art workshops, for 5s–13s;
Laurence Bradbury's lectures on
a theme, Christmas Pie, Ideas
Hatched from an Egg, again
guiding to enjoyment of
paintings, for young people,
children over 7, adults welcome.

*Open daily except Sunday mornings,
Tube Pimlico, BR Vauxhall.*
🏛️🎪🚌🔲

National Gallery Trafalgar
Square WC2N 5DN [071 839
3321]. The surprise in this
massive collection is to see a
familiar Rubens, Rembrandt,
Van Dyck, and realize it is the
original. Try the holidaytime
quizzes alongside the children,
3 levels, early readers, juniors
and seniors, with themes like
grandees, what's afoot, surprises.
Also lecture tours for 7s–14s and
competitions. Activities start at
Orange Street entrance.

*Open daily except Sunday mornings,
Tube Charing Cross, Leicester
Square.*
🏛️🎪🚌🔲

National Portrait Gallery St
Martin's Place WC2H 0HE [071
306 0055]. Likenesses of famous
Britons influencing national
history and culture since the
Tudors, arranged
chronologically. Holidaytime
events, say 7s upwards (can be
for families), like taking pinhole
portraits using biscuit tins,
creating hats from fuse wire,
pearls, netting, creating

vestments, 'making faces' with make-up, learning classical Indian dance.

Open daily except Sunday mornings, Tube Charing Cross, Leicester Square.

🏛️ 🚃 🌐

Guinness World of Records
Trocadero, Piccadilly Circus, Coventry Street W1V 7FE [071 439 7331]. 6 'worlds', Human (match your hand and foot to the world's tallest man, your weight to the heaviest), Animal (the flea is better than the frog at the high jump), Structures and Machines (the world's tallest structures), Sports (multi-screen computer taps into a data bank), Entertainment (songs, films), Our Planet Earth (exploration of space).

Open daily all year, adult £4.50, OAP £3.60, child £2.85, Tube Piccadilly Circus.

🎫 🚃 🌐

The Beatles Revolution
Trocadero, Piccadilly Circus W1V 7FE [071 437 1960]. Story told with sound, music, videos, dioramas and personal possessions, from Liverpool and Hamburg to Lennon's death.

Open daily all year, adult £4, OAP £3.50, child £2.50.

🎫 🌐

Cabinet War Rooms Clive Steps, King Charles Street SW1A 2AQ [071 930 6961]. Underground emergency accommodation for Churchill's wartime cabinet and chiefs of staff. Now a museum with his desk and 'hot-line' to US President Roosevelt. Map Room, Cabinet Room in suite of 21 rooms. Free adult and junior guide leaflets.

Open daily except Good Friday, May Day, Christmas, New Year and on state occasions, adult £3.50, OAP/child £1.75, Tube Westminster.

🎫 🚃 🌐

Barbican Centre Silk Street EC2Y 8DS [071 638 4141, recorded information 071 628 2295]. Art gallery, sculpture court, conservatory, library, theatre, concert hall, cinema (see under **Films**, page 264). August annual family week-long festival of fun 'Summer in the City' with sports like canoeing on the Barbican lake, dance, music, puppet shows, puzzles, clowns, a scavenger trail. Free except for children's workshops. Easter: Children's Fun Day, clowns, magicians, story-tellers, workshops. Christmas: Teddy Bears Concerts, 'The Snowman', family carol concert. Advice: get programmes beforehand to avoid children's disappointment when desirable event booked up. Silk Street Information Desk for what's on.

Open daily except December 24, 25, Tube Barbican.

🎫 🚃 🌐

Florence Nightingale Museum
2 Lambeth Palace Road SE1 7EW [071 620 0374]. Opposite

Houses of Parliament. The Crimean War nursing reforms with a reconstruction of the Scutari Ward, but also about the following years improving Army barracks and civil hospital, sanitation in India, influencing district nursing and health care. Audio-visual narration, historical relics like uniforms, furniture and a lamp. Sometimes nursing re-enactments.

Open all year Tuesday–Sunday, Monday bank holidays, except Easter, Christmas, New Year, adult £2, OAP/child £1, family ticket.
🏛 🖼 🎨

Imperial War Museum Lambeth Road SE1 6HZ [071 416 5000]. Story of 20th-century warfare from Flanders to Falklands, tanks, planes, a Dunkirk little ship, a trench re-creation with sounds/smells. 'Blitz Experience' (extra charge and arrive early, since popular), a replica blitzed street with air-raid shelter, 'near-miss', explosions, shaking floor, smell of burning. Not for the nervous. Touch screen videos tell more. Films and free children's quiz sheets weekends and school holidays.

Open daily except December 25–26, January 1, adult £3, OAP/child £1.50, free on Friday, Tube Lambeth North, BR Waterloo.
🏛 🖼

St Paul's Cathedral Ludgate Hill EC4 [071 248 4619]. By Wren, after predecessor destroyed in Great Fire of London. Whispering Gallery in the dome, whisper on one side and be heard on the other, but first climb over 600 steps. Charge. Exhibition on Royal Wedding includes marriage certificate showing that only the Prince of Wales's Dad's job was written in, Prince of the Realm, not his mother's. Charge. Wren, Lord Nelson, Duke of Wellington buried here. Tours.

Tube St Paul's.
🏛 🖼 🎨

Monument Monument Street EC3 [071 626 2717]. Wren column commemorating outbreak of Great Fire of London. Panoramic views of London if you can climb 311 steps; no lift.

Open April–September Monday–Friday, Saturday and Sunday afternoons, October–March, Monday–Saturday, adult £1, child 25p, Tube Monument.

Westminster Abbey Parliament Square SW1 [071 222 5152]. Royal coronations held here. Tombs and memorials of sovereigns, statesmen, poets. Grave of Unknown Warrior. Tours need booking.

Nave free, royal chapels, Poets' Corner, adult £2.20, OAP £1.10, child 50p, Tube Westminster.

Westminster Cathedral Ashley Place SW1 [071 834 7452]. Roman Catholic, seat of Cardinal of Westminster. Byzantine in style, marble from 100 countries.

Tower: charge, Tube St James Park, BR Victoria.

Madame Tussaud's Marylebone Road NW1 5LR [071 935 6861]. Waxworks from the 1770s to who's in who's out present day. Royals past in sumptuous costumes, to present, religious and political leaders, soldiers, artists, show business people. Long tradition of giving sittings and own clothes, including hanged multiple murderers for the Chamber of Horrors (not for the young), still creepy with the Jack the Ripper Victorian Street. 'Garden Party' with music, laughter, bird-song; mingle with guests like Pavarotti, Dame Edna Everage, Lenny Henry, Terry Wogan, Severiano Ballesteros. Developments: figures that can move, talk, walk, to complicate traditional guessing game of which seeming model attendant is alive.

  London Planetarium [071 476 1121], adjacent to Madame Tussaud's. The sky, stars, space, laser light shows to music, i.e. 'Solar Swoop' exploring the mysteries of the solar system through the eyes of two eagles,

say for 8s upwards. Astronomers' Gallery, lives of scientists.

Open daily except Christmas Day, Tussaud's adult £3.15, child £2.10, combined with Planetarium £7.25 and £4.85, family ticket, Tube Baker Street.

London Zoo Regent's Park NW1 4RY [071 722 3333]. Mammals, reptiles, birds, amphibians, insects. Events like Meet the Animals, Feeding Times, Demonstrations (could be elephant weighing), animal rides (a camel), also elephant tracking by satellite, the Discovery Centre, touch trolleys with displays, activities, Lifewatch Centre showing the zoo's history through film show and exhibition. Moonlight World reverses day and night so normally nocturnal creatures can be seen. Lifewatch, about wildlife conservation: Explorers' section for 4s–15s, membership £10 annually, provides *Explorer News*, free admission London and Whipsnade; special events like creepy-crawly afternoons in the Insect House and trips. 'Adopt an Animal' scheme: from £15 a year, i.e. a jellyfish's keep and feed.

Open daily except Christmas Day, adult £4.70, OAP £3.90, child £2.90, Tube Camden Town.

Buckingham Palace SW1. Sovereign in residence when royal flag flying. Changing the guard at 11.30 a.m. daily, alternate days winter (check with LTB, page 74), but get there at least by 11 a.m. for a good view.

Tube/BR Victoria.

Royal Mews Buckingham Palace Road SW1 [071 930 4832]. The sovereign's horses and carriages like the golden Coronation Coach and the Glass Coach used for royal weddings.

Open all year Wednesday and Thursday 2–4 p.m. except Ascot week, public holidays and royal occasions, adult £1, OAP/child 50p, Tube/BR Victoria.

Horse Guards Parade Whitehall SW1. Changing the guard 11 a.m. Monday–Saturday, 10 a.m. Sunday. Arrive a quarter of an hour beforehand but half an hour main tourist season and fine Sundays.

London Toy and Model Museum October House, 21–23 Craven Hill W2 [071 262 7905]. Teddies, dolls, dolls' houses, cars, boats, trains, 7000 exhibits, in 2 Victorian houses, something for every taste. In garden: play bus, vintage carousel, train layouts including ride-on trains for little ones, and raised tracks with electric trains running daily and steam trains on Sundays (you can take your own, requesting permission first). Quizzes available, with prizes. Events like Teddy Bears' Picnic, Model Boat Regatta (on the pond).

Open all year, Tuesday–Sunday, Monday bank holidays, except Christmas and January 1, adult £2.70, OAP £1.70, child £1.20, family ticket, Tube Queensway.

British Museum Great Russell Street WC1 3DG [071 636 1555, recorded information 071 580 1788]. Magna Carta, Rosetta stone, Elgin marbles, Lindow Man, Sutton Hoo treasure, lots of Egyptian mummies, among vast collections from Egypt, West Asia, Greece, Rome, China, pre-historic and medieval Britain. So advisable collect an available year-round children's trail like 'Lions at Large', 'Big Cats', 'Hunt the Hieroglyphs', 'Roman Britain', 'Asterix', say 8s upwards. Also in the holidays: films, say about Asterix and *Asterix the Gaul, Asterix and Cleopatra* (get programme, arrive early); workshops like 'Exploring Islamic Calligraphy', for 7s–11s, with story-telling, music; family events like Sumari stories, sword-polishing and trail.

Open all year except Sunday mornings, Good Friday, 1st Monday in May, Christmas, January 1, Tube Tottenham Court Road.

Museum of Mankind Burlington Gardens W1X 2EX [071 437 2224]. Ethnography Dept of the British Museum. Series of exhibitions illustrating the variety of non-Western societies and cultures. School holiday events for families or adult-accompanied children, say 7s upwards, like story-telling, professionals acting a traditional legend, making model rickshaws, paintings, or a board game allied to 'Traffic Art, rickshaw paintings from Bangladesh' exhibition or story-telling, songs, games, costume-handling, embroidering, allied to 'Palestinian Costume' exhibition.

Times as British Museum, Tube Green Park.

Syon Park Brentford, Middx [081 560 0881].

Syon House, remodelled by Robert Adam, London residence of Duke of Northumberland. Family portrait gallery will fascinate those interested in historic Royals and their courtiers. Needs interpretation for children. Gardens by Capability Brown, aviary, aquarium, 6-acre rose garden.

House open Easter–September Sunday–Thursday, adult £2.50, OAP/child £1.75, gardens open daily, combined house/gardens £3.75 and £2.50.

British Motor Museum, over 100 models tracing British production.

Open daily except Christmas, adult £2, OAP/child £1.25.

London Butterfly House, dazzling collection of free-flying butterflies from around the world in enormous tropical rain-forest. Will alight on your fingers, clothes. Can be seen courting. Watch foliage to see development from eggs to hatching. Also tarantulas, spiders, creepy-crawlies, terrapins. Outdoor wild garden to attract butterflies designed like a medieval tapestry.

Opening times, charges as Motor Museum. BR Kew Bridge, Tube Gunnersbury.

Royal Botanic Gardens Kew Road, Richmond, Surrey [081 930 1171]. 300 acres, 6 million plant species, superb vistas at any time of year, lots of wide open space, magnificent hothouses, pagoda, ducks. Guided tours for groups, school groups need booking well ahead.

Open daily 9.30 a.m.–dusk (7 p.m. summer, 4 p.m. winter) except Christmas Day, New Year's Day, admission £3.

Kew Palace – in the gardens, see page 78. Built in Dutch style 17th century, George III used it as a 'nursery' for royal children and lived in it himself with Queen Charlotte from 1802 waiting building of a new palace, never completed. He died and Queen Charlotte died here in 1818. Now decorated and furnished as during their habitation. Free education visits.

*Open daily April–September, 11 a.m.–
5.30 p.m., adult £1, OAP 75p, child
50p, Tube Kew, BR Kew Bridge.*
▦ ▣

Kew Bridge Steam Museum
Green Dragon Lane, Brentford,
Middx TW8 0EN [081 568 4757].
Imagine a steam engine you can
walk through while it's working.
Put it in a building like a
cathedral and that's only 1 of the
3 giant Victorian engines in this
restored water pumping station.
Also workshops, waterworks
railway. Special school Steaming
Days mid-week May and October.

*Open daily 11 a.m.–5 p.m. except
Good Friday, Christmas, Engines in
Steam weekends and bank holiday
Mondays: adult £1.80, OAP/child
90p, weekdays: (engines static) £1
and 50p, BR Kew Bridge.*
▦ ▣

Horniman Museum and Gardens
London Road, Forest Hill SE23
3PQ [081 699 2339]. Rich and
varied collection illustrating
worldwide cultures and
traditions through arts and crafts
(masks, puppets), musical
instruments (6000: sound tape
guide), natural history from the
100-year-old stuffed walrus to
birds, shells. Horniman
Workshops, Saturday and daily in
the school holidays for 8s
upwards (first 20 get in): pottery,
weaving, patchwork, basketry,
collage, badges, masks. Special
Interest Centre, open Saturday
to selected 8–14-year-olds to
study a topic of their choice.
Recorder Workshops, Saturday,

children recommended by their
schools perform together. Also
music sessions for parents and
toddlers, family events, origami,
making and testing boomerangs.
Sometimes fees for materials.
Summer entertainment bands,
clowns, magicians, Punch and
Judy. Garden: small zoo and
nature trails.

*Museum open daily except Sunday
mornings and December 24–26,
gardens open daily, BR Forest Hill.*
▤ ▦ ▣ ▩

Royal Air Force Museum
Hendon NW9 5LL [081 205
2266]. History of aviation from
pre-Wright brothers to present
day, so around 60 aircraft
including Spitfire and German
and American aircraft. Also
pictures, uniforms, memorabilia.
Continuous film shows. A
Tornado flight simulator. 'Battle
of Britain Experience', the battle
equipment, reconstruction of an
Operations Room, talking head
of Prime Minister Churchill, also
the home front, Home Guard,
ARP, and talking head of Gertie,
a Cockney mum, telling of her
Blitz experience.

*Open daily except December 24–26
and January 1, adult £3.60, child
£1.80, includes return visit, Tube
Colindale.*
▦ ▣ ▩

Wembley Arena and Stadium
Wembley, Middx [Wembley
Update 0898 600500, box office
081 900 1234]. In Arena
Christmas circus and ice shows.

Stadium 'Behind-the-Scenes' tours: a visit to players' changing rooms, go through the players' tunnel and be greeted by the roar of 80,000 cheers as on a big match day, see the famous pitch. Also memorabilia and learn about visits of famous including Pope John Paul II, Michael Jackson, Madonna. Note: not a case of dropping in. Tours restricted or cancelled for major events. Phone Tours Operations [081 902 8833] or write Wembley Stadium Tours, Wembley Stadium, Wembley, Middx HA9 0DW.

National Maritime Museum Greenwich SE10 9NF [081 858 4422]. Britain's seafaring heritage shown in actual and model ships, paintings, weapons, Cook and Nelson memorabilia, including uniform worn at Battle of Trafalgar, state barges, navigational instruments. Spectacular annual exhibitions like 'The Armada', 'Captain Cook – Explorer', 'Henry VIII – a European Court in England', accompanied by children's worksheets (maps, illustrations, quizzes) and interests for children. Example: Captain Cook exhibition had a Tahitian hut to play in, a native canoe to paddle, a replica ship to explore. Children learn to tie knots, follow a trail. Also: the Queen's House, restored as it might have appeared to Queen Henrietta Maria in 1662; the Planetarium, museum of astronomy and time (Greenwich Mean Time), shows, telescopes; the *Cutty Sark*,

moored outside. School holiday films. Planetarium shows.

Open daily except Sunday morning and December 24–26, Passport ticket to 4 sites £5.90, OAP/child £3.90, family £11.90, single tickets for each available, BR Greenwich, boats from Westminster, Charing Cross and Tower piers.

Thames Barrier Unity Way, Woolwich SE18 5NJ [081 854 1373]. Described as 'The Eighth Wonder of the World', as giant, gleaming 'knights' helmets', 'silver hoods', the world's largest movable flood barrier has to be seen to be believed. Take cameras. Raised viewing platforms at the Riverside Walk. Visitor Centre has exciting audio-visual show and working models to explain the engineering feat. Check with Centre for regular raising of the gates; the 4 main ones standing as high as a 5-storey building. You may prefer them closed and experience the excitement of a river cruise through the Barrier. Additional attraction, alongside the Centre, Hallett's Panorama, the Georgian city of Bath as viewed from a hot-air balloon, portrayed in oil paint and sculpture.

Open daily except December 25–26, January 1, Centre adult £2, OAP/child £1.20, Barrier cruise £1.25 and 90p, BR Charlton, regular river services from Westminster and Greenwich.

ANNUAL EVENTS IN LONDON

January *Lord Mayor of Westminster's New Year's Day Parade* Bands, floats, clowns, starting 12.30 p.m., going along Piccadilly, Regent Street, Oxford Street to Marble Arch into Hyde Park where there is entertainment. *London International Boat Show* Earls Court.

February *Clown's Service* Holy Trinity Church, Beechwood Road, Dalston E8. Clowns in full costume and traditional make-up. Free clown show afterwards. *Chinese New Year* Celebrated in Soho with decorations and Lion Dances through the streets.

March *Boat Race* Oxford and Cambridge universities race from Putney to Mortlake.

March/April – depending on Easter dates. *Easter Sunday, Easter Parade* Battersea Park SW11. Floats, marching bands, parade from 3 p.m. but entertainments and attractions from noon. *Easter Monday* London Harness Horse Parade, The Inner Circle, Regent's Park NW1. Working horses being polished and groomed from around 9.30 a.m., judging, ending with Grand Parade of winners at noon.

April *Marathon* From Blackheath/Greenwich to Big Ben.

June *Trooping the Colour* Horse Guards Parade. The Queen leaves Buckingham Palace around 10.40 a.m., going down the Mall to Horse Guards Parade by 11 a.m. After the spectacular ceremony she returns to appear on the palace balcony at 1 p.m. for RAF flypast. Rehearsals 2 Saturdays preceding ceremony. Tickets for Trooping and rehearsals (send SAE) Brigade Major (Trooping the Colour) Headquarters, Household Division, Horse Guards, Whitehall SW1A 2AX.

July *Royal Tournament* Earls Court Exhibition Centre SW5. Colour, pageantry, pomp, action-packed, by armed forces. Royals generally attend. *Swan Upping* Sunbury-on-Thames to Whitchurch. 6 skiffs catch Thames swan families to record and mark those belonging to 2 ancient Livery companies [071 236 1863 for details].

August *Notting Hill Carnival* August bank holiday Sunday and Monday. Steel and brass bands, spectacular costumes, floats, limbo dancing, West Indian food. Children's Carnival Sunday, competition for best costume.

September *Horseman's Sunday* Service St John's Church, Hyde Park Crescent W2, taken by vicar on horseback, 11.30 a.m. Followed by procession continuing into Hyde Park. Horse Show, gymkhana events Kensington Paddock, Kensington Gardens from 1.30 p.m.

November *Veteran Car Run* 1st Sunday. Starting Hyde Park Corner, 8–9 a.m. A23 road to Brighton arriving from 10.45 a.m. *Lord Mayor's Show* Floats, military bands, armed forces, gilded state coach, from the

Mansion House to the Law Courts [071 603 3030]. *Remembrance Sunday* Cenotaph Memorial, Whitehall SW1. Sunday nearest 11th. Armed forces, ex-servicemen and women, Royal family, government. *State Opening of Parliament* House of Lords SW1. Royal processions, state coaches, leaving Buckingham Palace around 11 a.m. along Mall, through Horse Guards Parade and Arch, Whitehall, to Parliament Square. *Christmas lights* Bond Street, Oxford Street, Regent Street till January 6.

Dates and times are available from Tourist Information Centres, where no contact number is given.

Thames
and Chilterns

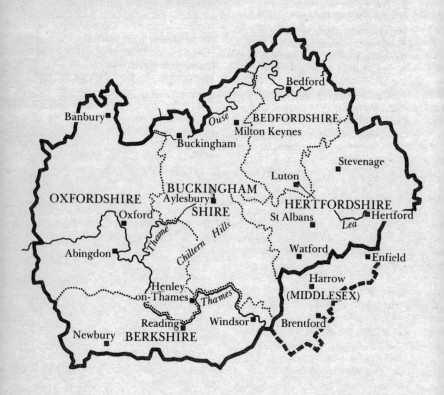

Berkshire

Windsor Castle Windsor [0753 831118]. Fortress here since the Conqueror but massive castle of today largely attributable to George IV. Castle lived in by the monarch and generally believed to be closed when she is in residence. Not so. On one visit I saw Her Majesty gathering corgis for their afternoon walk. Walls covered with weaponry, swords, guns, revolvers. State apartments display one of the finest private art collections in the world. Van Dyck, Holbein, Leonardo da Vinci, etc. You can walk all round Queen Mary's Dolls' House, even the servants had their own bathrooms. Late medieval St George's Chapel, burial place of 10 sovereigns, including beheaded Charles I, with Garter Knights' banners and heraldic badges. Children's quiz. Changing the Guard around 11 a.m. daily in summer, alternate days winter. Exhibition of the Queen's Presents and Royal Carriages: lots of large gold keys, huge gold and diamond-encrusted sword, the Princess Elizabeth's riding clothes, pictures made of feathers and shells, a glass state coach in a bottle.

Open daily except Good Friday, December 24–26, January 1, and for annual Garter ceremony, state visits, best check, State Apartments adult £2.80, OAP £1.80, child £1.20, Dolls' House £1.40, £1.20, 60p, Presents/Carriages £1.30, £1, 60p, Chapel £2, £1.

Royalty and Empire Central Station, Windsor [0753 857837]. Madame Tussaud's re-creation of Queen Victoria awaiting arrival of guests for her Diamond Jubilee, first in actual Royal Waiting Room, Royal Train outside. Then with daughter, grandchildren, approaching state landau, 70 Coldstream Guards forming the guard of honour. Audio-visual show 'Sixty Glorious Years' and moving, talking Victorians. Buses outside station for guided tours of Windsor, Eton and environs.

Open daily except Christmas Day, adult £3.95, OAP £2.95, child £2.80.

Windsor Safari Park Winkfield Road, Windsor SL4 4AY [0753 869841]. 'African Adventure', travel with a guide through animal reserves in Safari Roadtrains to see giraffes, rhino, zebra, tigers, a pride of lions. View elephants from 'Tree Tops'. The hippos and crocs in the 'Congo River', seen from the *African Queen* riverboat, are animated replicas. Shows: birds of prey, sea-lions, dolphins. Children's packs, quizzes, colouring sheets, on sale.

*Open daily except Christmas Day,
adult £5.99, OAP £3.99, child
£4.99.*

Courage Shire Horse Centre
Maidenhead Thicket,
Maidenhead, off A4 [0628
824848]. Very large horses,
familiar from TV and festivals.
Rosettes, gleaming harness on
display, working farrier some
days. Audio-visual presentation.
Also animals and birds
enclosure, playground.

*Open daily March–October, adult
£2, OAP/child £1.50.*

**Stratfield Saye House and
Wellington Country Park**
Stratfield Saye, Reading RG7
2BT. Between Reading and
Basingstoke [0256 882882].
House: family home of Dukes of
Wellington since 1817. House
and exhibition contain many
personal possessions and
mementoes of the Iron Duke
including his 18-ton funeral
hearse. Country Park: dairy
museum, children's animal farm,
deer park, nature trails,
boating/fishing. Unusual: 'dogs
very welcome'.

*House open daily May–September
except Friday, park daily
March–October and winter weekends,
house adult £3.25, child £1.60, park
£2.20 and £1.*

Oxfordshire

Didcot Railway Centre Didcot
OX11 7NJ. A4130 [0235
817200]. Reviving the golden age
of the Great Western Railway, re-
creation of Brunel's trackwork,
plus typical small country station,
original locomotive depot with
20 locos, various types, and work
going on by volunteers.
'Steamdays' with rides, first and
last Sunday each month from
March, bank holidays, all
June–August Sundays and all
August Wednesdays. Events like
Steamday for the Disabled,
Teddy Bears' Picnic, Santa
Steamings.

*Open weekends all year,
April–September Tuesday–Sunday
and Monday bank holidays, adult
£3.50, OAP/child £3.30.*

Pendon Museum Long
Wittenham, Abingdon. Off A415,
3 miles north of Didcot [086 730
7365]. A reproduction in
miniature in an indoor museum
of the English countryside
around 1930, with its styles,
colours, gardens, fields, rural
ways. So cottages, farms, of the
Vale of the White Horse; a
cavalcade of trains crossing a
Brunel-designed long viaduct on
the edge of Dartmoor, recording
the Great Western Railway of the
period; then Madder Valley, an
imaginary scene with hamlets,
castle, shops, warehouses, ships,
railway, drawn from real
originals. Naturally figures are
included, like farm workers,

children, chaps outside the pub, waiting passengers on train platforms, and a bike, buses, a horse, dog, rabbits. The Vale in particular is special because the modelled interiors, visible through windows, represent real originals. I heard of an elderly visitor enchanted to see her previous home, with all its small details, reproduced. Pendon is a charity, run by volunteers. Children's worksheets available. Viewing height unsuitable for very small children.

Open all year Saturday, Sunday, 2–5 p.m., Easter, May, August bank holidays 11 a.m.–5 p.m., closed around Christmas and New Year, adult £1.50, OAP/child £1.

Cotswold Wild Life Park Burford, Oxford. A361 [099 382 3006]. Rhinos, tigers, leopards, ostriches, gazelle, etc. in large paddocks, tropical birds in walled garden, aviary, reptile house and butterfly house, with 50-ft flight cage. Also pony/donkey and narrow-gauge railway rides in summer, and an animal brass rubbing centre. Events: falconry, archery displays, Snake Days (meet a snake). 'Junior Friends', up to 15s, magazine, badge, etc.

Open daily, adult £3.50, OAP/child £2.

Cogges Manor Farm Museum Witney OX8 6LA [0993 772602]. Manor-house dining-room,

kitchen, dairy, furnished in Edwardian style, livestock also typical of a farm of the period. Weekend (mostly) demonstrations include butter-making, sheep-shearing, bread and other farmhouse cooking, thatching, threshing. Nature and history trails. Activity guide on sale. Children's holiday activities.

Open daily April–October, entry charges.

Blenheim Palace Woodstock, Oxford. A34 [0993 811325]. Home of Duke of Marlborough, birthplace of Winston Churchill, an enormous house. State rooms, immense library, paintings, sculptures, etc.; Churchill exhibition (he's buried in nearby Bladon); trips on narrow-gauge railway or by boat on the lake created by Capability Brown. New, world's largest symbolic hedge maze in Garden Centre complex.

Open daily mid March–end October, inclusive: adult £5.50, OAP £4.20, child £2.80, park, butterfly house, garden centre, carful £3, pedestrian adult 70p, child 40p.

The Oxford Story 6 Broad Street, Oxford OX1 3AJ [086 790055]. Seated in a moving desk you spiral backwards into the past, and, with a commentary, learn about university life from the Middle Ages, books, ideas, the Reformation, the dissolution of the monasteries, the Civil War, the first women's halls, and the characters, John Wesley, Lewis Carroll, writer of *Alice's Adventures in Wonderland*, Lawrence of Arabia, more. Settings, furnishings, life-size figures.

Open daily except Christmas Day, adult £3.75, OAP £3, child £2.50, family ticket.

Oxfordshire County Museum Fletcher's House, Woodstock [0993 811456]. In a town house with garden. The story of Oxfordshire, its people, buildings and landscapes. Base for branch of Young Archaeologists Club, 9s up, magazine, monthly meetings with activities like field walking, visits to excavations: apply Education Section. Same source for children's holidaytime activities in various Oxfordshire museums.

Open October–April, Tuesday–Saturday, Sunday afternoon.

Pitt Rivers Museum South Parks Road, Oxford [0865 270927]. Diverse collection of the products of human art and ingenuity from all periods and cultures including extraordinary masks. Musical instruments to see and hear in nearby Balfour Building. Apply here (SAE to Dr H. La Rue) to join Oxmus Club for 8s–14s, meeting in Oxford museums for looking at fossils, an insect safari, animal games, graphic designing, for example.

Open all year, Monday–Saturday 1–4.30 p.m.

Buckinghamshire

West Wycombe Caves West Wycombe Park Office, West Wycombe [0494 24411]. Altered and extended 18th century by Sir Francis Dashwood. Winding passage to small chambers, some with lit-up artificial stalactites and stalagmites, others with life-size wax models of Sir Francis's friends.

Open February–May weekday afternoons, April Sundays and bank holidays, weekday afternoons, weekends May–October, adult £2, OAP/child £1.

Beckonscot Model Village Warwick Road, Beaconsfield HP9 2PL. Off A355 [0494 672919]. Could be the oldest model village, founded in 1929, covering some 40,000 square ft, gardens, town, villages, churches, castles, lakes, railways, of course, a miniature community. All in 1930s style. Queen Mary took *her* grandchild – now Queen Elizabeth II – to visit there several times. An example of a grandmother (I would hardly like to call her an OAP) saying 'Let's have a look at this!' I feel sure it was enjoyed by both generations. Take cameras. Children's quiz available.

*Open daily March–November, adult
£2, OAP £1.50, child £1.*

Bedfordshire

**Leighton Buzzard Narrow-Gauge
Railway** Pages Park Station,
Billington Road, Leighton
Buzzard. A4146 [0525 373888].
Once a sand-carrying railway,
now, through enthusiasts
rebuilding the track, station,
sheds, acquiring steam and diesel
engines, you can wend your way
on little trains through open
countryside, estates, both housing
and industrial. 5½-mile trip.

*Open April–October Sundays and
Monday bank holidays, mid
July–August Saturday and
Wednesday. Phone for fares.*

Whipsnade Wild Animal Park
Dunstable LU6 2LF [0582
872171]. 600 acres of parkland,
over 2800 animals, UK's largest
conservation centre specializing
in breeding certain endangered
species. Walk, drive round in
your car, or Roadtrains. 'Meet
the Animals' (pet a python,
cuddle a chinchilla), 'Animal
Encounters', 'Animals at Work'
(birds of prey, sea-lions,
elephants), at set times.
Discovery Centre, Children's
Zoo, steam railway, Adopt an
Animal, 'Lifewatch', under-15s
(members get magazine, free
admission). Events: 'Teddy
Bears' Party', Christmas with
Santa, his reindeer and sleigh.

*Open daily except Christmas Day,
adult £4.50, OAP £3.70, child
£2.70.*

Woburn Abbey Woburn. Off M1
[0525 290666]. The abbey itself,
of course, pictures, tapestry,
porcelain, plus Antiques Centre
with shop fronts rescued from
various parts of Britain. For the
young think not only of the
space, the deer park, but a study
trail which explains what is/was
in a stately home. Look also for
annual events, like flying your
own kite, a model helicopter
rally, more.

*Open January–February weekends,
daily March–October, adult £5, OAP
£4, child £2, family ticket, park only,
carful £2.50, pedestrian 50p.*

**Woburn Wild Animal Kingdom
and Leisure Park** Woburn MK17
9QN [0525 290407]. Britain's
largest drive-through safari park.
Tigers, lions, hippos, giraffes,
monkeys, camels. Working
elephant displays, sea-lion and
parrot shows. Roundabouts,
rides.

*Open daily March–October, inclusive
charge adult £6, OAP/child £4.*

Shuttleworth Collection Old
Warden Aerodrome,
Biggleswade. Off A1 [076 727
288]. Only collection of its kind
in Europe, point being to make
things work, veteran aeroplanes
and vehicles. Under cover

exhibition of transport history, also historic aeroplanes flying, weather permitting, various days May–October. Events like Twilight Aerial Display (some of the earliest), model planes flying and kite flying.

Open daily except Christmas–New Year's Day, adult £3.50, OAP/child £2, extra for special events.

Cecil Higgins Art Gallery and Museum Castle Close, Bedford [0234 211222]. English watercolours, prints, porcelain, glass, miniatures, textiles. Part set out as re-created Victorian mansion. Oakley Dolls' House, scale model of Russell family home. Children's holiday activities: making model rooms, fossil replicas, Christmas cards, murals, decorating a giant hat, quizzes, competitions, trails.

Open all year Tuesday–Sunday, Monday bank holidays, except Good Friday, December 25–26.

Hertfordshire

Standalone Farm Wilbury Road, Letchworth [0462 686775]. A working farm with a variety of animals, cattle, pigs, sheep, as well as fowl. Visitors see the seasonal farm work, like sheep being sheared. Most days except Saturday, a blacksmith at work. Hides to view wildfowl. Natural history exhibition. Also old farm

machinery, some days rides on a horse-drawn wagon, daily milking, a 'farm walk'.

Open daily Easter–October, adult £1.80, OAP/child 90p.

Knebworth House Knebworth [0438 812661]. Home of Lytton family since 1490, set in 250-acre deer park. Elizabethan portraits, 17th- and 18th-century furniture, various exhibits connected with famous visitors like Dickens, Winston Churchill. Delhi Durbar exhibition of Viceregal India including audio-visual show. 250 acres of parkland, 'Fort Knebworth' in adventure playground. Children's pictorial guide to house. Events: re-creation of Civil Wars, English and American, archery tournaments.

Open mid March–mid May, weekends, school holidays and Monday bank holidays, late May–September Tuesday–Sunday, Monday bank holidays, adult £3.50, OAP/child £3, park and playground only £2 each.

Hatfield House Hatfield [0707 262823]. Where Queen Elizabeth first heard she was just that. Personal possessions, portraits, paintings. Home of Cecil family. Re-creation of 17th-century gardens, around 3000 model soldiers since 1066 onwards. Extensive park with nature trails. Annual events include Living Crafts in May, Festival of Gardens in June.

Open late March–early October,
house closed Mondays, except bank
holidays, adult £3.90, child £2.70,
park, gardens and exhibitions only
£2.15 and £1.60.

Museum of St Albans Hatfield
Road, St Albans AL1 3RR
[recorded information 0727
59919]. Story of the city from the
departure of the Romans to the
present, monastery life, pilgrims'
badges, figures, medieval
knitting, a pillory to try for size,
craft tools, playing cards, straw
hats. Also wildlife, fossils and
minerals. Children's school
holiday activities like learning
about fossils, tracing changes in
animal life.

Open all year Monday–Saturday,
Sunday afternoons.

Verulanium Museum St
Michael's, St Albans AL3 4SW
[recorded information 0727
59919]. The life and times of a
major Roman city, over 400 years
of occupation. Mosaic floors,
household goods, personal
possessions, tools, coffins
including one with male
skeleton. Hypocaust, one room
of the bath wing of a Roman
town house, and sections of
Roman wall in the nearby park.
Children's illustrated quiz
available. Children's school

holiday activities like discovering
what life was like millions of
years ago.

Open all year Monday–Saturday,
Sunday afternoons.

Verulanium Roman Theatre West
of St Albans. Unique in Britain
in having a raised stage, unlike
an amphitheatre.

Open daily except December 25–26.

Zoological Museum Akeman
Street, Tring HP23 6AP [044282
4181]. Victorian natural history
collection of second Baron
Rothschild, elephant, rhino,
dinosaur, sea creatures, from
dressed fleas to hairless dogs.
Children's worksheets.

Open daily except Good Friday, May
Day, December 24–26, January 1,
Sunday mornings, adult £1,
OAP/child 50p.

Stevenage Museum St George's
Way, Stevenage SG1 1XX [0438
354292]. Local and natural
history, with live exhibits and
aquaria. Large hoard of Roman
coins, a doll's house 1920s-style,
domestic tools like lanterns,
lamps, irons, exhibition telling
the story of the New Town.
School holiday talks, workshops,
for families and children: drama,
straw-plaiting, creative maths,
discovering how clocks,
typewriters work and building
your own, paper play, town trails.

Open all year Monday–Saturday and bank holidays except Good Friday, December 25–26.

Paradise Wildlife Park White Stubbs Lane, Broxbourne EN10 7QA [0992 468001]. 17 acres, sheep, camels, wallaby, llamas, lions, Shetland ponies, reindeer, Vietnamese pot-bellied pigs. Woodland railway, pony rides, walk-through aviary, primate house, environmental education centre.

Open daily all year, adult £3, OAP £2, child £2.50.

Middlesex

Capel Manor Horticultural and Environmental Centre Bullsmoor Lane, Enfield EN1 4RQ [0992 763849]. 30 acres of richly planted, imaginative and informative gardens. Shows and events including dressing up, flying demonstrations of birds of prey. Farm, designed and stocked to help both adults and children understand more about farming at its best. Milking to be seen most days. Environmental Centre: 65 acres. Saturdays, all year, family activities like pond-dipping, Bats and Badgers, wildlife safaris, seeing young animals; Activity Days specially designed for children, including those with special needs, around the farm, feeding, cleaning, grooming, making homes for birds, bats, helping with young animals, night watch in the woodlands after dark. Operation Deer, summer holiday countryside activities from basket-weaving to scavenger hunts, pond-dipping to hay-making. Earth Education Programmes for 9s–12s residential, May spring holiday week and August: 'Sunship Earth', looking at nature and discovering how planet Earth really works; 'Earthkeepers' discovering the wonders of nature, advance booking essential.

Gardens open daily Easter–October, November–March weekdays only; farm Easter–October weekends and school holidays 1–6 p.m.; Environmental Centre, see programme, gardens adult £1.50, OAP/child 75p, farm same, Activity Days and Operation Deer accompanying adults free, child £1.

East Anglia

The Wash

Cromer

King's Lynn

NORFOLK

Norfolk Broads

Norwich

Yare

Great Yarmouth

Lowestoft

Peterborough

Nene

Great Ouse

Little Ouse

Thetford

Ely

CAMBRIDGESHIRE

Huntingdon

Bury St Edmunds

Cambridge

SUFFOLK

Ipswich

Saffron Walden

Stour

Colchester

Harwich

ESSEX

North Sea

Chelmsford

Southend on Sea

Thames

Essex

**Lee Valley Regional Park
Authority** PO Box 88, Enfield,
Middlesex. Covers 23 miles,
thousands of acres, from East
London into Essex and Herts.
Summer Camps for 5s–15s, day
or week, in the sports centres.
Also 'Pick n Mix', fun days out,
diverse activities, for groups of
all ages, in same centres, listed
below.

Park Countryside Centre, Abbey
Farmhouse, Crooked Mile,
Waltham Abbey, Essex EN9 1QX
[0992 713838]. Guided walks,
boat trips, orienteering,
countryside activity programmes,
nature trails, events.
Open daily summer, winter: check.

Eastway Sports and Leisure Centre
Quarter Mile Lane, Leyton E10
[081 519 0017]. All-weather
pitches, cycle circuit, multi-sports
hall.

Lea Bridge Riding School Lea
Bridge Road, Leyton E10 7QL
[081 556 2629]. Indoor and
outdoor, not under-7s.

Picketts Lock Leisure Centre Picketts
Lock Lane, Edmonton N9 [081
803 4756]. Swimming and dry
sports. Children's school holiday
activities.

Lazar Karting 44 River Road,
Barking IG11 0DW [081 594
2877]. Indoor go-karting.

Leisure Pool Old Nazeing Road,
Broxbourne, Herts [0992
446677]. 3s upwards.

Herts Young Mariner's Base
Windmill Lane, Cheshunt, Herts
[0992 24803]. Sailing, canoeing,
windsurfing.

Lea Valley Ice Centre Lea Bridge
Road, Leyton E10 7QL [081 519
0017]. 5s upwards. Countryside
Cabin [0992 713838] in car
park offers countryside
activities like pond-dipping. 7s
upwards.

Hayes Hill Farm Holyfield,
Crooked Mile, Waltham Abbey
[0992 892291]. Traditional open
farmyard and orchard where
children, even under-5s, can
wander among animals, fowl,
mostly young, and find out
about their care. Take your
wellies and some bad-weather
cover. Next door is Holyfieldhall
Farm, 435 acres, dairy and
arable, where the herd can be
seen milked the modern way,
around 3 p.m., and learn about
the farm year, sowing and
haymaking.

Open daily, adult £1.50, OAP/child £1.

⊞ ▤

Epping Forest Conservation Centre
High Beach, Loughton IG10 4AF
[081 508 7714]. Forest of nearly
6000 acres but the centre gives
clues to what you could be looking
at, for. Guided walks, lectures.
Children's holidaytime 'safaris'
7s–11s. At centre: a reconstructed
charcoal burners' encampment
and an Analemmatic sundial, the
only one in England. From centre:
a firm surfaced path through the
forest suitable for wheelchairs or
pushchairs. Planning worksheets,
etc. for children visiting with
families.

*Open Easter–October
Wednesday–Sunday, bank holidays
and winter weekends.*

▤ ⊞ ▤

Details from individual centres or
Lee Valley Regional Park
Authority address or 0992 700766.

Epping Forest District Museum
39–41 Sun Street, Waltham
Abbey EN9 1EL [0992 716882].
Social history for the whole of
the Epping Forest District.
Permanent displays from the
Stone Age to the 20th century
like oak panelling carved for the
Abbot of Waltham during Henry
VIII's reign and a fascinating
19th-century rural life display.
Many objects donated by local
people; paintings, photographs,
costumes, tools welcomed. 10–15
temporary exhibitions a year,

historical but also art/crafts,
photography, textiles,
complemented by
demonstrations, workshops,
worksheets. Children's quizzes,
competitions, on Fun Days, like
one discovering Archaeology is
Fun. School holiday activities:
paper sculpture, making and
performing puppets, Punch and
Judy, making models, story-
telling, say 5s upwards.

*Open daily 2–5 p.m., Tuesday from
noon, Wednesday/Thursday party
bookings only, except December 25,
January 1.*

▤ ⊞ ▤

Epping Bury Fruit Farm Centre
Upland Road, Epping Upland,
Epping CM16 5SA [0378 78400].
Pick your own strawberries and
mixed animal farm; meet and
touch rare breeds sheep, and
goats, cattle, poultry, pigs.
Observation beehive. Farming
interpretation centre. Nature
trail including lake.

*Open daily except Christmas, adult
£2, OAP/child £1.25.*

⊞ ▤ ▩

Mole Hill Wildlife Park
Widdington, nr Saffron Walden
[0799 40400]. Mammals
including first Canadian otters
bred in UK, owls, deer, wallabies,
chimpanzees and foxes; also
waterfowl, flamingos, and
domestic animals, ponies,
rabbits, goats. New Butterfly
Pavilion with free-flying
butterflies (*open only
March–October*).

Open all year except Christmas Day,
adult £2.75, OAP £2.25, child £1.75.

The Castle Colchester [0206
712481]. Built over the remains
of Emperor Claudius's temple,
destroyed by Boudicca, the
present enormous Norman keep
includes re-used Roman bricks,
after all Colchester is Britain's
oldest recorded town. Do go all
around the castle, which is
massive and its history includes
Civil War siege with an obelisk
marking the place where two
leaders were shot afterwards.
Inside look for the well, around
50-ft-deep shaft which once
continued up to the upper
floors so enemies couldn't get at
it at ground level. Look too for
early fireplaces with vents for
smoke, even a latrine. Among
the generously spaced exhibits
models of the castle in earlier
days, the Roman lead coffins,
looking all silvery, even
impression of a body; plus small
ones for children, which seem to
particularly appeal to children,
the cutaway section of earth
which tells like a jigsaw how the
bits and bobs of ordinary life,
buried in centuries of layers,
reveal the story of what life was
like. Audio-visual presentations.

Open April–October Monday–Saturday
and Sunday afternoons, adult 90p,
OAP/child 45p.

Hobbs Cross Farm Theydon
Garnon, Epping CM16 7NY
[0992 814862]. Working

livestock farm with sheep, lambs,
poultry and chickens, cows and
calves, ducks and geese,
breeding pigs. Occasional
holidaytime activities like August
Bank Holiday Fun Day.

Open daily except Christmas week
and January 1, adult £2,
OAP/child £1.50.

Colchester Zoo outskirts of
Colchester [0206 330253]. Big
cats and primates, elephants,
rhino, sea-lions, penguins, otters,
others, many viewed from
covered walkways. Handle a
snake, see parrot, penguin, sea-
lion, seal and falconry displays.
Also pony/donkey rides, farm
pets' corner, miniature railway
rides. Education Centre with
natural history exhibition.

Open daily except Christmas Day,
adult £4, child £2.

Mountfitchet Castle Stansted
CM24 8SP [0279 813237].
Reconstructed Norman wooden
motte and bailey castle and
Norman village of 1066, built on
its original site, where it was
attacked and razed in 1215. Re-
creation of what life was like
there in 1066, including animals,
defensive equipment.

Open daily March–November, adult
£3, OAP/child £2.

The House on the Hill adjacent
to Mountfitchet Castle [0279

813277]. Toys from Victorian times, animated displays, many activated by visitors: including the history of nursery rhymes, moving displays of toy cars, planes, boats, space exploration, fashion illustrated with dolls and dolls' houses.

Open all year Tuesday–Sunday, Monday bank holidays except December 24–26, under-14s must be adult-accompanied, adult £2.50, OAP £2, child £1.50.

Wat Tyler Country Park Wat Tyler Way, Pitsea, Basildon SS16 4UW [0268 559833]. Extensive events programmes for children: looking for animal tracks and signs, at plants, night walks with mammal trapping and bonfire, tracing wildflowers, blindfold walks, making corn dollies, spinning and weaving, pond-dipping.

Open daily. Charges for events.

Fossil Hall Boars Tye Road, Silver End, Witham CM8 3QA [0376 83502]. Scientific fossil replicas: vertebrates, invertebrates, plants, trace and pre-Cambrian fossils. Over 2000 exhibits in the museum, including dinosaur teeth, eggs, footprints and 50-million-year-old bats, frogs. Bookshop (60,000 items), museum shop (over 3000 items) including minerals, actual dinosaur bone, real fossil sharks' teeth, rocks, collecting trays and fossil

replicas. Not unexpectedly replicas of dinosaurs are among best sellers.

Open most Saturdays 10 a.m.– 5 p.m., other days appointment necessary, closed Wednesday and Sunday and during October, adult 50p, up to 2 accompanied children free.

East Anglian Railway Museum Chappel and Wakes Colne Station, Colchester [0206 242524]. 100 years of railway history. Platforms, sidings, workshops, signal boxes. Takes you behind the scenes to find out how things worked, railway signalling, steam engines. Steam trains operate on selected dates. Santa Specials with gifts in December. Schools' diesel and steam days. Children's worksheets.

Open daily except Christmas Day, adult £1.50, OAP/child 75p, double on steam days, family ticket. Special rates Santa Special.

Colne Valley Railway Castle Hedingham, Halstead CO9 3DZ [0787 61174]. Vintage steam and diesel locomotives and carriages in 5 acres woodland riverside area. Steam days, diesel days, steam rides in June: School Week Special for 6s–12s, Rising Five Special 4s–5s, Playgroup Special, 2s–4s in playgroups and Mother and Toddler groups, both pre-school events featuring Goldilocks and the Bears. Santa Specials in December with gifts.

Open daily March–December for static exhibits, adult £1.50, child 75p, steam days with rides £3 and £1.50, family ticket. Special events, special rates.

Suffolk

Kentwell Hall Long Melford CO10 9BA [0787 310207]. Tudor house, gardens, maze, working farm, with rare breed animals, costume exhibition. From late June to early July (weekdays for schools only, Saturday/Sunday for public), around 200 volunteers live as Tudors in the unique Historical Re-Creation of Tudor life. Meet characters from the 16th century, peasants and gentry. You easily fall into the same language, style, customs. Try a hand at spinning, kitchen or outdoor tasks, crafts, without mechanical aids. Try salves, concoctions, food and new dance skills. Compete in the Great Easter Egg Hunt Quiz

(Good Friday–Easter Monday), watch (and maybe join in) Tudor May Day Celebrations (May Day weekend). Smaller scale Historical Re-Creation Whitsun (spring bank holiday) weekend and August bank holiday weekend. Schools can book the Moat House for a day (say 40–50 children) and dress in Tudor costume (making instructions provided) to undertake Tudor activities using Tudor-style equipment.

Open noon (11 special events), mid March–mid June Sundays only, daily Easter, May Day and spring bank holiday weekends, daily mid July–September, October Sundays only, house, gardens and farm (except special events) adult £3, OAP £2.50, child £1.75, gardens and farm only £2, £1.75, £1.50.

Museum of East Anglian Life Stowmarket [0449 612229]. Re-erected buildings, all kinds of historic machinery, transport, tools (agricultural and domestic). Steam traction engines ('in steam'), working horse, a Suffolk Punch, and a water mill functioning. Also demonstrations, butter-making, spinning, lace-making, weaving, corn-dolly-making, sheep-shearing, wood carving, etc. on Sunday afternoons April–September. Also specific events for children during the summer school holidays, could be about ponies, or connected with Pooh, etc. . . . Also other special events, like Easter Sunday

egg hunt, special school days
(Children's Life 1900s).
Bioscope Show: historical film
about industries in the region.

*Open April–October,
Monday–Saturday from 11 a.m.,
Sunday noon, adult £2.75, OAP
£1.75, child £1.50.*

Easton Farm Park nr Wickham
Market. Off B1116 [0728
746475]. Victorian model farm
with over 40 species, Victorian
dairy, also lots of rural bygones,
but also working Suffolk horses,
blacksmith in his forge and herd
of cows milked the modern way
on view. Children can feed some
inhabitants, try the adventure
playground and the nature trail.

*Open daily Easter–October, adult
£2.75, OAP £2.15, child £1.50.*

Pleasurewood Hills Corton,
Lowestoft NR32 5DZ [0502
513626]. American Theme Park:
umpteen ways of spinning,
turning, soaring in over 50 rides;
The Land That Time Forgot
(dinosaurs), miniature railway,
mini-cars, sea-lion and parrot
shows, chairlift, entry charge
covers all this.

*Open Easter weekend and following
weekends, May Day weekend, daily
June–September 23, early October
weekend only, admission £7.*

Otter Trust Earsham, nr Bungay.
Off A143 [0986 893470].

Devoted to conserving otters,
especially British, to be seen in
semi-natural enclosures before
reintroduction to the wild; also
lakes with waterfowl, woods with
deer.

*Open daily April–October, adult £3,
OAP £2.50, child £1.50.*

West Stow Country Park
Icklingham Road, West Stow,
Bury St Edmunds IP28 5HE. Off
A1101 [0284 7287]. 125-acre
park showing range of Breckland
habitats, heath, woodland,
plantation, river and lake. Visitor
Centre, nature trail, bird hides.
Anglo-Saxon village
reconstructed on original site
(charge), where occasionally
enthusiasts in costume,
nobleman, slave, warrior, re-
enact village life: taped
commentary. Events: craft
demonstrations, spring Saxon
Market, using Saxon coins.
Children's Activity Book.

*Open daily all year. Free except
village.*

Norfolk

Thrigby Hall Wildlife Gardens nr
Filby, Great Yarmouth. A1064
[0493 369477]. Asian animals
and birds in 250-year-old
landscaped gardens, deer
paddocks, lake, tropical house,
aviaries, plus slide show
Whitsun–October.

Open daily all year, adult £2.50,
OAP £2, child £1.50.

Pettits of Reedham Feathercraft
and Falabella Miniature Horse
Stud Camp Hill, Reedham. Off
A47, then B1140 to Reedham
[0493 700094]. Gardens, lakes,
peacocks, pheasants, and tame
birds which youngsters can go
among and feed. Also the
making of pictures, flowers and
other objects from feathers can
be seen. Miniature train rides,
shows, snake slides.

Open April–October weekdays,
Sunday afternoons, adult £2.65,
OAP/child £1.80.

Bressingham Gardens and Live
Steam Museum nr Diss. A1066
[037 988 386]. Built from Alan
Bloom's 2 enthusiasms – creating
6 acres of informal gardens from
nothing and collecting steam
engines, now over 50 in all; with
an exhibition hall housing steam-
age relics, 5 miles of narrow-
gauge steam-hauled railway
rides, footplate rides on mainline
engines and steam-driven
roundabout. Norfolk Fire
Museum. Worksheets for visiting
children on sale.

Open Easter and various days
May–September, adult £3, child £2,
rides extra.

Banham Zoo and Monkey
Sanctuary Banham, nr Diss.
B1113 [095 387 476]. Camels,

sea-lions, otters, penguins, and
an extensive collection of rare
primates in over 20 acres.
'Woodland Walk', Roadtrain ride
around zoo. Events like: free
entry child carrying teddy,
Brownies/Guides, Cubs/Scouts
special free admission days.

Open daily except December 25–26,
adult £3.50, OAP £2.50, child £2,
Saturday 1 child free per
accompanying adult.

Norfolk Wildlife Park Great
Witchingham, nr Norwich.
A1067 [060544 274]. Emphasis
on conservation and breeding,
largest collection of British and
European mammals in the
world in near-natural
surroundings in over 50 acres of
parkland, everything from bears
to lynx, seals to otters. Also
waterfowl lakes, walk-through
aviaries. Children's adventure
play area with overhead
cableway and pets' corner.
Reindeer pulling their wheeled
sledge (not hot weather), giving
rides. Electronic Theme Hall
'The Dawn of Man and his
Animals'.

Open daily all year, adult £2.70,
OAP £2.20, child £1.40, Saturday:
children free, limit 2 per adult.

Norfolk Rural Life Museum
Cressenhall, Dereham. Off B110
[0362 860563]. Once a large
workhouse housing local poor,
now housing examples of rural
life over the past 200 years,

agricultural implements, tools, transport, clothing; in minor buildings reconstruction of forge, shop, wheelwright, bakery, plus furnished labourer's cottage with sewn samplers ('Home Sweet Home'), water jug and bowl and other contrasting domestic objects. Lots of outside space. Farm working as 1920s. Children's colouring sheets, quizzes, games, always available. Nature trail. Annual week-long summer holiday event for wide age range but younger children must be accompanied. Village life is main theme, could be doing the washing the old way, plus mangling or finding out about keeping clean with tin baths and washstands, or the work children did on the farm, cooking on a range, buying things from village shop with shillings and old pence, making scarecrows, feather pictures, old-style toys, cartoons, posters, games. Also learning about horses, tools, through farrier's demonstration. Lots of illustrated quiz/colour sheets.

Open April–September Tuesday–Saturday, Sunday afternoon, Monday bank holidays, adult £2, OAP £1.75, child 60p.

🏛 � 🈂

Thursford Collection Thursford. Off A148 [0328 878477]. Wonderful steam engines (a mix from the strictly functional to nostalgic show business, with fairground glittering splendour) in this extensive collection. 9 mechanical organs playing daily, mid-season live concerts on a

Wurlitzer, plus a small functioning steam railway.

Open daily April–September, October afternoons, adult £3.20, OAP £2.90, child £1.50.

🏛 🚂 🈂

Norfolk Shire Horse Centre West Runton Stables, West Runton, Cromer [026 375 339]. Shire and Suffolk horses; a talk, harnessing, working demonstration, twice daily followed by carthorse parade and children's wagon rides. Also film show on the subject and collection of horse-drawn machinery, wagons, carts. Special Working Days: sheepdogs, horse ploughing, foals, etc. Children's worksheets.

Open Good Friday–end October, Sunday–Friday, Saturday bank holidays, adult £2.50, OAP/child £1.25.

🏛 🚂 🈂

North Norfolk Railway The Station, Sheringham [0263 822045]. Steam railway over 5 miles to Weybourne and Holt. Museum exhibits, historic rolling stock.

Open daily Easter–October, short ride adult £2.20, OAP £1.80, child £1.10 (Sunday, daily in August), station only 40p/20p.

🏛 🚂

Glandford Shell Museum Glandford. B1156 [0263 740081]. Another resource when beaches are boring or chilly. Shells from all over the world, some carved or engraved. Also tapestry of this coast.

*Open January–February,
Monday–Thursday morning,
March–November,
Monday–Thursday all day, Friday,
Saturday afternoon, December,
Monday–Thursday morning, adult
25p, child 15p.*

Holkham Hall Holkham, Wells-
next-the-Sea [0328 710227]. My
main memory is of the adjacent
beach, seemingly empty because
it's so vast. Almost expected
camels to appear on horizon!
That is free of course. The hall is
the 18th-century home of the
Cokes of Norfolk. Marble Hall,
state rooms, splendid pictures
and statuary. 'Bygones', over
4000 items, tools, ploughs,
tractors, engines in steam.
Sunday and Thursday craft
demonstrations (extra charge).

*Open Easter, May, spring and
summer bank holiday Sunday,
Monday, daily except Friday,
Saturday late May–September, Hall
adult £2, OAP £1.75, child 75p.*
▦ ▦ ▦

Norfolk Lavender Caley Mill,
Heacham, King's Lynn. Off A149
[0485 70384]. 100 fragrant acres
of lavender, harvested to be dried
and distilled July/August for
ancient process of oil extraction.

*Open all year except December
24–beginning January, tours of
distillery during harvest-time (charge).*
▣ ▦

Sandringham House
Sandringham. B1440 [0553
2675]. Royal residence, much as

used (except no longer dining
table, laid out, since visitors
filched cutlery for souvenirs).
Museum with guns, trophies of
earlier Royals, historic state cars,
commemorative china, gifts like
a coronation picture made from
over 10,000 matchsticks. Of
interest to Royal-watchers rather
than children. Gardens (look for
dog cemetery) and lake.
Consider perhaps extensive
access to the country park, free,
and nature trails.

*Open late April–late September,
except mid July–early August and
when any member of family in
residence, Monday–Thursday and
Sunday, house/garden adult £2.20,
OAP £1.70, child £1.40, garden
only £1.70, £1.30, £1.*
▦ ▦

Wolferton Station Museum Off
A149 [0485 40674]. Once the
station for Sandringham.
Museum housed in former Royal
Retiring Rooms built for Edward
VII. Relics of royal train travel
including Queen Victoria's
travelling bed.

*Open April–September, weekdays,
Sunday afternoons, entry charges.*
▦

Houghton Hall Houghton,
King's Lynn [048522 569]. 18th-
century Palladian-style mansion,
belonged to Sir Robert Walpole.
Original furnishings, stables with
heavy horses and Shetland
ponies, coach house, 20,000
model soldiers, herd of white
fallow deer.

*Open afternoons Easter–September,
Sunday, Thursday and bank
holidays, adult £3, OAP £2.50,
child £1.50.*

The Kingdom of the Sea Marine
Parade, Great Yarmouth [0493
330631]. Walk along a glass-walled
tunnel to see 6 species of shark,
then other fascinating sea
creatures and plants in great tanks,
go beachcombing in the child-
height reconstruction of beach
habitat learning, for instance, how
to pick up a crab. Saturday Club
for 5s–11s. Learn about sea life
from marine biologists.

*Open daily all year, adult £3.95,
OAP £2.75, child £2.50.*

Living Jungle Marine Parade,
Great Yarmouth [0493 842202].
Free-flying butterflies from far-
away places, also Koi carp,
terrapins, tarantulas, scorpions.
Look for tiny colourful
humming birds.

*Open daily March–October, adult
£1.90, OAP £1.75, child £1.*

Merrivale Model Village Marine
Parade, Great Yarmouth [0493
842097]. Over 200 models in an
acre of landscaped gardens.

*Open Easter weekend, daily
May–September, adult £1.50, OAP
£1, child 50p.*

Tolhouse Museum Tolhouse
Street, Great Yarmouth [0493

858900]. Once the town gaol.
Dungeons including condemned
cell. Brass rubbing centre,
including a skeleton. Charge for
materials and instruction.

*Open daily June–September except
Saturday, October–May,
Monday–Friday.*

**Maritime Museum for East
Anglia** Marine Parade, Great
Yarmouth [0493 55746].
Lifesaving, shipbuilding, inland
waterways. Worksheets available.
Summer holiday practical
activities on general theme of the
sailor's life, all ages. So dressing
up, trying ropework, net-making,
using charts and navigational
tools, the stencil patterns that
marked herring barrels (and
designing your own), studying
sailors' crafts, ships in bottles,
dolls, woolwork pictures, objects
made by things collected on
voyages, and having a go at
some. Also sea stories and
poems, quizzes, painting and
drawing.

*Open May–September, weekdays and
Sundays, adult 50p, child 20p.*

Hunstanton Sea Life Centre
Southern Parade, Hunstanton
[0485 533576]. Walk through
Ocean Tunnel surrounded by
deep sea creatures, conger eel,
sting-ray; peer into tanks with
other marine life. Also seals,
deserted pups till well enough to
return to normal life. Saturday
Club for 5s–11s, chance to learn

about sea life from marine biologists.

Open daily all year except Christmas Day, adult £3.50, child £2.

Lynn Museum Market Street, King's Lynn PE30 1NL [0553 775001]. Natural history and geology including skeleton of Saxon warrior, pilgrim badges, farm tools. Christmas-time magic show or painting/drawing competition, also Easter-time chance to try Victorian gadgets, make an Easter bonnet, attempt worksheets, again with small prizes.

Open all year, Monday–Saturday, closed bank holiday, public holidays, adult 50p, child 20p.

Dinosaur Natural History Park Weston Estate, Weston Longville, Norwich [0603 870245]. Natural History Park with life-size dinosaurs in a natural setting. Wooded maze. Bygone Museum. Children's worksheets.

Open daily all year, adult £2.50, OAP/child £1.50.

Castle Museum Norwich NR1 3JU [0603 222222]. Medieval objects, armour, Norwich Snapdragons, natural history, archaeology, Egyptian mummies. Enter Royal Norfolk Regimental Museum through former prisoners' tunnel and reconstructed World War I trench, with sound effects (*50p and 20p*). Battlement and Dungeon Tours (*£1.20 and 60p, dungeons only 60p and 30p*). Week-long children's summer holiday activities including craft and art activities, quizzes and colouring. Occasional family activity days, variety of crafts when parents and children can create, perhaps jewellery or sculpture. Museum children's clubs meeting Saturday monthly during school term, topics from art to natural history and summer outings. Christmas puppet shows. Looking at objects for under-5s, pre-school sessions, including handling museum objects and related practical activities. Worksheets, also information about children's activities: Education Dept [630214]. Children's guide to Norwich Castle on sale.

Open all year Monday–Saturday, Sunday afternoon, adult £1, OAP 80p, child 20p, reduced winter.

Remember that museums/art galleries generally close Good Friday, Christmas, January 1.

Strangers' Hall Museum
Charing Cross, Norwich NR2
4AL [0603 667229]. Medieval
merchant's house with rooms
furnished in different period
styles. Costume gallery, toy
room, changing exhibitions.
Occasional Saturday children's
activity days, 4s upwards.
Children's worksheets.

*Open all year, Monday–Saturday,
adult 50p, child 20p.*

**Cockley Cley Iceni Village and
Museums** Cockley Cley, nr
Swaffham PE37 9AG. Off A1065
[0760 721339]. Reconstruction
of an Iceni settlement on site of
original, around 1st century AD.
Also East Anglian Museum,
exhibits and forge; carriage
collection; farm implements,
vintage engines over last 2
centuries; Saxon church. Nature
trail, butterflies, heron,
cormorant. Worksheets.

*Open daily April 1–end October,
adult £2.10, OAP £1.20, child 90p.*

**Pensthorpe Waterfowl Park and
Nature Reserve** Fakenham. Off
A1067 [0328 851465]. Unusual
since the lakes were created
from gravel pits. 200 acres, now
one of the largest collections of
ornamental water-birds in the
world. Fascinating to see
mapped that birds from as far
away as northern Russia have
discovered this attractive
wintering ground. A large part is
laid out specifically for
wheelchair/pushchair
movement. Visitor Centre, with
brass rubbings of birds. Torrent
ducks, only captive birds of the
species outside South America,
their name indicating habitat;
osprey, kingfishers, pygmy geese,
oyster-catchers, among the
enormous list of residents or
seasonal visitors. A duck decoy
illustrates how birds were once
caught for markets in their
thousands. Hides, nature trails
to see woodland wildlife,
meadow flowers. 'Waterfowl',
feeding methods, flight,
courtship, migration, a large
project pack for children
available.

*Open daily April 1–January 6,
except Christmas Day,
January–March weekends only,
adult £2.80, OAP £2.50, child
£1.10.*

Cambridgeshire

Duxford Airfield Cambridge.
A505 [0223 833963]. Long-time
RAF fighter station, aircraft
since 1916, also civil airliners,
tanks and midget submarine.
Also active flying/gliding
(pleasure flights in a Cessna
most summer weekends),
military vehicles regularly
demonstrated, and aircraft
restoration to be seen. Give the
ride simulator a try. Special
annual events. Free day for
children in August with extra
children's attractions.

Open daily except December 24–26, January 1, adult £4.50, OAP/child £2.25, family ticket, more for special events.

Wildfowl and Wetlands Trust Peakirk, nr Peterborough. B1443 [0733 252271]. Over 100 different kinds of birds including flamingos, ducks, geese, swans in 17 acres of water gardens. Nature trails. Food for feeding birds. Take cameras. Indoor film show and talks.

Open daily except December 24–25, adult £2.20, OAP £1.40, child £1.

Nene Valley Railway Wansford Station, Stibbington. Off A1 [0780 78285, Talking timetable 0780 782854]. 5 miles through the Nene Park from Wansford to Orton Mere, past sites of Roman villas, ancient churches, and through the fertile valley, drawn by steam locomotives from Europe and Britain. Special events: Teddy Bear Specials, Thomas in Steam.

Open Easter–end October, weekends, mid June–end August, Tuesday, Wednesday, Thursday, Santa Specials in December, station only adult 80p, child 40p, train fares £4 and £2.

Sacrewell Farm and Country Centre Sacrewell, Thornhaugh [0780 782227]. Working water mill, 530-acre farm, over 8000 bygones (like a primitive washing-machine, wooden-seated outdoor privy, butter churns, vintage typewriters, tools), 18th-century farm buildings, peacocks, swans in garden; watch out for free-ranging goats. Sand-pit with child-size pre-mechanization manual tools, sow/hoe. Aim, to tell story of farming, from sickle to combine harvester, enjoyably. Long trails and short ones. Look for signs: by beehive 'Do Beeware', though 'Beware of the dog' sits on one holding a toy dog. The whimsy elsewhere: trees bear labels, jolly useful to townees. Short trails: Trees; 'Over, Through, Under and In' takes you to find Collyweston slate, a hole in floor. Children's animals' names quiz.

Open daily, adult £2, OAP/child £1.50.

Flag Fen Bronze Age Excavation Fourth Drove, Fengate, Peterborough [0733 313414]. Ongoing excavation of a man-made defensive settlement some 3000 years old, pickled by water, so seeds, leaves, twigs, wooden ladle, bronze dirk, and the logs on which it was built survive. A reconstruction of what it must have looked like, informed guides, site tours, and Visitor Centre. Recommendation: choose a fine day or wrap up warm.

Open daily April–November, adult £1.75, OAP £1.55, child £1.25.

East of England Ice-Rink
Mallard Road, Bretton,
Peterborough [0733 260222].
Tuition courses

for adults and children, special
family sessions.

Open daily except at Christmas.

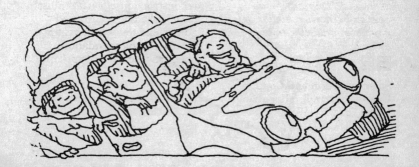

The English Shires

East Midlands Tourist Board

Glossop
High Peak
Buxton
Chesterfield
DERBYSHIRE
Mansfield
NOTTINGHAM-
SHIRE
Dove
Nottingham
Derby
Trent
Newark
Gainsborough
Louth
Lincoln
LINCOLNSHIRE
Skegness
Witham
Boston
The Wash
Grantham
Nene
Loughborough
LEICESTERSHIRE
Oakham
Leicester
Stamford
*North
Sea*
Kettering
Nene
NORTHAMPTON-
SHIRE
Northampton

Northamptonshire

Turner's Musical Merry-Go-Round Queen Eleanor Vale, Newport Pagnell Road, Wootton. B526 [0604 763314]. Unusual, but attracts right across the age range from those in pushchairs to those in wheelchairs. An indoor fairground, carpeted, more or less, from wall to wall, with historic functioning fairground organs going flash, bang, thump, also performances on the 'Mighty Wurlitzer' (mostly allied to tea dances, discos), rides on a refurbished giant roundabout.

Open all year, prior booking except Sunday, afternoon sight and sound spectacular, charges vary.

Holdenby House Holdenby, Northampton. Off A50 [0604 770241]. Where Charles I was imprisoned for 4 months, so King Charles's Walk in remains of one of largest Elizabethan gardens in England. He would surely have been puzzled to hear of nature trails. Throw in modest train rides, donkey rides, rare breeds of sheep and other creatures to gaze on, lots of small pets to delight in and plenty of space for letting off energies.

Gardens open April–September Sunday and bank holidays, afternoons, also July–August, Thursday, adult £2, OAP £1.50, child £1.

Wicksteed Park London Road, Kettering [0536 512475]. Indoor/outdoor, 140 acres; roller-coasters, steam train, dodgems, pony rides, commando course, minor car track, panoramic Cinema 2000, paddling, bird-spotting from hides, nature trail.

Open daily Good Friday–September. You pay only for certain amusements.

Boughton House Geddington, Kettering. Off A43 [0536 82248]. One of the homes of the Dukes of Buccleuch, since 1528. It's been described as 'a vision of King Louis XIV's Versailles transported to England'. So, magnificent ceilings, state rooms, splendid pictures, porcelain, furnishings, also heraldry and celebrated armoury. Possibly the main interest for children is in the several hundred acres, nature trails and adventure playground.

House open daily mid July–August, grounds daily mid April–September except Friday, house and gardens adult £3, OAP/child £2, grounds only £1 and 50p.

Deene Park nr Corby [078085 278]. Originally a medieval manor, transformed into Tudor and Georgian mansion by Brudenell family who still live there, so antiques among family mementoes. Famous owner the Earl of Cardigan who led Charge of the Light Brigade at Balaklava;

stuffed head of his charger among memorabilia of Crimean War. Large park, lake, gardens.

Open Easter Sunday/Monday, May bank holiday weekends, June–August Sunday, August bank holiday Monday, adult £3, child £1.

Naseby Battle and Farm Museum Purlieu Farm, Naseby NN6 7DD. Off B4036 [0604 740241]. Miniature layout of Naseby battlefield with commentary. Relics from battlefield. Also village history with agricultural tools.

Open Easter–September Sunday afternoon, groups other times by appointment, adult 80p, child 40p.

Daventry Garden Railway 11 Grenville Close, Southbrook Estate, Daventry [0327 704135]. 1600 ft of 00 gauge track, sidings and marshalling yard among rock gardens, pools, aviaries and rabbits.

Open May–October 1st Sunday in month, also May Day and August bank holiday Sunday, Monday, adult £1, OAP/child 60p.

Irchester Country Park Irchester, Wellingborough. Off B570 [0933 76866]. 200 acres, nature trail, ranger service, orienteering.

Irchester Narrow-Gauge Railway Museum [0234 750469]. Museum and engine shed housing 7 locos and rolling stock. 300 yards track in the park. Monthly steamings.

Park open all year, museum Sunday.

The Canal Museum Stoke Bruerne, nr Towcester NN12 7SE [0604 862229]. Insight into 2 centuries of life for working boatmen and their families in what was a grain warehouse beside the Grand Union Canal. Towpath. Boat trips nearby.

Open daily except Monday November–Easter and December 25–26, adult £1.50, OAP/child £1.

East Carlton Countryside Park East Carlton, nr Corby [0536 770977]. 100 acres of parkland with nature trail, interpretation centre. Rural craft workshops. **Steel-Making Heritage Centre:** craft workshops and forge.

Park open all year, centre closes Christmas week.

Lincolnshire

Burghley House nr Stamford PE9 3JY. On B1443 [0780 52451]. Built by William Cecil, first Lord Burghley, in 1587, still occupied by his descendants. Medieval kitchen with 260 copper utensils, Elizabeth I's bedroom, also Queen Victoria's, among 18 state rooms including the Heaven Room, a painted room, filled with treasures like silver fireplaces, tapestries, paintings. Deer Park, by Capability Brown, of course.

Open Easter–early October (closed early September for Horse Trials), weekdays, Sunday afternoons, adult £3.80, OAP £3.50, child £2.30.

🏛 🖼

Springfields Camelgate, Spalding. A151 [0775 724843]. 250 acres of landscaped gardens; millions of flowers in bloom in the spring; the spectacular Flower Parade (like a carnival, with floral floats, bands, etc., taking some hours to pass from the town centre to Springfields and back) takes place early May; then thousands of summer season roses, bedding plants. Add over 30,000 trees, shrubs, 4 miles of paths and roadways, woodland walks, a lake, a maze, glasshouses.

Open daily April–September, £2, accompanied child free, Flower Parade £2.50.

🏛 🔲

Belton House Belton, Grantham. Off A607 [0476 66116]. 17th-century house, paintings, furniture, Grinling Gibbons carvings, etc., also unique mementoes of Duke of Windsor since it was once owned by his friend and supporter Lord Brownlow. (National Trust, like many other places mentioned.) In 600-acre park, also gardens, an adventure wood for children, tree houses, etc., also lakeland

and woodland trails, boat trips, miniature railway.

Open 1 April–end October, afternoons, Wednesday–Sunday and Monday bank holidays, adult £3.50, child £1.70, expect extras for different attractions.

🏛 🖼

Boston Guildhall Museum South Street, Boston [0205 365954]. Former 15th-century town hall. Tells story of early Pilgrim Fathers' abortive attempt to leave England for religious freedom in Holland; original courtroom and dock which you can stand in, or go into the cells where they were imprisoned in 1607. Also 16th-century kitchen and domestic utensils, costumes, uniforms, weapons, from medieval to 19th century, and veteran cycles, agricultural implements.

Open all year Monday–Saturday, and April–September Sunday afternoons, except December 25–26, January 1, adult 70p, OAP 50p, accompanied child free, includes use of audio guided tour.

Manor House Folk Museum Manor House, West Street, Alford [0507 466514]. Thatched Elizabethan manor house. Connections with America, Thomas Paine who worked in the town and Pocahontas's John Smith who went to local grammar school, mementoes on display. Also 19th-century chemist's shop, cobbler's shop, vet's surgery, maid's bedroom, a sweet factory (not functioning unfortunately), a police cell and a railway room with ticket office, etc.

Open Monday–Friday, early May–late September, other times by arrangement. Craft market in grounds spring and August bank holiday weekends, adult 50p, child 25p.

Mablethorpe's Animal Gardens North End, Mablethorpe [0507 473346]. Over 200 animals in gardens and natural dunes; emphasis is on breeding small mammals. Various injured and sick animals/birds recuperate here. Walk through aviary.

Open daily early March–late October, adult £2, OAP £1.50, child £1.

Museum of Lincolnshire Life Burton Road, Lincoln [0522 528448]. History of county from 1800, domestic, industrial, agricultural, social. Edwardian room settings.

Open all year Monday–Saturday, May–September Sunday, November–April Sunday afternoons, adult 80p, child 40p.

Lincoln Castle Lincoln [0522 511068]. Views, gardens. Was used as a prison; hangings and burials took place. Unusual prison chapel where Victorian prisoners got a compartment which only gave sight of the chaplain! Historical reconstructions can cover

Romans, medieval joustings, the Civil War, etc.

Open all year except winter Sunday, adult 80p, OAP/child 50p.

Lincoln Cathedral Lincoln [0522 544544]. Hilltop, can be seen from miles away, especially lit up at night. Norman, shattered by earthquake, rebuilt 12th/13th centuries. Look for the imp. Tower trips mid July and August.

Open daily all year, voluntary contributions adult £1.50, OAP 50p, child free.

City and County Museum Broadgate, Lincoln [0522 530401]. Geology, birds and mammals including live displays. New archaeology gallery including cathedral's exemplar of Magna Carta.

Open daily except Sunday mornings, Good Friday, December 25–26, adult 50p, child 25p.

The Incredibly Fantastic Old Toy Show 26 Westgate, Lincoln [0522 20534]. Over 1000 toys, cars, trains, dolls, dolls' houses, teddies, games.

Open Easter–September Tuesday–Saturday and bank holidays from noon, October–Christmas, weekends and school holidays only, also by appointment, adult £1, child 50p.

Rutland Cottage Music Museum
Millgate, Whaplode St Catherine,
Spalding [040634 379]. Museum
of the Fairground Society.
Mechanical musical instruments
(played on conducted tour), from
music-boxes to fairground organs.
Also history of fairground and
travelling people. Marionettes
perform in Old Tyme Fairground
weekends from May.

*Open Easter–September Saturday,
Sunday and bank holidays,
July–September Monday–Friday
afternoons, adult £1.50, OAP/child
£1.*

Gainsborough Old Hall Parnell
Street, Gainsborough DN21
2NB. Centre of town [0427
612669]. Late medieval manor
house with fine medieval
kitchen. Different Royals stayed,
Richard III, Henry VIII,
Catherine Parr. Also meeting
place of Pilgrim Fathers. Family
portraits, furniture, dolls, period
dresses. Display on how built and
restoration. Richard III
exhibition. Kitchen as 1483 when
he stayed there.

*Open all year Monday–Saturday,
Easter–October Sunday afternoons,
except Good Friday, December 25–26,
January 1, adult £1, OAP/child 50p.*

> As well as addresses and locations
> I have tried to give telephone
> numbers. May I recommend that
> you *don't* ring to check extra facts
> at the *last* moment. Small staffs
> can mean someone will be trying
> to help visitors *and* answer your
> queries at the same time, or may
> be out of doors getting on with
> the job and not available to
> answer the telephone too.

Nottinghamshire

**Sherwood Forest Visitor Centre
and Country Park** Edwinstowe, nr
Mansfield. Off B6034 [0623
823202]. The ancient forest with
all the Robin Hood associations.
Visitor Centre includes exhibition
to do with him, slides, films, talks,
Tourist Information Centre; ask
about guided walks. Nature trail
for the visually handicapped.
Events like Easter Egg Trail, May
Day Merriment, Hunt the Outlaw,
Summer Robin Hood Festival.

*Open daily all year, though not
necessarily the Tourist Information
Centre.*

Sherwood Forest Farm Park
Lamb Pens Farm, Edwinstowe,
Mansfield NG21 9HL [0623
822255]. Rare breeds of cattle,
sheep, pigs, horses, goats in

lakeside setting with wildfowl. Aviary, pets' corner, tractor and trailer nature tours.

Open daily Good Friday—early October, adult £2, OAP £1.50, child £1.25.

Rufford Country Park Rufford Mill, Ollerton. A614 [0623 824153]. 25-acre lake with waterfowl, parkland, formal gardens, meadows with sheep, woodland walks. Restored Cistercian abbey with exhibition. Also craft centre in stable block of what was once stately home and craftspeople to be seen at work weekends. Charges for special events, games, puppets, dance, singing.

Open daily all year.

Newstead Abbey Linby NG15 8GE. A60 [0623 793557]. Byron, of course, so possibly for older children. Site goes back 800 years, 16th-century conversion to country house, then 19th-century restoration. Possessions, pictures, furniture, manuscripts of Lord Byron. Extensive parkland with lakes, water gardens, sub-tropical gardens, Monks' Stew Pond.

Open daily Good Friday—September, grounds all year, abbey/grounds adult £3, OAP/child £1.40, grounds only £1.20 and 60p.

D. H. Lawrence's Birthplace 8a Victoria Street, Eastwood. From Nottingham on A610 [0773 763312]. For older children. House furnished appropriately to time of Lawrence family occupation and his birth in 1885. Audio-visual presentation.

Open daily except December 24—January 1, adult 50p, accompanied child 25p.

The D. H. Lawrence *Sons and Lovers* **Cottage** 28 Garden Road, Eastwood. Off A608 [Enquiries: 0773 719786 or 051 653 8710]. Older children again. Home of Lawrence family 1887–91. Same garden layout and furnished ground floor as described in *Sons and Lovers*. Also display of mining family work and social conditions.

Open all year by appointment.

The Castle (and nearby cluster of attractions) Nottingham [0602 483504]. Dominates the city, presumably since medieval times. Inside a mixture of silver, glass, ceramics, military uniforms, flags, ethnic antique musical masks and instruments (look for one which seems to require 2 sticks to be swung to get air into drum-like cases, so you get music out of the pipes), also art gallery with pertinent information cards so you can look deeper into the pictures. Nottingham's history from prehistory to 1990. Outside pleasant gardens, the Robin Hood statue, and the entrance to 'Mortimer's Hole', a tunnel in the sandstone cliff through which a party of medieval noblemen went to arrest Roger Mortimer, Earl of March, the Queen's lover. Conducted tours of Hole and underground passages from 2 p.m. daily except Sundays.

Open daily except December 25, free except Sunday and bank holidays, adult 40p, child 20p.

Around the castle's cliff visit the Brewhouse Yard Museums (same phone number), look for the cane and the nit comb in the teacher's desk in the schoolroom, otherwise chemist's shop, grocer's, where everything was hand cut and packed, kitchen (look for ingenious cockroach-catcher) and lots of domestic and personal historic items on display. Add the nearby Museum of Costume and Textiles, 51 Castlegate (same phone number), furniture, clothes, fashionably dressed dolls, 18th–20th centuries.

Open daily except Christmas Day.

The Tales of Robin Hood 30–38 Maid Marian Way, Nottingham NG1 6CF [0602 483284]. In small moving cars you escape from the Sheriff of Nottingham into the greenwood to see the re-creation with figures, settings, the legends of the outlaws, with sounds, smells, commentary. Play the Silver Arrow Game. Study the presented research on who was Robin Hood. See

audio-visuals of those who played the outlaw in films. Medieval craft demonstrations, archery range.

Open daily except December 24–26, adult £3.95, OAP/child £2.50, family ticket.

Wollaton Park Wollaton Road, Nottingham. A mixture of indoors/outdoors. Vast parkland with cows, donkeys, deer, gardens, children's adventure playground, nature trail, freely open all year round. Also Wollaton Hall [0602 281333], magnificent Elizabethan mansion, now housing a natural history museum, immense stuffed apes, also fossils, birds, living fish, an ant colony, 19th-century camellia house. Also Industrial Museum [0602 284602] in 18th-century stable block, about Nottingham industries, so about hosiery, lace-making, pharmaceuticals, printing, engineering, transport including a great variety of historic bikes, and a giant Victorian beam engine which steams up, impressively goes into action, last Sunday each month.

Hall open daily except Sunday morning, and Christmas Day, museum April–September Monday–Saturday, October–March Thursday and Saturday, closed Christmas Day, free except Sundays and bank holidays, adult 40p, child 20p, for both.

Leisure Services
Nottinghamshire County Council, Trent Bridge House, Fox Road, West Bridgford, Nottingham NG2 6BJ [0602 823823]. Produces leaflets on guided walks, guided cycle rides, programmes at Rufford and Bestwood Country Parks and the Sherwood Forest Visitor Centre with details of events like finding out about spiders, mini-beasties, pond-dipping, making Christmas crackers and decorations.

Vina Cooke Museum of Dolls and Bygone Childhood The Old Rectory, Cromwell, Newark [0636 821364]. Victorian dolls, cots, toys, dolls' houses, costumes in 17th-century house. Also hand-made character dolls depicting Royal Family, TV and film stars.

Open daily except December 25–26, adult £1, child 50p.

▦

White Post Modern Farm Centre White Post Farm, Farnsfield, nr Newark NG22 8HL [0623 882977]. Part of a working farm with crops, cows, sheep, pigs, deer, angora goats, rabbits, llamas, ostriches. Tame animals to touch. Egg incubator. Indoor countryside 'walk' with exhibits.

Open daily, adult £1.95, OAP £1.50, child £1.20.

▦ ▭ ▩

Sundown Kiddies Adventureland and Pets Garden Treswell Road, Rampton, Retford DN22 0HX. Off

A57 [077784 274]. Theme park designed especially for under-10s. Miniature farm, animated nursery rhymes, Western street, Smugglers' Cove, toddlers' areas. Indoor play area planned.

Open daily except December 25–26, admission £2.

▦ ▭

Clumber Park nr Worksop. Off A57 [0909 476592]. Some 3800 acres including 2-mile 'Dukes Drive', Victorian chapel (closed Christmas Day), fishing, cycle hire, nature walks, lake.

Conservation Centre open April–October weekends, or by appointment, park open daily all year. Charges according to vehicle from cars £2 to coaches £5 (double weekends and bank holidays).

▦ ▭ ▩

Bestwood Country Park Bestwood Lodge Drive, Arnold, Nottingham. Off A60 [0602 670042]. 450 acres of parkland, lakes and woodland. Rangers give talks, lead walks. Events like 'The Real Mrs Tiggywinkle', meeting a real hedgehog, bird- and wildlife-watching, bat-watching, finding mini-beasts, Teddy Bears' Picnic. Electric buggies for disabled need pre-booking.

Open all year.

▣ ▦ ▭ ▩

Playworld Floralands Garden Centre, Catfoot Lane, off Mapperley Plains Road, Lambley. Off B684 [0602 670487].

Children's playpark with real fire engine, giant climbing net, assault course, Tarzan swing. Separate under-5s area.

Open daily Easter–September, and October half-term, adult £1, child £2.

Tumble Town 107 High Street, Arnold, Nottingham. Off A60 [0602 671161]. 3000-square-ft indoor play area. Climbing frames, slides, soft play, ball pools, supervised play.

Open Monday–Saturday, and Sundays September–April, adults free, child £2.

Derbyshire

National Tramway Museum
Crich, nr Matlock. A6 or A38 [077 385 2565]. Travel on trams (makes a change from steam trains) for a mile with scenic views. Here a collection of tramcars from Britain and elsewhere, built between 1873 and 1953. Also depots, power station, workshops, and Derbyshire lead-mining display, Edwardian street project.

Open two weeks over Easter, Easter–October weekends, bank holidays, May–September Monday–Thursday, August Fridays, but best to check, adult £3.30, OAP £2.90, child £1.90, includes unlimited tram rides.

Matlock Bath Aquarium 110–12 North Parade, Matlock Bath. Centre of town [0629 583624]. Once a thermal pool where people took the waters, now contains over 40 species of British and tropical freshwater fish. You can feed them. Hologram Gallery.

Open daily April–October and winter weekends, £1.20.

Peak District Mining Museum
The Pavilion, Matlock Bath, DE4 3PS [0629 583834]. Tape and slide-shows and exhibitions illustrate major industry, lead mining in the Peak District over 2000 years. Tools, methods, working conditions, massive engines. Visitors can climb mock shafts and operate pumps. Visits to underground mine sites also arranged, with guides, for parties.

Open daily except Christmas Day, adult 80p, OAP/child 50p.

Gulliver's Kingdom and Royal Cave Temple Walk, Matlock Bath. A6 [0629 580540]. Theme park, 60 attractions like dinosaur trail, model village, model railway, roundabouts, water ride, safari ride, roller-skating, BMX bikes, and sound and light tour of the show cave.

Open daily Easter–mid September, one price £3.95.

Heights of Abraham Matlock Bath. A6 [0629 582365]. Get

there by cable-car trip over Derwent Valley from the railway station! Then woodlands, a play area, a climb of Prospect Tower for spectacular views, or underground into Great Rutland Cavern Nestus Mine with re-creation of the atmosphere and sounds of a working lead mine in the 17th century, or into Great Masson Pavilion for multi-vision programme relating what the rocks can tell followed by underground visit to Cavern, where hurricane lamps are carried through long passages. So a fair choice according to age and inclinations.

Open daily Easter–late October, winter weekends, cable-car, tower, both caverns adult £4.50, OAP £3.75, child £2.50.

Hardwick Hall Doe Lea, nr Chesterfield. A617 [0246 850430]. Cavendish family's contemporary portraits, historic furniture, needlework, tapestries. But it's really notable because of that property-building Elizabethan lady, Bess of Hardwick (Countess of Shrewsbury), and obviously well known and favoured since access to the house can be limited at peak times to avoid congestion.

300-acre Hardwick Park is open daily all year. House, formal gardens including walled garden, nature walk, April–October afternoons, Wednesday, Thursday, Saturday, Sunday and Monday bank holidays, house/garden, adult £4.50, child £2.20, garden only £1.80 and 90p.

Chatsworth Bakewell. Off A619 and A6 [0246 582204]. Impressive 17th-century home of Duke and Duchess of Devonshire. Major art collections, pictures, books, furniture, historic relics of Cavendish family's home life. Usually an exhibition, add in special events mostly to do with country pursuits. Also the 100-acre gardens (Capability Brown), famous for elaborate waterworks, cascades, fountains. Farmyard with sheep, cattle, horses, pigs, poultry, live milking demonstrations with commentary daily around 3.30 p.m., exhibition on how Chatsworth Estate is managed. There is also an adventure playground.

House/garden open daily late March–end October, farmyard and adventure playground daily April–end September, house/garden adult £4.25, OAP £3.50, child £2, family ticket £11, farmyard and adventure playground £1.60.

Buxton Micrarium St Ann's Well, The Crescent, Buxton [0298 78662]. Specimens cover the whole natural world, animal, vegetable, mineral, with an extraordinary display of designs, shapes, colours, telling of the complexity of living systems. They are living, real, not in photographs or films, you can see a crystal growing as you watch, or see the activities of a normally invisible creature. You watch, not through peering through a microscope but on TV-size screens, with buttons to push, and find out how it all works, and why. Could be the only one of its kind; run by a family concern. Tends to get full, you can see why, on rainy days.

Open daily end March–early November, 10 a.m.–5 p.m., adult £2, OAP £1.50, child £1.

Sudbury Hall Sudbury, Derbyshire. A50 [028 378 305]. Hall, former home of the Lords Vernon, fine wood carvings, furniture. Museum of Childhood in one wing, illustrating life for children in an Edwardian nursery, a Victorian parlour, with copies of games to play, a poor child's home, and work (3 chimneys for climbing and a small mine tunnel), a schoolroom (school parties don pinnies/Eton collars for a lesson, or rags/clogs to attempt Victorian children's working tasks), add clothes, toys and fantasy, like the floor-level mouse-hole complete with mouse-house to view. Children's worksheets for Hall and museum.

Open April–October, Wednesday–Sunday and bank holiday Mondays, except Good Friday, Hall adult £2.80, child £1.40, museum adult £1, OAP/child 50p, joint ticket available.

Derby City Museum and Art Gallery The Strand, Derby DE1 1BS [0332 255586]. Paintings, porcelain, costume, social history, archaeology, natural history, coins, medals. Easter and summer school holiday activities: making parachutes, kites, rockets, masks, patchwork, mobiles, turning shells into decorative objects, competitions, here or in the Industrial Museum, see below, even outdoors.

Open daily except December 25–26.

Derby Industrial Museum The Silk Mill, off Full Street, Derby DE1 3AR [0322 255308]. The Rolls-Royce aero engine collection since 1915, models, sections, displays showing how aircraft fly and work. Gallery showing how Derbyshire's geology determined many industries like lead/coal mining, iron founding, limestone quarrying. New railway engineering gallery. Extensions in progress. Easter/summer school holiday activities, see City Museum (above).

Open daily all year, adult 30p, OAP/child 10p.

Pickford's House Museum
41 Friar Gate, Derby DE1 1DA
[0332 255363]. The
accommodation and furnishings
of a late Georgian professional
man, a change from stately
homes. The gentry, their
costume, bedroom with dressing-
room, then the kitchen, cellar,
pantry, housekeeper's cupboard,
Georgian servant's bedroom.
Cooking and laundry
demonstrations take place
regularly. School holiday
activities as under City Museum
plus cooking, laundry
demonstrations, study, drama
and design related to the
costumes and period displayed.

*Open daily all year, Sundays, bank
holidays from 2 p.m., adult 30p,
OAP/child 10p, Sundays free.*

**Elvaston Castle Museum and
Country Park** Elvaston, nr
Derby. Borrowash–Thurlston
Road B5010 [0332 573799]. A
working estate, how it was from
around 1910 onwards, some of
the earlier staff are still there.
Horses, pigs, chickens, a few
geese around, a ferret to study.
Lots of earlier transport, even to
the grave! Also functioning
workshops where you may see a
young farrier fitting new shoes, a
saddler or cobbler working
among his tools, other craftsmen
who are passing on their skills to
a new generation. Domestically
an imaginatively furnished
cottage; fire-heated irons, a
linen 'press', a glass wasp-
catcher, are all among many

relics of how it was once done,
where children can point to
grates, used for heating and
cooking, and ask 'What's that
black stuff?' Answer: coal. Also a
wash-house which explains some
of the laundering processes
before detergents and washing-
machines. Sometimes
demonstrations of skills like lace-
making. Otherwise 200 acres of
parklands/woodlands/footpath,
freely open.

*Museum: open mid March–October,
Wednesday–Saturday afternoons,
all day Sunday, bank holidays,
adult £1, OAP/child 50p, family
ticket.*

Peak Cavern Castleton, via
Sheffield. Off A625 [0433
20285]. Stalactites, subterranean
formations, underground
river reached by gentle walk through
Derbyshire's largest natural
cavern. Guided tour. 400-year-old
rope walks.

*Open daily late May–early September,
otherwise closed Monday, adult £2,
child £1.*

Speedwell Cavern Winnats Pass,
Castleton, Derbyshire.Off A625
[0433 20512]. Old Derbyshire
lead mine, entrance electrically
lit, parties taken in boats for
mile-long, 30-minute guided trip,
840 ft below surface.

*Open daily except over Christmas,
New Year, adult £3.50, child £2.*

Buxton Country Park Green Lane, Buxton. Off A515 [0298 26978]. 100 acres of woodland and nature trails. Visitor Centre with video show.

Open all year, Visitor Centre daily Good Friday–end October except Wednesday in April, May and October.

Poole's Cavern in Buxton Country Park, see above. Natural limestone caves, stalactites/stalagmites. Visitor Centre, video show. 'Show cave' since 1853, stalactites, stalagmites, etc., fantastic colours, 16-step access, electrically lit, new archaeological dig. Guided tours.

Open daily Good Friday–end October, except Wednesday April, May and October, adult £2.40, OAP £2, child £1.40.

Buxton Museum and Art Gallery Peak Buildings, Terrace Road, Buxton [0298 24658]. Full-size walk-through Coal Measure Forest. Cave with animal remains, dioramas and brown bear, crawl-in Roman temple. Local rocks, minerals, fossils, finds.

Open all year, Tuesday–Saturday, appointment only Monday.

Donington Park Castle Donington, Derby. A453 [0332 810048]. World's largest collection of single-seater racing cars on display, also racing motorcycles, adjoining the racing circuit.

Open all year except Christmas, New Year, adult £4, OAP/child £1.50.

Leicestershire

Belvoir Castle Grantham. A607 [0476 870262]. Home of Duke of Rutland. Special for the medieval-style jousting tournaments, 'ladies' favours' carried by the 'knights', one of whom is described as the 'JR of the Jousting Ring'; late May bank holiday, August bank holiday, and some other summer Sundays in between. Throw in lots of special events through the year, which can be maypole dancing, car rallies, marching bands, miniature steam model gatherings, pipers playing.

Open mostly late March–September, Tuesday–Thursday, Saturday, Sunday afternoons, Monday bank holidays, March and October Sunday, adult £3, OAP/child £2, 50p extra jousting days.

Stanford Hall Lutterworth LE17 6DH. Off B5414 [0788 860250]. 17th-century house, pictures, costumes of the Cave family, replica 1898 flying machine, collection of famous racing motorcycles and rare motors kept in running order for rallies, gardens and nature trail, tearooms.

*Open Easter Sunday–end September,
afternoons Thursday, Saturday,
Sunday, Monday bank holidays and
following Tuesday, house, adult
£2.50, OAP £2.10, child £1.20,
grounds £1.30, child 60p, museum
80p and 20p plus 'Grounds only'.*

Great Central Station Great
Central Road, Loughborough.
Off A60 [0509 230726]. Private
steam railway operating over
5 miles of countryside from
Loughborough to Rothley;
museum and locomotive depot
at Loughborough and new
extension to Leicester north.

*Open all year weekends and bank
holidays, May–September Wednesday,
regular daytime services. Round trip
adult £3.30, OAP/child £1.65,
family ticket available. Write for free
timetable.*

Rutland Farm Park Catmose
Farm, Uppingham Road,
Oakham [0572 56789]. Working
farm with rare and commercial
breeds of cattle, sheep, pigs,
poultry, Shetland and Exmoor
ponies. Attractive 19th-century
farm buildings, 18 acres park
and woodland with stream,
nature walk, even **Rutland
County Museum**, Oakham [0572
723654], domestic bygones,
agricultural tools, wagons,
archaeological finds, and
Oakham Castle [0572 723654],
large collection of horseshoes
left by Royalty and peers of the
realm, within short walking
distance.

*Open late April–September
Tuesday–Sunday, Monday bank
holidays, adult £2, OAP/child £1.*

Jewry Wall Museum St Nicholas
Circle, Leicester [0533 554100].
Spacious modern museum
facing on to remains of 2nd-
century Roman Baths and Jewry
Wall. Archaeology and history of
area to 1485; look for figures of
early British families, clothes,
activities.

*Open all year Monday–Thursday,
Saturday, Sunday afternoons, closed
over Good Friday and Christmas.*

Newarke Houses Museum The
Newarke, Leicester [0533
554100]. Set of houses telling
local history from 1485 in room
settings plus 19th-century street
scene, early 20th-century shop.
Toys, games, clocks.

Open same times as Jewry Wall.

**Wygston's House Museum of
Costume** Applegate, Leicester
[0533 554100]. Spotting it from
the car park, and being far too
early for a family wedding, I
popped in with daughter. We
enjoyed enticing reconstructions
of draper's and shoe shops of the
1920s plus displays of costume
and accessories from 1750 to
1940.

Open same times as Jewry Wall.

Rockingham Castle Market Harborough LE16 8TH [0536 770240]. Hilltop castle built by William the Conqueror, fortress for early Kings. Henry VIII granted it to Edward Watson; it's still the family's home. Interesting to trace domestic life, taste, upheavals through the centuries. Rockingham was captured by the Roundheads (Civil War armour in Great Hall) and so suitable as home of the Lacey family in BBC TV's *By the Sword Divided*, about the Civil War. Charles Dickens stayed, produced and acted plays, he's also reputed to have seen ghost of Lady Dedlock pass between the 400-year-old yew hedge (which is shaped like elephants!). Unusual for an inland castle: a naval exhibition with personal memorabilia of generations of sailors. Also 12 acres of gardens including the ravine through which the Roundheads attacked.

Open afternoons Easter Sunday–30 September, Sunday and Thursday, Monday bank holidays and Tuesday following, also August Tuesday, adults £3, OAP £2.40, child £1.50, gardens only £1.50.

Tolethorpe Hall Little Casterton, nr Stamford PE9 4BH [0780 54381]. Charming open-air theatre, seating 400 and with special canopy for wet weather, where Shakespeare's plays are performed mid June to mid August. But take a rug for chilly evenings [Box office 0780 56133].

Stoughton Farm Park Gartree Road, Oadby, Leicester LE2 2FB. On B667 [0533 710355]. Rare breeds, shire horses, modern milking parlour, audio-visual, exhibitions on countryside at work. Forge. Nature trails.

Open daily except December 25–26, January 1, adult £3, OAP £2.25, child £1.50.

Gorse Hill City Farm Anstey Lane, Leicester LE4 0FL [0533 537582]. Farm animals, farm buildings, with 'hands-on' experience of how a farm works.

Open all year except Wednesday.

Rutland Water Tourist Information Centre, Sykes Lane, Empingham, nr Oakham LE15 8PX [070 086 321]. Largest man-made lake in Western Europe. Trout fishing, sailing, canoeing, windsurfing, cycle hire, Drought Gardens and Arboretum. 2 adventure playgrounds for under-13s. Pleasure cruises. Nature reserve with bird-watching hides and self-guided trail. Normanton Church Water Museum, part of building under water.

Open all year, nature reserve Easter–September Tuesday–Sunday, Monday bank holidays, winter weekends, adult £1, OAP/child 30p, museum daily Easter–September, October–November weekends, adult 40p, OAP/child 20p.

Snibston Discovery Park Ashby Road, Coalville, Leicester [0530 510851]. Opening June 27 1992. 130 acres which will contain a nature reserve, nature trails, fishing lakes in the Country Park. Then 3 main themes. Industrial Heritage will have a working beam engine, remains of medieval mining, an 18th-century wheelwright's workshop, vintage vehicles, and the story of industries like boots and shoes and especially textiles, with work-them-yourselves exhibits. The Science Discovery Area will have 20 hands-on exhibits like Walk-Through Whirlwind, the Tin Recycle and the Cycling Skeleton. The Outdoor Science Play Area will contain big experiments such as pendulum swings, level seesaws and sound mirrors.

Open daily 10 a.m.–6 p.m. except December 25–26, adult £3, OAP/child £2, family ticket £8.

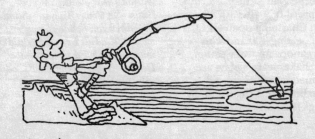

Heart of England

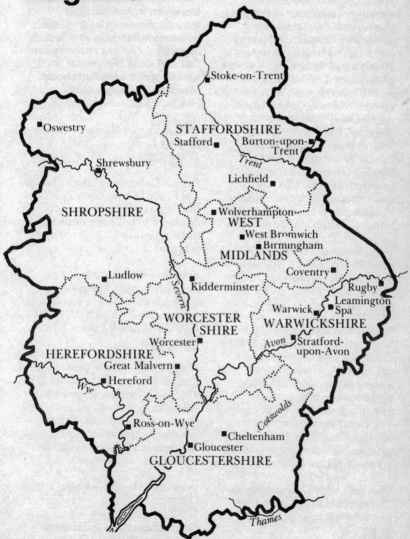

Oswestry

STAFFORDSHIRE

Stoke-on-Trent

Stafford

Burton-upon-Trent

Shrewsbury

Trent

Lichfield

SHROPSHIRE

Wolverhampton

WEST

West Bromwich

Birmingham

MIDLANDS

Ludlow

Coventry

Severn

Kidderminster

Rugby

Warwick

Leamington Spa

WORCESTER
SHIRE

WARWICKSHIRE

Worcester

Avon

Stratford-upon-Avon

HEREFORDSHIRE

Great Malvern

Hereford

Wye

Ross-on-Wye

Cotswolds

Cheltenham

Gloucester

GLOUCESTERSHIRE

Thames

West Midlands

Black Country Museum Tipton Road, Dudley [021 557 9643]. Past brought to life in living, working community with homes, shops (baker's, chemist's, hardware), chapel, workplaces like a bakery in 26-acre site. Watch a nail-maker, chain-maker, glass-cutter. Try the rides, stalls in 1920s fairground. Ride on the electric tramway. Take a trip in a narrow boat (maybe try 'legging', lying on your back to walk the walls) in the canal tunnel to the cathedral-size Singing Cavern and the limestone mines. Also underground reconstruction of Victorian drift mine, with figures, noise. Children's Activity Guide.

Open daily except Christmas Day, adult £3.75, child £2.50, family ticket, joint ticket with zoo £5.50 child or adult, £16.50 family.

Dudley Zoo and Castle 2 The Broadway, Dudley [0384 252401]. Ruins of medieval fortress with audio-visual of its turbulent history. Some 1000 mammals, birds, reptiles in surrounding grounds. Landtrain up to castle. The Geochrom, re-created Silurian Coral Reef 400 million years ago (Dudley Bug), tropical area with plants, butterflies.

Open daily except Christmas Day, adult £3, OAP/child £1.50, family ticket, joint ticket with museum, see above.

Birmingham Museum of Science and Industry Newhall Street, Birmingham [021 236 1022]. Working stationary steam engines and hot-air engines, locomotives, historic cars, aircraft, bikes, working demonstrations of scientific apparatus. Engines run on steam first and third Wednesday each month, steam weekends held March and October plus similar events.

Open daily except December 24–27, January 1.

Patrick Collection Patrick House, 180 Lifford Lane, Kings Norton, Birmingham. Motor cars displayed to tell story of social history. Children's go-karts and play area.

Open November–mid March, Sunday, otherwise Wednesday, weekends, bank holidays and school holidays, adult £3.50, OAP £2.50, child £2.10, family ticket.

Birmingham Nature Centre Pershore Road, Edgbaston. [021 472 7775]. Small wildlife park, foxes, badgers, owls, etc., fishponds, duckponds, aviaries, honeybee observation hive. Indoor natural history exhibits and school project room.

Open daily March–November.

Birmingham Railway Museum 670 Warwick Road, Tyseley,

Birmingham B11 2HL [021 207 4696]. A dozen steam locos from *Clun Castle* to *Henry*, tiny industrial tank engine. Fully operational turntable, repair workshops. Steam Days with rides Sundays Easter–December. Events include Gala Days, August Teddy Bears' Picnic, December Santa Steam. 'Henry Club' for children with badge, magazine.

Open daily January–March, October–December except Saturday, December 25–26, January 1, daily April–September, adult £2, family £5.

▦ ▨

Birmingham Museum and Art Gallery Chamberlain Square, Birmingham [021 235 2834]. Paintings, sculpture, costumes, jewellery, ceramics, textiles. Wonderfully varied attractions in the school holidays for families covering a wide age range who just drop in, and could include demonstrations of many arts, like making embroideries, historic dolls and their fashion styles, but also joining in, helping decorate the Christmas tree, printing a Christmas card, making a tile mosaic, a collage. Lots of sessions specifically designed for particular child age-ranges, generally requiring bookings; could be about cave paintings, about teapots, about toys, life in ancient Greece or in bygone Birmingham, creative writing, drama, mask-making, music-making, and all kinds of collecting which could include buttons, fossils, rocks, pebbles.

Generally a special holiday session for under-5s with accompanying adults. Add gallery tours for 8s to 14s; quizzes for children also available. But remember events during school holidays could be happening in Chamberlain Square, or at **Aston Hall** (furniture, herbs, how children lived), **Blakesley Hall** (toys and games), **Weoley Castle**, **Sarehole Mill**, **Birmingham Nature Centre** (making a fish collage, looking at life in rivers and streams, also at rodents, butterflies.

Open daily except Sunday mornings, December 25–26, January 1.

▤ ▦ ▨ ▨

Cadbury World Bournville, Birmingham [021 433 4334]. No moving river of chocolate, as some visitors anticipate. Story of chocolate told in tableaux from Montezuma (and the chance to taste an Aztec-style chocolate drink) to the Victorian Cadbury family. No modern production line either but chocs being hand-made by staff who chat about their work. Anticipate strong desire for chocolate. The 'Alternative Exhibition' in the car park, and free, houses Willy Wonka-style machinery.

Open daily except Christmas Day, adult £4.50, child £3.50, family ticket.

▦ ▨ ▨

Sandwell Park Farm off Salters Lane, West Bromwich [021 553 0220]. Queen Anne farm building, visitor and interpretive centre for Sandwell Valley. Functioning 19th-century farm, enormous dovecote, farm animals. Valley, 1400 acres, many sports, nature trails, Benedictine monastery, lakes, woodlands, wildlife.

Open all year.
🏛️ 🏫 🚊 ⊞

Midland Air Museum Coventry Airport, Baginton [0203 301033]. Open-air museum illustrating the jet age, wartime Meteor to supersonic Lightning. Exhibits include giant Argosy freighter. In contrast also, plane-spot modern aircraft operating from the airport.

Open daily April–October and winter weekends, adult £1.75, OAP £1, child 75p.
🏫 🚊

Coventry Cathedral Priory Row, Coventry [0203 224323]. 20th century with outstanding modern works of art and Visitor Centre with audio-visual story of the destruction of the medieval cathedral alongside, holograms, treasury.

Cathedral open daily except during services, donations welcome, Centre closed Sunday mornings, adult £1.25, OAP/child 75p, family ticket.
🏫 🚊 ⊞

Museum of British Road Transport St Agnes Lane, Hales Street, Coventry [0203 832425]. Over 400 cars, motorcycles,

cycles (Hobby Horses to BMX), with period street scenes (horseless carriages), royal cars, racing cars. Film *World Landspeed Record Story* has a dramatic finale I will not reveal.

Open daily April–October, otherwise Friday–Sunday, adult £2, OAP/child £1.
🏫 🚊 ⊞

Coventry Toy Museum Whitefriars Gate, Much Park Street, Coventry [0203 227560]. Tiny lodge in ancient gate houses personal collection of toys of every description, tinplate, trains, games. Gas mask on doll could cause thought.

Open daily 2–6 p.m., closed winter, adult £1, OAP/child 50p.

Ryton Gardens Ryton-on-Dunsmore, Coventry CV8 3LG [0203 303517]. National Centre for Organic Gardening. Appeared on TV *All Muck and Magic*. Green issues here, compost, natural pest control. Wildflower garden, pond, wildlife conservation area, bee garden with observation hide. Children's play area. Delicious organically grown food.

Open daily except December 25–26, adult £2, OAP/child £1.
🏫 🚊 ⊞

Herbert Art Gallery and Museum Jordan Well, Coventry [0203 832381]. Coventry's history. Unusual: living creatures to study including vivarium.

Open daily except Sunday mornings, Good Friday, Christmas.

Warwickshire

Bosworth Battlefield Visitor Centre and Country Park nr Market Bosworth. B585 [0455 290429]. Where Richard III lost his crown. Visitor Centre with models, films, replica flags/shields. Illustrated battle trail available; you can see where Richard drank before the battle, where he died. Mini-trail, following boards, covers part of battle trail. Visual and printed explanations. Incidentally you can also take a boat trip, horse-drawn or motorized through the historic countryside, direct from/to the battlefield [0455 212061]. Events: Battle re-enactments, jousting, falconry displays, extra charge, July–September.

Open: battle trail daily all year, Visitor Centre March–October, Monday–Saturday afternoons, also bank holiday Sunday/Monday. Trail free, except car parks, centre, adult £1.20, OAP/child 80p.

Warwick Castle Warwick [0926 495421]. Medieval, and what everybody thinks a castle should look like. State rooms, dungeon, torture instruments, armoury, ghost tower; 'A Royal Weekend Party – 1898' by Madame Tussauds, splendidly dressed figures in 12 rooms including making their toilettes and formally socializing in the drawing-room, when Edward VII was visiting. Also 60 acres of grounds with peacocks, woodland walks, nature trail. The Red Knight, mounted, tours precincts in summer, and amiably co-operates in photo-opportunities. New: Caesar's Tower open 140 ft, so walk the ramparts for panoramic views. Special events: Morris dancers, bands, mummers, displays of historic soldiery, drilling/mounting guard.

Open daily except Christmas Day, adult £5, OAP £3.40, child £3.25.

Warwick Doll Museum Oken's House, Warwick [0926 495546]. Antique dolls, dolls' houses, prams, but also books, puzzles.

Open daily Easter–September and school holidays, adult 75p, child 50p.

Shakespeare's Birthplace Henley Street, Stratford-upon-Avon [0789 20416]. Restored building with period furnishings, exhibits on his life and work. BBC TV Shakespeare Costume Exhibition. Visitor Centre. **New Place/Nash's House** Chapel Street [0789 292325]. Last home, with local archaeological and historic material. **Hall's Croft** Old Town [0789 292107]. His daughter's home including Elizabethan doctor's consulting room. **Anne Hathaway's Cottage** in Shottery. Off A422 [0789 292100]. Thatched farmhouse. **The Shakespeare Countryside Museum** and **Mary Arden's House** Wilmcote. Off A34 [0789 293455]. Home of his mother, now furnished in Victorian/Edwardian domestic style, plus outside museum of farming and country life including dovecote with 600 nesting holes. Walking tour from Birthplace.

5 properties open daily except November–March Sunday morning, Good Friday morning, December 24–26 and January 1 morning, inclusive ticket adult £5, child £2, separate admission charges of course, Birthplace and Anne Hathaway's Cottage not easy for disabled.
▦ 🚐 ▩

Stratford Brass Rubbing Centre Summer House, Avonbank Gardens, Stratford-upon-Avon [0789 297671]. Replicas of brasses of mostly county knights, ladies, scholars, merchants, priests.

£1–£6 charge for rubbings materials. Open daily April–October, March weekends only.
▤ ▦ 🚐 ▩

Stratford-upon-Avon Butterfly and Jungle Safari Tramway Walk, Stratford-upon-Avon [0789 299288]. Europe's largest live butterfly safari, tropical with birds, free-flying butterflies, world's largest waterlily. Insect City behind glass, scorpions, leaf-cutting ants, world's largest spider.

Open daily except Christmas Eve/Day, March–November, adult £2.75, OAP/child £2, less December–February, family ticket.
▦ 🚐 ▩

Teddy Bear Museum 19 Greenhill, Stratford-upon-Avon [0789 293160]. Giant, tiny, mechanical, musical, amusing, old, famous (Pooh, Rupert, Paddington, Sooty, Aloysius from *Brideshead Revisited*), owned by the famous and lent by the famous including Royals.

Open daily all year, adult £1.75, child 85p.

Ragley Hall Alcester, nr Stratford-upon-Avon. Off A435 [0789 762090]. 300-year-old house; treasures include a large modern mural. 400-acre park with Adventure Wood, 3D maze, stables, farm, woodland walk.

Open mid April–September Tuesday–Thursday, Saturday–Sunday and Monday bank holidays, adult £3.50, OAP/child £2.20, garden and park only £2.50 and £1.20, family ticket.
▦

The Battlefield Line Shackerstone Station, Shackerstone, Nuneaton. Off A444 [0827 880754]. Station houses railway relics. Collection of steam locos. Regular steam-hauled train service between

Market Bosworth and Shackerstone Station. Extension to Shenton near Bosworth Battlefield nearing completion.

Museum/site open weekends all year, adult 50p, child free. Service April–October Sundays and Monday bank holidays, return adult £2.25, OAP/child £1, family ticket.

Cadeby Rectory Nuneaton. Off A447 [0455 290462]. Cadbury Light Railway, probably the smallest working narrow-gauge (2 ft) in the country. Steam museum, road engines, model railway.

Open second Saturday each month, engines in steam from 1 o'clock.

Gloucestershire

Cotswold Water Park south of Cirencester. Off A419 [Ranger's Office 0285 86459]. 1500 acres of lakes offering wide variety of sports, such as watersports, walking, horse riding, cycling. For families: Keynes Country Park, angling, windsurfing, walks, playground, nature reserve, children's beach [0285 861459]; Neigh Bridge Country Park, playground, lakeside walk; Somerford Lakes Reserve [770226], children's pirate parties, for 5s–10s with trip around lake leading to treasure on Pirates' Island.

Keynes open daily all year, children's beach end May–September, £1.50 per car weekdays, £2.50 weekends and bank holidays.

Corinium Museum Park Street, Cirencester [0285 655611]. Full-size triclinium (dining-room) of Roman town house plus kitchen complete with menus. Mosaics, artefacts. Chronological sequence through Cotswold history and archaeology. Recent finds: fossil remains of mammoth and other prehistoric animals.

Open daily except Sunday mornings and October–March Monday, adult 80p, OAP 50p, child 40p.

Cheltenham Art Gallery and Museum Clarence Street, Cheltenham [0242 237431]. Arts and Crafts Movement collection, paintings, ceramics, social history and archaeological material. Ask for toddler stools to see into display cases. Look for slot containers in galleries holding children's quiz sheets, trails. School holiday activities: painting and printing, various crafts here, or dressing up at the Pittville Pump Room.

Open all year Monday–Saturday except Monday bank holidays, May–September Sunday afternoons.

Cotswold Farm Park Guiting Power, Cheltenham. B4077 [045 15 307]. Historic breeds of British farm animals, going back to Stone Age man, plus poultry and rabbits popping up. 1000-acre Cotswold farm, offering also pets' corner, cart rides, farm trails about crops, viewing seasonal activities like harvesting, sheep-shearing, indoor study centre with audio-visuals.

Open daily May–September, adult £2.40, OAP £1.75, child £1.20.
🏛 🚃

Model Railway Exhibition Box Bush, High Street, Bourton-on-the-Water [0451 20686]. Over 400 square ft of model railways among various landscapes, operated by push-button. (Look also on same street for model of the actual village.)

Open daily April–September, otherwise weekends, bank holidays, school holidays, adult £1, OAP 90p, child 80p.
🏛 🚃 ▦

Cotswold Countryside Collection Northleach. A40/A429 [0451 60715]. Housed in a 'House of Correction' (prison), with reconstructed cell block, and modern galleries, the story of rural Cotswold life, agricultural instruments, skills, the domestic side. Regular rural craft demonstrations, Morris dancing. Children's activities half-terms like Pondwatch.

Open daily April–October except Sunday morning, adult 80p, OAP 50p, child 40p.
🏛 🚃

Cotswold Falconry Centre Batsford Park, Moreton-in-the-Marsh [0386 701043]. Flying demonstrations of eagles, owls, hawks, falcons. 'Owl Wood', 'Hawk Walk', deer park.

Open daily mid March–November, adult £2, OAP £1.50, child £1.

National Waterways Museum Llanthony Warehouse, Gloucester Docks [0452 307009]. Story of transport on British rivers and canals. Working exhibits, live demonstrations.

Open daily except Christmas Day, adult £3.75, OAP/child £2.75, family ticket £9.50.
🏛 🚃 ▦

Museum of Advertising and Packaging Albert Warehouse, Gloucester Docks [0452 302309]. Around 100 years of history told through Robert Opie's 200,000 collection of containers, packages, from family shopping baskets, larders, meal-times. Continuous screening of TV commercials since 1950s.

Open all year Tuesday–Sunday, August Monday, bank holidays except December 25–26, adult £1.50, OAP £1.20, child 75p.
🏛 🚃 ▦

House of the Tailor of Gloucester 9 College Court, Gloucester [0452 422856]. The building illustrated in the Beatrix Potter story; inside kitchen re-created, scenes of tailoring mice, etc.

Open all year, Monday–Saturday.

Wildfowl and Wetlands Trust
Slimbridge. Off M5 [045389
333]. World's largest collection
of wildfowl, 2500 of some 180
different kinds. Attractive in all
seasons: in winter months skies
are alive with those wintering
here, to be seen more closely
from comfortable hides. Plenty
too in grounds in summer.
Visitor Centre, Tropical House,
exhibitions, cinema. 100-acre
site, also headquarters for
Wildfowl and Wetlands Trust.
Braille Trail. Special family days:
making masks, models and
mobiles, carrying out
experiments, pond-dipping,
children's trails.

*Open daily except over Christmas,
adult £3.50, OAP £2.50, child
£1.90.*

**Royal Forest of Dean's Mining
Museum** Clearwell, nr Coleford.
Off B4228 [0594 32535]. Warren
of tunnels stretching under the
forest, worked until 1945. Mining
equipment and vintage engines.

*Open daily March–October, also
December 1–24, 'Santa's Secret
Workshop', adult £2, OAP £1.50,
child £1.*

Dean Heritage Centre Camp
Mill, Soudley, nr Cinderford. On
B4227 [0594 822170].
Reconstructed cottage and mine,
beam engine and water wheel,
pigs, domestic fowl, 15-frame
observational beehive, wood
ants' nest, charcoal burning,
nature trails.

*Open daily all year, adult £2.25,
OAP £1.50, child £1.25.*

Dean Forest Railway Norchard
Steam Centre, New Mills,
Lydney. B4234 [0594 843423].
Lots of railway track where you
can take steam-train rides in full-
size railway engines and coaches.
Run by volunteers.

*Static displays open daily all year
round, steam-train rides Easter
weekend, spring/August bank
holiday, April–September Sunday,
June–July Wednesday, August
Tuesday–Thursday, steam days adult
£2.50, child £1.50, other days 35p
and 15p.*

Falconry Centre Newent. Off
B4216 [0531 820286]. Take
cameras to photograph historic
birds of prey in open ground:
sometimes they're even seen
rearing their young. Flying
demonstrations, weather
permitting, of eagles, falcons, etc.
Tethered in hawk walk (no wire).
Museum with photographs,
exhibits, books on subject.

*Open daily February–November,
adult £3.50, child £1.95.*

**Newent Butterfly and Natural
World Centre** Springbank,
Birches Lane, Newent [0531

821800]. Tropical butterfly house, insect menagerie, reptile area, waterlife exhibition. Also pheasants and aviaries.

Open daily Easter–October, adult £2.25, OAP £1.85, child £1.45.

Berkeley Castle Berkeley. Off A38 [0453 810332]. Over 800 years: Cromwell's troops knocked it about, Henry VIII had a honeymoon (Boleyn), Elizabeth I flounced out leaving some possessions. Scene of Edward II's murder. Great Hall, great kitchen. Look for fly embedded in confessional, 'Time flies'! Also: Butterfly House in walled garden, free-flying beautifully coloured creatures, feeding, mating.

Open April Tuesday–Sunday afternoons, May–September Tuesday–Saturday, Sunday afternoons, Monday bank holidays, October Sunday afternoons, adult £2.90, OAP £2.60, child £1.45, includes Butterfly House.

Sudeley Castle and Gardens Winchcombe. Off A46/B4632 [0242 602308]. Once the home of Henry VIII's widow, Catherine Parr. Visited by Elizabeth I and Lady Jane Grey. Treasures like Catherine Parr's prayerbook, canopy made by Anne Boleyn for her daughter and the christening robe. Castle inspiration for P. G. Wodehouse's *Blandings*. Falconry exhibition. Events: re-enacting history.

Open daily April–October, adult £4.20, child £2.20, family ticket.

Hereford

Wye Valley Open Farm Goodrich, Ross-on-Wye [0600 890296]. Same family since 1650. Traditional stone farm buildings, chickens, ducks, geese, pigs, goats, cattle, horses. Woodland walks by River Wye.

Open daily Easter–October, adult £3, child £1.50.

World of Butterflies Symonds Yat West, Whitchurch. Off A40 [0600 890360]. Free-flying butterflies in tropical atmosphere, plants, pools.

Open daily Good Friday–October, adult £1.80, OAP £1.40, child £1.

Jubilee Maze Symonds Yat. B4164 [0600 890360]. Traditional hedge maze and world's first maze museum.

Open daily Good Friday–October, adult £2, child £1.

The Lost Street Museum Palma Court, 27 Brookend Street, Ross-on-Wye [0989 62752]. Edwardian street with shops displaying period photographs, musical boxes, radios, toys, dolls. Old amusement machines. Quizzes.

Open daily February–November,
December–January Friday–Sunday,
adult £1.50, OAP £1.25, child £1,
family ticket.

Worcestershire

Severn Valley Railway The
Railway Station, Bewdley [0299
403816]. Two parts: UK's largest
working collection of standard
gauge steam and diesel
locomotives. Steam trains to
Kidderminster and along river
valley to Bridgnorth. Model
railway on station. Gala
weekends and Santa Specials.
Station open all year.

Trains daily mid May–end September,
mid March–December weekends and
public holidays, adult £1, child 50p
refunded when train ticket bought.

West Midland Safari and
Leisure Park Spring Grove,
Bewdley. A456 [0299 402114].
Go on safari through 200 acres
of wild animal reserves, no
safari bus and pedestrians not
admitted. Then Cinedome, you
feel you are speeding along
motorways/rivers, a trapeze
show with visitors trying it
themselves, sea-lion antics, train
trip, boats/canoes, skating,
various fairground rides.

Open daily April–October, £3 per
person, extra for rides.

Birtsmorton Waterfowl
Sanctuary Birtsmorton, nr
Malvern [068 481 376]. Children
can walk among the birds in
natural surroundings and feed
them.

Open daily except Christmas Day,
adult £1.25, child 50p.

Broadway Tower Country Park
Broadway. A44 [0386 852390].
55-ft tower, 18th-century folly,
gives spectacular views from top.
Nature walks, rare animals and
birds, children's farmyard,
adventure playground. Giant
chess and draughts.
Picnic/barbecue area.

Open daily Easter–October, adult £2,
OAP/child £1.25, family ticket.

Shropshire

Ironbridge Gorge Museum
Ironbridge, Telford [095 245
3522 weekdays, 2751 weekends].
Where Abraham Darby first
smelted iron, using coke as fuel,
in the 18th century. History of
the industrial revolution told in
a number of museums in 6
square miles along the tree-
lined banks of Severn Gorge.
Peak summer months Park and
Ride. I have listed those most
likely to interest children.
Advice: contact Visitor
Information Service (address,
phone number above) for
leaflet, details.

*Open daily except December 24–25,
but some sites other times. Passport
gives entry to all museums in any
order and on return visits, adult
£6.50, OAP £5.50, child £3.80,
family passport.*

*Museum of the River and Visitor
Centre* Like mini-castle. 40-ft
model of Gorge in 18th century.
Video on the industrial
revolution. Furnished sections of
period homes. Slide/tape show
on the way the river is managed
now compared to in the past.
Intro to various sites.

Adult £1.20, child £1, see passport.

Ironbridge Tollhouse Walk the
Iron Bridge. There is a
certificate obtainable
confirming you have been in
Tollhouse housing exhibition
about bridge.

Blists Hill Open Air Museum
Re-creation of Victorian town.
Staff dressed in period clothes.
Chemist (pill-making machine,
like rolling pastry then pilling,
colouring, bowl of leeches,
blood-letting bowl) with
dentistry section; bank (change
money); printing on ancient
machine; locksmiths,
carpenter, sweet shop;
squatter's cottage with outdoor
lav. Coal mine, cage worked
with primitive machinery.
Working wrought ironworks.
Horse and cart transports
fodder or visitors. Tub boat
canal.

*Adult £4.50, OAP £3.80, child £3,
see passport.*

Tar Tunnel 100-yard-long tunnel
into hillside with wells of natural
bitumen discovered 1786.

*Open daily in summer, adult 75p,
child 50p, see passport.*

Rosehill House Darby Road,
Coalbrookdale. Furnished in way
of life of early 19th-century
ironmaster.

Adult £1.20, child £1, see passport.

*Museum of Iron and the Darby
Furnace* Story of iron- and steel-
making and of Coalbrookdale.
Sound and light display.

*Adult £2.50, child £1.50, see
passport.*

Weston Park nr Shifnal [095 276
207]. 17th-century house,
treasures include tapestries, fine
art collection. Home of Earls of
Bradford. Weston Park Railway
from Adventure Playground
provides a tour of park which
also offers a tropical butterflies
attraction in an enormous
greenhouse, plus insect house,
the aquarium with freshwater
and maritime creatures, Museum
of Country Bygones, pets' corner.
Nature trails. Special events.

*Open April, May and September
weekends, bank holidays, daily
spring bank holiday week, daily June
and July except Monday and Friday,
daily August, house and garden
adult £3.50, OAP/child £2.10,
garden and museum £2.50 and
£1.50.*

Aerospace Museum RAF
Cosford, Wolverhampton. A41
[0902 374872]. Aircraft, aero
engines, rockets, missiles, from
different countries. One of the
largest aviation collections in the
UK. British Airways Hall tells
story of civil air transport from
DH4A to Concorde. Also
missiles, engines, uniforms,
memorabilia.

*Open daily except December 24–26,
January 1, adult £3.30, OAP/child
£1.50.*

**Acton Scott Working Farm
Museum** Wenlock Lodge, Acton
Scott, nr Church Stretton. A49 or
B4371 [06946 306]. Working
farm in man/horse tradition
before electricity/petrol engine.
19th-century-style mixed farm
including horses, sheep, pigs,
poultry. Mostly outdoor site so
wrap up for weather, take wellies,
to see what it was like. Butter-
making, other traditional crafts
demonstrated. Broad-wheeled
invalid chairs available.

*Open daily April–October, adult £2,
OAP/child £1, family ticket.*

**Midland Motor Museum and
Bird Garden** Stanmore Hall,
Stourbridge Road, Bridgnorth.
A442 [074 62 61761]. Unusual
mix: over 85 sports, racing cars,
motorcycles, then 8 acres with
800 birds in 70 aviaries,
paddocks, lakes. Small mammals
on show, apart from pets' corner.

*Open daily except Christmas Day,
adult £3.30, OAP £2.65, child
£1.65.*

Staffordshire

Drayton Manor Park and Zoo
nr Tamworth. A4091 [0827
287979]. Another mix, zoo in
wooded parkland with primates,
reptiles, big cats, penguins, and
farm section, then fairground
rides, mini-railway, jungle cruise,
pedal boats, life-size simulated
dinosaurs, even a parachute
tower.

*Open daily April–October, adult £2,
child £1, plus charges for rides.*

Shugborough Hall
Shugborough, nr Stafford [0889
881388]. Ancestral home of
Earls of Lichfield. Staffordshire
County Museum housed in
previously servants' quarters.
Seasonal demonstrations old-
style spring cleaning. Domestic
side like brewhouse, coach
house, laundry, costume, crafts.
Farm is a working museum with
equipment, herds of rare breeds.

Open daily late March–October,
mansion, museum, farm, adult £5,
OAP/child £3, single site £2, £1.50.

Children's Farm Ash End House
Farm, Middleton Lane,
Middleton, nr Tamworth [021
329 3240]. Off A409. Farm
animals, rare breeds, shire
horses. Guided tours for
playgroups, play schemes,
Cubs/Brownies, schools.

Open all year, per child, includes
bucket of food for animals, badge or
balloon, pony ride and fresh egg
when available, £1.80, adult 90p.

Alton Towers Alton. Off B5032
[0538 702200]. Extraordinary
number of ways to be swung,
turned, twisted upside down
including Log Flume, Black
Hole, Alton Beast. Magnificent
historic gardens, large model
railway, Wildlife Museum, Dolls'
Exhibition (large and varied toy

museum), theatre with
performance entirely of water
effects to music, supervised
adventure playgrounds
(admission by height), vintage
car museum, lots more.

Open daily mid March–mid
November, adult £9.50, child £7.50
(all-in ticket).

Chatterley Whitfield Mining
Museum Tunstall, Stoke-on-
Trent. A527 [0782 813337].
700 ft underground in 'cage' to
see coal mining techniques, old
and new, around 1¼ hours,
conducted by experienced
miners. Advisable to wear
serviceable clothing, stout shoes;
protective equipment such as
helmets, cap lamps, provided.
Underground locomotive ride.
Pit ponies. Working steam locos.

Open daily, adult £3.75, child
£2.75, family ticket.

North West

Lune

Lancaster

Ribble

Clitheroe

LANCASHIRE

Blackpool

Preston

Blackburn

Irish Sea

Southport

Bury

Bolton

Wigan

Oldham

GREATER MANCHESTER

St Helens

Manchester

Tame

MERSEYSIDE

Warrington

Liverpool

Stockport

Birkenhead

Mersey

Runcorn

Macclesfield

CHESHIRE

Dee

Chester

Weaver

Crewe

Cheshire

Jodrell Bank Science Centre and Tree Park Macclesfield SK11 9DL. A535 [0477 71339]. Easily located by the Lovel Radio Telescope almost the size of St Paul's Cathedral. Interactive hands-on gallery with infinity mirrors (see yourself to infinity) periscope, curved mirror (shake your own hand), corner reflector (see yourself as others see you), sound reflectors (whisper your message over 75 yards), gyro chair, gravity hollow, model radio telescope. Talking head of Sir Isaac Newton and life-size version of his telescope. Exhibition about telescopes, space (a space suit), satellites, modern astronomy. Video wall and holograms. 35-acre Tree Park contains a scaled layout of the solar system as well as nature trails. Planetarium (not under-5s): regular presentations plus 'Star of Bethlehem', from mid December, with the sky as it was over Bethlehem nearly 2000 years ago, as the Wise Men (the scientists of their time) saw it, and the chance to consider whether there was a shooting star, a comet, Jupiter, or a legend.

Open daily Easter–October, November–Easter weekends, plus the Christmas show opening, adult £2.75, child £1.50.

Quarry Bank Mill in Country Park Styal, Wilmslow [0625 527468]. Life 150 years ago. Giant water wheel built to power 4 floors of weaving looms.

Apprentice House for 100 pauper children working in the mill and going to school at night. Their garden too and the school and chapel the mill owner built for the workers. Try spinning, 18th-century schooling. 250-acre country park. Events include children's school holiday activities, helping the skivvies cleaning the Apprentice House with period cleaning materials, workshops in painting, printing, weaving, Teddy Bears' Picnic.

Mill open daily April–September, October–March Tuesday–Sunday, Apprentice House and garden daily Easter, July–September, Christmas period, otherwise closed Monday, December 24–25, one price £3.75, mill only £2.75, family ticket, National Trust members free.

Tatton Park Knutsford WA16 6QN [0565 54822]. Mansion includes state rooms, nursery, servants' rooms, cellars. Home farm, horses and other animals, worked as 50 years ago. Mysterious Old Hall, audio-visual of Tatton's history through 5 centuries. Try your hand at threshing. Deer park and nature trails. Special events include August Children's Week, Christmas on the Farm, historical re-enactments.

House open Easter–September, farm also winter Sundays, park and gardens all year, all closed Mondays. Entry charges.

Lion Salt Works Ollershaw Lane, Marston, Northwich. B5075 [0606 40555]. Adjacent to Trent and Mersey Canal. The last open-pan salt works in Great Britain making cut lump salt from brine. Operating from 1842 to 1986 the works are being restored and will have developing exhibits as work proceeds. Groundwork Discovery Centre on site: information on Vale Royal, its attractive countryside and rich industrial heritage. Also cycle hire: Easter–October weekends, daily July–August.

Open daily all year from 2 p.m., voluntary donations.

Salt Museum 162 London Road, Northwich CW9 8AB [0606 41331]. Story of salt-making in Cheshire from Roman times to present day. Audio-visual introduction to displays in old workhouse.

Open all year Tuesday–Sunday 2–5 p.m., July–August Tuesday–Saturday 10 a.m.–5 p.m., Monday bank holidays, except Good Friday, December 24–26.

Chester Zoo Zoological Gardens, Upton-by-Chester. Off A41 [0244 380280]. 110 acres with spacious enclosures, family groups of rare species in summer. Penguin pool with underwater viewing, tropical house with birds in free flight, summer waterbus trips, to view wild waterfowl, free guided tours, children's farm, children's worksheets. UK's largest garden zoo.

Open daily except Christmas Day, adult £4.60, OAP/child £2.30, wheelchairs for hire.

Chester Toy and Doll Museum 13a Lower Bridge Street, Chester [0244 346297]. Over 5000 exhibits, tinplate, cars, planes, lorries, dolls and bears, games, boats, battery toys, puppets, from 1830. Largest collection of Matchbox toys on public display in the world. Representation of a toy shop window some 30 years ago. Dolls' hospital, dolls and teddies restored, recuperation ward. Children's play area, old toys to play with. Events concerning antique toys.

Open daily, adult £1.50, OAP/child 70p.

Grosvenor Museum 27 Grosvenor Street, Chester CH1 2DD [0244 321616]. The organization of the Roman Army, Roman tombstones and inscriptions, dioramic model of the Roman Legionary Fortress at Chester, replica of armour worn by the Legionaries 1st century AD. Also natural history, local history and archaeology of Chester and Cheshire. Children's school holiday activities, say 6 upwards: painting, calligraphy, cooking, paper-making, printing, making models on themes like Romans, natural history, theatre, an art exhibition.

Open all year Monday–Saturday,
Sunday afternoons, except Good
Friday, Christmas.

Lady Lever Art Gallery Port
Sunlight Village, Wirral [051 645
3623]. World-class gallery set in
early 20th-century high-standard
village planning. A lot of
Wedgewood (plaques, vases,
fireplaces), sculptures, furniture,
paintings (Reynolds, Turner,
Constable, the Pre-Raphaelites),
Chinese art from 200 BC,
enamels, clocks, needlework.
Unaccompanied under-16s not
admitted. School holidays:
quizzes, generally with a theme,
select and guide through the
abundance.

Open daily except Sunday mornings,
Good Friday, December 24–26,
January 1.

Have you read **A Plea**, to check
that your destination is open
before you depart (page 11)?

Merseyside

The Boat Museum Dockyard
road, Ellesmere Port, South
Wirral. Off M53 [051 355 5017].
How people lived and worked on
the inland waterways. After
puzzling how a family managed to
cook, sleep and eat in a narrow,
traditionally decorated canal
boat, remember everybody
worked, including the children.

Over 60 different craft, to be
compared with ships passing on
adjoining Manchester Ship Canal,
also audio-visual presentations,
boats being restored, and steam
engines once providing dock
power 'in steam' first Sunday of
the month and summer bank
holidays. Indoor exhibitions tell
the story of canal building and
the life of the boat people
(narrow, mine boat, navvies' hut);
'The Horse on the Cut', for
pulling the canal boats; the
building of the Manchester Ship
Canal; 'Canal Carrying' (cargoes
and the chance to handle some).
Terrace of cottages showing how
dock workers lived from Victorian
times to 1930s. Trips in narrow
boat with commentary in
summer. Craft workshops.
Worksheets for children. Videos
for deaf. Resources pack for
blind.

Open daily April–October,
November–March
Saturday–Thursday, except December
24–26, adult £3.60, OAP £2.50,
child £2.30.

Merseyside Maritime Museum
Albert Dock, Liverpool [051 207
0001]. Waterfront story of
historic docklands with loading
machinery even from sailing-ship
era. Maritime Park with historic
vessels. River Room where you
can see/understand activities on
the river today, Boat Hall with
restoration going on and
craftsmen at weekends
demonstrating skills like sail-
making, net-making, fancy

ropework, and probably the world's only Maritime Brass Rubbing Centre with replica brasses, even the *Titanic* and the *Victory.* 'World of Models' over 200 from a few inches long to a 10-ft liner. 'Emigrants to a New world', walk down a reconstruction of an 1850s street into the interior of an emigrant ship, to learn story of the 9 million who emigrated through Liverpool between 1830 and 1930, with sound effects, videos, tapes. Guidelines on tracing emigrant ancestors. Events for families: studying marine life with microscopes; handling and experimenting with marine objects; theatrical re-enactments of port life in the past including the emigrants' grim ordeals.

Open daily except Good Friday, December 24–26, January 1, admission £1.50, family ticket.
🚻 🚃

Liverpool Museum William Brown Street, Liverpool L3 8EN [051 207 0001]. Collections from the wonders of the Amazonian rain-forests to outer space. Natural History Centre: some 10,000 specimens, shells, insects, fossils, minerals, local birds, for handling, examining, using video cameras and microscopes, with staff to answer questions. Young children can find out about animal shapes and colours while others can tackle quizzes.

Open all year Tuesday–Saturday and Monday bank holidays 1–4.30 p.m. and Sunday 2–4.30 p.m.

Planetarium: programmes like *In Search of Other Worlds* and *Nightwatch* about what stars and planets to see in the sky that night. *Tuesday–Friday 3.15 p.m.: school holidays several performances most days: adult 80p, child 40p.* Adjacent exhibition on satellites, watch American TV. Aquarium. School holiday events: 'Play and Learn', activity sessions for 3–7-year-olds in summer; quizzes; imaginative activities for families allied to current exhibition, i.e. Bulgaria, so folk dancing, making 'Koukeri' masks, decorative celebratory twigs. 'Project Explorer '91': club for 7s–12s with magazine (quizzes, competitions), introduction to collections from a duck-billed platypus to bed bugs, free entry to Maritime Museum, membership £2 a year.

Open daily except Sunday mornings, Good Friday, December 24–26, January 1.
♿ 🚻 🚃

Walker Art Gallery William Brown Street, Liverpool L3 8EL [051 207 0001]. Paintings from 14th century. European Old Master, Victorian and Pre-Raphaelite pictures, sculptures. Children's holiday activities: quizzes, usually with a theme, say Christmas; an artist at work in a studio ready to talk, answer questions.

Open: as Liverpool Museum.

Animation World Britannia Pavilion, Albert Dock, Liverpool, L69 5BJ [051 507 1828]. 'Castle Duckula, with bad jokes and Duckula's coffin, 'The Wind in the Willows', the countryside and Toad Hall, 'B.F.G.' Street with shops, houses and big feet. In addition to sets and characters, how it's done shown in pre-production area with scripts, sounds, post-production where it all comes together, model studio, original sets, models and drawings, workshops with puppets, props, paint, hands-on exhibits.

Open daily all year 10 a.m.–6 p.m., adult £3, child £2.50, family ticket.

The Beatles Story Britannia Pavilion Vaults, Albert Dock, Liverpool L3 4AA [051 709 1963]. A street in Hamburg, the Cavern Club, the height of Beatlemania with screaming fans, the flower-power period, a walk through Yellow Submarine with real fish beyond the portholes, Beatles music and film footage. 'Beatle Brain' computer.

Open daily except Christmas Day, adult £3, OAP/child £2, family ticket.

Croxteth Country Park Croxteth Hall Lane, Liverpool [051 228 5311]. Within the city boundary, 530 acres of a working country estate once owned by the Earls of Sefton. So lots of tearing around and picnicking space plus the Hall, with furniture and displays of aristocratic formal dress from turn of the century (audio-visual *The Way They Lived*), a Victorian walled garden which once fed the gentry (you can buy produce in season), and a Victorian-style farmyard with pigs, sheep, horses and some other animals which city-raised children can touch and feed (so when did *you* last see chickens pecking around in the open?). Add guided walks which illuminate bird and plant life, many festivals, demonstrations, displays, children's 'Fun Days'. Adventure playground and miniature railway.

Outer park open throughout the year free. Inner park, Hall, walled garden, farm, open daily Easter–October, some winter openings, except Christmas/New Year, adult £2, OAP/child £1, or tickets for each attraction.

Knowsley Safari Park Prescot, Merseyside. A58 [051 430 9009]. Look for lions, tigers, elephants, rhinos, monkeys, zebra, camels, on your drive through the Game Reserves. Also Dolphinarium, children's amusement park and pets' corner with animals to feed.

Open daily Easter–September, Game Reserves, car with all passengers, £4.50, then various, like safari buses, adult £1.80, child £1, extras for Dolphinarium, pets' corner.

Lancashire

Wildfowl and Wetlands Centre
Martin Mere, Burscough,
Ormskirk, Lancashire. Off A59
[0704 895181]. 45-acre waterfowl
gardens, 1600 species from all
over the world, 300-acre wild
area with comfortable hides to
see geese, swans, etc. in winter.
Visitor and Viewing Centre. Brass
rubbing, worksheets, quizzes,
holidaytime family activities.

*Open daily except December 24–25,
adult £3, OAP £2, child £1.50.*

Museum of Childhood Church
Street, Ribchester PR3 3YE.
B6245 [0254 878 520]. Around
250,000 exhibits. 300 teddy bears
including tiny one rescued from
the *Titanic*. Working model of an
Edwardian fairground. Costume
dolls from 80 countries and
Warneken collection of 200
needlework figures. Victorian
and Edwardian dolls' houses,
Professor Tomlin's Famous Flea
Circus, the fleas being trained to
duel, dance, push a lawnmower.
Trains to drive yourself, toys to
play with. 'General Tom
Thumb', 25 in high,
memorabilia.

*Open all year Tuesday–Sunday and
Monday bank holidays, adult £1.75,
child £1.*

**Museum of Childhood and
Gillow Furniture Museum**
Church Street, Lancaster [0524
32808]. Barry Elder doll

collection, games, toys, dolls of
past 3 centuries; Victorian
schoolroom, Edwardian
nurseries. In Gillow Museum
period room settings, for gentry
and servants. Children's
worksheets, summer quizzes.

*Open Easter–October
Monday–Saturday, adult 70p, child
35p.*

University of Lancaster Bailrigg,
Lancaster [0524 65201]. Rare
example of university sports
facilities open to the community,
like the pool, squash courts,
water sports, and much more.
Special sessions for children in
school holidays, termtime
parent/child classes, children's
swimming.

*Open most of the year but
students/university staff given
priority in termtime.*

Wigan Pier Wigan [0942 323666,
recorded information line 0942
44888]. 'The Way We Were',
1900 brought to life by actors, so
be a child (any age) in a
Victorian classroom, visit the
collier's family where grief, joy,
drama are enacted, sing a song
in the pub, repent at the
temperance meeting, be
entertained in the Music Hall,
have fun at the annual Wakes
Week at the seaside, bargain in
the market, talk to the young
volunteer just off to the Boer
War. Walk the canalside or take
the waterbus to Trencherfield
Mill, to see and hear the sound

of the cotton industry, view the world's largest original working mill steam engine.

Open daily except December 25–26, adult £5.10, OAP/child £3.10, family ticket £13.30.

🏛️ �᎒

City Museum Market Square, Lancaster LA1 1HT [0524 582000]. History and archaeology of the city. King's Own Royal Regimental Museum too. Children's worksheets, quizzes Easter, summer holidays, with prizes.

Open all year Monday–Saturday, closed Christmas, New Year.

🏧 🏛️ �᎒

Maritime Museum St George's Quay, Lancaster [0524 582000]. Former 18th-century Custom House tells of port's history and the local fishing industry with boats, cargoes, displays. Lancaster Canal and the ecology of Morecambe Bay dealt with in adjacent warehouse, more boats, also sound, smells, computers and an audio-visual show. Children's worksheets, quizzes Easter summer holidays, with prizes.

Open daily Easter–October 11 a.m.–5 p.m. (admission charge), daily November–Easter from 2 p.m. free.

🏛️ �᎒ 🔲

Camelot Theme Park Charnock Richard, Chorley, Preston, Lancashire. Off M6 [0257

453044]. There is of course a castle and Merlin's Cave. But add an Indian Village with children's tepee, indoor playroom for 5–6-year-olds, Valley Forge Fort with Cowboy Shoot-Out show, Uncle Tom's Cabin, and a spread-out adventure playground with rope tunnel, water tube slide (wet – take bathing suit) or ball bath (dry), also different size roller-coasters. Add too a children's circus, rides in all sorts of vehicles, and Aquatic World with fish on display.

Open Easter, some dates April, May, June Wednesday–Sunday, daily July–August, September weekends and some other times, adult £6.95, OAP £3.95, child £5.95.

🏛️ �᎒ 🔲

Blackpool Pleasure Beach Promenade, Blackpool [0253 41033]. Own railway station. Ways of going down, up, over, round like Tagada, the Black Hole, water chute, log flume, big dipper, swamp buggies. Funshireland park for children 2–10. Ice shows.

Open daily April–November, admission free, you pay per ride.

🏛️ �᎒ 🔲

Blackpool Sea Life Centre Golden Mile Centre, Promenade, Blackpool [0523 22445]. Walk through a tunnel to see sea creatures like sharks, octopus, look down on other fish in large tanks.

Open daily all year except Christmas Day, adult £4.25, child £2.25.

Blackpool Tower Promenade, Blackpool [0253 22242]. Tower-top ride, holograms, satellite TV from America, Tiny Tots Soft Play Area (1–4-year-olds), Jungle Jim's Adventure Playground (5–12-year-olds), Undersea World Aquarium, Dungeon, Tower Ballroom.

Open daily May–November, adult £4.75, child £3.75.

Sandcastle South Promenade, Blackpool [0253 404013]. Sub-tropical temperature. Pools with water slides, water chute, floating islands. Shallow 'Kiddies' Harbour' for little ones. Giant inflatables. Supervised children's (dry) play area.

Open daily May–November, £4.20.

Greater Manchester

Cornerhouse 70 Oxford Street, Manchester M1 5NH [061 228 2463]. Centre for visual arts. 3 cinemas, exhibitions of photography, sculpture, paintings, courses and workshops. Events for children like films in the school holidays.

Admission free, charge for cinemas. Phone for details.

Granada Studios Tour Water Street, Castlefield, Manchester M60 9EA [061 832 9090]. *Coronation Street*, walk the set, view 30 years of the programme; the Sherlock Holmes set in Baker Street, interior and exterior; outside of No 10 Downing Street; House of Commons and the chance to debate; Kingdom of the Giants with chairs looming over you; behind-the-scenes make-up techniques, special effects; magic show.

Open mid March–mid September Tuesday–Sunday and Monday bank holidays, winter Wednesday–Sunday, closed December 24–25, adult £6.96, child £4.75.

Museum of Science and Industry Liverpool Road, Castlefield, Manchester M3 4JP [061 832 2244]. World's largest collection of working steam engines and locos; 'The Making of Manchester', the city's story; 'Underground Manchester', a reconstructed sewer pipe; Air and Space Gallery, aeroplanes, try the simulator; 'Xperiment!', hands-on experiments like 'Electronic Fleas', a demonstration of static electricity, 'Upside-Down Periscope' which you ride, 'Optical Snooker' to play, magic with mirrors.

Open daily all year, adult £2, OAP/child £1.

Chinese Arts Centre 36 Charlotte Street, Manchester [061 236 9251]. Chinese art, craft, people and customs. Also the Imperial Chinese Archway in Faulkner Street (ceramics, gold leaf, lacquer) and Ornamental Garden, designed by Chinese. 2 pavilions for viewing the bamboos, maple, junipers.

Arts Centre open all year Tuesday–Sunday.

City Art Gallery Mosley Street, Manchester M2 3JL [061 236 9422]. Reconstruction of Lowry's sitting-room and studio. Paintings, drawings, watercolours including Stubbs, Constable, Turner, Oriental works of art, pottery and silver, Greek and Egyptian pottery, Victorian arts and crafts. Athenaeum Gallery, next door, long-time location for imaginative children's holiday activities. Worth checking to find out if resumed.

Open all year Monday–Saturday, Sunday afternoons.

Manchester Police Museum Newton Street, Manchester M1 1EF [061 855 3290]. Charge office of the 1920s with figures; cells of the 1880s (note: warm and a toilet, so far superior to occupants' home conditions); mug shots; uniforms; night stick (banged on railings to get help before personal radios); offensive weapons confiscated at football matches *then* (darts, spiked metal balls, knuckle-dusters), a forger's den.

Open by appointment only.

Manchester Museum University of Manchester, Oxford Road, Manchester [061 275 2634]. Egyptian mummies, with X-rays, information about disease, diet. Fossils, plants, animals, Greek and Roman coins, Mammal Gallery, vivarium, aquarium.

Open daily except Sunday.

Manchester United Museum Warwick Road North, Old Trafford, Manchester M16 0RA [061 872 1661]. The first purpose-built museum in British football. Tells the club's story from 1878 including the 1958 plane crash at Munich.

Open daily except Saturday, adult £1.50, OAP/child £1.

Library Theatre Central Library, St Peter's Square, Manchester M2 5PD [061 236 7110]. High-standard family Christmas shows, *The Adventures of Huckleberry Finn, Sleeping Beauty*. Half-term puppet shows. Manchester Youth Theatre performances. Children's painting competitions. 'Playdays', behind the scenes, workshop, tour.

Phone for details.

Forum Theatre Wythenshaw [061 437 9663]. *As Library Theatre.*

Pankhurst Centre 60–62 Nelson Street, Manchester M13 9WP [061 273 5673]. Home of Emmeline Pankhurst, where the Women's Social and Political Union formed in 1903. 'Pankhurst Parlour' and gardens in Edwardian style. Story of the suffrage movement 19th–20th centuries.

Open all year Monday–Friday and afternoons first Sunday in month.

Manchester Cathedral Brass Rubbing Centre Manchester [061 833 2220]. You pay for the materials you use, instruction included, say from 50p.

Open all year Monday–Friday.

Museum of Transport Boyle Street, Cheetham, Manchester. A665 [061 205 2122]. Story of public transport in the area, over 50 buses and other vehicles representing 100 years of local transport history.

Open all year Wednesday, weekends and bank holidays, adult 70p, child 30p.

Gallery of English Costume Platt Hall, Platt Fields, Rusholme, Manchester [061 224 5217]. Georgian house, costumes from 1600 to present day, from haute couture to working clothes. Special exhibitions on particular aspects of fashion.

Open all year Monday, Wednesday–Saturday and Sunday afternoons.

Yorkshire and Humberside

North Yorkshire

York Minster Deangate, York YO1 2JA [0904 624426]. Largest Gothic cathedral in England. Much medieval stained glass including famous Rose Window, reassembled after fire damage. Look for ceiling bosses including *Blue Peter* competition winner. Medieval Chapter House (charge), Central Tower, 275 steps, children accompanied (charge). Undercroft: the Minster stands on the central part of a Roman legionary fortress, then came the Saxons, and the Normans who built a vast cathedral. The archaeological finds over the centuries can be seen, and the massive concrete collars now supporting the Minster. Large-scale models help understanding (charge).

No sightseeing permitted Sunday before 12.30, restricted during Evensong. Admission, donations.

▦ ▭ ▨

York Story Castlegate, York [0904 628632]. History and architecture told in sound and vision, including representation of the Shambles, York's narrow medieval street and church with figure. Unusual introduction to city.

Open daily except Sunday mornings, Christmas and New Year, adult £1, OAP/child 50p.

▦ ▭ ▨

Castle Museum Clifford Street, York [0904 653611]. Housed mostly in ancient prison buildings, including cell which held Dick Turpin, here is a folk story told in rooms furnished with commonplace objects, Victorian, Georgian, Stuart, even 1953, the Queen's coronation year. Also reconstructions of entire Victorian streets, with furnished, stocked, shops, Kirkgate perhaps the most famous with its cobbles and horse-drawn vehicles. Add galleries with toys, ladies, children's costumes on figures, military garb from armour to World War I, on figures. Lots more. Working water mill April–October.

Open daily except December 25–26 and January 1, adult £2.75, OAP/child £1.35, family ticket.

▦ ▭ ▨

Jorvik Viking Centre Coppergate, York YO1 1NT [0904 643211]. Unique interpretation of history. You travel in 'time-cars', hearing a commentary, through a reconstructed Viking settlement, the market street with stalls and products displayed, past houses with rubbish-choked yards, and latrines, pigsties, scavenging domestic fowl, a cargo boat, all with people, tools, furnishings, smells. Then you travel through the excavated site of where it actually happened. Out of the time-cars you reach the laboratory where Viking period seeds, bones, insects, pots are identified. When you reach a display of some of the objects found, dress, jewellery, textile/metal/glass products you view them understanding they were once a familiar part of everyday life. Visitors can stamp a coin the old way, with a hammer. New: a figure based on the skull reconstruction of an actual contemporary Viking Age person, a revolutionary development which could lead to the current figures in the subterranean street being replaced by those recognizable by their descendants. Warning: long queues in summer school holidays.

Open daily April 1–October 31 9 a.m.–7 p.m., November 1– March 31 9 a.m.–5.30 p.m., adult £3, child £1.50.

Assembly Rooms Blake Street, York [0904 24604]. 18th-century ballrooms, open, free, except when events are happening like the annual Model Railway Show over the Easter weekend, Saturday, Monday, Tuesday, with some 18 railway layouts to enjoy and lots of displays of what's going on, what's new, to interest modelling addicts.

City Walls 13th-century ramparts, say some 2¹/₂ miles, but there are 4 gateways, various different period walls, towers, i.e. Roman, medieval, on the way.

Open daily dawn–dusk, weather permitting.

Clifford's Tower Tower Street, York YO1 1SA [0904 646940]. 13th-century keep of York Castle. Once a 19th-century prison. Climb to top for view.

Open daily except December 24–26 and January 1, adult 80p, OAP 60p, child 40p.

Yorkshire Museum Museum Gardens, York YO1 2DR [0904 629745]. Anglo-Saxon and Viking Age sculptures, leatherwork, jewellery, medieval treasures. Roman Life galleries: statues, tombstones, wall paintings, mosaics, a kitchen, jewellery, even the auburn hair of a Roman lady. Life-size figure of a Roman soldier. Ask for worksheets about the legions, fashion, food, industry, devised for schools. Interesting temporary exhibitions.

Open all year Monday–Saturday and Sunday afternoons, adult £1.50, OAP/child 75p, family ticket.

Friargate Wax Museum Lower Friargate, York YO1 1SL [0904 658775]. Royals through the ages, replica Crown Jewels, historic and literary characters plus animation and special sound and lighting effects.

Open daily February–December, adult £1.75, OAP/child 85p.

Rail Riders World Station Rise, York YO2 2AB [0904 30169].

Adjacent to York Station. One of Britain's largest model railway layouts including night scene, some 3000 little people, sound effects, famous engines.

Open daily late March–December 23, adult £1.50, OAP/child 75p, family ticket.

🏛 🚃 🏵

Jorvik Viking Festival [Information JVF Office, Clifford Chambers, 4 Clifford Street, York YO1 1RD: 0904 611944.] Annual February spectacular with fireworks display, drama, warriors staging battles and torchlight processions, replica Viking ships.

Museum of Automata Tower Street, York [0904 65550]. Wonderful collection of 18th- and 19th-century mechanically animated figures brought to life and action, such as circus acts, magic tricks, on video screens. Start modern pieces yourself, like the Mad Professor's Musical Instrument, Madame Eva the Fortune Teller, a contraption to make waves without water, or the end-of-pier attractions including a chap falling into the loo.

Open daily all year, adult £2.30, OAP £1.50, child £1.30.

🏛 🚃 🏵

The ARC Archaeological Resource Centre, St Saviourgate, York [0904 643211]. Hands-on. Match up excavated animal bones, piece together pots, sort bones, shells, teeth, figure out

Viking padlocks, sew Roman sandals, weave Viking way on a replica loom. Computer quizzes and screens that transport you to a dig site. Archaeologists in attendance.

Open daily April–October, Sundays from 1 p.m., November–March weekdays, closed Good Friday, December 24–26, January 1, adult £2, OAP/child £1.

🏛 🚃 🏵

National Railway Museum Leeman Road, York [0904 21261]. Full-size, steam, diesel, electric locomotives in 2-acre Main Hall, assembled round 2 turntables. Stock includes ornate royal saloons which can be peered into from outside. Changing displays. Also show-cases telling about technical, social and economic developments to do with railways worldwide. Railway scene in miniature in the Model Railway Gallery. Replicas of the latest trains. Events: working locomotives, steam days, the narrow-gauge passenger-carrying steam railway.

Open daily except December 24–26, January 1, adult £3.20, OAP £2.10, child £1.60, family ticket.

🏛 🚃 🏵

Castle Howard Coneysthorpe, York. Off A64 [065384 333]. 18th-century stately home by architect Sir John Vanbrugh, still stunning many more of us when seen in the TV series *Brideshead Revisited*. Still lived in by same (real) family. Paintings by Rubens, Gainsborough, Holbein, furniture by Chippendale, Adam, Sheraton. Interest for most children lies in largest privately owned costume collection in Britain. Add family carriages, replicas of Crown Jewels, much more. Also 1000 acres of parkland with rose gardens, lake, nature walks with birdlife.

Open daily March–October, adult £5, OAP £4, child £2.
🏛 🚻 ♿

Nunnington Hall Nunnington [04395 283]. Manor house with long history, on banks of River Rye, now mainly Tudor, Stuart periods. Collection of miniature rooms gathered, commissioned, by Mrs Kitty Carlisle over 40 years and around 10,000 pieces of miniature furniture, furnishings to be seen.

Open April–June, September–October weekends only, July–August, Tuesday–Thursday, weekends, bank holidays, best check, Hall and garden adult £1.80, child 90p, gardens only 60p, 30p.
🏛 🚻 ♿

Flamingo Land Kirby Misperton, Malton YO17 0UX. Off A169 [065 386 287]. 375 acres with around 1000 animals. Dolphin show, parrot show, sea-lion show. Children's and thrill rides, Corkscrew, Log Flume, etc.

Open daily Easter–October, one price £6.
🚻 ♿

Eden Camp Malton. Off A64 [0653 697777]. In a prisoner-of-war camp. Story of World War II told in reconstructed scenes, with sound, light, smells: fashions in a wartime street, Home Guard, musical hall with puppet shows, rationing, munitions factories, a coal mine (Bevin Boys) to explore, a trapped U-boat, more. Assault course for youngsters.

Open daily February 14–December 23, adult £3, OAP/child £2.
🏛 🚻 ♿

North Yorkshire Moors Railway Pickering Station, Pickering YO18 7AJ [Talking timetable on 0751 73535]. Originally built by George Stephenson in 1830s with coaches, trucks, horse-drawn until the advent of steam. Involvement open to all and volunteers wanted to help run the railway. A varied route which takes you into the National Park where other modern transport cannot go, but also includes stops as in Pickering, Levisham (also appearing in *Brideshead Revisited*), Newtondale Halt leading to its forest with waymarked paths, Goathland where you can meet blackfaced sheep, Grosmont where restoration of engines can be viewed. And there is much more, like the chance to stop off and continue your journey later, with information about local attractions to explore available from the station shops. Steam Gala Days. Children's illustrated guide.

Open daily April–October, also Santa Specials in December, adult return from £4.10, child £2.10, family ticket.

🏛 🚃 🎢

Ryedale Folk Museum Hutton le Hole, York YO6 6UA. A170 [07515 367]. In some 2½ acres there are houses brought from elsewhere and reconstructed including thatched and cruck-framed. Purpose-built craft workshops like wheelwrights, saddlers, foundry. In the summer (mostly Sundays) around 20 craftspeople operating, like cobbler, spinner, wood carver, blacksmith, tinsmith, etc. Special events: folk and maypole dancers, World Merrils Championship (also known as Nine Men's Morris) with junior section. Annual summer schools' project.

Open daily mid March–mid October, adult £2, OAP £1.50, child £1, family ticket.

🏛 🚃 🎢

The Moors Centre Danby, Whitby [0287 660654]. Start here for information on North York Moors National Park. In 13 acres, adventure playground, woodland nature trail, quizzes, brass rubbing historic replicas. 'Moorland Experience', exhibition on largest area of heather moorland left in England/Wales, wildlife, clog-making, pack ponies. Family activities: talks, demonstrations, have-a-go sessions on countryside topics, summer Sunday afternoons.

Open daily Easter–end October and winter Sundays noon–4 p.m.

🏛 🚃 🎢

Lightwater Valley Theme Park North Stainley, nr Ripon. A6108 [0765 85321]. 125-acre country park with white knuckle thrills, live entertainment, Grand Prix go-karting, BMX bikes, boat and steam train rides. Longest (1½ miles) roller-coaster in the world.

Open mid March–mid October (not daily), £4.99.

🏛 🚃 🎢

Fountains Abbey and Studley Royal Park nr Ripon. Off B6265 [076586 333]. Think big, and outdoors. Most complete 12th-century monastic ruin in Europe; some 650 acres, gardens mostly water gardens but with temples, statuary, vistas, 400-acre deer park with avenues of trees, waterfowl on lake.

Abbey and grounds open daily except November–January Friday and December 24–25, adult £1.90, child 90p, deer park open all year, free.

🏛 🚃 🎢

Ripley Castle Ripley, nr Harrogate. Off A61 [0423 770152]. Ancestral home of Ingilbys since 14th century (and lived in now), so some family ancestors to be seen in effigy in the church, many portrayed, telling of history around the castle, which is everyone's idea of what a castle should look like. Visitors have included James I and Oliver Cromwell. Priest hole, lots of background on the Civil War, armoury, weapons, treasures, Capability Brown gardens. Recommend current Sir Thomas Ingilby's booklet about the many characters in the family including the lady who watched Cromwell, with pistols, all night, and the Ingilby who remodelled the village in the style of Alsace-Lorraine – you cannot miss that or the market place and stocks. Children's guidebooks.

Castle open April, May and October weekends, June–September Tuesday–Thursday, weekends and Monday bank holidays, gardens daily April–October, adults £2.75, child £1.50.

Skipton Castle Skipton [0756 2442]. Fully roofed and floored, but not furnished, medieval fortress. Tour sheet tells you where you are going, what to look for, and about living conditions adapted to the needs of defence. Goes back to the Normans, a large building, massive Tudor gatehouse.

Open daily except Sunday mornings, Christmas Day, adult £1.60, child 80p includes tour sheet, under-18s free, Skipton Castle Explorer's badge.

Staintondale Shire Horses East Side Farm, Staintondale, nr Scarborough. Off A171 [0723 870458]. 18th century. Working farm. Harnessing the big horses demonstrated, pets' corner, goats, miniature Shetland ponies, lambs,

doves, chickens. Old-fashioned dairy, cottage museum with domestic bygones, blacksmith's shop. Panoramic views.

Open bank holidays, mid May–mid September Tuesday, Wednesday, Friday, Sunday, adult £1, child 50p.

Kinderland Burniston Road, North Bay, Scarborough [0723 354555]. Traditional play structures and activities especially developed with children and young people up to 14 years in mind. No slot-machines or electronic wizardry. Special surfaces for extra safety. So: waterchute, log roll, maypole, swings, toddlers' climbing village, sand-pits, rocking horses, junior trampolines, giant outdoor chess/draughts, cycle track, roller-skating rink, boating lake, adventure play structure, more. Indoor 2-tier play centre with dry swimpool, superbounce mat. Even more unusual, play equipment for disabled. No dogs except guide dogs for the blind. Under-7s must be accompanied.

Open daily Easter–September, one price covering activities, top rate summertime £3.25, less other seasons and also after 4 p.m.

Old Mother Shipton's Cave and The Petrifying Well Prophesy House, High Bridge, Knaresborough HG5 8DD [0423 864600]. An odd one, a well (probably the only one of its kind in Britain) where lime, sulphate and other elements in the water turn porous objects into stone! Obviously all sorts of things are displayed, petrified, like royal shoes, 19th-century hats, teddies. Also birthplace of Mother Shipton, born 1488, a prophetess, with cave, museum, her predictions; a wishing well; grounds, adventure playground. Set along River Nidd.

Open daily mid March–October, adult £2.65, OAP £2.25, child £1.95, family ticket.

West Yorkshire

Harewood House Harewood, Leeds. A61/A659 [0532 886225]. Home of the Lascelles family for over 200 years with a royal connection through Princess Mary. Interior designs by Robert Adam; furniture by Chippendale; Turner, Reynolds, pictures. Lord Harewood's personally recorded tour of his house can be hired. Bird garden with aviaries, walk-through Tropical House with simulated rain-forest. Original landscape gardens by Capability Brown with 30 acres of gardens and woodland and an adventure playground. Children's worksheets.

Open daily April–October, check winter opening, adult £3.85, OAP £3.20, child £1.80, grounds only adult £1.75, child 75p.

Temple Newsam Home Farm Temple Newsam, Leeds LS15 0AD [0532 645535]. Rare Breeds Centre with 400 head of cattle from endangered British breeds. Piglets, hens, turkeys, etc. around the farmyard. Farming equipment and events. Walled gardens, lakes, in 1000-acre estate around Tudor/Jacobean house, where Lord Darnley, husband of Mary Queen of Scots, was born.

Open daily all year except Monday in winter.

Abbey House Museum Kirkstall Road, Leeds. A65 [0532 755821]. A 12th-century gatehouse where late Victorian period brought to life with 3 full-sized streets, shops, workshops, cottages, transferred here from around Leeds. Furnished rooms, including domestic tools side, toys and games, even herb garden. Try the early slot-machines using real old pennies.

Open daily except Sunday mornings, adult 65p, OAP/child 30p.

Leeds Industrial Museum Armley Mills, Canal Road, Leeds [0532 637861]. Enormous 19th-century woollen mill. Walk through a woollen mill, a clothing factory, a downtown tailoring suburb. Watch films in the 1920s cinema. Restored locos driven around on open days.

*Open Tuesday–Saturday, Sunday
afternoons, Monday bank holidays,
adult 75p, OAP/child 35p.*

🏛 📽 🎞

The World and Sooty Exhibition
Windmill Manor, Leeds Road,
Shipley, Bradford [0274 531122].
Sets, small-scale props and
effects, of Sooty, Sweep and Soo
over 35 years, in restored former
school where Harry Corbett
once staged his shows. Shows on
film and TV. Fan Club, Saturday
Morning Club (cartoons), play
area with puppet theatre and
jigsaw puzzles.

*Open Monday–Thursday, Fridays in
school holidays, adult £1.25,
OAP/child 75p.*

🏛 📽 🎞

Victoria Reed Organ Museum
Victoria Hall, Victoria Road,
Saltaire, Shipley [0274 585601,
after 5 p.m.]. Private collection
of around 50 from lap-top to
large pedal-playing, with material
from period including an
organist's instructions in
numbers so anyone could press
by number and play for a service.
Organists can ask curator for
chance to play.

*Open all year Sunday–Thursday,
except 2 weeks over Christmas/New
Year, adult 75p, OAP 65p, child
50p, family ticket.*

🏛 📽

**National Museum of
Photography, Film and Television**
Prince's View, Bradford [0274
727488]. Just about everything
you would want to know about
taking pictures, early still
photography up to latest
technology. Try your hand at
being a TV newsreader. In a
studio set operate the cameras
and discover the skills. Fly the
'Magic Carpet' over land and sea
(camera effects). Watch (again,
first time) Andy Pandy, early
What's My Line?. IMAX, imagine a
screen 1000 times bigger than
your TV. Feels like you are actually
there in films like *To The Limit,
Grand Canyon, The Dream is Alive*
(be an astronaut). Cliff-hanging,
nail-biting stuff, only the brave
(schoolboys) sit on front seats.

*Open all year Tuesday–Sunday,
Monday bank holidays, except May
Day, free; IMAX adult £3, child
£1.50.*

🏛 📽 🎞

Colour Museum 82 Grattan
Road, Bradford BD1 2JB [0274
390955]. What is colour? Why is
it so important? Would you eat a
plateful of blue food? Visitor-
operated exhibits explain. See
how the world looks to a dog, a
fish, mix coloured lights,
experience colour illusions, use
computerised technology for a
dye-making factory.

> Groups should always book
> beforehand. It's difficult to
> believe, but I have heard of
> classes of schoolchildren just
> turning up. When a place is
> already busy they are unlikely to
> get full attention or full pleasure
> from the visit.

Open all year Tuesday–Friday 2–5 p.m., Saturday 10 a.m.–4 p.m., small charge.

Industrial Museum Moorside Road, Bradford [0274 631756]. Former 19th-century spinning mill. Now tells of industrial past, also a collection of transport vehicles and a reconstructed mill owner's house. School holiday activities like practical workshops in calligraphy.

Open all year Tuesday–Sunday, Monday bank holidays.

Cartwright Hall Lister Park, Bradford [0274 493313]. Dramatic baroque-style building housing 19th- and 20th-century paintings and sculpture. School holiday activities like using different media and materials to make your self-portrait.

Open all year Tuesday–Sunday, Monday bank holidays, except Good Friday, December 25–26.

The Manor House Castle Yard, Ilkley LS29 9DT [0943 600066]. Elizabethan with Roman artefacts, history of the town and furnishings in manner of 17th- and 18th-century farmhouse parlour, kitchen. School holiday activities: sculpture, blown egg-decorating, pottery, young historians, historic cooking.

Open all year, Tuesday–Sunday, Monday bank holidays.

Cliffe Castle Spring Gardens Lane, Keighley BD20 6LH [0274 758231]. Natural and social history, geology, minerals, pottery, toys and games. Life-size reconstruction of a giant newt-like creature lurking in a forest of primitive vegetation. School holiday activities: bird identification games, prehistoric man/woman's tasks, making bird/bat boxes, studying minerals, fossils.

Open all year Tuesday–Sunday, Monday bank holidays except Good Friday, December 25–26.

Keighley and Worth Valley Railway Haworth Station, Keighley [0535 45214]. 5 miles, Keighley to Oxenhope with historic trains, workshops, railway museum, picnic areas. Access to Brontë Parsonage.

*Open all year weekends, bank
holidays, daily July–August, adult
£3, OAP/child £1.50 returns, family
ticket.*

🖼 🚃

Brontë Parsonage Museum
Haworth, Keighley BD22 8DR
[0535 42323]. Georgian building
where Brontë family lived,
furnished in Victorian manner,
where the sisters wrote novels,
poems, songs, stories.
Memorabilia includes the
miniature books they made as
children. Village: Brontës'
Sunday school, burial place,
Branwell's drinking hole and
druggist's store.

*Parsonage open all year except 3
weeks from late January and
December 24–26, Easter–September
adult £1, OAP/child 50p, less other
times.*

🖼 🚃

Haworth Museum of Childhood,
West Lane, Haworth [0535
43825]. Fascinating collection of
toys, dolls, games from Victorian
times to present. Working
models and trains.

*Open daily April–October,
November–March weekends, adult
60p, child 40p.*

🖼 🚃

Shipley Glen Tramway Prod
Lane, Baildon, Shipley BD17
5BN [0274 589010]. Saltaire to
the glen by narrow-gauge, cable-
hauled trams. Opened in 1895
and once 'a penny up and a
halfpenny down' fare. Run by

volunteers. Countryside Centre
at top.

*Open Easter–October weekends,
Monday bank holidays, June–July
Wednesday, 15p uphill, 10p
downhill, 20p return.*

🖼 🚃

Yorkshire Mining Museum
Caphouse Colliery, New Road,
Overton, Wakefield WF4 4RH
[0924 848806]. Underground
tour of real coal mine so warm
clothes, sensible shoes. Audio-
visual theatre, machinery,
paddy train rides, pit ponies.
Under-5s not admitted
underground.

*Open daily except December 25 and
January 1, adult £3.75, OAP
£3.15, child £2.90.*

🖼 🚃 🎛

Red House Museum Oxford
Road, Gomersal, Cleckheaton
BD19 4JP [0274 872165]. Home-
like effect in 1830s style of Taylor
family. Charlotte Brontë , friend
of Mary Taylor, visited and
featured house/family in *Shirley*.
Costumed figures. Family and
children's (6–14) activities most
months: block printing,
historical games, marbling.

Calderdale Industrial Museum
Square Road, Halifax [0422
358087]. 'Clock-in', hissings,
rumblings, clattering, tell you
what it was like to work in the
mills. Smells, from toffee boiling
at Mackintosh's. Crawl through a
coal mine. Events like 'Great
Rowntrees Sweetie Hunt'.

Open Tuesday–Saturday, Sunday afternoons, adult £1, child 50p.

Piece Hall Halifax [00422 59031]. Market, art gallery, art/craft shops, Pre-Industrial Museum (domestic cloth manufacture). Entertainment: bands, jugglers, dance, theatre groups, Christmas celebrations with Santa's Grotto.

Open daily all year.

Bankfield Museum Akroyd Park, Halifax HX3 6HG [0422 354823]. Large costume and textile collection, Duke of Wellington's Regimental Museum, toys, natural history. School holiday events: 'Calderdale at War' (food, clothes, shelters), 'So You Wanna Be in Pictures?' (making motion pictures), green issues explored through drama workshops.

Open Monday–Saturday, Sunday afternoons, except December 25–26, January 1.

Eureka! The Children's Museum, Discovery Road, Halifax HX1 2NE [0422 330069]. The first children's museum of its kind in the UK, designed specifically for 5s–12s and accompanying adults opening spring 1992 on an over 12-acre site. Follow dinosaur or gorilla footsteps to the new building, thread your way through a tile maze, follow your nose along a scented trail, discover the hidden technology under your feet because even the building reveals how it works, the structure, heating, air flow. 3 permanent exhibitions. 'You and Your Body' – climb inside a giant human body to discover how organs, the brain, senses, work. 'Living and Working Together' – a mini-town with house, shop, factory, bank, garage, café, gardens, for learning about how industry, commerce, goods, services, work can affect everyday life, through making toys, driving a simulated car, role-playing, even flushing a transparent toilet to see how that functions. 'Creating and Inventing' – theme that everyone is capable of inventing and creating. About problem-solving. Unusual inventions to try, heated socks. Children can make their own broadcasts, work both sides of the camera in the TV studio, publish a newspaper, design their own objects, package, promote them. All about touching, exploring, even in the special 'safe' area for under-5s who can explore a tactile jungle with 'musical flowers', 'whispering stones'. Events programme: performances, demonstrations, competitions. Resource centre for parents, teachers, children providing more information, sources of help for children with special needs, and about career opportunities within industry or the professions.

Shibden Hall West Yorkshire Folk Museum, Godley Lane, Halifax

HX3 6XG. 15th century. 17th-century room settings with figures, dining-room, nursery. Farm buildings now 19th-century village with pub, clogmaker, saddler, wheelwright and craft demonstration weekends. Horse-drawn vehicles. 90 acres with miniature steam railway, tractor train, orienteering.

Open all year Monday–Saturday, Sunday afternoons, February Sunday only, adult £1, child 50p.

Colne Valley Museum Cliffe Ash, Golcar, Huddersfield HD7 4PY [0484 659762]. Pre-industrial weavers' house living downstairs and working at the top of the house. Mid 19th-century living-room, flagstoned with peg-rugs, centred round the range with fire (lit) heating the oven, hot water and flat irons. Mangles and rubbing boards are in the wash-kitchen. The museum is run by volunteers who may be lace-making, spinning, cropping (the cloth), raising the nap with teasles, or working the Spinning Jenny or the looms in the top floor, where there is also a gas-lit Clogger's Shop, still producing. You can try a pair. School groups can enjoy spinning, weaving, baking, cooking, washing, ironing, some even a bath (stored on the wall) before the fire.

Open all year Saturday–Sunday and public holidays 2–5 p.m., adult 70p, OAP/child 35p.

Museum of Myths, Legends and Horrors, Valley Road, Hebden Bridge [0422 845690]. Dark passages with lit tableaux illustrating gruesome killings like Jack the Ripper's, Vlad the Impaler, so gore, shrieks, dramatic music. Not for the sensitive who can conveniently slip out and wait in the café.

Open all year Tuesday–Sunday and Monday bank holidays, adult £1.80, child £1.20.

World of the Honey Bee Hebble End Works, Hebden Bridge [0422 845557]. 3 colonies of honeybees at work, enclosed in glass tanks so they can be seen in industrious action.

Open weekdays except Tuesday, 11 a.m.–4.30 p.m., weekends, bank holidays 10.30 a.m.–5 p.m., small admission charge.

Walkley Clogs Canal Wharf Sawmills, Burnley Road, Hebden Bridge [0422 349174]. Clogmakers at work so the stages of production can be seen. Also craftsmen/women at work and other attractions like 'Enchanted Wood', grotto and tableaux.

Phone for opening times.

> Remember: a royal visit to necessary repair work can cause a short or long closure. Always check before you go.

South Yorkshire

Abbeydale Industrial Hamlet
Abbeydale Road South,
Sheffield. A621 [0742 367731].
How it used to be, casting steel,
finishing large agricultural tools
like scythes, sickles, reaping-
hooks, long replaced by
mechanical methods. Now a
museum with Victorian counting
house, manager's house,
workman's cottage, how things
were made even earlier like the
tilt forge, forging blades with
twin water-powered tilt hammers.
3 of the 4 water wheels operate at
intervals during the day, water
supply permitting. Visit to
Shepherd Wheel, in Whiteley
Woods off Rustlings Road, takes
you back even further, to 16th
century; also functioning water
wheel. Hamlet puts on several
working days during the year,
also an annual crafts fair.

*Open daily, Wednesday–Sunday and
bank holiday weekends, adult £1.80,
OAP/child 90p, family ticket.
Working days £2, £1.*

Mappin Art Gallery Weston Park,
Sheffield [0742 750875]. British
painting and sculpture 18th–20th
centuries. Long-standing
imaginative holiday-time
programmes here. Booking
essential. Mostly over a day so
packed lunch advisable. Minimum
age 7. Events such as embroidery
and patchwork workshops, a hat-
making week, 'White Elephants',
meaning in white silk, with snake
charmers, the Taj Mahal;

'Fabulous Legends', inventing
stories, making magic, making
tableaux; 'Into the Garden',
drawing, painting, modelling;
'Water Works' meaning a
workshop about things that float,
creatures of all kinds, boats made
from paper, cloth, cardboard,
strange exotic plants, even
dwellings, shells, burrows, pods.
Add Saturday classes (as unschool-
like as possible), younger from 7s
up in the mornings, afternoons
say from 12s up.

*Open all year Tuesday–Saturday,
Sunday afternoons.*

Graves Art Gallery Surrey Street,
Sheffield [0742 734781].
British/European paintings and
sculptures, also Indian and
Japanese art. Saturday morning
children's classes.

Open all year Monday–Saturday.

Sheffield City Museum Weston
Park, Sheffield [0742 27226].
Cutlery, of course, also clocks,
sundials, weather-recording
instruments, coins, birds,
mammals, Bronze Age finds.

Open daily all year.

Museum of South Yorkshire Life
Cusworth Hall, Doncaster DN5
7TU. Off A638 [0302 782342].
18th-century, now reveals local
and social history, domestic
equipment, what life was like.
Lots of exhibits still coming in

from local families to expand what to see about transport, crafts, agriculture, folk life, toys, costume and mining community life. Temporary exhibitions on wide variety of local and social history themes. Add park with space. Events include children's Easter egg decorating and rolling competition and children's activities every holiday (quiz competition in summer) and half-term except Christmas. Christmas family evenings, when participants usually dress Victorian-style, so popular now additional Sunday afternoon with carol singing, mummers' play, parlour games. School groups dress in reproduction costumes, act out an old-fashioned school day. Facilities for visually/hearing handicapped.

Open daily except Sunday mornings.
🏛 🎪 🚎 🏵

Sandtoft Transport Centre
Belton Road, Sandtoft, nr Doncaster DN8 5SX [0724 711391]. Country's largest collection of trolleybuses and motor-buses. Working trolleybus system. Miniature steam railway.

Open some dates March, April, May, June, July, August, check, adult £1.20, child 70p.
🎪 🚎

The Dome Bawtry Road, Doncaster DN4 7DP [0302 370888]. Lagoons, two-level ice-rink, bowls, sports from badminton to basketball, 5-a-side football to gymnastics, theatre, dance, music. Mums and toddlers

swimming sessions. Crèche. After school badminton, trampolining, gymnastics, basketball, squash, snooker for 7s–16s. Kids Club, for 5s–10s, with Saturday morning films, games, competitions, newsletter, discounts.

Open daily all year.

Humberside

Elsham Hall Country Park
Elsham, Brigg DN20 0QZ. B1206 [0652 688698]. Birds and giant carp; you are encouraged to feed. Also trout fishing, pony-trekking, nature trails, a butterfly garden and bird garden. Lots of space and thinking about children. Arts/crafts centre.

Open daily Easter–September, other months Sundays except Good Friday, December 25–26, adult £2, child £1, less in winter.
🎪 🚎 🏵

Normanby Hall Normanby, nr Scunthorpe DN15 9HU [0724 720215]. Regency mansion, furnished in period with costume displays. Park: 350 acres of gardens, parkland and nature trails. Countryside interpretive centre, riding school, deer park, ducks, miniature railway.

Hall open Easter–October Monday–Friday, Sunday afternoons, bank holidays, adult 70p, OAP/child 40p, park closed only Christmas Day.
🏛 🎪 🚎 🏵

Burton Constable Hall Sproatley, North Humberside. B1238 [0964 562400]. Stunning mellow Elizabethan house, many treasures; Hall remodelled through the years, with additions by Adam, Lightoller, gardens of course by Capability Brown. Set in 200 acres with 25 acres of lakes.

Open Easter Sunday, Monday, spring bank holidays, June–July Sunday, mid July–September Sunday–Thursday, adult £2.50, OAP £2, child £1.20.

Museum of Army Transport
Flemingate, Beverley HU17 0NG [0482 860445]. Army road, rail, sea and air exhibits in 2 exhibition halls. Restored military vehicles driven/demonstrated last Sunday May–August and Monday bank holidays May and August.

Open daily all year, adult £2, OAP/child £1.

Hornsea Museum Burns Farm, 11 Newbegin, Hornsea HU18 1AB. Off M62 [0964 533443]. One family occupied Burns Farm for 300 years. Now it's a small folk museum with figures of Victorian period and kitchen, bedroom, sitting-room, parlour, dairy. Also tools of various local trades, displays about local people and activities.

Open daily Good Friday–October afternoons, mid July–September Monday–Saturday all day, Sunday afternoons, adult 70p, OAP/child 50p.

Hornsea Pottery Edenfield Works, Hornsea HU18 1UD [0964 534211]. Functioning pottery, so you can see how things are actually made. Birds of prey, butterfly farm, car collection, gardens, children's playground, a model village with harbour, houses, shops, farms, castle.

Open daily except Christmas week. Pass: adult £3.99, OAP £2.50, child £2.99, or pay for individual attractions.

Humber Bridge Country Park
Hessle [0482 641989]. Woodlands, meadows, water. Adjacent to Humber Bridge. Programme of guided walks, offering local and natural history, Sundays and some Wednesdays. Under-14s should be adult-accompanied. WATCH groups for children. [Events: Countryside Section, Leisure Services Dept, Prospect House, Prospect Street, Hull HU2 8PU, 0482 212828.]

Open daily all year. Free. Walks: adult £1, OAP/child 50p.

Millington Wood 1 mile north-east Millington village. As Humber Bridge Country Park.

Portminian Model Village
Sewerby, Bridlington YO15 IEL

[0262 606414]. Landscaped, 1-acre site with over 200 stone-faced buildings creating a miniature rural seaside community. Hundreds of hand-made model figures. Work of Geoff and Carol Sooper.

Open daily late May–September 31, adult £1, OAP/child 50p.

⊞ 🚋 ⊞

Sewerby Hall Park and Zoo
Sewerby, Bridlington YO15 1EA [0262 673769]. Zoo, aviary, children's corner, museum, art gallery, Amy Johnson collection. Novel train from park to Bridlington.

Park and zoo open daily all year, museum Good Friday–late September. Entry charges.

Cumbria

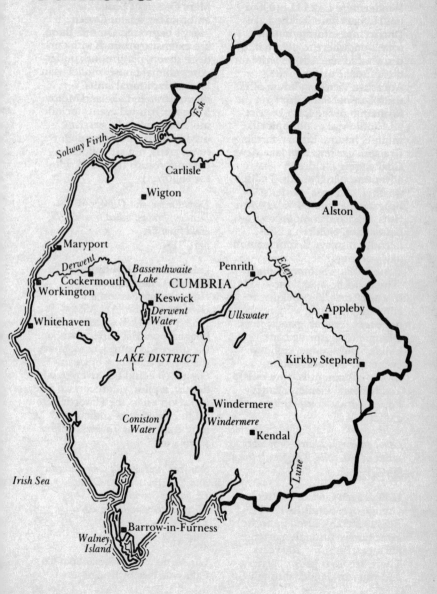

Lake District National Park Visitor Centre Brockhole, Windermere LA23 1LJ [09662 6601]. Start here for the Lake District and information on what's on, where to go, what to do, what to see. Advice: write for the annual *Events* booklet. Attractive Victorian house offers the 'National Park Story' on the formation of the Lake District and audio-visuals on topics like wildlife, natural history, farming. Graceful gardens with lake views. Challenging children's adventure playgrounds. Trails: weather, compass, gardens. Programme: guided walks, farm visits, map and compass courses, batwatches, children's films, falconry displays, demonstrations like working sheepdogs, dry-stone walling. Summer holiday 'The Brockhole Sett' for 7s–11s, treasure trails, kite-making, rock climbing, drawing, wildlife discovery sessions, games, story-telling. Easter, spring bank holiday and summer holiday events for families: puppet shows, talks on owls (with owls), Teddy Bears' Picnics, Beatrix Potter stories, competitions, games.

Open daily mid March–September, adult £1.90, child 90p, family ticket.
🏛 � 🌐

Holker Hall Cark-in-Cartmel, Grange-over-Sands LA11 7PL [05395 58328]. Lived in by the same family, through marriage alliances, for some 300 years. There are no ropes or barriers, and you can wander through rooms which include a Wedgewood dressing-room, Mary Queen of Scots' embroidery, a later Queen Mary's bedroom. Outside there are extensive grounds with tame deer, sheep, playground, under-cover animal house, model train layout, traditional crafts demonstrated, Lakeland Motor Museum. Annual events include model aircraft rally, carriage driving trials, show jumping, horse trials, hot-air balloon championships (tethered rides for children).

Open Easter–end October, Sunday–Friday, adult from £1.95, child from £1.
🏛 � 🌐

Lakeside and Haverthwaite Railway Company Ltd Haverthwaite Station, nr Ulverston LA12 8AL. A590 [05395 31594]. You can be off a boat and on to a puffer train, or the other way round, or just have the fun of travelling by steam engine (it could be driven by a dentist, a pilot, volunteers do a lot). Don't miss the Haverthwaite Engine Shed, gets addicts muttering about *Thomas the Tank Engine*, etc.

Site open daily except some Saturdays and Christmas, trains Easter, Christmas Specials, daily May–October, adult £2.20, child £1.15.
🏛 � 🌐

Windermere Iron Steamboat Co Lakeside, Newby Bridge,

Ulverston LA12 8AS [05395 31188]. Cruise the 10½ miles of water and scenery, watch out for the ferry (otherwise folk would have to go all the way round!).

Open daily Easter–November, single fares Round the Lake £6, discounts OAP/child.

⌘ ⊟ ⊞

Windermere Steamboat Museum Rayrigg Road, Windermere [09662 5565]. Boats, many salvaged from lake beds like *Dolly*, the oldest mechanically powered boat in the world, now in working order. Look for gleaming attached 'kettles' (you raised steam and the cuppa simultaneously); Beatrix Potter's surprisingly cumbersome rowing boat; steam yacht *Esperance*, better known as Captain Flint's houseboat in the film *Swallows and Amazons*.

Open daily Easter–end October, adult £2, child £1, family ticket.

⌘ ⊟ ⊞

Hawkshead B5285/6. Picturesque village, dating from Elizabethan times. Look for the grammar school 1585–1909, now a museum showing that boys not only carved quill pens but their names on every available bit of wood, including William Wordsworth. Schooldays 6 a.m. to 5 p.m.! On sale, slates to be written on by slate (screech). Charge. The National Trust Information Office was once owned by Beatrix Potter who used it to

illustrate the shop where Tabitha Twitchit gossiped. Beatrix Potter Gallery, in what was her husband's office, Main Street [09666 355]: original drawings and illustrations.

Open daily April–November, adult £1.80, child 90p.

Ravenglass and Eskdale Railway Ravenglass [06577 226]. England's oldest narrow-gauge railway, maintained by volunteers of all ages, known as 't'laal Ratty'. It looks child-size but is big enough to carry adults too, through 7 miles of fine scenery including Muncaster water mill. Museum at Ravenglass (small fishing village), walks from Eskdale.

Open daily Easter–November, some weekends earlier and later and Christmas period, adult £4.40, OAP £3.90, child £2.20, returns, family ticket.

⌘ ⊟ ⊞

Muncaster Castle Ravenglass. A595 [06577 614]. Has belonged to the Penningtons since 13th century. Among the gruesome bits is a silver-mounted gourd from melted down buttons found on a chap washed ashore; another oddity is the elaborate medal given by the Emperor of Ethiopia to a schoolboy in the family, for teaching the Emperor how to use a lawnmower! Annual exhibitions. Owl Centre with close-circuit TV of owls and an extensive collection of owls. Nature trails available.

*Open late March–end October, owls
and grounds daily, castle closed
Mondays except bank holidays,
castle, grounds and owls adult
£3.25, child £1.75, grounds and
owls £1.75 and £1.25.*

**Cumberland Pencil Museum
and Exhibition Centre** Southey
Works, Keswick CA12 5NG
[07687 73626]. Where the first
pencils were made in
Elizabethan times. Graphite
(actual writing bit), when
mined locally, was once so
precious that soldiers guarded
it against pilferers. See how
pencils were made then and
now, including coloured ones
(innards look like coloured
spaghetti); tiny capsules
containing map and compass
fitted into pencils for World
War II Bomber Command, also
sent in prisoner-of-war parcels;
see the largest pencil in the
world – 7 ft. Try your hand in
the art section, materials
provided.

*All year except December 25–26,
January 1, adult £1, OAP/child
50p.*

Lowther Leisure Park
Hackthorpe, Penrith. A6 [09312
523]. Stevenson's Crown Circus,
BMX bikes, boats, train, Tarzan
trail, in acres of park.

*Open daily Easter–mid September,
adult/child £3.95, OAP £2.75.*

**Ancestral Research and Leisure
Centre** Holesfoot, Maulds
Meaburn, Penrith CA10 3HX
[07683 51458]. Tracing the
family tree, brass rubbing,
Victorian bakehouse. For
children: BMX track, roller-
skating, grass sledging, indoor
bowls, maze.

*Open Easter, then daily early
May–September, £2.20.*

South Tyndale Railway Railway
Station, Alston CA9 3JB [0434
381696]. Narrow-gauge railway
from riverside setting through
North Pennines. Preserved
steam and diesel locos.

*Open Easter weekend, May weekends
and bank holidays, June and
September Tuesday–Thursday and
weekends, daily July–August, other
times so best check, adult £1.20,
child 60p.*

Holme Farm Sedbergh LA10
5ET [05396 20654]. Working
farm, sheepdogs, sheep, poultry,
calf-rearing, pigs and goats. Old
farm machinery. Guided tours
2 p.m.

*Open daily April–September, adult
£1.50, child £1.*

Birdoswald Roman Fort Wall and
Turret, west of Greenhead. Off
B6318. Section of Hadrian's Wall
with fort, late Roman buildings,
stone and turf walls and
excavations in progress.

Site open all year, exhibition may close winter months, adult £1, child 50p.

Settle–Carlisle Railway [0228 44711]. Long-fought campaign has kept this going. 70 panoramic miles through the Yorkshire Dales, over the Pennines, into the Eden Valley.

Ring for times, fares.

Carlisle Castle Carlisle [0228 31777]. Border stronghold constantly changing hands from Scotland/England and back, walls built of stones from Hadrian's Wall, real portcullis still in 14th-century gatehouse. Climb staircases to lofty towers, walk the high ramparts for memorable views, study prisoners' graffiti. Mary Queen of Scots was held here. Museum of Kings' Own Border Regiment, more about people than weapons. In the gatehouse you can get a mirrored view of a cell and 'prisoner'.

Open daily April–September, October–March Tuesday–Sunday, except December 24–26, January 1, adult £1.60, OAP £1.20, child 80p.

Tullie House Castle Street, Carlisle CA3 8TP [0228 34781]. The turbulent history of the English/Scottish Borders. Stroll through Roman Carlisle, climb Hadrian's Turf Wall, come face to face with a reiver (see below), experience 'Cumbria outdoors', peep into a clifftop cave with birds of prey, see where Isaac Tullie could have been recording the Roundheads' siege of the city, recall the days of steam locos. The names of the lawless reiver families who stole each other's goods, herds, over 3 centuries are recorded. Maybe yours is among them?

Open daily except Christmas Day, adult £2.80, OAP/child £1.40.

Northumbria

Berwick-upon-Tweed

Tweed

Holy Island

Alnwick

Cheviot Hills

Coquet

North Sea

NORTHUMBERLAND

North Tyne

Morpeth

South Tyne North Shields

Newcastle upon Tyne South Shields

Hexham *Tyne* Gateshead

TYNE AND WEAR

Pennines Sunderland

Durham

Wear

DURHAM Hartlepool

Bishop Auckland

Tees Stockton-on-Tees Middlesbrough

Darlington CLEVELAND

Durham

Raby Castle Staindrop, Darlington. A688 [0833 60202]. Looks like a castle, with places from which defenders poured boiling oil on besiegers. Long history includes plotting for Mary Queen of Scots, a Civil War stronghold. Family history includes 'The Rose of Raby' marrying Richard Plantagenet. It is still a family home. Medieval Great Kitchen, used till recently, equipment mostly Victorian, servants' hall, coach houses with 18th- and 19th-century vehicles. 200-acre deer park. Annual June Home Farm Open Day. (Also major waterfall some eighteen miles from castle.)

Open Easter–September, bank holiday weekends and Monday, Tuesday, May–June Wednesday and Sunday, daily July–September except Saturday, castle (from 1 p.m.), park and gardens adult £2.50, OAP £1.95, child £1.20, park and gardens only 80p, 60p, 60p.

🏛 🚉

Darlington Railway Museum North Road Station, Darlington [03254 60532]. On route of world's first steam-worked public railway. So here you have *Locomotion* built by Stephenson in 1825, first steam loco to work a public railway, plus *Derwent* built in 1845, lots of other engines, model railway layout, lots of railway memorabilia, steam train rides on certain dates.

Open daily except Good Friday, December 25–26, January 1, adult £1.20, OAP 80p, child 60p.

🏛 🚉 ▦

DLI Museum and Durham Art Gallery Aykley Heads, Durham [091 3842214]. Unusual combination. Museum: story of Durham Light Infantry since 18th century told through uniforms, weapons, including jeep (military vehicle rally, August bank holiday). Art Gallery: arts/crafts exhibitions, events, workshops, videos, concerts. Brass band concerts outside summer Sunday afternoons. Children's quizzes, worksheets/workshops allied to some exhibitions. Exhibitions booked with holiday periods in mind, i.e. Disney at Christmas with workshops.

Open Tuesday–Sunday, Monday bank holidays.

🏛 🚉 ▦

Bowes Museum Barnard Castle [0833 690606]. Huge, French château style, built in 1860s to house collections of John and Josephine Bowes who travelled and bought even job lots which legend has it once included the El Greco costing £8. So art galleries, ceramics, textiles, furniture, tapestries, costume (including crinolines), children's section with dolls, dolls' houses, model boats. Life-size silver swan in entrance hall in action 4 p.m. to 'swallow' a fish, others seemingly swimming along. Below hall level: Roman artefacts, medieval daily life, local wildlife, a large Victorian kitchen, a model of a lead mine, a grotto of minerals collected by a local miner, a 2-headed, 6-legged calf (ugh). Surrounded by large gardens.

Open daily Monday–Saturday from 10 a.m., Sunday 2 p.m. except week before Christmas and January 1, adult £1.75, OAP/child 85p.

Hall Hill Farm Satley, nr Lanchester. B6296 [0388 730300]. Working farm, farmyard animals including pets' corner. Woodland and riverside trails. Farm trailer rides.

Open Easter weekend for special lambing events, late May–end August Sunday and bank holidays, 1–5 p.m., adult £1.60, child 80p.

Beamish the North of England Open Air Museum Beamish. A693 [0207 231811]. 300 acres, with re-erected buildings from the region furnished as they were and costumed staff to demonstrate that way of life. Travel by old electric tramcar to the Town, a Co-op (with hardware, grocery, drapery departments), dentist's home and surgery, solicitor's office, pub, stables, stationer's shop and printer's. At the railway station locos are often in steam. The Colliery Village has a row of furnished pit cottages and an underground 'drift' mine with a guided tour of how coal was worked. Home Farm has old

breeds of cattle, poultry, pigs and in the large farmhouse kitchen the farmer's wife demonstrates traditional cheese-making. Other demonstrations like bread-baking in coal-fired ovens, mat-, quilt-, lace-making. Special events. Free camera loan service. Accessible to wheelchair users but exhausting; make enquiries.

Open daily Easter–October, November–Easter Tuesday–Sunday, check Christmas period, adult summer £5, OAP/child £4, winter £3 and £2.

Killhope Wheel A689 Stanhope-Alston road [0388 537505]. Lead was mined in the North Pennines possibly from Roman times. Restored lead mine and crushing mill. 34-ft-high wheel turning again. Story of mining and miners, such as miners sleeping 4 to a bed, cooking, eating in same room, in stinking squalor. New Visitor Centre's exhibition shows daily life of the time when boys left school at 8 to work in the mines, girls stayed on till 14. Woodland trail with displays of mining through the ages. Pan for lead in the stream, and be astounded at the sheer drudgery in achieving enough lead to get paid.

Open Easter–end October, otherwise for parties, adult £1.50, OAP/child 75p.

> Remember admission charges are subject to alteration. Why not assume they have increased? You may have the pleasure of discovering they have not.

Cleveland

Captain Cook Birthplace Museum
Stewart Park, Ladgate Lane,
Marton, nr Middlesbrough. A174
[0642 813781]. Close to site
where he was born, traces his
early life as son of farm labourer,
conditions on 18th-century
sailing ships, epic voyages with
smells and sounds like the
creaking of ship's timbers. Start of
a 'trail' through Captain Cook
country, Great Ayton where he
went to school, Staithes, where he
worked in a shop, Whitby where
he learnt his sailing skills.

*Open Tuesday–Sunday, Monday
bank holidays, adult 60p,
OAP/child 30p.*

🏢 🎹 🚌 🔲

Newham Grange Leisure Farm
Coulby Newham. B1365 [0642
300202]. Working farm
presenting farm life past and
present, cattle, calves, pigs and
weaning pens, poultry, chicks'
incubation house (see them
hatching), farm pond with
ducks, geese. 19th-century vet's
surgery, saddler's shop. Re-
created farmhouse kitchen.
Visitor Centre. Wildlife
interpretive room. Children's
play area. Children's worksheets.

*Open summer daily except Mondays,
winter Sundays only, adult 60p,
OAP/child 35p.*

🎹 🚌 🔲

Preston Park Museum Yarm Road,
Stockton-on-Tees TS18 3RH [0642
781184]. Re-created Victorian

High Street with period shops and
working craftsmen, like resident
farrier and blacksmith daily and
Northumbrian Small Pipe-maker
most Sundays. Hall: life as it was in
Victorian times and exhibits like
armour, costume, children's toys.
100-acre park along banks of River
Tees; wildfowl walk, bird aviary,
Stockton Railway Heritage Trail,
annual Historic Vehicle Rally,
Family Fun Run.

*Museum open daily except Sunday
mornings, park always open.*

🏢 🎹 🚌 🔲

Tyne and Wear

**The Wildfowl and Wetlands
Trust** District 15, Washington.
Off A19 [091 416 5454]. 1200
birds, many wandering freely and
can be fed on corn for sale. Also
wild refuge with hides for bird-
watchers, rain shelters, children's
play area in 100-acre park. Flock
of Chilean flamingos all named
after characters in Catherine
Cookson's books. Available for
fostering. Illustrated Discovery
Sheets make the visit even more
interesting for children. Events
like Pond Day, looking at pond
life, Downy Duckling Days (the
young), Migration Mysteries.

*Open daily except December 25–26,
adult £2.60, child £1.30.*

🎹 🚌 🔲

Ryhope Engines Museum
Ryhope, Sunderland. Off A1018
[091 521 0235]. How water was

provided from late 19th century for a century, pumping engines conserved, maintained by volunteers, all ages. As well as 160-ft chimney, possibly tallest listed ancient monument in England, a light-hearted display of sanitary ware, which was what it was about. Engines in steam public holidays Easter to autumn, and other times.

Open Easter, May holidays, August–October, daily 2–5 p.m., adult £1, child 50p.

Museum of Science and Engineering Blandford House, Blandford Square, Newcastle-upon-Tyne NE1 4JA [091 232 6789]. How things work and the pioneers of Tyneside industry. The Motive Power Gallery, man's search for energy – the windmill to the modern jet engine, with working models. 'From Dugout to Dreadnought' gallery, the maritime story of the River Tyne with 40-ft-long model of the river and models of ships built here, like the *Mauretania*. 'Pioneers of Industry' gallery, lives and works of engineers George and Robert Stephenson, Swan (electric light), Parsons (turbine). Also Science Factory, hands-on, keeping a ball up with air, changing the colours of shadows, checking sound waves, fun with mirrors.

Open all year Tuesday–Saturday.

Museum of Antiquities The Quadrangle, Newcastle University, Newcastle-upon-Tyne NE1 7RU [091 222 6000]. Regional antiquities 6000 BC to AD 1600, particularly Roman inscriptions, tombstones, jewellery, coins. Models of Hadrian's Wall and life-size figures of Roman soldiers. Audio-visual: reconstruction of the Temple to Mithras. Worksheets and shop has colouring sheets. Occasional special days for children with handicaps or learning difficulties. Roman sculpture's open display helpful to visually handicapped.

Open Monday–Saturday, except Good Friday, and December 24–25, January 1.

Grindon Museum Grindon Lane, Sunderland [091 528 4042]. Edwardian period rooms, with figures, cook surrounded by day's washing preparing evening meal, child in the nursery with her toys and games, the lady of the house laying out her clothes, jewellery, in the big bedroom. Also reconstruction of an Edwardian Post Office, cobbler's workroom, dentist's surgery and chemist's shop. Children's quiz sheets available.

Open all year Monday–Wednesday, Friday, Saturday, June–September Sunday 2–5 p.m., except bank holidays, closed lunch-time.

Monkwearmouth Station Museum North Bridge Street, Sunderland [091 567 7075].

Imposing (1848) façade. Inside step back into the Edwardian era with porter, top-hatted passenger, trunks. Sidings contain 1915 guard's van. Platform gallery with models, bicycles. View of modern railway.

Open daily except Sunday mornings.

Shipley Art Gallery Prince Consort Road, Gateshead [091 477 1495]. British and Old Master paintings, also decorative art and local history collections. Craft classes and workshops, sometimes for children in the school holidays.

Open daily except Sunday mornings.

Northumberland

Hadrian's Wall The Romans built it against the northern tribes, over 70 miles, once up to 20 ft high and 9 wide, and forts, turrets, signal towers. Much of the Wall still exists. English Heritage produce a leaflet and map on the sites. Members get free admission to its properties.

Corstopitum Roman Fort Corbridge. A69 [043 471 2349]. Roman site on York to Scotland route, dating from 1st to 4st centuries, museum with excavated finds including the Corbridge Lion. Excavated remains include foundations of best-preserved granaries in Britain. See system of grain ventilation.

Open daily Good Friday or April 1, whichever is earlier–September 30, otherwise Tuesday–Sunday. Closed December 24–26, January 1, adult £1.40, OAP £1.05, child 70p. English Heritage.

Housesteads Roman Fort nr Bardon Mill. B6318 [0434 344363]. 5-acre fort with remains of granaries, commandant's house, barrack blocks, latrines and gateways. North wall part of Hadrian's Wall. Museum with artefacts found and large model of the fort. Considerable stony surface walk from car park so not for pushchairs. Toilets only at car park level, none on site. Junior Guides available. Open air so appropriate clothing, footwear. English Heritage.

Opening times and admission charges as Corstopitum Roman Fort.

Chesters Roman Fort and Museum Chollerford. B6318 [0434 681379]. Built for 500 cavalrymen. Bathhouse with underfloor heating system. Also barrack blocks, commandant's house, museum with collection of Roman sculpture.

Opening times and admission as Corstopitum Roman Fort. English Heritage.

Vindolanda Roman Fort Bardon Mill [049 84 277]. Excavations, museum set in ornamental gardens, replica section of Hadrian's Wall. Full-scale reconstructions of a stone turret and gate tower. Waterlogged conditions preserved timber, leather, writing tables found in museum. Steep access to museum (and return). Toilets only at car park. Junior Guides available. Open air except museum.

Open daily all year.

Roman Army Museum Carvoran, Greenhead [0697 747485]. Life-size figures displaying armour, weapons and uniforms. Audio-visual presentations including film showing a guided tour of the Wall.

Open daily March–October, otherwise weekends.

Alnwick Castle Alnwick [0665 510777]. Border fortress. Home of Duke of Northumberland's family since 1309. Keep, Armoury, Guard Chamber, dungeon, state coach, Museum of British and Roman Antiquities. Pictures, heirlooms. Children's illustrated guide leads to some fascinating historical exhibits and to thought about how things worked, like the drawbridge, or how the upper tier of books are reached in the library.

Open daily late April–October except May and September Saturday, 1–5 p.m., adult £2.50, OAP £2, child £1.

Alnwick Fair [0665 602552]. Re-enactment of medieval fair held annually for a week starting last Sunday of June. Townspeople don period costumes. Craft demonstrations in the market place, strolling minstrels, Market Courts with swift justice in the ducking stool, stocks. Tournament finale. Organized events for children.

Grace Darling Museum Bamburgh [066 84 310]. Her heroic story, when with her father she rowed through a storm to save ship survivors, is told in exhibits including father's log book, the Northumbrian fishing coble used for the rescue, gifts sent by admirers, and a selection of the commemorative souvenirs produced at the time. A very small museum. Monument in churchyard.

Open daily Easter–October, free but donations to Royal National Lifeboat Institution appreciated.

Bamburgh Castle Bamburgh. B1340 [066 84 208]. Majestic citadel, first castle in Europe to succumb to gunfire (Wars of the Roses). Furniture, pictures, armour. Overlooks extensive sandy beach.

Open daily April–October from 1 p.m. and July–August from noon, adult £2, child 90p.

Farne Islands off north Northumberland coast. Boats

from Seahouses, B1340.
Information from National Trust
Centre, 16 Main Street,
Seahouses [0665 720424]. Home
for 18 species of seabirds, puffin,
eider-duck, kittiwake, etc., a
colony of grey seals. Some
clambering over rough ground
to get ashore; take food, and
there's minimum lavatory
provision.

Open daily April–September,
restricted access during breeding
season May–August when
disturbance would be detrimental,
adult £2.80, child £1.40, tickets
bought on island; outside breeding
season £2 and £1. Nature trails
obtainable. School parties must have
permit to land, by post, in advance:
Warden/Naturalist Farne Islands,
8 St Aidans, Seahouses,
Northumberland NE68 7SR, add
boat tickets, Boatman W. Shiel, 4
Southfield Avenue, Seahouses [0665
720308], £3. Rough weather can
prevent sailing.

Holy Island between Berwick-
upon-Tweed and Bamburgh,
opposite Beal. Reached by a
causeway at low tide. Island not
accessible from 2 hours before
until 3½ hours after high tide.
Tide tables posted at each end of
causeway. Lindisfarne Castle
[0289 89244], built 1550,
restored by Sir Edward Lutyens
in 1903. Lindisfarne Priory
[0289 89200], ruins of a
Benedictine priory refounded
11th century after St Aidan's
destroyed by Vikings, and smaller
version of Durham Cathedral.
Small museum. Island, famed as
the birthplace of Christianity in
Britain, also rich in natural
history, large and varied species
of birds and interesting flora.

Castle: open daily April 1–September
except Friday (open Good Friday)
and October Wednesday and
weekends, 1–5 p.m., £2.80. Priory:
open daily except December 24–26,
January 1. Entry charges.

Kielder Water Falstone NE48
1BX [0660 40396]. On Scottish
Border. Visitor Centres: Forestry
Commission, Kielder Castle
[0660 50209], displays on forest,
walks and drives in forest, large
play area; Tower Knowe, Yarrow
Moor [0660 40436]. Wide choice
of outdoor activities, pony-
trekking, cycling, walking,
orienteering, windsurfing,
canoeing, waterskiing, fishing,
wagon rides, bird-watching.

Open daily except December 25–26,
January 1–2.

Scotland

Wick

North Sea

Stornoway

Ullapool

WESTERN
ISLES

HIGHLAND
REGION

Elgin

Skye

Inverness

GRAMPIAN
REGION

Loch
Ness

Spey

Aberdeen

Dee

Fort William

TAYSIDE REGION

Tay

Dundee

Mull

Oban

Perth

St Andrews

CENTRAL
REGION

FIFE REGION

Loch
Lomond

Stirling

Kirkcaldy

Jura

LOTHIAN
REGION

Atlantic Ocean

STRATHCLYDE
REGION

Edinburgh

Islay

Glasgow

Clyde

Kintyre

Arran

Lanark

Galashiels

Tweed

Ayr

BORDERS REGION

Hawick

DUMFRIES AND
GALLOWAY REGION

Dumfries

Stranraer

Battlefields and ruins of abbeys, of castles, tell of ancient wars.
The centuries of fighting, feuding, cattle-rustling on the
Borders, once the hotly disputed, ravished and ravaged
territory straddling England and Scotland, could be compared
with the romanticized legends of the Wild West. The massive
Fort George, once described as 'the most considerable fortress
in Great Britain' was built after Culloden in 1748, as the
garrison for George II's Hanoverian Army, costing over
£200,000, the equivalent of £1 billion today, and unnecessary.
There were also of course the conflicts around the throne;
Mary Queen of Scots' story is far more extraordinary than a
fiction writer could devise. All food for thought. The settings
are all there to be seen, often in great houses, castles, that
survived, often, remarkably, still inhabited by the original
families. They are also generally surrounded by large estates
which visitors can now enjoy. There are also numbers of
country parks where walkers can take pleasure in the wildlife
and woodlands. Other countryside locations offer
opportunities for a variety of active sports, Aviemore being an
obvious example.

Then there are single attractions to be seen, considered,
photographed, which do not constitute a day's outing but
could be combined, with planning, with others. Carleton
Castle, Girvan, now a ruin, is famous because the owner is said
to have disposed of 7 of his wives over a cliff, the 8th disposing
of him. Among innumerable commemorative tablets, obelisks,
there are two separate stones each recording a victory over the
English by Robert the Bruce. I must mention in this category
the highest beech hedge in the world, planted south of
Meikleour in 1746, now nearly 600 yards long and 100 ft high.
Numbers of such single attractions can be found with 'Touring'
map references in 1001 *Things to See in Scotland*, £4.40 including
postage and packing, published by the Scottish Tourist Board,
23 Ravelston Terrace, Edinburgh EH4 3EU [031-332 2433]
which, unusually for such guides, now contains a special
section of information on attractions of interest to children.

Borders

Bowhill Selkirk. Off A708 [0750 20732]. Victorian house, one of Scotts of Buccleuch homes. Pictures by such as Van Dyck, Canaletto, Gainsborough, furnishings, portrait miniatures. Audio-visual presentation, theatre, Visitor Centre. Adventure woodland play area, riding centre, nature trails.

House open daily in July, otherwise by appointment for study purposes, adult £3, child £1.
Grounds/playground daily late April–August, except Fridays, £1.

Traquair House Innerleithen, Peebleshire. B709 [0896 830323]. Goes back to 10th century, said to be oldest continuously inhabited house in Scotland. 27 Scottish, English monarchs have visited, including Mary Queen of Scots, so lots of relics, paintings, embroideries, porcelain, manuscripts, also massive staircase, winding passages, priest's room, secret stairway for escape during religious troubles, 18th-century library, the Bear Gates closed after Prince Charles Edward Stuart passed through them, an 18th-century brewhouse which still produces ale. Much more, like woodland walks, craft workshops, a maze, and annual events.

Open afternoons Easter weekend and following week, then daily late May–September, grounds open from Easter.

Biggar Gasworks Museum
Gasworks Road, Biggar [031-225 7534 – Royal Museum of Scotland]. Buildings, plant, displays, video show, guided tours, tell the story of the coal-gas industry. Working exhibits and live steam on special occasions.

Open late May–September, Monday–Thursday afternoons.

Gladstone Court Street Museum
Biggar, Lanarkshire [0899 21050]. Shop windows from period 1850–1920, in a museum laid out as a street, with shops, offices, school, bank, telephone exchange, and peopled with appropriately dressed life-size figures.

Open daily except Sunday morning, Easter–October, admission charges, (under-8s free).

Mary Queen of Scots House
Queen Street, Jedburgh [0835 63331]. Her death mask, and since Max Factor himself was let loose on it, resembling a thirties filmstar. Sad relics include her communion vessels last used to self-administer since a priest of her religion was refused. Note narrow circular staircase, defendable by one man (you could not prod a pike round it) and the small room for her attendants, the four Marys. How did they fit in, remembering all

those skirts? Visitor Centre explains a lot.

Open daily, Easter–mid November, adult £1, OAP/child 50p.

Castle Jail Castlegate, Jedburgh [0835 63254]. Turrets, battlements but only built 1825. Illustrates with figures 19th-century prison life when relatives cooked for the inmates. Death cell with viewing balcony for jailers to prevent suicide. The statutory 'unmarked graves' I was told lie in a dell in the left-hand corner in grassy area.

Open all year, weekdays, Sunday afternoons, adult 60p, OAP/child 30p.

Thirlestane Castle Lauder [05782 430]. Bonnie Prince Charlie slept here after Battle of Prestonpans in 1745 while his troops camped out front. He apparently even got a warming-pan. Vast children's nurseries now housing quantities of toys from Pollocks Toy Museum. Box of dressing-up clothes for modern visiting children. Old kitchens and laundry show domestic working conditions. 'Border Life' exhibitions illustrate outdoor estate life, for gentry and staff.

Open Easter week, May, June and September Wednesday, Thursday and Sunday, July–August daily except Saturdays, from 2 p.m., adult £2.50, OAP/child £2, family ticket.

Border Collie and Shepherd Centre Tweedhopefoot, Tweedsmuir [08997 267]. Tiny school, used 1900–37 for 12, surely tightly packed in, shepherds' children. A wildflower meadow, picnic space, puppies, and unspoilt acres. Craft shop in shepherd's bothy. Yes, the loos are for 'Shepherds' and 'Shepherdesses', and nothing seen on TV compares with seeing Geoff or Viv Billingham putting their collies through their paces rounding up sheep.

Open all year, sheepdog-handling demonstrations 11 a.m., 2 p.m. and 3.30 p.m. daily except Saturday, adult £1.50, child £1.

Dumfries and Galloway

Robert Burns Centre Mill Road, Dumfries [0387 64808]. Housed in 18th-century mill now 70-seat theatre with exhibition on Burns's life in Dumfries, audio-visual presentations, so for older children.

Open April–September Monday–Saturday and Sunday afternoons, October–March Tuesday–Saturday, theatre 50p, child 25p.

Little Wheels Portpatrick [077 681 536]. Over 100 metres of model railway track. Children can usually drive some of the trains.

*Open daily Easter–October, adult
90p, child 70p, family ticket.*

Blowplain Open Farm
Balmaclellan, Castle Douglas
[06442 206]. Guided tours
illustrating day-to-day life on a
small hill farm, the different
types of animals and their roles.

*Open daily Easter–end October from
2 p.m. except Saturday, adult £1.50,
child 70p.*

Wildfowl and Wetlands Centre
Eastpark Farm, Caerlaverock
DG1 4RS [038777 200]. Over
12,000 barnacle geese from far
beyond the Arctic Circle winter
in the Solway Firth area. In an
area 1400 acres, an observatory,
3 towers and 20 hides. Other
geese, peregrines, merlins, roe
deer, foxes. Also home to the
most northerly colony of
natterjack toads remaining in
Britain. Farmed in summer so
closed to the public.

*Open daily September 16–April 30,
except December 24–25, adult £2.20,
child £1.20.*

Strathclyde

Culzean Castle and Country Park
nr Turnberry. A719 [065 56
269]. Castle: 18th century and
the 'Eisenhower Presentation'
explains the General's
association. Country park: first in
Scotland, over 500 acres with
Interpretation Centre,

exhibition, in farm buildings.
Outdoors, walled gardens,
camellia house, aviary, swan
pond, etc. Also guided
walks/talks. Induction loop.

*Castle open daily April–October,
adult £2.40, child £1.20. Country
park: grounds always open.*

Burns Cottage and Museum
Alloway, Ayrshire. B7024 [0292
41215]. Where he was born, in
thatched cottage built by his
father, and lived as a child, with
adjacent museum of Burnsiana.

*Open all year Monday–Saturday,
and Sunday afternoons April, May,
September, October, adult £1.40,
child 70p, includes the Burns
Monument, near River Doon.*

Land O'Burns Centre Alloway
[0292 43700]. Exhibition,
theatre showing a presentation
on Robert Burns. Start of Burns
Heritage Trail, places where he
lived, where he married, where
he died, his inspirations.

*Open daily all year, small charge for
audio-visual.*

The Tenement House 145 Buccleuch Street, Garnethill, Glasgow [041-333 0183]. A Victorian flat in a tenement, with furnishings, fittings, of family who lived there for over 50 years.

Open daily April–October, afternoons, otherwise Saturday and Sunday afternoons, otherwise groups by appointment. Adult £1.20, child 60p.

Glasgow Zoo Calderpark, Glasgow. Off M73/74 [041-771 1185]. Lions, leopards, elephants, camels, bears, wallabies, reptiles.

Open daily all year, adult £3, OAP/child £2.

Art Gallery and Museum Kelvingrove, Glasgow GE 8AG [041-334 1131]. The main one, with natural history, archaeology, decorative and fine art. School holidaytime competitions, say for 5s upwards, especially annual art competition, also quizzes, slide/tape shows. Add Saturday termtime activities like Puppet Club, art classes, etc.

Open daily all year except Sunday mornings, December 25 and January 1.

Museum of Transport Kelvin Hall, Bunhouse Road, Glasgow [041-357 3929]. Reproduction of 1938 Glasgow street. Walk-in Motor Car Showroom with cars from 1930s. Glasgow trams, buses and a subway station. Also cars, fire engines, horse-drawn vehicles, cycles like oldest one in the world, locos. Details as Art Gallery.

People's Palace Museum Glasgow Green [041-554 0223]. Victorian, tells the people of Glasgow of their history, political (including women's suffrage), cultural, industrial. Details as Art Gallery.

Haggs Castle 100 St Andrew's Drive, Glasgow [041-427 2725]. 16th-century castle, acquired by Glasgow Council in the 1970s, restored, developed as museum of social history for children. Reconstructed 16th-century dining-room with models of inhabitants, John and Marion Maxwell of Pollock, reconstructed kitchen same period, Victorian nursery. Period gardens. School holiday activities for 4-year-olds upwards, in specific groups as appropriate. Could include making biscuits, rag dolls, stained-glass windows *to eat*, butter (shake, rattle and roll), your own heraldic shield, lavender bags, marzipan, gingerbread, Easter bonnets, cards, traditional fare or pressed-flower pictures, pincushions, samplers, flags, bookmarks, kites, tiles, fans, puppets and much more. Also croquet, Victorian entertainments, weaving, story-times, nature trails, make-up, shell work, street games, dressing up, Christmas-time carols, decorating, making cards, presents, food. Bookings essential. Advice: get programme as soon as available.

Open daily all year except Sunday mornings, December 25 and January 1.
 school holiday activities

The Dome of Discovery South Rotunda, 10 Govan Road, Glasgow G51 1JS [041-427 1792]. Interactive science centre with around 60 exhibits offering visitors 'hands-on' experience, finding out, like making sound waves on a vibrating string or on water, creating a vertical wave, multiple reflections, an anti-gravity wheel, mirror drawing. Weekend events programme like scientific experiments to repeat at home, taxidermy and making your own plaster casts, under headings including physics, biology, chemistry, the environment, generally with audience participation.

Open all year Tuesday–Sunday and Monday bank holidays, adult £2, OAP/child £1.20, family ticket.

Hunterian Museum Glasgow University [041-330 4221]. Dinosaur footprints, Plesiosaurus skeleton, Triceratops skull, minerals, prehistoric dugout canoes, exhibits brought back by Captain Cook, a coin gallery.

Open all year except public holidays, Saturday and Sunday afternoons November–April.

Inveraray Castle Inveraray, Argyll [0499 2203]. Seat of Clan Campbell chiefs, later Dukes of Argyll. Present building 18th century, the Adam family involved, damaged 20th century by fire but restored. Fairy-tale exterior. Inside has armoury hall with 1300 items, painted rooms, portraits by such as Gainsborough, Raeburn, tapestries, china, family relics. Also gardens, woodland walks, spectacular scenery beside Loch Fyne.

Open April–June, September–October daily except Friday and Sunday morning, July–August daily except Sunday morning, adult £2.50, OAP £2, child £1.50, family ticket.

Inveraray Jail Inveraray [0499 2381]. 19th-century prison with life-like figures, sounds, smells and trials in progress. Exhibitions.

Open daily all year, adult £2.45, OAP £1.30, child £1.10.

Argyll Wildlife Park Dalchenna, Inveraray [0499 2264]. 60 acres with one of Europe's largest collection of wildfowl. Large owl collection.

Open daily all year, adult £2.50, OAP £2.25, child £1.

Auchindrain Old Highland Township A83 south-west of Inveraray [049 95 235]. West Highland farming township, now folk museum, with 18th- and 19th-century homes and barns, furnished/equipped in period and operating in 19th-century style with traditional crops and livestock. Displays explain how life has changed. Flax growing, vegetable dyeing shown.

Open daily Easter–September except April, May, September Saturdays. Adult £2, OAP £1.50, child £1.20, family ticket.

Blackshaw Farm Park nr West Kilbride. B781 [0563 34257]. Working farm, so you can see calves fed, cows milked, sheep dipped, sheared. Nature trails, tractor and trailer rides, 4-wheeler motorbikes, grass-sledging play area.

Open daily Easter–August, and September Saturday, Sunday, Monday, adult £1.80, child £1.20, or £5 per carload.

Calderglen Country Park Strathaven Road, East Kilbride [03552 36644]. 300 acres, nature trails, woodland, river with large waterfalls. Children's zoo. Visitor Centre interprets the landscape and includes natural history displays.

Park always open, Centre from noon, weekends only in winter.

Dean Castle and Country Park Dean Road, Kilmarnock [0563 22702]. 14th–15th century with battlements, dungeon, medieval arms and armour. 200-acre park with rivers, nature trail, children's corner, fawns.

Castle open daily from noon except December 25–26, January 1–2, adult £1, children free, park all year.

Kelburn Country Centre nr Fairlie. Off A78 [0475 568685]. Estate of Earls of Glasgow. 18th-century farm buildings form a village with craft shops. Nature trails, waterfalls, adventure course, assault courses, children's stockade, pets' corner.

Open daily Easter–mid October, adult £2, OAP £1.40, accompanied child £1.

Summerlee Heritage Trust West Canal Street, Coatbridge [0626 31261]. Museum with working historic machinery, reconstructed buildings, working electric tramway, excavations of Victorian ironworks.

Open daily all year except 2 weeks at Christmas.

Central

Doune Castle and Motor Museum A84 [castle 031-244 3101, museum 0786 841203]. Castle a preserved ruin, tied into Scottish history since medieval times. Look for bridge in village built by James IV's tailor because ferryman refused to transport him! Motor museum houses Earl of Moray's collection including second oldest Rolls-Royce in the world.

Castle closed Friday and alternate Saturday, October–March, museum open daily April–October, castle adult £1, OAP/child 50p, museum adult £1.90, OAP £1, child 90p.

▦ ▥

Stirling Castle Stirling [031-244 3101]. On 250 ft great rock captured and recaptured way back to the 13th century. Ancient royal residence, Mary, James VI, etc. Various rebuilding, but still parts going back to 16th century like the hall, Chapel Royal. Useful Visitor Centre with audio-visual which tells of old battles, say as a foot soldier following Robert the Bruce, or the racket of firing guns when General Monk attacked, but also about life in the castle and the town for knights jousting or people suffering from the plague.

Open daily all year, adult £1.75, OAP/child 85p. Visitor Centre, same times, adult 50p, child 25p.

▦ ▥ ▨

Bannockburn Heritage Centre Bannockburn. Off M80, south of Stirling [0786 812664]. Equestrian statue of Robert the Bruce, indoor audio-visual explains events prior to the 14th-century battle and Scottish victory. Exhibition 'The

Kingdom of the Scots'. Induction loop.

Centre open daily April 1–October 28, adult £1.10, child 55p.

Scotland's Safari Park Blair Drummond. A84 [0786 841456]. Lions, tigers, camels, zebra, monkeys. Drive yourself or a safari bus. Boat safari round chimp island. Pets' farm, performing sea-lion shows, penguin pool. Adventure playground.

Open daily April–September, phone for charges.

▦ ▥ ▨

Scottish Deer Centre near Cupar. A91 [033781 391]. Many species. Feed, stroke, photograph on ranger-led tour. Multi-media exhibition, audio-video show. Farm walks. Adventure playground includes treetop walk and maze.

Open daily April–October, November–March weekends but special openings Easter and Christmas, adult £2.50, OAP £2, child £1.50.

▦ ▥ ▨

Lochure Meadows Country Park nr Ballingry. On B920 [0592 860086]. Land and water sports, bird-watching, wildlife study, trails, ancient historical remains, children's adventure playground. Ranger-guided walks, displays, tell story of reclamation of loch from coal mining waste.

Open daily all year.

Vane Farm Nature Reserve Loch
Leven. B9097 [0577 62355].
Nature centre displays interpret
countryside and loch. Wild geese
and duck feed and rest here late
September–April. Binoculars
provided. Observation hide,
nature trail. RSPB.

*Open daily except Christmas, New
Year, adult £1, child 50p.*

Weavers' House and Highland
Trust Museum 64 Burrell Street,
Crieff. A822 [0764 5202].
Restored 18th- and 19th-century
houses with working tartan
handloom weavers', spinners'
produce for sale. Scottish clan
and family archives with records
of over 2000 tartans. Children's
dressing-up chest and Victorian
games in the museum.

*Open daily except Sunday, adult
£1.50, OAP £1, child 50p.*

Lothian

Kinneil Museum Bo'ness, West
Lothian. A904 [0324 24911 ext
2472]. Converted 17th-century
stables contain local industrial
history, pottery, cast-iron work,
salt pan implements. Exhibition
'2000 Years of History', the story
of the Kinneil Roman Fortlet,
excavated for public viewing in
the estate's grounds; medieval

house, village remains, James
Watt's cottage.

*Open April–September
Monday–Saturday.*

Bo'ness and Kinneil Railway off
Union Street, Bo'ness [050
6822298]. Steam trains of course,
because of the Scottish Railway
Preservation Society. Historic
rolling stock housed at Bo'ness
and a regular service operating
Easter–September weekends but
other times according to
timetable.

Return adult £2, OAP/child £1.

Hopetoun House nr South
Queensferry [031-331 2451].
Splendid Robert Adam mansion,
though originally started in 17th
century; home of Hope family,
now Marquesses of Linlithgow.
So, magnificent apartments,
furnishings, paintings including
Rubens, Rembrandt, Canaletto.
Rooftop viewing platform with
panoramic views. Also museum
with Scottish features, extensive
grounds with deer parks, black
sheep with four horns, birds,
etc., a nature trail.

*Open Easter–September, adult £2.80,
child £1.40.*

Palace of Holyroodhouse Royal
Mile, Edinburgh [031-556 7371].
Now official residence of
monarch in Scotland. Origins go
back to at least 12th century, and

King David, grateful for surviving a crash with a stag. Any number of high-level folk had a hand in its various rebuildings, reshaping, or are linked with its story, James IV, Cromwell, Charles I, Charles II, etc. Steeped in stories like the funeral of the Marquis of Montrose, executed on Cromwell's orders, and his various parts displayed around the country. These, limbs, head, etc. were reassembled for the obviously extraordinary event, attended by 14 earls. Even with that stunner, and there are more, Mary Queen of Scots still dominates the scene. Her story always seems more like fiction than fact. Here is where she lived when her Italian secretary, David Rizzio, was dragged away and stabbed to death by a group including her second husband Lord Darnley, later also to reach a sudden end. See her rooms, her tapestries, also state apartments, refurnished, used, by 19th- and 20th-century royals, picture gallery of 100 Scottish kings.

Open daily April–October with later, 11 a.m., Sunday opening, and daily November–March except Sunday. Also closed during state visits so check between May and July. Adult £2, OAP £1.50, child £1.

Royal Commonwealth Pool
Edinburgh [031-667 7211]. 50-metre swimming pool, diving pool, teaching pool. Nautilus Flume Complex.

Adult 90p, child 55p. Flume extra. School holiday events.

Royal Observatory Visitor Centre Blackford Hill, Edinburgh [031-668 8405]. Through models, historic instruments, the story is told of astronomy, its history, techniques as far as Australia and Hawaii. Largest telescope in Scotland to be viewed. Videos and computer games. Fine views to be seen in the normal fashion.

Open daily all year, weekends and public holidays in afternoons, adult 75p, OAP/child 45p.

National Museums of Scotland Chambers Street and Queen Street, Edinburgh [031-225 7534]. Chambers Street: Main Hall in this Victorian building reminiscent of the Crystal Palace. Something here for all tastes: evolution, with dinosaurs, minerals, silver, wildlife (British and foreign), fossils, costume, Egyptology, arms/armour, and, on the technical side, various push-button working models of steam engines as well as an actual giant 19th-century water wheel which is in operation at specified times. Queen Street: History of Scotland, from various angles, since Stone Age; archaeological exhibits include Bronze Age, Roman and Viking periods; from medieval times forward there is silver, costumes, weapons, even a beheading machine called 'the Maiden'. School holiday activities, mainly in Chambers Street, annual art and poetry competitions for under-16s, films, Discovery Room exploration of jaws, masks, seashells, printing, workshops on these and sculpture, weaving, spinning.

Open daily all year except Sunday mornings, December 25–26, January 1–3.

Museum of Communication James Clerk Maxwell Building, Mayfield Road, Edinburgh [0506 824507, ext 3674]. Electrical communication is the theme so early hearing aids, dictaphones from the twenties, also what could be coming. All handleable and some exhibits in working order.

Open daily except Christmas and New Year.

Camera Obscura Outlook Tower, Castle Hill, Edinburgh. Between Castle and Lawnmarket [031-226 3709]. Victorian device projects spectacular image of the city on to a viewing table high in the Outlook Tower. Also holography, laser images, pin-hole photography, and more.

Open daily except December 25–26, January 1–2, adult £2.20, OAP £1.45, child £1.10.

Museum of Childhood High Street, Royal Mile, Edinburgh [031-225 2424]. Said to be first in world devoted to history of childhood and certainly not a place where children are expected to be seen but not heard. Exhibits not only of historic toys but telling about children's lives, clothing, education, etc. 'Time Tunnel' with schoolroom, fancy dress party, nursery. School holiday activities like workshops say 6 upwards making copies of authentic original Christmas cards or optical toys (thaumotropes, zoetropes, flicker books).

Museum open all year daily except Sunday, December 25–26, January 1–2.

Brass Rubbing Centre Trinity Apse, Chalmers Close, Royal Mile, Edinburgh [031-225 2424]. Brass rubbing centre offers replicas moulded from ancient Pictish stones, rare Scottish brasses and medieval church brasses. Robert the Bruce included of course.

Open all year except Sunday (open afternoons during Edinburgh Festival), December 25–26, January 1–2. You pay for materials, instructions for brass rubbing.

Calton Hill off Regent Road, Edinburgh [031-225 2424]. Magnificent views. Uncompleted reproduction of the Parthenon, also 102-ft-high Nelson Monument.

*Open all times, free. Monument
April–September 55p.*

**Edinburgh Butterfly and Insect
World** Dobbies Garden Centre,
Lasswade, nr Edinburgh
[031-663 4932]. Rain-forest with
tropical plants, waterfalls, lily
ponds where butterflies from all
over the world can be observed
at close quarters. Also tarantulas,
scorpions, huge green beetles,
behind glass. Children's
playground.

*Open daily mid March–October,
adult £2.25, OAP £1.75, child
£1.10.*

Gorgie City Farm Project
51 Gorgie Road, Edinburgh
[031-337 4202]. On 2¹/₂ acres,
animal pens, farm kitchen with
workshop/craft.

Open daily all year.

Edinburgh Zoo Corstorphine
Road, Edinburgh [031-334
9171]. Over 1000 mammals,
birds and reptiles. Penguin
colony and Penguin Parade daily
at 2.30 p.m. Adventure
playground.

*Open daily all year, adult £3,
OAP/child £1.50.*

The People's Story Museum
Canongate Tolbooth, Edinburgh
[031-225 2424]. Tells of the lives,
work and leisure of ordinary
people in Edinburgh from late
18th century to modern times.
Reconstructions of a cooper's
workshop, a 'steamie', a 1940s
kitchen.

*Open all year Monday–Saturday
and Sunday afternoons during
Edinburgh Festival.*

Edinburgh Castle Royal Mile,
Edinburgh [031-244 2903]. For
centuries the fortress has
dominated the city, and today
makes a marvellous scene for
the floodlit August military
tattoo. A royal residence since at
least the 12th century, and
therefore involved in all sorts of
happenings, and people regal,
upper class, lower class,
including 19th-century
prisoners-of-war who set up craft
sidelines like forging banknotes.
Fascinating tumultuous history,
stuffed with famous names. Look
for James IV's Great Hall, room
where James VI of Scotland, I of
England, born, the Scottish
regalia long concealed in same
room, and much more.

*Open almost daily, adult £2.20,
OAP/child £1.10, family ticket.*

Greyfriars Bobby corner of
George IV Bridge and
Candlemaker Row, Edinburgh.
Statue of the Skye terrier who,
after his shepherd master's death
in 1858, watched day and night
over his grave (which can be
seen in the nearby Greyfriars
Churchyard) for 14 years.

Memorial to the dog in the
churchyard too.

Museum of Flight East Fortune
Airfield, North Berwick, East
Lothian. B1347, 22 miles from
Edinburgh. Enquiry point
National Museums of Scotland
[031-225 7534]. Former RAF
wartime station, varied collection
of aircraft since thirties including
a Spitfire, a Comet open to walk
through, the Blue Streak rocket,
a wind tunnel, and working
exhibits.

Open daily April–September.

Scottish Mining Museum
Prestongrange. On B1348,
8 miles from Edinburgh
[031-663 7519]. Cornish Beam
Pumping Engine House, steam
locos, steam crane, colliery
winding engine. Steam Days first
Sunday of each month
April–October. Self-drive Coal
Heritage Trail to Lady Victoria
Colliery, see below.

*Open all year Tuesday–Friday,
weekends from noon.*

Lady Victoria Colliery
Newtongrange. A7 [031-663
7519]. Pithead tour. Visitor
Centre with life-like display of
life in a Victorian pit village.

*Open as Mining Museum, adult £1,
child 60p.*

Fife

Scottish Fisheries Museum
Harbourhead, Anstruther, Fife
[0333 310628]. In 16th–19th-
century buildings, all about
fishing: methods explained in a
diorama, an aquarium holding
local fish, boats in the courtyard
or in the harbour, a furnished
interior with figures.

*Open all year except Sunday
mornings, December 25–26,
January 1–2, adult 50p,
OAP/child 25p.*

St Andrews Sea Life Centre The
Scores, St Andrews [0334 74786].
Come eye to eye with sea
creatures behind glass, view
others in large tanks designed to
emulate their natural
environment. Also an outdoor
seal pool and a British sharks
display.

*Open daily February–December,
adult £3.60, child £2.50, family
ticket.*

Tayside

Scone Palace Perthshire. Off
A93, north of Perth [0738
52308]. Family home of the
Earls of Mansfield. Notable of
course for site of coronation-
linked Stone of Scone, 9th
century, taken by English to
Westminster Abbey 13th
century, even seized back 20th

century. Otherwise bed hangings worked by Mary Queen of Scots, porcelain, furniture, ancient clocks, agricultural implements and a collection of rare conifers.

Open Easter–October Monday–Saturday, adult £3, child £2.

Broughty Castle Museum St Vincent Street, Broughty Ferry, Dundee [0382 76121]. 15th-century castle. Displays tell its history and the ecology of the River Tay. Also whaling relics, arms, armour.

Open all year except public holidays and Fridays, Sunday mornings (except July–September).

Camperdown House and Country Park Dundee. Off A923 [0382 23141]. Victorian mansion. 395 acres of parkland, tennis, horse riding, adventure playpark. Wildlife centre, bear, wolves, foxes, golden eagle, wildfowl ponds.

Open daily all year, free, Wildlife Centre adult 90p, OAP/child 55p.

Barrack Street Museum Dundee [0382 23141]. Natural history, wildlife of area including Highlands. Skeleton of Tay whale.

Open all year Monday–Saturday.

Shaw's Sweet Factory Fulton Road, Dundee [0382 610369]. 1940s-style using traditional methods. Demonstration, explanation. Mini-museum on sweet-making.

Mid June–mid August Monday, Tuesday, Thursday, Friday, March–mid June and mid August–Christmas Thursday, from 1.30 p.m. Groups other times by appointment.

Frigate *Unicorn* Victoria Dock, Dundee [0382 200900]. A 46-gun wooden frigate launched in 1824, now Britain's oldest warship afloat and being restored as a floating museum, telling of its history and about shipbuilding and the Navy in the golden age of sail.

Open daily April–October except Tuesdays and Sunday mornings, adult £1.25, child 75p.

Mills Observatory Balgay Hill, Balgay Park, Dundee [0382 67138]. Astronomical observatory with small planetarium, displays on astronomy and space exploration, telescopes. Sky-viewing possible according to weather. Audio-visual programme.

Open all year weekdays and Saturday afternoons, closed public holidays.

Royal Research ship *Discovery*
Victoria Dock, Dundee [0382
201175]. Captain Scott's famous
Antarctic exploration vessel,
built in Dundee.

*Open daily April–September but
opening times vary, adult £1.75,
OAP/child £1.25.*
▦ 🚍 ▨

Glamis Castle A928, south-west
of Forfar [030 784 242]. 14th-
century, added to, with all kinds
of literary (Duncan's Hall,
legendary setting for *Macbeth*)
and other connections, like
birthplace of HRH Princess
Margaret. Main connection, of
course, HM Queen Elizabeth the
Queen Mother, her childhood
home. China, tapestry, furniture,
nature trail.

*Open daily Easter, mid April–mid
October from noon, other times by
arrangement, adult £3, OAP £2.40,
child £1.50.*
▦ 🚍 ▨

Barrie's Birthplace 9 Brechin
Road, Kirriemuir, Angus. A926
[057 52 2646]. With some of the
personal possessions of Peter
Pan's creator including early
costumes, his first theatre. Audio
programme.

*Open Easter weekend, late
April–September, Monday–Saturday,
Sunday afternoons, adult £1,
OAP/child 50p.*
▦ 🚍 ▨

Blair Castle Blair Atholl,
Perthshire. Off A29 [079 681

355]. Seat of Duke of Atholl,
only British subject allowed to
maintain a private army. Oldest
part of turreted castle is the 13th-
century tower. Last castle in
Britain to be besieged, in 1746.
Mary Queen of Scots, Prince
Charles Edward Stuart, Queen
Victoria among famous guests.
Attractively furnished period
rooms, Jacobite relics and of
course lots of arms and armour.
Deer park, pony-trekking, nature
trails.

*Open daily Easter–mid October,
April, May and October Sunday
afternoons only, adult £3,
OAP/child £2.*
▦ 🚍 ▨

Fairways Heavy Horse Centre
Walnut Grove, nr Perth. Off A85
[0738 32561]. Working and
breeding Clydesdale horses. 40
brood mares in summer
months, foals. Wagon rides
pulled by a team. Videos show
them at work and being shod by
a blacksmith.

Open daily April–September.
🏠 ▦ 🚍 ▨

**Pitlochry Power Station and
Dam** Pitlochry. Off A9 [0824
251]. Exhibition and video.
Salmon to be seen through
windows on the fish ladder.
Children's quiz. Boating and
fishing.

*Open daily late March–late October,
free, small charge for exhibition.*
▦ 🚍 ▨

Grampian

Aberdeen Art Gallery Schoolhill, Aberdeen [0224 26333]. Collections include 18th–19th-century artists and contemporary ones, also sculptures, silver and glass. Many activities for the young. Termtime Saturday mornings Children's Class in studio workshop. Young Friends of the Art Gallery, 12s upwards, meet Thursday evenings; print workshop, TV, artist/dancers in residence. Easter, summer and October half-term school holidays, 6 upwards, could be on whales, building one from cardboard, on the Japanese tea ceremony, writing, poetry, costume, kite-making, or on watercolours, textiles, allied to current exhibitions. Wednesday evenings, drama group for the handicapped, say 15 upwards.

Open all year Monday–Saturday and Sunday afternoons, except December 25–26 and January 1–2.

Marischal Museum University of Aberdeen, Broad Street, Aberdeen [0224 273131]. From local archaeology including Bronze Age burials to collections of antiquities from many parts of the world. One impression: *'lots of monstrous, in style not size, exhibits'.*

Open all year daily except Saturdays, Sunday mornings and public holidays.

Jonah's Journey Rutherford Celebration Centre, Rosemount Place, Aberdeen AB2 4YW [0224 647614]. Family museum. Unusual, even a rarity. Designed to give a practical insight into life 3000 years ago, through participation, like dressing up, making lamps and grinding corn, spinning and weaving, using ancient writing materials, sketching and drawing. Leaflet provided asks you questions, suggests things to do: in what kind of boat did Jesus sail, try tools of the time, how was the weaver's workshop built, when only boys went to school what did the girls do, how were clothes made, try making garments from just a rectangle of cloth, why did the nomads travel, why were towns built on a hilltop, can you make a shoe from a piece of leather and thong? Puppet theatre. Special plays at Christmas and Easter. Games and quizzes. Activity sheets on various topics.

Open all year Monday–Friday 10 a.m.–4 p.m. (but closes October–March Tuesdays at 2 p.m.) weekends by arrangement, child £1, adults half price.

Anderson's Storybook Glen Maryculter, Aberdeen. Off B9077, around 5 miles west of Aberdeen [0224 732941]. Some 30 acres with gardens, waterfalls, life-size models of such as Old MacDonald's Farm (with goats, sheep, Shetland ponies, etc.), or Tower of London. You may see

Jack/Jill going up the hill, or Snow White and the dwarfs, Tom, Tom the piper's son, or come across the 3 bears' house, Mummy, Daddy, Baby, porridge, etc.

Open daily March–October, weekends November–February, adult £1.75, child 80p.
🏛️ 🚃 🌐

James Dun's House Schoolhill, Aberdeen [0224 26333]. 18th-century town house, now museum, with exhibitions of particular interest to families.

Open all year Monday–Saturday.
🚹 🏛️ 🚃 🌐

Provost Skene's House Guestrow, Aberdeen [0224 641086]. 17th-century town house, with a painted gallery with religious subject matter, and rooms furnished in different periods, Cromwellian, Restoration, Georgian, Regency, etc. Video explains its history.

Open daily all year except Sunday and December 25–26, January 1–2.
🚹 🏛️ 🚃 🌐

Aberdeen Maritime Museum Provost Ross's House, Shiprow, Aberdeen [0224 585788]. Telling story of Aberdeen and the sea through illustrations, audio visuals, and models such as fishing boats, a clipper that rivalled the *Cutty Sark*, a very large one of an oil rig and a life-size one of a herring packer. Quiz sheet for children.

Open all year Monday–Saturday.
🚹 🏛️ 🚃 🌐

Stratosphere The Discovery Place, Justice Mill Lane, Aberdeen [0224 213232]. Science and technology centre with nearly 100 hands-on experiments exploring sound, light, energy. Science-based toys in shop.

Open daily all year except Tuesdays and Sunday mornings, adult £2, OAP/child £1.
🏛️ 🚃 🌐

Pitmedden Garden and Museum of Farming Life Pitmedden. B999, north of Aberdeen [065 13 2352]. National Trust for Scotland. Immense garden with fountains, elaborate flower designs, also livestock, agricultural tools, farmhouse, sheds, reconstructed as they were, 'Thunder houses'. Visitor Centre. One-hundred-acre estate, woodland, farmland walks.

Garden, museum, Visitor Centre open daily April–September, adult £1.90, child 95p.
🏛️ 🚃 🌐

Balmoral Castle nr Ballater, Aberdeenshire. A93 [033 84 334]. You cannot tour the castle, a royal family holiday home since Queen Victoria, only the grounds, gardens. But the Balmoral Castle Ballroom Exhibition depicts the castle in Victoria's time with paintings, objects. Walks. Pony-trekking.

Open daily May–July, closed Sundays and when family in residence, adult £1.50, OAP £1.10, child free.

Braemar Castle Aberdeenshire. A93 [03397 41219]. Turreted, originally built in 17th century, burnt, rebuilt 18th century. Apart from antiques, family relics, castle includes a central tower, spiral stair, underground pit prison and massive cairngorm, a semi-precious stone weighing 52lb, on display.

Open daily early May–October, adult £1.30, child 65p.

North-East of Scotland Agricultural Heritage Centre Aden Country Park. On A950, 30 miles north of Aberdeen [0771 22857]. In restored Home Farm, interpretation of 20th-century estate life with audio-visual programme, horseman's house, costumed guide. Also 'Weel Vrocht Grun' exhibition with dioramas, soundtrack, video, illuminates 200 years of north-east farming life. 250-acre country park with ranger service, exhibitions, woodland walks, adventure playground.

Open: Centre May–September, October–April weekends only, park all year.

Crathes Castle and Gardens Off A93, East of Banchory [033 044 525]. Towers here dating from 14th century and rooms with names like Chamber of the Nine Nobles, Chamber of the Nine Muses. 18th-century gardens. Nature trails. Grounds, 7¹⁄₂ miles of wayfaring trails, Visitor Centre.

Castle, Visitor Centre open daily mid April–October, garden and grounds all year (NTS), adult £3, child £1.50, grounds only £1.10 and 60p.

Fort George Ardersier. B9039 off A96 west of Nairn [031-244 3101]. Big, the mile-long rampart encloses 42 acres. Built as Highland garrison fortress for George II's Army, completed at vast expense in 1769 and never a shot fired in anger. In the museum relics from different periods, different wars up to World War II and a bit of Hitler's desk. Historic barrack-rooms with figures illustrate that soldiers in 1780 slept 2 to a bed, 8 to a room, some with wives and children too. Conditions were much better by 1868. The soldiers' guard room is also re-created, a communal wooden shelf-bed at first, later replaced by single beds. Standing orders required them 'not to suffer people to wash at the pumps'. The Powder Magazine, stacked with now-empty barrels was designed to keep powder dry. Casemated barrack-rooms for use in sieges had little ventilation. Displays of arms and heavy guns. Regimental Museum of the Queen's Own Highlanders, medals, uniforms.

Open daily all year except Sunday mornings, Regimental Museum closed October–March Saturdays, adult £1.75, OAP/child 85p, family ticket.

Grampian Transport Museum

Alford. A944 [09755 62292]. Historic road vehicles. Climb-aboard exhibits include giant Mac snowplough, vintage road roller. Video bus with road transport history. Driving simulator. Adventure playground. Summer events.

Open daily April–September, adult £1.50, OAP £1.10, child 70p.

Cawdor Castle and Gardens

Cawdor. B9090 [06677 615]. Shakespeare's Macbeth was Thane, castle one of traditional settings for Duncan's murder, so older children will find interest here. 14th-century tower, surrounded by 16th-century buildings. Gardens and nature trails.

Open daily May–September, adult £2.90, child £1.50.

Highlands

Landmark Highland Heritage and Adventure Park

Carrbridge. A9 [047 984 614]. North of Aviemore. 3-screen audio-visual show tells of turbulent Highland history from the clan period, and exhibition provides some of the objects of day-to-day life. Forestry Heritage Park, with steam-powered sawmill, 65-ft viewing tower, demonstrations of forestry skills in summer, forestry trail. Pine Forest Nature Centre is an introduction to the local wildlife to be seen on a boardwalk trail (features on special panels) and on the Tree Top Trail which rises through the pine branches to some 20 ft. The Adventure Playground includes the balancing trail, giant woodland maze, the tube slide, 50 ft of twisting steel tunnel. Centre, nature trail and maze, wheelchair accessible.

Open daily all year, adult £3.45, child £2.15.

Strathspey Railway

Aviemore, Speyside [0479 810725]. Route part of former Highland Railway, now a Victorian-style passenger steam train service run by volunteers. Some splendid locomotives, tank engines, coaches and more to restore. Museum and carefully restored station at Boat of Garten. Magnificent scenery includes mountains, forest.

Open Easter weekend, April Wednesday, Sunday, May Wednesday, weekends, late May–September daily, October weekends, write or ring for times, fares.

Aviemore Centre Aviemore, Inverness-shire. A9 [0479 810624]. Well, just lots, like any number of water or land sports, summer or winter; a spectacular ride on the summer chairlift; go-karts; cycles to be hired; worth writing, ringing, for information.

Highland Wildlife Park Off A9, south of Aviemore [05404 270]. Drive through reserve with red deer, bison, Highland cattle. Walk to see eagles, wolves, wildcats. Exhibition on 'Man and Fauna in the Highlands' in Centre.

Open daily except winter, car and passengers £7.

Highland Folk Museum Duke Street, Kingussie, Inverness-shire [0540 661307]. Houses like a Lewis Black House, a Clack Mill, a turf-built kail-yaird, and more. Indoor farming museum about dairy, stable, Highland tinkers. Also weapons, costume, musical instruments.

Open April–October Monday–Saturday and Sunday afternoons, November–March Monday–Friday, closed Christmas and New Year, adult £1.50, child, 75p.

Glencoe and Dalness A82 runs through glen, scene of 17th-century massacre. National Trust for Scotland Visitor Centre [085 52 307] for information. Now noted for mountaineering, wildlife, walks, ski centre with chairlift, magnificent views and tows. All needing careful checking on skills, times, etc.

Centre open daily April–October, adult 30p, child 15p.

Glencoe and North Lorn Folk Museum Glencoe Village. Off A82 [085 52 332]. In restored cottages, historic relics from Jacobite period, also weapons, costumes, toys, agricultural and industrial tools.

Open May–September Monday–Saturday.

The Official Loch Ness Monster Exhibition Drumnadrochit. On A82 [04562 573]. 40-minute multi-media presentation of the story of the search for the monster.

Open daily main season, also other times so best check, adult £2.75, OAP/child £1.50.

Cairngorm Reindeer Centre Reindeer House, Loch Morlich. A951 from Aviemore [047 986 228]. Guided tours to see free-ranging herd. Reindeer Centre in the house.

Open daily all year, subject to weather, at 11 a.m., afternoons in high season, adult £2, child £1.

Culloden Moor B9006, east of Inverness [National Trust for

Scotland 0463 790607]. Where
Prince Charles Edward in 1746
finally lost, with heavy casualties
illustrated by simple headstones
and a great memorial cairn
raised in 1881, apart from
the English dead also
commemorated. Large stone
from which Duke of Cumberland
is reputed to have watched the
battle. Museum. Visitor Centre.

*Site open all year, Visitor Centre daily
April–October, adult £1.40, child
70p, including audio-visual.*

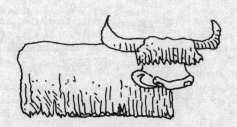

Wales

Castles of course, over 100 to be visited, especially Edward I's
chain of fortresses as a defence against the Welsh. They were
the focus of long-ago dissensions, rebellions. Then there are
mines, no longer producing, once major sources of fuel and of
metals, gold, silver, copper, lead. We can go underground today
and find out about the endurance of those who worked them.
But consider the considerable difference in the physical ability
of a small child, a grandparent, or even between a questing,
curious primary-school child and one in secondary school.
Think of mountains and splendid views and the unusual ways
of seeing astonishing panorama, like when emerging from the
Sygun Copper Mine, climbing to over 3000 ft on the Snowdon
Mountain Railway, Britain's only rack and pinion railway, or
travelling on a spiralling track, though not so high, through
the Snowdonia National Park on the Ffestiniog Railway.

  There is a lot of unspoilt scenery, coastal and inland, some
unusual museums, open working farms, evidence of sundry
invaders, Romans, Vikings, Normans, and still some of the old
crafts practised. Useful publications from bookshops or from
Wales Tourist Board, Brunel House, 2 Fitzalan Road, Cardiff
CF2 1UY [0222 499909]: *A Tourist Guide to North Wales, A Tourist
Guide to Mid Wales, A Tourist Guide to South Wales*, £2.95 each. In
them you will find information on coastal resorts, safe beaches,
outdoor pursuits, nature trails, crafts, towns and villages. In
hotels, farmhouses, guest houses, look for 'Bedroom Browsers'
with leaflets about nearby attractions.

Dyfed

Manor House Wildlife and Leisure Park St Florence, Tenby. B4318 [0646 651201]. Rare and exotic birds; animals; fish and reptiles. Pets' corner. Playground with remote-controlled boats and go-karts, roundabouts, 'pig-train', Giant Astraglide/slide. Model railway exhibition. Children's worksheets. Falconry displays 2 p.m. and 4 p.m. except Saturdays.

Open daily all year, adult £2, OAP/child £1.

Rheidol Power Station Cwm Rheidol, Aberystwyth SY23 3NF [097084 667]. Landscape and technology. Nature trail, walks short or long (2½ miles round the reservoir), lakeside picnics, scenic drive, fishing. Tour the power station (leaflet explains what is going on) and fish farm. Look for the fish lift and ladder.

Open daily Easter–October, rest of year for booked parties, adult £1.25, OAP 75p, child 50p.

Vale of Rheidol Railway Aberystwyth. Adjacent to British Rail Station. (Enquiries c/o Brecon Mountain Railway, see page 217). Opened in 1902 to serve lead mines and timber traffic. Rails half an inch under 2 ft apart yet the 3 steam locos are more than 8 ft wide. Aberystwyth–Devil's Bridge, about an hour each way with height difference of over 600 ft. Ask at bridge directions to Mynach Falls, Jacob's Ladder, Devil's Punchbowl.

Open daily late March–September, adult return £9, child £4.50, with under 16 child travelling for £1 with adult fare-payer.

Llywernog Silver-Lead Mine Ponterwyd, nr Aberystwyth SY23 3AB [0970 85620]. Open-air museum in 6 acres, so best in good weather. 'Miner's Trail' self-guided tour to see several working water wheels, a rock crusher, an old prospecting tunnel, an audio-visual. Main building contains re-created underground scenes and the 'California of Wales Mining' exhibition, about the hunt for gold/silver in the Welsh hills. You can go underground to old mine levels, cleared and lit. Special 'hands-on' area for children, with pumps, panning, jigging, wheelbarrows and a real tramwagon to push. You will learn about Winzes and Plats, Round Buddles and that ore was Jigged and Buddled. Mining Adventure Trips: half-day underground guided trips arranged to other bigger local mines.

Open daily Easter–October, winter for special events (Santa's Grotto, December) and pre-booked groups, adult £2.50, OAP £1.95, child £1, family ticket.

West Glamorgan

Swansea Leisure Centre
Oystermouth Road, Swansea
[0792 49126]. Activities for all
age ranges including squash,
badminton, table tennis, roller-
skating, swimming.

Open daily all year, various charges.

Penscynor Wildlife Park Cilfrew,
nr Neath SA10 8LE. Off A465
[0639 642189]. Tropical birds,
monkeys, penguins, sea-lions,
parrots, tropical aquaria. Feed
5000 rainbow trout. Also alpine-
slide reached by a chairlift to the
clifftop, radio-controlled cars,
bumpa-boats. Extra charge for all
rides. Worksheets.

*Open daily except Christmas Day,
adult £2.75, OAP/child £1.50.*

Mid Glamorgan

Brecon Mountain Railway Pant
Station, Merthyr Tydfil. A465
[0685 4854]. Narrow-gauge line.
4-mile round trip (around 50
minutes including 20-minute
stop at Taf Fechan Reservoir for
a walk, snack, or stay longer and
catch later train back) steam-
hauled into the Brecon Beacons
National Park.

*Open 2 weeks around Easter, May
Bank holidays and daily
June–September, half-term, **with some
omissions,** and Christmas specials,
adult £3.40, child £1.70, 1 child
free for each adult fare-payer.*

Rhondda Heritage Park Lewis
Merthyr, Coed Cae Road,
Trehafod. Off A470 [0443
682036]. Sprinter from Cardiff
Central. 'Black Gold – The Story
of Coal.' At the beginning of
World War I the Rhondda Valley
was the largest coal-exporting
region in the world. In 1986 the
last coal was brought to the
surface. Heritage Park opened
1991 with the pithead buildings
as industrial theatres to tell the
stories of the men and women
who lived and worked in the
Rhondda during the heyday of
coal, with multi-media
presentations, exciting special
effects, realistic scenes re-created
from first-hand accounts,
authentic sights, sounds, smells,
and extraordinarily life-like
figures of past times. Visitor
Centre, engine houses, pithead
machinery. Over the coming
years: 'Black Gold II – the
Underground Experience', a
reconstructed 1920s mining
village, valley's chapel, country
park, Educational Resource
Centre, cycle paths, adventure
play area. Already worksheets for
children and information packs.
Events: the music of choirs and
brass bands; July Pithead Festival;
August programme of events for
the family; Christmas
celebrations.

*Open daily all year, adult £2.75,
OAP/child £1.75.*

🏛 🚃 🔲

South Glamorgan

Welsh Folk Museum St Fagans,
Cardiff. 3 miles west of Cardiff
[0222 569441]. Fascinating and
as fantastic in its own way as
Portmeirion. The life and
culture of Wales to be seen
through its buildings of many
economic and historic levels,
having been lifted from original
sites and set down here in
around 100 acres, such as an
Elizabethan mansion, also
cottages, a farmhouse,
demonstrating the lifestyle,
generally with furnishings,
appropriate gardens. Add
tannery, tollhouse, cockpit,
forge, chapel, and working
woollen and flour mill. Craft
demonstrations on Saturdays in
the summer. 30-page illustrated
children's Activity Guide takes
them through different buildings
picking out furniture, fittings,
their purpose, games, children's
domestic and school life, asking
them to think about the
differences. School holiday
activities like craft workshops.

*Open all year Monday–Saturday,
Sunday afternoons except Good
Friday, May Day, Christmas and
January 1, adults £3, children £1.50.*

🏛 🚃 🔲

**Welsh Industrial and Maritime
Museum** Bute Street, Cardiff

[0222 481919]. In Cardiff's
docklands large outdoor exhibits
tell the story of 2 centuries of
industrial history: cranes, a pilot
cutter, a canal boat, railway
footbridge, a working replica of
the Penydarren locomotive.
Some school holiday activities.

*Open daily all year,
Monday–Saturday, Sunday
afternoons, except on public holidays as
under St Fagans, adult £1, child 50p.*

🏛 🚃 🔲

National Museum of Wales
Cathays Park, Cardiff [0222
397951]. The story of Wales,
plants, animals, geology, arts,
industry. Look for largest turtle
ever found (on Harlech beach),
9 ft long, also dinosaurs, whales.
Children's quizzes. Spacious
presentation. Family expeditions,
April–October, informal walks
with members of staff, children
in care of adults especially
welcomed. You can drop out
whenever you wish, or under
pressure of child needs. Subjects
include archaeology, botany,
geology, zoology, industrial and
local history. Waterproof clothing
and footwear recommended,
binoculars useful. School holiday
activities like creative writing,
making your own print, camera,
handling artefacts, fossil-seeking
trips, talks.

*Open all year Monday–Saturday,
Sunday afternoons, except Good
Friday, May Day, Christmas and
January 1, adult £1, child 50p.*

🏛 🚃 🔲

**Welsh Hawking Centre and
Wildlife Park** Weycock Road,
Barry, South Glamorgan. On
A4226 [0446 734687]. Lions,
leopards, waterfowl, talking
parrots, and for the younger
children rabbits, guinea pigs,
chickens, chicks, in 12½ acres.
But also 200 birds of prey, eagles,
owls, hawks, falcons, houses in
mews and breeding aviaries. Birds
flown hourly from noon, weather
permitting. Take your cameras.

*Open daily all year, adults £2.75,
OAP/child £1.75.*

National Sports Centre for Wales
Sophia Gardens, Cardiff CF1
9SW [0222 397571]. Swimming,
tennis, football, archery,
badminton, trampolining,
gymnastics, netball, squash, short
tennis, canoeing, snorkelling,
among the courses for children,
say 6 upwards, in the main school
holidays. Generally too multi-
activity sessions providing a taster
to at least half a dozen sports.

Open daily, various charges.

Techniquest 72 Bute Street,
Pierhead, Cardiff CF1 6AA [0222
460211]. No one says 'don't
touch', just the opposite in this
hands-on science centre with
some 70 exhibits where you can
discover science and technology
while having fun. Illusions,
mirrors, magnets. Design a
computer tree, create electricity
under your own power, learn
how aircraft fly. Frequent special
events like STARLAB (guided

tour of the night sky in an
inflatable planetarium). Some
children's holidaytime activities.
Shop sells specially designed
scientific goodies.

*Open all year Tuesday–Friday from
9.30 a.m., weekends and bank
holidays from 10.30 a.m., adult
£2.50, child £1.25, family ticket.*

Gwent

Penhow Castle nr Newport. On
A48 [0633 400800, recorded
information 0633 400469].
'Wales' Oldest Lived-in Castle.'
Full restoration since 1973 still
going on. 15th-century Great
Hall with minstrel's gallery, 12th-
century Norman bedchamber,
Restoration-period bedchamber,
17th-century kitchen, Victorian
housekeeper's room, all set out
and furnished as to the times.
Look for medieval meat bones
thrown into the moat about the
time of Richard III. Walkman
tours included in admission with
choice of Grand Tour of the
fascinating history; Cook's Tour
through the centuries; or for
those who don't like guided
tours, Concert Tour, period
music recorded on authentic
instruments; Young Adventurer
Tour for children accompanied
by imaginative worksheets.

Open Good Friday–September Wednesday–Sunday and bank holidays, Wednesday only in winter, adult £2.75, child £1.50.

Model Farm Folk Museum
Wolvesnewton, nr Chepstow. Off B4235 [02915 231]. 18th-century Duke of Beaufort's 'model farm', rare breeds of farm animals, also museum of Victorian life and working craftsmen. Quiz trail and badges for children.

Open daily Easter–October, adult £1.20, OAP 80p, child 60p.

Big Pit Mining Museum
Blaenavon, Gwent NP4 9XP. Off B4248 [0495 790311]. A real coal mine, working till 1980, now open to the public. Again a question of your children's ages; under-5s are not admitted, nor under-7s in school groups, nor anyone not prepared to wear the safety helmets with cap lamps to go down the 300-ft shaft, in a cage, to the 100-year-old workings to find out what life was like for generations of South Wales miners, taking about an hour, guided by ex-miners (sensible shoes and clothes). If you don't want to go down under with your children (the museum assured me that children are fascinated), surface interests include workshops, pithead baths, miners' cottages, an exhibition on the history of the mine, its own steam train in steam over weekends. New: simulation of underground work and conditions to walk through.

Open daily all year except week before Christmas but check January/February for closures for bad weather, adult £4.25, OAP £4, child £3.

Roman Legionary Museum
Caerleon [0633 423134]. Life-size figures of Roman soldiers in full armour and evidence of life 2000 years ago from gemstones to children's milk teeth. Nearby remains of Roman amphitheatre. Occasional school holiday activities.

Open weekdays all year except Good Friday, May Day, Christmas and January 1, adult £1.25, child 75p.

Powys

Dan-Yr-Ogof Showcaves
Avercrave, Glyntawe, Swansea SA9 1GJ. On A4067 [0639 730284]. In Brecon Beacons National Park, 2 massive spectacular caves, claimed to be the largest in Europe. Wear warm clothing. Concrete paths can take pushchairs but there are some steps. Add in the Dinosaur Park (some 15 life-size replicas), the Bone Cave (taking only small groups to get some understanding of how animals/humans lived some 3000 years ago), plus the chance to try skiing on an artificial slope. Look for model showing dinosaur's innards. Museum and audio-visual theatre. Handling of exhibits. Worksheets

available. Nearby: Craig-Y-Nos Country Park.

Open daily Easter–November generally but also wintertime openings, adult £3, child £2.

Centre for Alternative Technology Pantperthog, Machynlleth, Powys. A487 [0654 702400]. Something different. Working demonstration of solar, wind and water power like conservation house (and how to build one yourself), solar-heated exhibition hall. Organic garden, ecological garden with pond, goats, ducks, chickens, maze. Children's worksheets. Water-balanced cliff railway.

Open daily all year except Christmas, adult £2, OAP/child £1.20.

Clwyd

Chwarel Wynne Mine and Museum Glyn Ceiriog, nr Llangollen and church, Clwyd. Off A5 [069 172 343]. Half-hour guided tours through disused slate mine, also a video theatre and museum telling of mining, quarrying, and about domestic life in the Ceiriog Valley. Set in 12-acre site. Nature trail.

Open daily Easter–end October, otherwise by appointment for groups, adult £2, OAP £1.50, child £1.

Canal Museum and Passenger Boat Centre The Wharf, Llangollen [0978 860702, bookings: 0691 75322]. A horse-drawn boat journey takes you back 100 years to a quieter age; anyway, an unusual experience. Canal Museum tells about the canals period and about those who worked and lived on them.

Open: museum daily Easter–end October (weather permitting), boat trips every weekend Easter–end September, and daily July and August. Museum: adult 70p, child 45p, boat trips adult £1.80, child £1.

Deeside Ice Rink and Leisure Centre Queensferry, Deeside CH5 1SA. Off junction A55 North Wales Expressway [0244 812311]. Ice-rink, indoor and outdoor sports, crèche for the young. School holiday sessions.

Open daily except Christmas and New Year.

The Knights Caverns 38–41 West Parade, Rhyl [0745 338562]. Walk through supernatural, mythological North Wales to a spectacular presentation of turbulent historic times, castles, warrior Kings, knights, dragons, a 14th-century battle, special effects. Not for the very young.

Open daily all year, adult £1.80, OAP £1.40, child 90p.

Farmworld Sontley, nr Wrexham LL13 OYP [0978 840697]. 300-acre working farm. Audio-visual introduction. Milking parlour, museum with modern and historic tools and their uses, Farm Control Centre (computerized), calf-rearing unit, animal hospital, Mill and Meal House (learn how to mix the meal). Adventure park and animal paddocks, lambs, geese, ducks, deer and hens, to meet and touch. Bird sanctuary and nature walk.

Open daily all year, adult £2.50, OAP/child £1.25, family ticket.

The Ribbon Plate Restaurant Boat Trevor Wharf, Trevor, Llangollen LL20 7TP [0978 823215]. Cruises by narrow boats over the Pontcysllte Aqueduct, passing 126 ft high above the River Dee, under a lift bridge and through a tunnel.

Open daily April–September. A meal is included in the trip price. Ring for costs.

Eirias Park Colwyn Bay [0492 515271]. 50 acres, by the sea, with all-weather tennis courts, golf, bowls, and many other activities. Leisure Centre [0492 533223] offering a long list of activities, yoga, trampoline, gymnastics, judo, keep fit, several different forms of dance, squash, weight training, swimming, much more, over a wide range. Easter and summer school holiday activity courses for children.

Open daily all year.

Dinosaur World Eirias Park, Colwyn Bay [0492 518111]. Over 35 life-size fibre-glass models. They are set in parkland, and growl and roar! Also Neanderthal People's figures, cave, and Cave Bears. The 'Tiny Tot's Dinosaur Play Area' has more friendly-looking creatures. Children's worksheets.

Open daily Easter–September, weather permitting, adult £1.50, OAP/child £1.

Harlequin Puppet Theatre Cayley Promenade, Rhos-on-Sea, Colwyn Bay [0492 58166]. First permanent puppet theatre to be built in Britain, 1958. Traditional full-length marionettes. Performances for families, starting at 3 p.m., over an hour, with interval, can be a classical fairy-tale, a musical with a circus story, a presentation which shows children how marionettes are worked, selected according to age range. One programme Tuesday–Thursday, another Friday–Sunday. Adult show 8 p.m., Tuesday–Friday.

Open Easter season, Whitsun season (late May) and July–September, and school half-terms, closed Mondays, schools other times by arrangement, adult £3, child £2.

Welsh Mountain Zoo and Flagstaff Gardens Old Highway, Colwyn Bay LL28 5UY. B5113, A55 [0492 532938]. Elephants, lions, bears, leopards, ostriches, penguins, otters, red squirrels in 37 acres with magnificent panoramic views of Snowdonia, North Wales coast, and attractive informal gardens. Children's farm, Alligator Beach, Tropical Houses, Reptile House. Jungle Adventureland and Tarzan Trail for families. New: Chimpanzee World with robots Professor MacFergie and the Cheeky Chimp (realistic-looking robots) introducing an audio-visual; two glass-panelled walk-in viewing areas give an unparalleled view of the animals in action outside; Chimp Hall is an indoor jungle clearing furnished with artificial termite mound. Children's worksheets. Summer fun days like Teddy Bears' Picnic. Free-flying eagles (weather permitting). Sea-lions performing tricks. Mini-bus service from Colwyn Bay Station to the zoo.

Open daily except Christmas Day, adult £4, OAP/child £2.

Theatre Clwyd County Civic Centre, Mold CH7 1YA [0352 55114]. 3 theatres under 1 roof. Regular programme of films, concerts, exhibitions, and live theatre. Saturday morning drama classes for 6s–16s. Children's films in the school holidays.

Bodelwyddan Castle Bodelwyddan LL18 5YA. A55 [0745 584060]. Magnificent Victorian castle, outstation of National Portrait Gallery so collection of 19th-century portraits in appropriately furnished settings. Walled garden with aviary. Maze. Adventure Woodland for teenagers and play/activity area for younger children. Imaginative activity sheets bring the portrait collection to life for children with questions, drawings to attempt, even bubbles where they write in the thoughts of, say, explorer David Livingstone. Events during and beyond school holidays such as a non-animal circus, a puppet theatre, with children's workshops to learn circus or puppetry skills.

Open mid March–October Tuesday–Sunday and bank holiday Mondays, in winter weekends but also open other times, adult £3, child £1.50, addition for events.

Gwynedd

Conwy Visitor Centre Rosehill Street, Conwy [0492 59 6288]. Exhibition and colour film introduces you to historic town and castle, over 700 years old. Children's worksheets. Plus brass rubbing centre with over 70 replicas of brasses to try your hand on (you pay for materials and instruction).

Open mostly daily except in January, also closed February–May and October–December Wednesday, film and exhibition adult 50p, child 35p, family £1.20.

Conwy Castle Conwy [0492 592358]. Impressive, a masterpiece of medieval architecture, built by Edward I to subdue the Welsh. 125-ft-long Great Hall. Apartments prepared for Edward and Queen Eleanor. Outside the gates, over three-quarters of a mile of town walls with 22 towers, 3 gateways.

Open all year Monday–Saturday, Sunday afternoons, Sunday mornings also in summer, except Christmas and New Year, adult £2, child £1.

Penrhyn Castle Bangor. On A5122 [0248 353084]. 19th-century furnished castle, fine views, open park and walled garden, also railway museum, exhibition of dolls and natural history. Audio tour available which guides you round in an informative and entertaining way. Children's activity sheets: 'Nobility', 'Servants', 'Architecture', 'Industrial Railway Museum'. Braille guides. Golf buggy (pre-booked) for disabled garden tour. National Trust.

Open daily April–November except Tuesdays, and afternoons only early and end of season, adult £3.80, child £1.90, family £9.50.

Plas Arthur Leisure Centre Llangefni, Anglesey [0248 722966]. Swimming, squash, badminton, tennis, etc. Children's school holiday sessions, single coaching or mixture of activities.

Open daily.

Museum of Childhood 1 Castle Street, Beaumaris, Anglesey. Off A5 [0248 712498]. 150 years of family nostalgia through 2000 toys, playthings, pastimes, early visual and audio equipment played hourly; helps you remember how adults can share their pleasure with their children. Special display of teddy bears. Rocking horse rides for under-5s. Children's 'Spotter Packs'.

Open Easter–Christmas Monday–Saturday and Sunday from noon, other times by arrangement, adult £2, OAP £1.50, child £1.

Anglesey Sea Zoo and Farm Brynsiencyn, Anglesey LL61 6TQ. A4080 [0248 430411]. Undersea world, under cover. Large and small seascapes. Walk through a shipwreck where conger eels swim around you. Special 'tide tank' where the ebb and flow can be seen. A wave tank where you get wet if you're too close. Touch pools where you could find a crab under a rock. Look for mermaids' purses. The sea creatures are local. Adventure playground, toddlers upwards, radio-controlled model boats, playboat floating on a sea of bark. Children's Activity and Colouring Book (Congers and Ladders game!) £1.75.

Open daily all year except December 23–27 and January 1–6, adult £3.50, OAP £3, child £2.50, family ticket.

Beaumaris Castle Beaumaris, Anglesey. A545 [0248 810361]. Last big one built by Edward I in North Wales. Looks much as it did in 14th century, except that then ships could sail up to the main gate. Look for platform from which boulders or boiling oil hurled on attackers. Good view by walking the outer walls.

Open all year Monday–Saturday, Sunday afternoons, Sunday mornings also in summer, except Christmas/New Year, adult £1.50, child 90p.

Caernarfon Castle Caernarfon. Centre of Caernarfon [0286 77617]. Lots of Welsh castles but this one not only started out 700 years ago, it was also the birthplace of first English Prince of Wales, son of Edward I. Has its own well. Basement of Eagle Tower, walls 18 ft thick. To **Regimental Museum of Royal Welsh Regiment** and exhibitions on the castle, add audio-visual, sound and lighting effects, of the stately investiture of the current Prince of Wales, with HRH Prince Charles contributing his reactions. Includes the Princess

of Wales presented to the country for the first time.

Open as Beaumaris Castle, adult £3, child £1.50, family ticket.

The Power of Wales and the Museum of the North Llanberis LL55 4UR [0286 870636]. Merlin, the Welsh wizard, resorting to sophisticated gadgetry in a multi-media exhibition, guiding from early civilization in Wales to the 19th century with special effects, films, and animated costumed models of such as Roman warriors, Celtic saints, Owain Glyndwr, Henry VIII, David Lloyd George. Museum: industrial archaeology and history focus on gold, slate, coal, iron and steel; natural sciences about how North Wales formed and its plants, wild animals; holidays in the age of steam, the railway station, but also holiday souvenirs of the past, 'Present from . . . '. Temporary exhibitions. You can also take a trip to the nearby Dinorwic Power Station (leaving museum on hour and half-hour) including an exciting underground film presentation.

Museum open daily except Good Friday, Christmas; power station trip daily February–October, museum adult £3, OAP £2.25, child £1.50, trip additional £1, 75p and 50p.

Welsh Slate Museum Llanberis [0286 870630]. Quarry closed late sixties but machinery, plant, atmosphere preserved. Largest water wheel in Wales. Film depicts quarrymen's work. Exhibition shows social background of the industry. Land-Rover trips to Dinorwic quarries.

Open daily Easter–September Monday–Saturday and Sunday afternoons, Sunday mornings in summer, except Good Friday, May Day, adult £1.50, OAP/child 75p.

Snowdon Mountain Railway
Llanberis. A4086 [0286 870223]. Britain's only rack and pinion railway, opened in 1896, operated mostly by steam, some diesel, locomotives climbing over 3000 ft in approximately 5 miles. Incredible views on a fine day but colder up there than down below so dress appropriately. The 2¹⁄₂-hour return journey includes a half-hour stay at the summit. But snow, ice and other difficulties can mean getting only three-quarters of the way. Normally mid May before it can reach the summit.

Open daily March 15–November 1, first train 9 a.m. (8.30 peak periods), regular service unless insufficient passengers turn up, return fare adult £11, child £8, lesser early morning economy fares and also 'Stormy Weather' fares, part way.

Padarn Country Park Llanberis LL55 4TY [Warden's office 0286 870892]. Once part of the huge

Dinorwic Slate Quarries. You can now explore on footpaths created by the quarrymen. Visitor Centre and Quarry Hospital [0276 870892]. Hospital has collection of surgical equipment and woodland display. Steam train 40-minute trip alongside the large lake [timetable 0286 870549]. Craft workshops with people at work [0286 871366]. Watersports Centre including canoeing, windsurfing, abseiling.

Park open all year, Visitor Centre, Easter, daily spring bank holiday–September, railway daily early March–late October, crafts daily March–October, watersports daily spring bank holiday–September, park, Hospital Visitor Centre, free, railway adult fare £3.20, child £2.

Caernarfon Air Museum
Caernarfon Airport, Dinas Dinlle, Caernarfon LL54 5TP. Off A499 [0286 830800]. Climb into cockpits, take the controls, handle the 'Varsity' instruments. Planes and helicopters in landscaped settings, ejector seats, wartime memorabilia. Cinema with aviation shorts or full-length films. Over 200 model aircraft. Adventure playground built round an aeroplane and helicopter. Pleasure flights from here.

Open daily March 1–November 30, limited opening other months, pre-booked groups any time, adult £2.50, child £1.50.

Llechwedd Slate Caverns
Blaenau Ffestiniog, LL41 3NB
[0766 830 306]. Surface:
exhibitions include slate-splitting,
Victorian shops. 'Miners'
Tramway' takes you into side of
mountain through spectacular
caverns with tableaux. You can
explore on foot. Deep Mine
involves a ride in steep incline
passenger railway then you walk
in the footsteps of a Victorian
miner, his life portrayed in
sound/light presentations.
Children's worksheets.

Open daily all year, surface free,
single tour adult £3.75, OAP £3.25,
child £2.75, both: £5.75, £4.75, £4.

Gloddfa Ganol Slate Mine
Blaenau Ffestiniog [0766 830
664]. Museum on the industry,
view of open-cast blasting
operations from observation
gallery, miners' cottages over last
100 years, also processing of slate
into such as roofs, hearths, etc.
Also a walk into enormous
underground chambers blasted
from mountain by miners
working by candlelight, and see
tableaux, figures, with a voice-
over explaining how it was in the
past. Natural history centre and
Britain's largest narrow-gauge
railway collection.

Open daily Easter–October, otherwise
Monday–Friday and bank holidays,
adult £3, child £1.50.

Ffestiniog Railway Porthmadog.
A470 [0766 512340]. Steam locos
on narrow-gauge track from sea
level at Porthmadog, through
the fine scenery of the
Snowdonia National Park, to
slate town Blaenau Ffestiniog, an
hour's journey and over 700 ft
above sea level. Children's
worksheets.

Open daily late March–early
November, also Christmas/New Year,
some winter days, adult return fare
£9.80, OAP/child half price, 1 child
free with each grown-up.

Porthmadog Pottery Snowdon
Street, Porthmadog [0766
512137]. Watch pottery being
made and painted. Make your
own pot, paint a plate, all to take
away. Guided tours, worksheets
by arrangement. Look for
massive wall mural depicting
characters like Lawrence of
Arabia, Lloyd George.

Open Easter–end September
Monday–Friday, free entry. Throw a
pot £1.75, guided tours 50p.

Portmeirion Penrhyndeudraeth. Off A487 [0766 770228]. Italian-style waterside village, a fantasy created by Sir Clough Williams-Ellis. So shops, cottages, sandy beaches, also an exhibition and half-hourly audio-visual film show. But you pay to go into village. No dogs. Bathing dangerous.

Open daily mid March–early November, adult £2.50, OAP £2, child £1; daily, early November–mid March, adult £1.25, child 50p.

▦ ▤ ▩

Welsh Highland Railway Gelerts Farm Works, Madoc Street West, Porthmadog LL49 9DY. Adjacent British Railway main line [0766 513402]. Once a 22-mile journey, currently ³/₄ mile steam- or diesel-hauled, through pleasant countryside, operated by volunteers, to Pen-y-mount, with views of Snowdonia in a half-hour round trip.

Open April–October weekends and bank holidays, daily July–early September. Ring for fares.

▦

Maes Artro Village Llanbedr, nr Harlech [0341 23 467]. Once living quarters for RAF Fighter Squadrons so RAF Museum with memorabilia, films. World War II air-raid shelter with sound/light effects. Sea Life Aquarium holding local marine life. Workshops of the past and craft shops of the present, 19th-century Welsh street. Children's assault course. Nature walks. Children's worksheets and quizzes.

Open daily Easter–October, adult £2.30, OAP/child £1.70.

▦ ▤ ▩

Harlech Castle Harlech [0766 780552]. One of Edward I's chain of fortresses, cunningly sited with the sea once coming up to the base of the rock. Huge gatehouse, optional climb of 143 steps to top, domestic buildings. Walk the walls. Jackdaws to be seen and heard.

Open all year weekdays, Sunday afternoons, and Sunday mornings too in summer, adult £2, child £1.

▦ ▤

Talyllyn Railway Tywyn. A493 and B4405 [0654 710472]. From the coast inland into Snowdonia National Park, steam-operated, opened 1866. Chances for forest walks (folders available). Narrow-gauge railway museum at Tywyn with display of locos (widely used in quarries, mines) wagons, signals. Step into the cab of Victorian steam loco *Jubilee 1897* and try your hand operating the controls. Children's worksheets. Allow over 2 hours for full return journey.

Open daily Easter–October and Christmas, New Year, return £4.90, child £2.45, family ticket.

▦ ▤ ▩

Fairbourne and Barmouth Steam Railway Beach Road, Fairbourne, Dolgellau LL38 2PZ [0341 250084 recorded information]. From Fairbourne to Porth Penryn seeing splendours of the

estuary, mountain backdrop.
Period coaches with closed or
open cars, even observation
saloon by first class. Period
stations. Ferries to Barmouth. At
Fairbourne, Butterfly Safari, free-
flying butterflies, also lemurs,
racoons and coatimundis.

*Open daily April–October, return
first class £3.10, child £1.85, less
second, Butterfly Safari £1.80, child
£1.*

Sygun Copper Mine Beddgelert,
Caernarfon LL55 4NE. A498
[076 686 595, recorded
information 076 686 564].
Abandoned in 1905, though the
mountainside was the site of the
Chinese village in 1958 film *The
Inn of the Sixth Happiness*, with
Ingrid Bergman. Now you can
explore the old workings on foot
(not really suitable for toddlers),
wearing helmets, through
tunnels, large caverns, dazzling
stalactite and stalagmite
formations, seeing veins of
precious metals. Victorian
working conditions brought to
life with figures of miners, tools,
sound/light effects and taped
commentaries. The quarter-mile
route rises 140 ft via stairways to
the Victoria level and panoramic
views of the Gwynant Valley.
Sensible shoes recommended.

*Open daily all year, adult £3, OAP
£2.40, child £1.60.*

Cae Du Farm Park Beddgelert
LL55 4NE [076 686 345].
Working farm in 300 acres in
Gwynant Valley. ½-mile trail to
see Shetland ponies and big
shire work horses, cattle,
different breeds of sheep and
pigs, domestic rabbits,
ornamental ducks on the lake.
Look too for pheasants,
buzzards, mountain goats.
Hillside fort remains, named
after Merlin. Gelert's Grave,
legendary resting place of a
Welsh Prince's faithful hound.

*Open daily all year, adult £1.50,
child £1.*

Henblas Country Park
Bodorgan, Anglesey LL62 5DL.
B4422 [0407 840 152]. 200 acres
with considerable under-cover
elements. 17th-century manor
house with audio-visual on the
estate's history. Woodlands
nature trail including Neolithic
Burial Chamber, carp pond and
animal pens. Supervised
undercover children's play area
with aerial runways, ball pool but
also pets' corner, a blacksmith,
cart or tractor rides. Welsh Shire
Horse Centre, and daily parades.
Falconry displays. Worksheets.

*Open daily Easter–October, pre-
booked parties in winter, adult
£2.90, OAP £2, child £1.85, family
ticket.*

Segontium Roman Fort Museum
Caernarfon [0286 5625]. On site
of excavated fort. Impressive
model of Roman soldier. Displays
of Roman artefacts, coins,
illustrate day-to-day life of the fort.

*Open all year Monday–Saturday
and Sunday afternoons.*

Anglesey Bird World Dwyran,
Llanfairpwll, Anglesey LL61 6RP.
Off A4080 [0248 79 627]. Over
1000 tropical birds from 4
continents. Walk-in aviaries,
outdoor aviaries, breeding
programme of Parakeets, a pair
of South African ostriches. Tame
waterfowl can be fed. In pets'
corner children can cuddle a pet
lamb, feed a baby goat. 'Loopy
Track' for children and toddlers'
play area with mini-trikes,
rocking boats, barrel slides.

*Open daily all year, adult £2.25,
OAP/child £1.25, family ticket.*

Northern Ireland

Ah yes, I thought, categorizing, in Scotland you go up –
mountains – in Wales you go down – mines. Then in Northern
Ireland you are on level ground. So lots of wide open space for
resident or visiting children to enjoy. There may be only 1 zoo,
1 safari park, but there are 60 forests, 8 country parks. Then I
remembered Northern Ireland has mountains too, as well as
lakes and extraordinary rock formations, like the Giant's
Causeway. It also has various ways of telling about the people
who made their mark, their fame, in other parts of the world.
So, no, I cannot categorize. Each has its own special attractions,
and surely one for younger children is travelling across the sea
but not having to deal with a foreign language.

More information from Northern Ireland Tourist Board,
River House, 48 High Street, Belfast BT1 2DS [0232 246609],
or 11 Berkeley Street, London W1X 5AD [071-493 0601]. See
their publications like *Northern Ireland*, including map with
attractions marked, or *Northern Ireland Stop and Visit*, about
different attractions including forests and parks and their
recreation facilities, and *On the Move*, about getting around by
bus, train or boat. For information about steam trains: the
Railway Preservation Society of Ireland, Excursion Station,
Whitehead, Co Antrim (SAE please).

Co Fermanagh

Fermanagh County Museum and Royal Inniskilling Fusiliers Regimental Museum Castle Keep, Castle Barracks, Enniskillen [0365 25050]. 2 museums in remodelled 16th-century keep, known more informally as Maguire's Castle. County: mostly archaeological with dioramas but also an audio-visual on 'The Maquires of Fermanagh and the Town of Enniskillen'. Regimental: [0365 23142] uniforms, battle trophies, arms, colours.

County Museum open Monday–Friday, Saturday afternoons May–September and spring/summer bank holidays, closed July 12, Christmas, January 1. Regimental museum open all year Monday–Friday, adult 50p.
🏛 🎫

Lakeland Visitor Centre Shore Road, Enniskillen [0365 323110]. Convenient for lakeside. Information available on fishing, cruising, historic monuments, archaeological sites such as nearby Devenish Island, and its 12th-century Round Tower, and White Island, Lough Navar Forest Drive (7 miles through conifer forest on the lookout for deer, wild goats, red squirrels, even a peregrine falcon), Belleek Pottery (Ireland's oldest), holidays afloat. Boat trips in the summer from Round O jetty.

Centre open daily all year.
🏛 🎫 🚻 ⊞

Marble Arch Caves Marlbank Scenic Loop, Florencecourt, Enniskillen. A32 [0365 82777]. 'Over 300 million years of history.' Technically the etching away of millions of tons of Dartry limestone by acid rivers and streams. The result a wonderfully ornamental underworld of lakes, waterfalls, stalactites, natural sculptures, and extraordinary effects. New walkways and lighting have opened it to all. Conducted underground journey of around 1½ hours.

Open daily Easter–October, weather permitting, from 11 a.m. Always check beforehand, wear sensible shoes and a woollie, closing times vary, adult £3, OAP £2, child £1.50, family ticket.
🎫 🚻

Co Tyrone

Ulster-American Folk Park Camphill, Omagh BT78 5QY. Newtownstewart/Omagh Road, A5 [0662 243292]. Originally ancestral home of Mellon family, who emigrated to America, made immense fortunes, financed art galleries and contents, hotels, canals, and this outdoor museum. It's a gathering of reconstructed or re-created buildings to explain how people lived 18th/19th centuries in Ulster and then emigrated to United States. Start at Matthew T. Mellon Building, with exhibitions, audio-visuals. Progress through Old World, the

Mellon farmstead, 18th-century Presbyterian Meeting House, local school, a weaver's cottage, blacksmith's, also thatched cottage, boyhood home of Archbishop John Hughes who built St Patrick's Roman Catholic Cathedral, New York. In the reconstruction of an early 19th-century 2-masted 'brig', the crammed 'tween decks' conditions for steerage passengers are revealed in creaking timbers, foul smells, roughly constructed berths, sparse cooking utensils. Dockside buildings, moved here and rebuilt, include an 18th-century typical boarding house providing lodgings before the sea voyage. New World with such as a wagon, meaning home as well as transport, a farmstead with extras like the log barn (note cows in with the family), corn crib, smoke house, spring house, more, to illustrate agricultural and domestic techniques. Children's work booklets, colouring cards.

Open daily Easter–early September, Monday–Friday to pre-Easter, except Christmas, January 1, adult £2.50, OAP/child £1.25, family ticket.
🏛️ 🚌

Sperrin Heritage Centre 274 Glenelly Road, Cranagh, Gortin. On B47 [066 26 48142]. Natural history and gold mining. Be a forty-niner. You can hire a Klondike-style gold pan and try your luck in the iron pyrite stream. Put your questions about the area into computers. Exhibitions.

Open April–September Monday–Friday from 11 a.m., Saturday from 11.30 a.m. and Sunday from 2 p.m., October–March Monday–Saturday from 11 a.m., adult £1.25, OAP free, child 50p, family ticket, pan hire 50p, child 30p.
🏛️ 🚌 🔲

Parkanour Forest Park Off A4 west of Dungannon [086 87 58256]. Herd of white fallow deer. Nature trail with Victorian garden, wishing well. Exhibition.

Open daily all year, car £1.

Lisahoppin Open Farm 2 Leap Lane. On B158 3½ miles SE of Omagh [0662 42502]. Dairy farm. Guided tours, nature trail, riverside walks. Milking sessions can be viewed from a gallery. Children can bottle-feed young animals.

Open daily all year 11 a.m., milking 4–6 p.m., adult £1.50, OAP/child £1.

Ulster History Park Cullion, Omagh BT79 7SU. On B48 [06626 48188]. Human history of Ulster, from the first primitive settlements some nine thousand years ago to the 17th century. Find out how people lived in the full-size replicas of the houses and monuments, a mesolithic camp, a ring fort, etc. You must admit that it is unusual to hear that 'an early Norman castle' is to be built in the park. Visitor Centre with

interpretive exhibition.
Adjacent to the Gortin Glen
Forest Park, orienteering, bird-
watching, deer and wildfowl
enclosures.

*Open April–September
Monday–Saturday from 11 a.m.,
Sunday from 1 p.m., October–March
Monday–Friday from 11 a.m., adult
£1.50, child £1.*

Co Londonderry

Foyle Valley Railway Centre Foyle
Road, Londonderry [0504
265234]. Audio-visual
programme. Railway history of
Derry, particularly the narrow-
gauge 3 ft Londonderry and
Lough Swilly Railway. Trip on
thirties' diesel railcar on a mile of
track.

*Open Tuesday–Saturday and
Sunday afternoons May–September.
Phone for details.*

Walls of Derry They withstood
several sieges. Views from the top
of the walls which encircle the
old city, a circuit of 1 mile.

*Open all the time, and free.
Within the walls: O'Doherty Tower in
Magazine Street has temporary
exhibitions and city views from the
roof platform.
Open June–September
Tuesday–Saturday, adult 50p, child
25p.*

Co Antrim

Portrush Countryside Centre
Bath Road, Portrush BT56 8AP
[0265 823600]. Acts as
interpretive, information centre,
for adjacent fossil ammonites,
nature reserve, Lansdowne
Crescent. 'Are You Just Visiting',
exhibition looking at animal
migration. Small aquarium with
rock pool animals during
summer months. Stuffed
specimens of sea-birds and
waders. Continual videos
showing local and international
films. Worksheets and quiz sheets
for children. 'Rock Pool Safaris'
at low tide and bird-watching
groups led by staff (telescopes
available). *Times for both to be seen
in Centre.*

*Open daily June–mid September at
1 p.m. except Tuesdays.*

Giant's Causeway B146, 9 miles
east of Portrush. Somewhere
around 40,000 basalt rock
columns, 4-, 5-, even 8-sided,
some 40 ft high, closely packed,
providing giant stepping stones
from the cliff into the sea. Result
of prehistoric volcanic activity. A
walk, signposted by illustrated
information panels, can take you
round the 'Honeycomb',
'Wishing Well', the 'Giant's
Granny', the 'King and His
Nobles', 'Port na Spaniagh'
where the gold and silver
treasure from Spanish Armada
ship was recovered in the sixties
(now in Ulster Museum, Belfast),
'Lover's Leap' and up a wooden

staircase to Benbane Head and clifftop. Depending on the family ages you might gaze astounded rather than do a full walk. You might get there by the Bushmills Bus (Bushmills being the world's oldest legal distillery), open-topped, travelling from Coleraine bus station to the Causeway via Portstewart, Portrush, Portballintrae, Bushmills, partly on historic hydro-electric tramway route; *ring Ulsterbus [Coleraine 43334] for times, fares, say £2 return, OAP/child half price. Always open.*

Giant's Causeway Centre

Causeway Head. 2 miles from Bushmills [026 57 31855]. Displays of region's geology, flora, fauna. Replica of old hydro-electric tram running between Portrush and the Causeway till 1951. Audio-visual on local history. National Trust guide to wreck site of Armada treasure ship, 35p, and leaflet about Whitepark Bay nature trail.

Open daily all year except Christmas week, audio-visual £1, child 50p, static exhibition only, 50p and 30p, family ticket.

Causeway Safari Park 28

Benvarden Road, Ballymoney. 6 miles from Causeway, on Coleraine/Ballycastle road. B67 [02657 41474]. Drive through the lion reserve, walk through the zoo to see pumas, tigers, zebras, llamas, chimps, leopards, camels. Aviary and farmyard. 12 rides, bumper cars, giant slide, miniature railway.

Open Easter Saturday and for 9 days, April–May weekends including bank holidays, daily June–August, September Sunday, entry charge for lion reserve only, adult £2, OAP/child £1, including car, admission to zoo, amusements, etc, free.

Carrick-A-Rede Rope Bridge A2

west of Ballycastle. A swinging rope bridge with handrails, spans a 60-ft-wide chasm, 80 ft over the sea, to provide access to the island for salmon fishermen during the season.

Bridge erected early May, taken down mid September.

Larne District Historical Centre

Old Carnegie Library, Victoria Road, Larne [0574 79482]. What life was like in early 20th century, shown through a country kitchen, its furnishings, its open peat hearth, or in a milk house where butter was made, or in a smithy. Family history material.

Open all year Tuesday–Saturday afternoons.

Railway Preservation Society of Ireland

Whitehead Excursion Station, Whitehead [09603 53567, answerphone outside office hours]. Steam trains, of course. The *Portrush Flyer* is the star turn. It commemorates an express train of the same name in the thirties. Train formed from society's preserved coaches including dining car, drawn by vintage locomotive. Unusual in that it gives the family time out at the seaside, with a different style of travel, *on selected Saturdays July and in August*. A round trip starting at Whitehead at 8 a.m., or Belfast (York Road) at 9 a.m. and, with countryside travel, takes you to Portrush and returns you later in the day, usually about 7 p.m. in Belfast. *Fares around £9 with reductions for children, OAPs, parties.* But there are also steam rides, *Sunday afternoons, in July, August, while the Easter Bunny visits Easter Sunday, Monday, Tuesday and Santa December Sunday*. But add in 'Steam Enterprise', round trips to Dublin from Belfast *in September (fare around £15, reductions as above)*, and various other chances to travel by steam. Also, of course, especially weekends, see the Whitehead Centre. But write for information/programme (with SAE), or phone.

🎫 🚌

Glenariff Forest Park Off A43 Ballymena/Waterfoot road [026 673 232]. Spectacular glen with 3 waterfalls. Scenic path round sheer sides of the gorge. Waymarked walks and trails to mountain viewpoints. Visitor Centre.

Open daily all year, car £1.50, pedestrian 50p, child 25p.

Leslie Hill Historic Farm and Park Ballymoney BT53 6ZL. Off Macfin Road, a mile west of Ballymoney [02656 63109]. 300 years of agriculture. 18th-century outbuildings, blacksmith's shop, horse and trap rides, horse-drawn machines, farm museum, carriage display. Also a working farm with animals. Pets' corner, adventure playground. Children's information packs and quiz sheets.

Open Easter–June and September, Saturday, Sunday and bank holidays, July–August Wednesday–Sunday, 2–6 p.m., adult £1.50, OAP/child 90p.

🎫 🚌 ⊞

Watertop Open Farm Ballyvennaught Road, Ballycastle. On A2 6 miles SE of Ballycastle [026 57 62576]. Farm animals, poultry and ornamental game birds. Farm museum. Paddy wagon tours and sheep-shearing (July–August). Boating, pony-trekking.

Open Easter weekend, daily July–August, or by arrangement, adult 60p, OAP/child 40p.

🎫 🚌

Carrickfergus Castle Carrickfergus [096 03 51273]. Largest, best-preserved Norman castle in Northern Ireland. Great hall, impressive dungeons and 37-ft-deep well. Figures all over the castle representing defence through the ages (longbowman, crossbowman, musketeer etc.), history (John de Courcey first builder – 12th century, Con O Neill – a prisoner who escaped, more). Winter 'A day in a Castle' for schools, acting as lords, ladies, soldiers, entertainers.

Open all year Monday–Saturday, Sunday afternoon, except Christmas, New Year's Day, adult £1, OAP/child 50p.

Shane's Castle Railway and Nature Reserve Randalstown Road, Antrim. Off M2 [084 94 63380]. Northern Ireland's only narrow-gauge steam railway, meaning small, nostalgic, story-book trains. You travel through woods, along Lough Neagh to Shane's Castle, where rolling stock is stored. Add in a fairground, the deer park and especially the nature reserve including nature trails and observation hides. Special events include steam rallies, car rallies.

Open April–May Sunday and bank holidays, June Wednesday, Sunday and bank holidays, July–August Wednesday, Saturday, Sunday and bank holidays, September first 3 Sundays. Phone for times, fares.

Best to assume entry charges change. Well, it can be a pleasure if they have not.

Ulster Museum Botanic Gardens, Belfast BT9 5AB [0232 381251]. Thousands of years of natural and human history, interestingly set out in a spiral interior so you start with the Dinosaur Show and move on and up to local history, antiquities (look for the treasures from the Armada shipwreck *Girona*), natural sciences and art galleries. 3 working water wheels and 3 big steam engines. Local history includes secret society badges, uniforms, regalia and a large coin section. Look for 'Made in Belfast', the Egyptian mummy, the 'Living Sea' and rare specimen of the coelacanth, the 'living fossil' fish. Children's Activity Sheets on sale. Weekend events and some holiday programmes for families and children.

Open all year weekdays, Saturday, Sunday afternoon only.

Botanic Gardens Belfast [0232 324902]. The bulbous-shaped Palm House is older than the Great Palm House at Kew Gardens, houses coffee, banana, cotton plants. In the Tropical Ravine House, completed 1886, you view from a balcony with tall plants at eye level, since they grow in a sunken glen. Bananas again, sugar cane and rice by a lily pond.

Open all year weekdays, afternoons weekends.

Belfast Zoo Antrim Road, Newtownabbey BT36 7PN [0232 776277]. Innovative modern zoo using its dramatic location on the slopes of Cavehill for specialized open and naturalistic enclosures. Underwater viewing of sea-lions and penguins. Many rare animals including spectacled bears, red pandas, tamarins and marmosets. Free-flight aviary. Large African enclosure. Children's farm where young animals may be seen. Adoption scheme. 'Zoo Crack', free, reports on different creatures, on breeding, and has included a children's quiz competition. The Children's Page has had illustrated information on the young and contributed poems. Summer school holiday activities for the family, successfully launched, will be a regular event if funds allow, like feeding and handling sessions, guided tours, watching elephants' bathtime, Zoolympics comparing your athletic abilities with animals'.

Open daily all year except Christmas Day, adult £2.80, OAPs free, child £1.40, less in winter.

Transport Museum Witham Street, Belfast [0232 51519]. 200 years of Irish transport, street trams, fire engines, vintage cars, motorbikes, penny-farthing bikes. There is also a yacht and the Amphicar which drove the 30 miles across the North Channel from Scotland to Ireland in 1968. Railway exhibits over 130 years, industrial, passenger, different gauges, includes giant *Maeve*, Ireland's largest steam loco.

Open all year Monday–Saturday, adult 60p, child 40p.

Dundonald Old Mill 231 Belfast Road, Quarry Corner, Dundonald [0232 480117]. 18th-century corn mill housing huge water wheel measuring over 30 ft in diameter. 168 wooden buckets power 3 sets of millstones.

Open all year Monday–Saturday and Sunday from 11 a.m.

Have you read **A Plea** page 11 about checking before you set off?

Streamvale Open Dairy Farm 38 Ballyhanwood Road, Dundonald [0023 18 3244]. Milking can be viewed from a gallery. Children can bottle-feed a lamb in pets' corner. Nature trail. Donkey rides.

Open daily June–August from noon, September–May Wednesday, Saturday, Sunday, bank holidays from 2 p.m., closed Christmas Day, milking 3 p.m., small animals fed 4 p.m., adult £1.50, OAP/child £1.

Giant's Ring off Ballylesson Road, South Belfast. A mile south of Shaw's Bridge. Extraordinary, probably neolithic, ceremonial place being an embanked enclosure 600–700 ft across with central dolmen of basalt boulders.

Co Down

Ballycopeland Windmill On B172 near Millisle [0247 861413]. Only working windmill in Ireland. Original millstones and wooden machinery. 18th century. Visitor Centre in miller's house with electrically operated model and hands-on experience of milling.

Open Easter–September Tuesday–Saturday, Sunday afternoons, otherwise Saturday and Sunday afternoon, adult 60p, OAP/child 30p.

Murlough National Nature Reserve between Dundrum and Newcastle. Off A24 [039 675 311]. Sand dunes and heathland, always open. Also Information Centre [039 67 24362] with displays and guided walks which help you look for wildlife.

Open daily afternoons June–September.

Ulster Folk and Transport Museum Cultra Manor, Holywood. A2, Belfast/Bangor Road [0232 428428]. In 180 acres, homes, water mills, a church reconstructed here. Fascinating variety of homes: one with 'bed outshot' so as not to take up living space, another with dwellings for relatives, several where the cows were not physically separated from the family, but then linen weavers worked in their own homes, with a watch-tower where an armed watch was kept on the spread-out-for-bleaching linen against thieves or wandering cattle, and terrace houses include a shoemaker's workshop. Add working places like a forge, a flax-scutching mill, and a school where today's children can try woodwork, weaving, churning, by arrangement. Also purpose-built gallery with video shows of traditional farming activities, exhibitions on both domestic and agricultural techniques. Earlier tools for getting things done had names like 'harnen stands', 'noggins', 'piggins', 'creepies'. Also Transport Museum, from donkey creels and pony traps to old aircraft, a schooner. Horse and carriage rides, £1, 50p. Events.

Open all year Monday–Saturday, Sunday afternoons, adult £2, OAP/child £1.

Castle Ward nr Strangford. On A25 [039686 204]. 700-acre country estate on south shore of Strangford Lough. 18th-century mansion, façade and furnished interior in 2 styles. Stable yard about below stairs in Victorian times. Laundry and garments of the period. Pastimes Centre:

dress in replica costumes and play with Victorian toys and games. Farmyard. August workshops for children, also nature walks. Barn, centre for National Trust Wildlife Scheme, 'touch table' for children, story of Strangford Lough, (wildfowl and marine life, including seals), bird-watching. Young Wildlife Club [0238 510721], meetings and activities for up to 12s.

House: Easter week daily, April, September and October weekends only, May–August daily except Thursdays, from 1 p.m., barn: Easter week daily, April–June and September weekends and bank holidays only, July and August daily except Thursdays, from 2 p.m., estate and grounds open all year, house adult £2, child £1, barn free, estate £2.50 per car, November–Easter £1.

Castle Espie Centre 78 Ballydrain Road, Comber [0247 872517]. Wildfowl and Wetlands Trust. Ireland's largest collection of ducks, geese and swans. Enjoy feeding the birds. View from hides, waterfowl gardens. Natural and local history exhibits.

Open daily except December 24–25, adult £2, OAP/child £1.10.

Scrabo Country Park Newtownards [0247 811491]. Old quarries, walks, Scrabo Tower, head of Strangford Lough, countryside centre with 122 steps to the top.

Park always open, tower daily June–September except Monday from noon.

Quouile Pondage National Nature Reserve Off A25, near Downpatrick [0396 615520]. Visitor Centre next to ruins of 16th-century Quoile Castle: how a flood-control barrage has changed the saltwater estuary to fresh water, the fish and insect life. Guided walks, trails, talks.

Centre open April–September Tuesday–Sunday from 11 a.m., otherwise weekends from 1 p.m., grounds always open.

Northern Ireland Aquarium The Ropewalk, Castle Street, Portaferry BT22 1NZ [02477 28062]. Around 70 marine species in over 20 large tanks, and found in Strangford Lough, from octopuses to conger eels. Illustrations of the lough's different habitats. Arranged guided tours and shore walks. Also wildfowl pond, woodland walks, sports facilities.

Open April–August Monday–Saturday, Sunday from 1 p.m., otherwise closed Monday and 10 days at Christmas, adult £1.20, OAP/child 60p, family ticket.

Seaforde Tropical Butterfly House Seaforde Nursery, Seaforde. A24 [039 687 225]. In large flight area hundreds of free-flying exotic butterflies to be seen. Also behind glass, insects and reptiles from 4 continents.

Open April–September Monday–Saturday, Sunday from 2 p.m., adult £1.90, child £1.

Co Armagh

Armagh County Museum The Mall, Armagh [0861 523070]. Victorian schoolhouse, now small museum and contains art gallery, natural history room, Victorian doll collection, even railway collection like uniforms, badges, lamps, models, telling of the time when we travelled on tracks rather than roads. Children's worksheets.

Open all year Monday–Saturday.

The Planetarium College Hill, Armagh [0861 523689]. 'What is a Planetarium?' Answer: 'A communication medium designed to help explain many of the important concepts of astronomy and space science through a combination of methods and styles.' This is neatly summarized as 'an astronomical information centre'. So here you have Encyclopaedia Galactica, with over 6000 images accessible by computer with topics: Shuttle, Mars, Sun, Planets, Earth,

Jupiter, Constellations. Models of the *Gemini* spacecraft, Galileo probe, Viking Mars landing. Meteorite collection. Interactive starshows with audience participation, video projection on the dome showing spectacular effects from the Big Bang to the end of the universe. Public telescope for viewing on certain nights October–March. Occasional special competitions. Inflatable planetarium for hire. Children's school holiday activities especially Easter, Hallowe'en and Christmas.

Open all year Monday–Saturday from 2 p.m. except over Christmas week and 12 July. Very much worth getting programme details, especially for Star Shows, Saturday afternoons and July/August daily. Charge for shows (reservations advised), adult £2, child £1.50.

Ardress House Annaghmore BT62 1SQ. On B28 [0726 851236]. 17th-century farmhouse, farm implements, livestock in cobbled farmyard. Woodland walks, playground.

Open daily Easter week, April–June and September weekends and bank holidays, July and August daily except Tuesdays, from 2 p.m., house, grounds, farmyard £1.50, child 65p, grounds and farmyard only £1, child 50p.

British Tourist Boards

Channel Islands: Jersey Tourist Information Office 35 Albemarle Street, London W1 [071 493 5278], also **Information Office** Liberation Square, St Helier, Jersey [0534 78000]; **States of Guernsey Tourist Committee** Crown Pier, St Peter Port, Guernsey, by post PO Box 23, White Rock, St Peter Port [0481 726611].

Cumbria Tourist Board (covering county of Cumbria) Ashleigh, Holly Road, Windermere, Cumbria LA23 2AQ [096 624444]. Written and phone enquiries only.

East Anglia Tourist Board (counties of Cambridgeshire, Essex, Norfolk and Suffolk) Toppesfield Hall, Hadleigh, Suffolk 1P7 5DN [0473 822922].

East Midlands Tourist Board ('The English Shires', counties of Derbyshire, Leicestershire, Lincolnshire, Northamptonshire and Nottinghamshire) Exchequergate, Lincoln, Lincolnshire LN2 1PZ [0522 531521]. Written and phone enquiries only.

Heart of England Tourist Board (counties of Gloucester, Hereford and Worcester, Shropshire, Staffordshire, Warwickshire and West Midlands) Woodside, Larkhill, Worcester, Worcestershire WR5 2EQ [0905 763436]. Written and phone enquiries only.

Isle of Man Tourist Board 7–13 Victoria Street, Douglas, Isle of Man [0624 674323].

London Visitor and Convention Bureau (LVCB) (Greater London area) 26 Grosvenor Gardens, London SW1W 0DU [071-730 3488]. Various services; see under London.

Northern Ireland Tourist Board River House, 48 High Street, Belfast BT1 2DS [0232 231221]. Also office at 11 Berkeley Street, London W1 [071-493 0601].

Northumbria Tourist Board (counties of Cleveland, Durham, Northumberland, Tyne and Wear) Aykley Heads, Durham DH1 5UX [091-384 6905].

North West Tourist Board (counties of Cheshire, Greater Manchester, Lancashire, Merseyside and the High Peak District of Derbyshire) Swan House, Swan Meadow Road, Wigan Pier, Wigan, Lancashire WN3 5BB [0942 821222]. Written and phone enquiries only.

Scottish Tourist Board 23 Ravelston Terrace, Edinburgh EH4 3EU [031-332 2433]. Also office at 19 Cockspur Street, London SW1 [071-930 8661].

South East England Tourist Board (counties of East Sussex, Kent, Surrey and West Sussex) The Old Brew House, Warwick Park, Tunbridge Wells, Kent TN1 1NH [0892 540766].

Southern Tourist Board ('South of England', counties of Hampshire, Eastern and Northern Dorset and Isle of Wight) 40 Chamberlayne Road, Eastleigh, Hampshire SO5 5JH [0703 62006].

Thames and Chilterns Tourist Board (counties of Oxfordshire, Berkshire, Bedfordshire, Buckinghamshire and Hertfordshire) The Mount House, Church Green, Oxfordshire OX8 6DZ [0993 778800].

Wales Tourist Board Brunel House, 2 Fitzalan Road, Cardiff, CF2 1UY [0222 499909]. Also office at 34 Piccadilly, London W1 [071-409 0969].

West Country Tourist Board (counties of Avon, Cornwall, Devon, West Dorset, Somerset, Wiltshire and Isles of Scilly) Trinity Court, 37 Southernhay East, Exeter, Devon EX1 1QS [0392 76351].

Yorkshire and Humberside Tourist Board (counties of North Yorkshire, South Yorkshire, West Yorkshire and Humberside) 312 Tadcaster Road, York, North Yorkshire YO2 2HF [0904 707961].

> Countryside Tourist Information Centres are always worth a call for guides, maps, mini-guides on the locality, sometimes free. Look for TIC signs.

Part two: Children in mind

Introduction

So what's the difference between part one about family outings, and this one? Well, there are loads of fascinating things for *families* to see and do throughout the country and there is increasing understanding of the sheer *energy* of children, which is why you may find an adventure playground in the acres surrounding a stately home. I would take it as said that public swimming pools offer facilities right across the age range. Theatres, particularly at Christmas time, also put on shows to attract all ages from children to grandparents.

This is about what's on *specifically* for children, meaning planned and designed for youngsters and relating to their mental, physical and emotional development. It's what I would rather think of as fun, what childhood is about, but backed by careful thinking of what they can take in at different ages.

I am delighted to see that there is much more thought about the young. More working farms are open to give children a closer acquaintance with animals and some understanding of agriculture and how food gets to the table. Then there are city farms in urban districts. More of the events in country parks are for children. Most steam railways have Easter (eggs, bunnies) and Christmas (Santa and little gifts) programmes. The majority of the Wildlife and Wetlands centres have school holidaytime activities like making masks, rubbings, of birds or, for the very young, working on large-piece jigsaws. The country's first children's museum, after so many years of campaigning, effort, planning, has at last been achieved in **Eureka!**, in Halifax. Meantime there has been the expansion of a positive chain of 'hands-on' science and technology centres, truly learning through playing, doing, experiencing, at London's Science Museum, in Bristol, Cardiff, Buxton and more. All these are listed under their areas. More attractions

provide children's worksheets, or quizzes, or activity books,
which select, draw attention to, interpret, single exhibits
among the sometimes bewildering abundance displayed. Ask
for these. Demand might be met with supply. Taped personal
Walkman guides, a marvellous innovation in my view, are
sometimes available in a children's version.

I must emphasize that, because some happenings in this
section are listed as appropriate for certain ages, this does not
necessarily mean for the children by themselves, without
adults. This refers especially to theatres, concerts and
exhibitions. For adults I would say do go, here is a refreshing
entertainment, something different. Then visits to museums or
art galleries, and some out-of-school holidaytime events, can be
for accompanied children, or for children delivered and
collected – depends on the age. And watch the specified age
carefully; I hear often about children being left unsupervised,
even by siblings, for events for which they are too young.

Don't ever assume that you can leave young unsupervised;
check whether this is an event for a particular age range and
for them alone, professionally supervised, or to be enjoyed with
a parent. You will probably have to make bookings anyway,
though the events can be free; when word of this gets around
the demand can be considerable.

About what's offered: often I think, 'Oh great, really
marvellous, this is inspiration' about a particular place, then I
think well, if you live a couple of hundred miles away, you don't
count it into the possibilities for your own child. It can still be a
seed; somebody somewhere is trying to float activities for
children, probably parent-backed.

Museums and art galleries

Children get the best service in museums and art galleries. This may surprise some parents who may have noted a less-than-friendly eye from staff as little ones enjoy charging up and down in the spaces between all those cabinets and displays, into which they and older siblings are peering.

Let's divide the service roughly into that for schools and that suited to the school holidays or other leisure times, so there is then an organized time-pattern for the young.

Either way nobody is assuming that you KNOW. This jelled for me when, by invitation, I accompanied groups of schoolchildren visiting the National Gallery. Here, of course, an adult will inevitably be constantly taking a second look sideways at famous paintings, long known and many times reproduced. Thrill is that this is the *original*, but what do you know about it other than its fame? The children, inspired, encouraged and drawn out by an education officer, were looking at many more paintings, considering effects, what was going on, what was being said.

Highlight of the visit: study of *Balthazaar's Feast*, pretty large, lots of discussion about costume, the occasion, use of colours, especially to focus on the main drama depicted, which was what it was about, why the carry-on, about impending loss of treasures. 'He'd nicked 'em,' declared a short-trousered boy, who had obviously been closely following the artist's ideas. Then we all trooped off to the next consideration and dissection of another major work. With this sort of refreshing approach, are you surprised that I take advantage of my journalist status to join in?

Then there are all kinds of happenings when school's OUT, on holidays and weekends. Looking at historical objects, yes, but not just looking, also trying the physical things like what jobs children were expected to do in country areas, or the washing/mangling (no washing-machines, launderettes, helpful manmade fibres); or what the schools were like; all kinds of evidence about how people lived in villages, towns, cities and celebrated traditional festivals.

So very much a-doing, and finding-out-about-the-past-by-doing, which could be making Easter bonnets or Hallowe'en masks, cooking all kinds of edibles associated with different traditions, designing your own heraldic device, creating cards, presents, pressed flowers, puppets, toys, embroideries, working models of machinery, or ornamental objects. You can also discover the 'servant-style' or 'leisure-style' living of not so long ago, make a study of a district, expressing what's needed by the next generation. There are all kinds of activities offered and they are wonderfully varied.

You may regard museums and art galleries as mostly glass cases and Old Masters, with a few jolly exceptions, in which case you are remembering the cultural institutions of your own childhood, when 'interpretation' consisted largely of a printed label on an enclosed case. There has been a revolution in many museums, castigated by some as Disneyland style. I regard it rather as opening up our cultural heritage to a much wider clientèle. Exhibits are now presented in settings, that we take for granted in the theatre, to show their place in human, natural, animal life or in history, their workings, functions, role, in a lively style that draws us, entices us to find out more, discover, learn. Instead of strict instructions *not to touch* we now find the opposite. We are invited to stroke, hold, examine, or to make things work. We shall see this approach in all its glory with the opening of our first children's museum, **Eureka!** in Halifax in 1992.

For adults art galleries have not changed but children in the school holidays can go on specifically arranged tours, see an artist at work, try their hands at sculpture, paintings, quizzes.

Most museums or art galleries arranging programmes for children give careful age-interest definitions – meaning those who can cope with what is offered. Depending on district, children may need to be delivered and collected. But there may be a wider age range. This does not mean museum staff are childminders, only that the museum offers interests and activities for younger children. Always check whether they should be accompanied.

Because of sheer demand it is as well to watch what your local museum is offering, so that you get the programme well in advance and can book in places.

I have written about happenings over recent years but always accept that because of staff changes, shortage of resources, rethinking, facilities can shrink – or with more generous funding, even expand!

Museums and art galleries are listed under their districts because they have become so much more attractive as family outings. You will find also whether children's activities are organized. Remember that many close over Good Friday, Christmas and New Year.

> The majority of national museums and art galleries are still free though more are charging for entry and occasionally there may be small fees for participation in events, like the cost of materials or, with expeditions, the cost of coaches.

Theatre

More than just the panto at Christmas is my definition here. Not decrying a pantomime; a seasonal visit by the entire family, including grandparents, can be an occasion. But the age target is very wide.

Children's theatre is for children, carefully matched to age ranges. Does that sound dry? I can assure you it's not, it's care about what different ages can assimilate from their experience so far and drawing them on with colour, drama, spectacle and extraordinary effects. The plots can be traditional or set in present-day situations.

An occasion? Oh yes, very much yes. You want to be there! I have been to quite a few but I especially remember, as a journalist rather than as a mother, a Whirligig performance at London's Sadlers Wells, seated down among the school groups; pre-start, the number of bulbs in the massive candelabra was being counted, the whole ambience of a theatre for those who had never been in one was new, interesting; in the interval they offered me their sweets and talked about the plot, the effects, what could happen next. I wondered whether the grand dramatic finale might bother some; I heard them discussing the theme and how the effects were achieved as they left, preparing for writing about it in school.

Schools figure strongly in children's theatre, either going to theatres in termtime or having touring companies coming to schools. There is a certain amount of sponsorship to keep ticket prices down, but I'm sure everyone would say not enough. After all it is a straight question of whether you sustain into another generation the concept of going to the theatre, so different from watching television. Theatre for children was badly hit by the Education Reform Act which confused parents by requiring contributions instead of the straightforward charge. Many children's theatre companies survive on a financial knife-edge anyway. Children's playwright David Wood: 'Maybe one day we will see a National Children's Theatre.' Ah . . . The few – like Little Angel Marionette, Polka or Unicorn – actual theatres for children are mostly based in London, but there are touring companies and theatres who present themselves throughout the year, or especially in school holiday times. So watch your local theatre.

But this is also *by*, as well as *for*, children.

As an adult I would say don't go as a chore, dutifully keeping the children occupied, culturally educated. You could be astonished, enchanted, get a completely fresh view of all kinds of things you have previously taken for granted or maybe never even thought about. Children's theatre is, of course, about showing the next generation the magic, the mystery of live theatre. This generation, meaning attending parents, could well start saying this is fun, amazing, extraordinary, and discover for themselves a whole new aspect to theatre-going.

> **Note:** indication of age suitability is usual but never assume this means the child alone. Always check.

London-based, but many tour around the country

Vanessa Ford Productions 62 Uverdale Road, London SW10 0SS [071-352 1948]. Family shows touring in regional theatres with a Christmas season in a London theatre. The Narnia stories, *The Lion, the Witch and the Wardrobe, The Horse and His Boy, The Magician's Nephew* but also *A Christmas Carol, Winnie the Pooh, Noddy*.

Little Angel Marionette Theatre 14 Dagmar Passage, Cross Street, London N1 2DN [071-226 1787]. Converted into a theatre seating 100 from a bomb-wrecked temperance hall by John and Lyndie Wright and opened in 1961. Devoted to puppetry in all its forms. Resident company also travels, with acclaim, worldwide and lots of visiting companies from Britain and other countries can, therefore, be seen at the theatre. So a very nice variety of theatre from different areas, different countries. The age range is always carefully defined. Almost always a show suitable for 3s–5s on Saturday mornings, but otherwise all kinds of age variations offered and especially at weekends, in school holidays and half-terms (also weekday shows for schools).

The list of titles is long, like Oliver Goldsmith's *The Prince and the Mouse*, Menotti's *Amahl and the Night Visitors, Babar the Elephant, Hans the Bellringer* (from Holland), *The Fisherman and His Soul* (Oscar Wilde), Hans Andersen's *The Little Mermaid* and *The Marsh King's Daughter, The Bewitched Baobab Tree* (an African fairy-tale). For 3s–5s, *Snitchity Titch, Rapunzel, Bandicoot, Three Billy Goats Gruff*. Fortunately lots of repeats of the popular shows, so very much worth checking on what's going on, apart from always booking seats. **Note:** Dagmar Passage not marked in *London A to Z*, so look for Dagmar Terrace.

London Bubble 5 Elephant Lane, London SE16 4JD [071-237 4434]. A large tent, bright yellow in appearance, a travelling theatre performing for a week or two June-August in London's local parks and open spaces, since 1972. Expect music, informality, audience participation. Examples: *Bugs and Slugs or a Trip Inside David Bellamy's Head* for 5s–12s, about the inhabitants of a tiny world above and below us; *Peacemaker* for 5s–18s about how the Reds and the Blues come together in dance, circus skills; *Operation Elvis* for 8s–12s, about a boy, disbelieved when he says he's Elvis Presley so he jumps on a bus and heads off to Memphis, Tennessee. Tent wheelchair-accessible and fitted with induction loop. Bubble company also appears at Christmas, indoors.

Molecule Theatre of Science Bloomsbury Theatre, 15 Gordon Street, WC1H 0AH [071-388 5739]. This was founded by Lord and Lady Miles, is now a separate registered charity. The idea is to present scientific facts to 7s–11s in show-business style, that is to say with goodies and baddies, a storyline, plot, lights, costumes, lots of music and songs, a chance for the audience to be cheering goodies, hissing baddies, great fun, but also illuminating (no pun intended) when, say, I have seen electricity demonstrated on stage in what looks like a large fish tank, or the workings of a light bulb shown with a loaf, two rods and some wiggly wire!

Tours theatres all over Britain and Ireland. Recent titles: *Safety in Numbers*, about maths; *It's All in the Stars*, about seasons, time, tides, phases of the moon, the solar system; *Gremlins in the Works*, about telecommunications. Additionally: week-long residencies with 30 children *from the same class* developing a theme like astronomy, pollution, genetics; 12s–13s with actor-teachers. Teachers' project notes for follow-up work provided for both.

When sponsorship allows, you may come across **Molecule**'s workshops for 11s–12s in museums in half-terms.

Movingstage Marionette Company 78 Middleton Road, London E8 4BP [071-249 6876 – box office 0836 202 745]. Puppet theatre barge, rare, a full-scale marionette theatre built on an old Thames barge, with child-high brass portholes, raked seating for 50, toilets, central heating, refreshments. Autumn and spring (Christmas, Easter, May bank holiday weekend) moored at Little Venice, Blomfield Road, London W9 (nearest Tube Warwick Avenue), summer moves to Wallingford, then Henley, then Marlow, then Richmond. Shows: *The Hare and the Tortoise and Other Tales from Aesop*; *Sir Gawain and the Green Knight*, Arthurian times; *Monkey Business*, they perform breathtaking tricks; *The Birdman*, about an old man who rescues a small bird.

National Youth Music Theatre Sadler's Wells Theatre, Rosebery Avenue, London EC1R 4TN [071-278 6563]. President HRH The Prince Edward. Formerly the Children's Music Theatre started in 1976. 8s–16s, a mixture of children from different backgrounds, from all over Great Britain act, sing, dance, make music, take on backstage like wardrobe, make-up, lighting, sound, or front-stage work like box office, publicity. Children are drawn from schools private and public, all parts of the country. Tours, performances are during the school holidays and these are widespread, say from Edinburgh to Jersey, including famous theatres, festivals, but also have included Yugoslavia, Hong Kong. Sample productions to be *involved in, or to see*; have happened or will no doubt be repeated: *Helen Come Home, or Achilles the Heel* (enjoy some ghastly jokes); *Powder Monkeys*, about a 12-year-old in Nelson's Navy; *Captain Stirrick*, child gangs Regency-style; *Drake*, a big-band musical comedy, with a cast of 40; *Pal Joey*; *Oliver*; *October's Children*, set in the 1917 Russian Revolution; *Once Upon a War*, Channel Islands' wartime occupation; *The Ragged Child*, about destitute Victorian children who were given new opportunities in the Ragged Schools. If you have seen NYMT shows on TV you will know the quality, skill, sheer exuberance. Annual auditions held, national and local. Also around 6 2-day residential workshops, exploring all forms of music theatre, held annually.

National Youth Theatre of Great Britain 443–445 Holloway Road, London N7 6LW [071-281 3865]. Patron HRH The Prince Edward. Founded in 1956. Aims: to give young people practical experience of the theatre, to set them high standards and in doing so to offer them a valuable form of teamwork. Offers both acting and technical experience to 14s–21s. Presents annual seasons of both contemporary and classical plays in London, also tours in this country and abroad. Some titles: *Murder in the Cathedral, Romeo and Juliet, Troilus and Cressida, The Royal Hunt of the Sun, A Man for All Seasons, Freedom of the City* (civil rights), *Shakespeare and the Supernatural* (the playwright's and his contemporaries' preoccupation with the subject). Among those who acted in NYT: two 007s (Sean Connery and Timothy Dalton), Simon Ward, Ben Kingsley, Helen Mirren and, on the technical side, Kate Adie. Annual auditions London and regional centres.

Parasol Children's Theatre Garden House, 4 Sunnyside, Wimbledon, London SW19 4SL [081-946 9478]. Director Richard Gill, playwright, puppetmaster and creator of Polka, see below; actors, rod, shadow and glove puppets, touring regional theatres and arts centres, say 6s upwards. New London theatre planned. Titles: *The Wind in the Willows, Alice in Wonderland, The Jungle Book* (notable for its huge puppets). Teachers' notes for school groups cover making puppets, putting on a show.

Playboard Puppets 94 Ockendon Road, London N1 3NW [071-226 5911]. Recycling long before it became fashionable. The Spoon family travel in their baked-bean can spaceship to Button Moon. All the puppet characters are made from household objects like empty plastic bottles, wooden spoons, funnels, tubes (Drainpipe Castle) and loo brushes. Shows touring the length and breadth of the country, mostly in regional theatres. Suitable 4s–9s. *Mr Spoon on Button Moon*, with the Singing Hotpots, landing on Tabletop Mountain where Queenie Jelly is holding a Royal Circus followed by the panto *Cinders and the Magic Beans* with two Rag Bag sisters playing the Ugly sisters; *Button Moon and the Moon Monsters* when a Flying Wok full of bright green monsters even capture the spaceship. New: *The Spooks That Live on the Hill.* Also to be seen on TV and on videos.

Polka Children's Theatre 240 The Broadway, Wimbledon, London SW19 [081-543 4888]. The theatre building is an enticement even before you get to the shows; like an outdoor playground, a café with food coming round on little trains and seats in train-style apartments, a display of puppets from all over the world, an exhibition of toys of Britain, craftsman-made, a booth selling all kinds of interesting, different, pocket-money-price toys. Performances, puppets and humans, with light music, continue all year, partly for schools but also for the public on Saturdays and especially through the school holidays.

Examples: *The Wind in the Willows,* David Wood in his Magic and Music Show, a Grand Festival of Punch and Judy, The Wild Animal Song Contest, *Shoshok,* a Russian play, *Roli,* the adventures of a puppet, *Helen,* about Helen Keller, blind, deaf, dumb, and her victory over the handicaps, *The Giant's Baby,* a delight. Performances are always carefully categorized according to age range, could be 6–100 (!) but could also be tightened into 5s–9s or 7s–11s, worth paying attention. In the Adventure Room, Saturdays, for 3s–5s: shows like *Rosy the Clown, The Adventures of Stardog, Major Mustard, Pipsqueak,* a variety of

puppet companies. Free story-telling sessions first Saturday each month at 1 p.m. Annual Open Day, free, to see behind the scenes, plus entertainment. Induction loop. Add in too the holidaytime workshops, carefully set into age groups from, say, 3s–15s. These workshops could be about magic, drama, marionettes, story puppets, shadow puppets, rod puppets, mime and masks. You always need to book for a performance, but there is so much to see happening here, so I would advise phoning or writing (SAE) for a programme well in advance of school holidays so you'll know what's coming up for your children's age range, and so that you get the maximum from a day's visit, with or without a performance. Must repeat that the Polka Company tours, all over the country, different times of the year, performances carefully balanced to an age range. So watch your local theatre.

Riverside Studios Crisp Road, Hammersmith, London W6 [081-748 3354]. Saturdays at 2.30 p.m. Shows: *Funky Circus,* clown skits; *Neptune's Cavern and the Ugly Baby,* an unhappy baby crocodile; *Escape,* about Houdini; *Fabulous Beasts,* wild acrobatics, by humans. Age suitability given in each case. Also: school holiday workshops which can be music, movement, drama, concluding with a performance, or trying clowning, juggling. Advice: get leaflet *Saturday For Kids* with details of shows, workshops and films.

The Anna Scher Children's Theatre 70–72 Barnsbury Road, London N1 0ES [071-278 2101]. A charity. Started as a school's drama club in 1968. Aims to develop artistic abilities but not necessarily for professional careers, though children have appeared on stage/TV. Classes in mime, improvisation, movement, dance, singing, also theatrical history, theory, technique, production, after school, in groupings from 6 upwards. Summer projects open to those attending classes. Over 2-year waiting list. But school groups do get one-off sessions with Anna in termtime. Here a matter of theatre-interested families being involved, knowing what's going on, when the open days, festivals, happen.

Theatre Royal Stratford East Gerry Raffles Square, Newham, London E15 1BN [081-534 0301]. Youth Theatre Saturday afternoons for 8s–14s, workshops on theatre and drama skills; Monday evenings for 14s plus, the same programme working towards a production; both onstage and backstage roles.

Tricycle Theatre 269 Kilburn High Road, London NW6 7JR [071-328 1000]. Saturday shows, each designed for an age group, 3s upwards. Under 7s must be accompanied by someone 16 or over. Many of the performers/companies

mentioned elsewhere but also Play in a Day, put on a show and video it; songs and drama games; discovering how to play thumb piano, bamboo, cow bells and perform as a traditional Afro-Caribbean ensemble; puppet workshops and putting on a show; clowning, stilt-walking, juggling. Holiday and termtime workshops with mime, story-telling, circus skills, more. Youth Theatre, 16s upwards, onstage and backstage, improvisation, workshops, and 2 shows produced each year. Young People's Programme, Education, Youth Theatre [071-372 6611]. Induction loop, wheelchair access and space.

Unicorn Theatre for Children Arts Theatre, Great Newport Street, London WC2H 7JB [071-836 3334]. Founded by Caryl Jenner over 30 years ago. Commissions top-quality plays, also presents musicals, shows by writers here and abroad. Among titles, *Asterix and the Great Divide*, *Meg and Mog*, *The Gingerbread Man*, *Noggin the Nog and the Firecake*. Other theatre companies visit so attractions can include a magic show, puppet presentations from other countries or say from Polka or Birmingham's Cannon Hill. In summer the Unicorn Theatre Company tours schools, parks, playgrounds with such as *Robin and the Tree Trick*, music, songs, action for a story not unlike Robin Hood's but updated to a conservation theme. Shows are matched to different age groups, as appropriate, between 4 and

12 years. Unicorn offers performances to schools Tuesday–Friday afternoons in termtime, with teachers' notes.

Unicorn is a club theatre. Temporary membership for non-members, 20p. So anyone can enjoy a Unicorn show, and that includes the deaf through an induction loop system, and a performance with simultaneous sign language by an interpreter.

But 4s–12s can join the Unicorn Club, have birthday tea parties in the restaurant with arranged activities, see plays in the Studio, receive *Unicornews*, a little magazine with competitions, articles, information about new productions and especially about the workshops. These happen Saturday/Sunday and during the school holidays: magic, find out how it's done; make-up, find out how to change your face through greasepaint, older, younger, nicer, nastier; stage-fighting, the tricks of the stunts people; clowning, juggling, falling about, slapstick; puppets, that is, not only making them but getting together a play with all the props, scenery; masks, making them, weird or beautiful; making a play, of course; scene-painting, meaning how the effect, ballroom, space ship, beach is created; story games, for younger ones, acting stories, playing games. Add 'Jumbo Days', with 2 different workshops, a full day including lunch, and 'Double-Decker Days', with morning workshop, lunch, and the current Unicorn play. Worth writing for details, joining form. [Unicorn Club number: 071 379 3280].

Whirligig Theatre 14 Belvedere Drive, Wimbledon, London SW19 7BY [081-947 1732]. A touring company to look for in regional theatres and also in London during autumn and winter. Formed by David Wood, actor, writer, composer, musician, producer (with fellow Oxford graduate John Gould). Aim to give children the experience of live theatre. David, father of 2, quotes figures like '90% of the people in this country never go to theatres, so you can't expect them to take their children', or '70% of our audience have never set foot in a theatre before'. David also expounds on the very high standard demanded by children from writers and actors, not just wanting entertainment, 'a challenging audience'. I have seen what he means in sheer physical terms when the dramatic point of the play depended on the audience reaction, creating wind effects, a roof-raising storm (whooh, whooh) to drive away the baddy, an astounding, multi-coloured figure.

Whirligig plays largely to schools and the arrival of more and more crocodiles of children coming off coaches into a theatre is something to see. But if your children miss out, a pity, so look for usually weekend performances; if they saw it, reckon they would want to see it again, talk to you about it.

Children usually get a leaflet, to colour, to take further, to think about the background theme of the show. Most of David Wood's musical plays for children have a message, I think. Like road safety in *The Ideal Gnome Expedition*, the ecological problem in *The Selfish Shellfish*, and what about the dangers of paper and fire in *The Papertown Paperchase*, with such characters as the Litterbug, Lady Carrier Bag, Spike the Pen, Professor Paperback? And what about the dangers of the Paperclip Forest, Scissors Gorge, the River Ink?

Many of David Wood's musical plays for primary school children have been launched in the Whirligig circuit (now well over 25 titles), but happily you can come across them in various theatres interested in children. Like: *Gingerbread Man*, taking place on a Welsh dresser, where the newly baked Gingerbread man meets such as Herr Von Cuckoo, who has a sore throat, and sundry villians like Sleek the Mouse and the Old Bag, meaning an old teabag who lives in a teapot; or *Jack and the Giant*, where Jack, his sister, their mother, get involved with spacemen and Silver Giant, Baby Giant, who live at the top of a silver baked-bean tin tree; lots more like *The Plotters of Cabbage Patch Corner*, *Meg and Mog Show*, *Nutcracker Sweet*, *The Owl and the Pussycat Went to See . . .* , *There Was an Old Woman*, *Mother Goose's Golden Christmas* (big bad wolf, bigger badder wolf!). *The See-Saw Tree*, another environmental piece, *Save The Human*, well just turn upside down our campaigns about endangered species. Add: *The Old Man of Lochnagar* based on the book by HRH The Prince of Wales, and in 1991, by coincidence just after Roald Dahl died, *The BFG (Big Friendly Giant)*, where the puzzle word square for children in accompanying programme required finding 'Gizzardgulper' 'Frobscottle', 'Phizzwizard'.

Young National Trust Theatre
36 Queen Anne's Gate, London SW1H 9AS [071-222 9251].
A professional Theatre-in-Education Company of actors/musicians who each year invite hundreds of schoolchildren from across England, Wales and Northern Ireland to join them at National Trust properties where they explore a chosen historical theme. The main emphasis is on the children's full participation in the action and they dress appropriately for the occasion in fluted caps and other home-devised bits and bobs to get into the mood. In the course of the drama they experience at first hand the atmosphere and issues of the historical period in question. Working with the actors the children are encouraged to make decisions and take actions which will affect the outcome of the show. An educational experience aimed at pupils from 9 to 16 and supporting the new English and History National Curriculum recommendations and GCSE's

emphasis on investigative learning.

In the summer the YNTT caters for an even larger audience with its Family Shows which are part of the National Trust's Events Programme.

Regions

Biggar Little Theatre Broughton Road, Biggar, Lanarkshire ML12 6HA [0899 20631]. The International Purves Puppets in a Victorian house in 9 acres (croquet, French bowls, painting areas) of grounds, the coach-house, stables, converted into a 100-seat Victorian theatre in miniature. All types of puppetry. You may well see a line of miniature costumes on the washing-line. Fabric scraps always welcomed. Some shows: *Nessie The Loch Ness Monster*, a tall tale about Hughie, Mari and her wicked Uncle Naggie with Nessie herself saving the day (Haggis Band); *The Nutcracker*, how did the Prince become a Nutcracker?; *Johnny and the Space Machine*, Johnny and his faithful donkey are kidnapped, taken to the Purple Planet where they meet Professor Snodgrass with his flying saucer (including the cup) and his great invention the Scintintinabulator. Workshops 'The Magic of Puppetry', with the chance to try your hand at working puppets too, for groups, different ages, or creating their own show, for the school. Guided tours behind the scenes, with a talk. Facilities for the handicapped like blind visitors meeting the puppets first to touch and gauge their size, shape. Closed Wednesday.

Cannon Hill Puppet Theatre MAC, Cannon Hill Park, Birmingham B12 9QH [021-440 3838]. Director John M. Blundall. Puppets from small hand-held figures made from household objects to large elaborate rod puppets and marionettes designed and constructed in the theatre's workshops. Performs here, tours, and organizes workshop seasons in local primary schools. 5 annual productions. Performances all year, appropriate ages indicated. Shows: *Dragon Tails*, 3s–6s; *Giants, Witches and Fighting Men*, forerunner to Arthurian tales, 7s–12s; *City Fox*, a tale of wildlife in the City, 4s–7s. Arrangements can be made for parties to see the puppets being made and visit the stores where all puppets from the past over 20 years are kept – an extraordinary sight. Disabled access, induction loop.

Contact Theatre Company Oxford Road, Manchester M15 6JA [061-274 3434, box office 061-274 4400]. Founded to provide a building-based theatre for younger audiences, presenting plays which are accessible and relevant. Over 60% of the audience is aged between 14 and 25 with adaptations of children's classics for Christmas, *The Snowman, The Red Balloon, The Weirdstone of*

Brisingamen, attracting a family audience. Contact Youth Theatre, for 12s–25s living in Manchester. No auditions. Grouped in ages, after-school and evening, termtime weekly workshops. Visits to professional productions, performance projects through the year. Annual 'Playdays' examining the main themes of plays being studied for GCSE and A-level. Induction loop, wheelchair facilities.

East 15 Acting School Hatfields, Rectory Lane, Loughton 1G10 3RU [081-508 5983]. Actors of the school, used to working with children, run Young People's Theatre Workshops in the Easter and summer school holidays for 7s–16s. Each week a different project including making plays through mime, improvisation and movement with the opportunity to become involved in other theatre skills and crafts. 2-week summer course for 13s–16s. Motivation is important. Weekends with presentation to family/friends in Corbett Theatre, a converted medieval tithe barn. Workshops are in the grounds or in Hatfields, the adjacent Georgian house. Also **Galtres Theatre Company** and **East 15 Acting School** residential summer schools for 17s upwards at Sheriff Hutton Park, York with text study and research into the life and times of each play: Shakespeare, Ibsen, Chekhov, modern playwrights.

Harlequin Marionette Theatre Rhos-on-Sea, Colwyn Bay, North Wales [0492 48166]. The Eric Bramall Marionettes in the first permanent puppet theatre to be built in Britain, opened 1958. Traditional full-length figures worked by strings. Opens Christmas, Easter, spring holiday, half-terms and July–September, and for school groups any time. Some 50–60 shows. Afternoon family show will consist of 3 features, for example the *Mikado, King Neptune's Daughter,* and *Harlequin in Toyland,* a classic, a fairy-tale and a presentation where children can see how it all works. 2 shows a week, Tuesday–Thursday, a change Friday–Sunday. An adult evening show. Closed Monday. Those who went as children are now taking their children. Caters for handicapped.

Harrogate Theatre Oxford Street, Harrogate HG1 1QF [0423 502710]. Theatre courses for young people. Easter 9s–18s, improvisation, acting, voice, movement and mask. Summer 8s–11s, mornings, as above plus make-up and concluding with a presentation. Summer 11s–18s, as above plus fencing, simulated unarmed combat, script work, stage management, lighting, design, concluding with a presentation; this one non-residential or with accommodation.

National Association of Youth Theatres The Bond, 180–182 Fazeley Street, Birmingham B5 5SE [021-766 8920]. An umbrella organization which provides services and support for the around 700 Youth Theatres (involving 60,000 young people) throughout the UK. Membership scheme: monthly newsletter, free publications, preferential fees for attendance at its workshops and conferences, access to free script-loan scheme and any specific advice or support. Age range catered for in member theatres somewhere between 10 and 30, usually meeting on a weekly basis, maybe working towards a group-devised performance, or learning a wide variety of skills in workshops such as lighting, set design, music, mime, dance, mask-making, administration, circus skills.

Norwich Puppet Theatre
St James, Whitefriars, Norwich NR3 1TN [0603 629921]. Purpose-built theatre, seating 200 in tiered auditorium, inside a medieval church, a most unusual setting. Exhibition gallery. Designs and builds high-quality puppet productions in the workshops adjacent to theatre. Productions: E. Nesbit's *The Enchanted Castle*, Dahl's *James and the Giant Peach*, *The Travelling Storyteller*, *Sleeping Beauty*, *Just So*, *Owl and Pussycat*, *Brer Rabbit*. Repertoire constantly extended. Open during every school holiday and at other times. Regular workshops for children, and adults, in design, making, performance, lighting and stage management, voice, movement. Pre-school and school groups welcomed especially for the

Christmas show (November–February). Wheelchair facilities.

The Playhouse The High, Harlow, Essex [0279 424391, box office 431945]. Harlow School of Ballet, ballet and modern classes in the Studio, children accepted from age 6. Ballet Club founded in 1959 for those who dance purely for pleasure or those who go on to professional work. Summer workshop with school and club activity, followed by young choreographers' new ballets for public presentation. Also **Molecule Theatre of Science** presentations. Wheelchair access.

Queen's Theatre Billet Lane, Hornchurch, Essex RM11 1QT [040 24 56118]. 9-week Christmas family spectacular like *The Wizard of Oz*, or David Wood's *Mother Goose's Golden Christmas*, plus other family-orientated productions at different times. Children's Saturday shows: magic, clowning, puppets, a make your own puppet workshop, *Amazing Exploding Punch and Judy*, *Mr Spoon on Button Moon*, each age graded. Junior Theatre-Goers Club: badges, stickers, newsletters, competitions, for 3s–14s. School groups. Induction loop and wheelchair access.

Theatr Clwyd, Mold, Clwyd CH7 1YA [0352 55114]. Saturday Morning Drama, for 6s–16s every Saturday during school terms.

Theatre Royal Westgate Street, Bury St Edmunds, Suffolk 1P33 1QR [0284 755127]. Performances for young people at half-term, high-standard children's theatre. Youth Theatre and Dance Summer School in August for 14s upwards, technique, choreography, and a performance. The theatre has its own Dance Animateur who runs Sidekick, a youth dance company, for 14s upwards, meeting Thursday evenings, all year. All kinds of dance and an annual performance.

The World and Sooty Exhibition Shipley, see page 170.

Films

Times and customs change, including cinema-going, even the very existence of cinemas, changes to be seen in the history of the **Children's Film and Television Foundation**, household television and videos being a major effect. Yet there are still a few places where films of real children's stories are screened and even films made by children.

Children's Film and Television Foundation Ltd Goldcrest, Elstree Studios, Borehamwood, Herts WD6 1JG [081-953 0844]. The production of films especially for children was started in 1944 by the Rank Organization with the intention of combating growing delinquency among children whose home life was disrupted through evacuation and the absence of parents on war work. In 1951 the film industry formed the non-profit-making Children's Film Foundation. By the 1969 silver jubilee celebration of children's films, it was despatching features, serials, shorts, about 800 copies each week to be seen by about half a million customers between 5 and 11 who paid 6d (old pence) entry, to the Saturday cinema event.

Generally the films have children as the main characters so that children could identify with the action. The films were professionally made and many eminent actors and actresses appeared. Sometimes there is an inherent message but the crux is adventure, happening in all kinds of settings.

Some of the CFTF films appear on TV; recent screenings on the BBC resulted in viewing figures averaging over 4 million and 8 million at Christmas. CFTF notes that cartoons, serials and magazine programmes for children are plentiful on TV but full-length filmed stories are not.

Making the simplest 90-minute economically budgeted story film today would be in the region of half a million pounds, now far beyond its resources but it is still able to promote, pump-prime, occasionally part-finance feature films especially suitable for 5s–12s, in short, the family film. It sees the need for children's films of real quality to be greater not smaller. The CFTF is there to help producers fulfil that need. it is emphatically in the market for good stories.

Glenbuck Films Ltd, Glenbuck Road, Surbiton, Surrey KT6 6BT [081-399 5266]. Distribute CFTF 35 mm and 16 mm films. Only around 10 cinemas in the UK today screen them for Saturday matinées. But an extensive film library is available for hire in 16 mm, some in video format, some videos for sale, catalogue available, which could be of interest to playgroups, or to those organizing children's holiday events.

A new development from Canada, 'Tales For All', has won many international awards for its feature films designed for young people. Glenbuck Films has a selection for hire, films/videos. They feature the adventures of children in such as *Bach and Broccoli*, *The Case of the Witch who Wasn't*, *Tadpole and the Whale*, *Summer of the Colt*.

London-based

Barbican Centre Silk Street, London EC2Y 8DS [071-638 8891]. Barbican Children's Cinema Club, meets Saturdays; films and cartoons for 6s–12s. Films have included *The Secret of Nimh*, *The Muppet Movie*, *The Wizard of Oz*, *Charlotte's Web*, *Born Free*, *Flash Gordon*, *Treasure Island*, *Moonwalker*, *Labyrinth*, *The Railway Children* and the *Superman* epics.

Children join, membership fee, and may take 2 guests. No unaccompanied adults admitted. Advisable to book tickets, as performances regularly sell out.

Children's Film Unit Studio 4, 192 Queenstown Road, Battersea, London SW8 3NR [071-622 7793]. By and for up to 16s, accepted by interview and audition at the beginning of each year. Not only acting but camera, sound, lighting, make-up, continuity, prop-making, script-writing and more. Founded by Colin Finbow,

secondary school teacher, whose Forest Hill School Film Unit made many films over 10 years, including the internationally praised *The Custard Boys*, about World War II evacuees in a Suffolk village. You may still come across it.

CFU runs Saturday workshops covering camera operation, sound recording, film editing, costume and set design. The CFU makes an annual full-length feature film in the school holidays. The team is recruited from faithful attenders at the workshops, who have essentially, demonstrated serious commitment. Some may have career ambitions front- or backstage, but for many an exploration of ideas, discovering the intricacies, problems of the media.

Films: 1981, *Captain Stirrick*, filmed largely in London's Westminster School quadrangle (world premier at London Institute of Contemporary Arts, also shown on Channel 4); 1982, *A Swarm in May*, filmed in Rochester Cathedral (shown on Channel 4 on Boxing Day 1983); 1983, *Dark Enemy*; 1984, *Take Cover*, a documentary about insurance for teenagers, and a feature film, *Mr Skeeter*; 1985, *Daemon*, about a disturbed boy; 1986, *Time to Talk*, about the Samaritans' helping role, and *School for Vandals*; 1987, *Infantile Disorders*, London gang warfare; 1988, *Under The Bed*, a 'scary' tale, and *Hard Road*, about runaways; 1989, *Doombeach*, an environmental thriller.

Professional actors join in (ploughing fees back into Unit's finances), parents join in, especially for the crowd scenes.

Institute of Contemporary Arts The Mall, London SW1Y 5AH [071-930 0493]. ICA's Children's Cinema runs through the year, weekends, school holidays. Membership free with the first ticket bought and children receive a membership card and a regular newsletter. Here you could see films made by British children like *Captain Stirrick*, or *A Swarm in May* and *Mr Skeeter*, made by the Children's Film Unit; an extravagant musical like the Dr Seuss-based *The 5000 Fingers of Dr T* (featuring a giant piano with 13,200 keys, the biggest in the world, with some 500 boys bowed over the keyboard in the academy); *The King and Mr Bird*, made by French animators, with the tyrannical king outwitted by Mr Bird, shepherdess and just about everybody else including the king's lions; Gerry Anderson films, think of *Fireball XL5*, *Stingray*, *Thunderbirds*, *Captain Scarlet*, *Terrahawks*, once with the puppetmaster himself, Mr Anderson, appearing to explain, talk, demonstrate. Other series have included all the *Superman* films. Once the entire *Captain Marvel* serial was shown, lasting 3½ hours. Lots more, including *Spiderman*, *Batman*, *Flash Gordon*.

National Film Theatre South Bank, Waterloo, London SE1 8XT [071-928 3232]. Long-time Junior NFT section for under-16s, at weekends. Can be on a monthly theme like *Just William, Creatures of Fantasy*, Puffin book films, Walt Disney. Children's programme notes. Sometimes there are workshops or talks. The Junior London Film Festival, autumn half-term, is a showcase of the best new films from around the world. Sometimes an opportunity to talk to film-makers, also workshops about aspects of production like Script to Screen TV Drama Workshop, where children can meet experts and help film a drama; a video workshop on soap opera, a model animation session led by animators. Adults only admitted to Junior NFT if accompanied by children. Membership charge but include just-for-a-day type and waived for the Festival; family ticket.

Riverside Studios Crisp Road, Hammersmith, London W6 9RL [081-748 3354]. Saturday morning films for children, each programme about 1½ hours. Some titles *Asterix and the Big Fight*, *The Wizard of Oz*, *Charlotte's Web*, *Back to the Future*.

Regions

MAC Cannon Hill Park, Birmingham B12 9QH [021-440 3838]. Children's films in the school holidays like *An American Tale*, *Land Before Time*, Disabled access, induction loop.

National Museum of Film, Bradford, see page 170.

Theatr Clwyd County Civic Centre, Mold, Clwyd CH7 1YA [0352 55114]. School holiday-time films and Saturdays: *Snow White and the Seven Dwarfs, Bigfoot and the Hendersons, All Dogs Go To Heaven.*

Tyneside Cinema 10 Pilgrim Street, Newcastle-upon-Tyne NE1 6QG [091-232 8289]. Saturdays and school holidaytime films: *Asterix in Britain, Return of the Jedi, Little Mermaid, Batteries not Included, The Princess Bride, Bigfoot and the Hendersons.*

Music

Introduction of children to classical music through concerts goes back decades. There were pioneers. It is great that there is now a new wave presenting a wide range of music to children in a way that they can absorb even quite young, mostly through narrative, explanation, story-telling, accepting their short attention span. But, enjoyably, there are all kinds of audience participation which can mean singing, acting parts, trying quizzes, taking along your own instruments and joining the professionals on stage; well the distinction between stage and audience is also undefined.

But let's also think of children making music, playing instruments, not for certificates, not to become international stars, but just to enjoy the sound of music, created or listened to.

So here is music for and by children.

> **Note**: indication of age suitability is usual but never assume this means the child alone. Always check.

London-based

Fun with Music 2 Queensmead,
St John's Wood Park, London
NW8 6RE [071-722 9828]. Ann
Rachlin is a story-teller, to music.
Let's start with her school
holidaytime presentations,
(including autumn half-term,
occasionally in or around
London) in carefully defined age
groups. She sits in a splendid
high-backed peacock chair and
tells the stories she creates.
Participation? Well, on the
summertime Thames river trip
retracing King George I's
journey in 1717 to hear the first
performance of the *Water Music,*
other Thames travellers are
surprised when parents and their
children of 7–11 stand for the
Halleluja chorus as did that
King, and my daughter and I.
Once Upon the Thames is
performed in July and August.
Other, onland events can include
Musically Ever After or the *Magical
Musical Feather* for 5s–7s, or *Papa
Haydn's Surprise* or *Naughty Boys*
for 7s–11s, mostly at the Mayfair
Theatre, London, and with
music from Ravel, Prokofiev,
Rimsky-Korsakov, Debussy,
Strauss, Smetana, many more
and with the children in the
audience helping to act out the
story, on stage.

Then all year she can appear at
festivals, schools, theatres, round
the country, enchanting 5s–11s
(and adults) with a repertoire
which includes Heckerty the
musical witch who lives in her
attic, or *Beethoven's Birthday Party,*
with sundry birthday cakes as

appropriate, or the fascinating
tale of *Mozart the Miracle Maestro,*
and many more explorations
into how musicians lived,
survived.

Ann started telling the human
stories of famous classical
musicians back in the sixties,
what they got up to, their
problems, for her own children,
backed by music. That led to **Fun
with Music** with youngsters
coming to her own London
home after school for tea, stories
to music, quizzes, the under-5s
trying toy-size instruments. They
came from far and wide, more
than can be crammed into a
home.

Fun with Music classes now take
place in termtime in the Perry
Gore Room, St John's Wood
Church (on the roundabout at
Lord's). Children from all
backgrounds, colours, creeds,
say around 24 nationalities, sit
round her tea table, what she
calls a 'Musical United Nations'.
Divided into 3 groups, 3½s–5s
early afternoon, 5s–6s and
7s–11s after school. There is a
waiting list! Pupils: The Prince
and Princess of Wales's sons,
Prince William and Prince
Harry, Lord Frederick Windsor,
son of the Prince and Princess
Michael of Kent; the children of
the King and Queen of Greece,
Peter O'Toole, Judi Dench,
Edward Fox. Some now send
their own children, some have
become famous in their own
right.

In her spare time (?) Ann's
hobby is the Beethoven Fund for
Deaf Children, raising money

through music concerts to buy musical instruments which are used in schools for the deaf to teach children to speak.

Some of the **Fun with Music** EMI/HMV CDs and cassettes, packaging designed by children: *Once Upon the Thames, Happy Birthday, Mr Beethoven!, A Musical Journey to the Moon* (*Holst's Planet Suite*), *Mandy and the Magic Butterfly* (3s–6s), *The King who Broke his Promise, Nurse Goose and the Magic Doors.*

Ernest Read Music Association
9 Cotsford Avenue, New Malden, Surrey KT3 5EU [081-942 0318]. Ernest Read, Professor at the Royal Academy of Music, started a regular series of Children's Concerts in London in 1945 to inspire youngsters through the opportunity of hearing live music in the concert hall. These are now held at the Royal Festival Hall on Saturdays during an October–May season. Programmes are designed particularly to appeal to children in the 7–12 age range and both choice of music and the style of its presentation take account of a child's limited span of concentration. Even so, parents are advised not to take children under 6.

Different orchestras from London and elsewhere play for different concerts and include, on occasion, more specialized ensembles like the orchestra of the Royal Opera House or the orchestra of Birmingham Royal Ballet. Programmes feature movements from standard classics – like the *New World Symphony* and Beethoven's *Fifth Symphony* – music from opera and ballet such as *The Magic Flute, Swan Lake* and *Coppelia,* often with a linking and 'voice-over' story told by narrators like Johnny Morris and David Kossoff, as well as special children's favourites like *Peter and the Wolf* and *The Sorcerer's Apprentice.*

Children also take an active part. Gifted youngsters from the country's specialist music schools often perform concertos with the orchestra and everyone in the audience takes part in a song rehearsed at the beginning of the concert and performed in the course of it, helped along by a 120-strong children's unison choir, who also perform a song of their own. Songs are sometimes purely recreational ('Drunken Sailor', 'John Brown's Body', etc.) and sometimes contribute to a broader musical scheme – such as 'The Toreador's Song' as one item in the *Story and Music of Carmen.* For the Christmas concert a mixed-voice schools' choir is formed of 13s and upwards.

There is an annual song competition for under-14s in 3 age groups, working singly or collaborating with others. A concert magazine is on sale at the concerts with programme notes and illustrations, short articles, a story, puzzles, even a cartoon strip of Weedy Reedy, the pest of the Festival Hall, who gets into various scrapes, as well as pages of contributions from the young concert-goers themselves.

As a natural progression a series of 3 Family Concerts is presented each season designed to appeal to children over 10 as well as to adults. One is a Family Christmas Concert at the Royal Festival Hall with a first half of orchestral music – such as a Suite from Humperdinck's *Hansel and Gretel*, *Winter* from Vivaldi's *Four Seasons*, Tchaikovsky's *Sleeping Beauty* suite, etc. – and a second half of carols and seasonal choral music. The other 2 concerts, held at the Barbican Hall, have featured, variously, Music for Stage and Screen, Ballet Music and Opera. Singers, choirs and dancers appear with the Ernest Read Symphony Orchestra at the concerts which include not only introductions to the music but also some simple explanations and demonstrations by a leading dancer of the 'language' of movement and mime in the danced extracts.

General enquiries about concerts, brochures, details and application forms for choirs and the song competition should be made to ERMA. Tickets can be booked through ERMA or from the box offices, early application advisable.

Teenagers of 15–16 upwards are also accepted at the annual ERMA Summer School held July–August at Wantage, Oxfordshire, offering courses for 2 symphony orchestras, choral singers, student conductors and listeners. Brochure from ERMA.

Additionally an annual Junior Orchestral Summer Course for 12s–18s has been organized in association with ERMA. This is held over a week at Bradfield College, near Reading, Berks. 3 Orchestras and a concert band rehearse during the morning and late afternoon (participants have opportunities for outdoor sports in the afternoon); there are weekend concerts. Brochure (large SAE please) from John Morrell, Course Organizer, 403 Pinner Road, North Harrow, Middx HA1 4HN.

Yorke Trust A charity, about making and providing child-size double basses for children, so think of this as mini-bass, in the same way as small children learn on suitable-size violins, violas, cellos. But also very much about bringing in teachers, and child musicians in various courses in various locations, workshops, recitals, master-classes. Details from Rodney Slatford, 31 Thornhill Square, London N1 1BQ [071-607 0849].
Additionally: the new Royal Northern College of Music Junior Strings Project will give the highest possible quality string training to children from the age of 6. Enquiries: School of Strings, RNCM, 124 Oxford Road, Manchester M13 9RD.

Regions

Aldeburgh Foundation High Street, Aldeburgh, Suffolk 1P15

5AX [0728 45935]. Wonderful for schools: Snape Sounds for Schools bring together children from 17 Suffolk schools for *Enchanted Places*, based on A.A. Milne's poems, performing at Snape Maltings and the Bury St Edmunds Theatre Royal; A Celebration of Schools' Music, nearly 2000 Suffolk pupils in music, dance and visual arts projects at Snape. Then the Britten-Pears School for Advanced Musical Studies at Snape offers young singers and musicians from all over the world the chance to gain a foothold in the professional music world.

Special children's and family concerts are a regular part of the concert series throughout the year and especially in the school holidays. Example: 'Percussion Party!', at Christmas, for 4s upwards, invited to take a drum and participate in a specially written piece before hearing *The Snowman* with the story narrated by Nerys Hughes. Accompanying adults admitted.

Avril Dankworth National Children's Music Camps Write: Mrs Y. Speller, Ye Barn, Spinney Lane, Aspley Guise MK17 8JT [0908 583025]. Avril Dankworth, freelance music educator, is dedicated to helping everyone enjoy the pleasures of music and of making music. The camps, which she founded in 1970, are held in the school summer holidays at Wavendon, Buckinghamshire, home of Avril's brother John, and Cleo Laine. The aim is to bring together children of all musical levels to share their enjoyment of music in a social environment. Everyone lives under canvas; all activities are in the open air, weather permitting.

No stipulated grade of entry. Avril: 'Musically, these holidays are unique, since there is no qualification for entry; we want to attract all children interested in music-making, providing a training ground for complete beginners and further study for the experienced and the timetable is tailored to the participants' instruments, ability and interests.'

4 1-week camps: 2 for 13s–17s, 2 for 8s–12s. A wide range of musical interests and experiences is offered. Workshops graded according to instrument(s), age, ability: strings, woodwind, brass, percussion, guitar, recorder, keyboards, also a camp orchestra, vocal, jazz and pop groups. Teenagers have a chance to try steel drums, handbells, harmonica, piano, accordion, composition. For everyone the programme includes sports, swimming, dancing, concerts, camp fire. Part of each day is devoted to rehearsing an operetta, performed at week's end, to which everyone contributes, singing, playing, acting, dancing, making costumes, props and scenery.

Finchcocks: Living Museum of Music Finchcocks, Goudhurst,

Kent TN17 1HH [0580 211702]. Richard Burnett weaving a tapestry of sound on the open days (see page 70). Special events for young people, like a recital for families on keyboards, horns of all kinds; a recital by up to 18s, soloists, small chamber groups, small choirs (auditions held throughout the season, keyboard players perform on instruments from the collection and can receive tuition and practice facilities beforehand); workshops, master-classes, chamber music and recitals by soloists, singers and chamber musicians and tutors. Then schools have a demonstration on the instruments with keyboard players welcome to try them out.

Gerard and Jean Jean Phillips playing the piano, Chopin, Bach, Debussy, Prokofiev, Grainger, Beethoven, Schubert, etc. Gerard Benson telling the story, well, acting the story. Lots of audience participation, especially singing, concerts always begin with a song, but otherwise opportunities for joining in like making the sound-effects, a creaking gate, an exploding dragon, a flowing river (!). The Christmas event includes carols, songs, poems, jokes, riddles, Gerard and Jean's *Mummers' Play* with Gerard playing all parts, with 7 or 8 rudimentary costumes, plus props, on stage, and everybody rounds it all off with singing titles such as 'Star-Eyes and the Sneezing King', 'Mr

Noselighter', 'A Trunk Full of Elephants', 'The Gingerbread Man', 'Epaminondas and His Aunty', 'The Stolen Turnips', even 'Little Red Riding Hood'. Family entertainments, parents, grandparents, children 5s–10s (children are not left). Have given 200 concerts at London's Purcell Room. Now, short regional tours including festivals – Cumbria, Nottingham, Kent, even Kenya. More information: Jean Phillips, Gothic Cottage, 22 Orchard Street, Canterbury, Kent CT2 8AP [0227 767282].

National Association of Youth Orchestras Ainslie House, 11 St Colme Street, Edinburgh EH3 6AG [031-225 4606]. Formed in 1961 to represent youth orchestras and inter-school orchestras, chamber, symphonic wind, swing, whether independent or under local authorities. So very much an interchange of ideas not only national but international, and an information source.

NAYO presented the first Festival of British Youth Orchestras in Edinburgh during the Edinburgh International Festival in 1980, giving orchestras a wider audience, a new experience, and have repeated this since. The Glasgow Festival of British Youth Orchestras, running concurrently with the Edinburgh event, was started in 1988 and this too continues on an annual basis. It is hoped that by presenting such programmes of youth orchestral concerts the association will enable the public to have a more comprehensive idea of the standards at which the youth orchestras throughout the country are aiming. A highly successful Conducting Bursary was held in 1985, 1987 and 1989 and it is now alternating annually with the British Reserve Insurance Conducting Prize so that NAYO is offering 2 valuable biennial opportunities to young conductors for study abroad. A new benefit for members is the British Reserve Insurance Youth Orchestra Awards Scheme, started in 1990, when 2 youth orchestras were awarded financial assistance for special projects. NAYO gratefully acknowledges financial assistance from many sources. Every summer the association organizes an Anglo-German Youth Music Week, meeting alternately in Germany and England. The emphasis is on providing the opportunity for musicians between 15 and 25 of both countries to join in playing a programme of music biased towards the 20th century which is liable to be known by repute but for the rehearsal of which little possibility would be available in their normal environment. NAYO's publications include a comprehensive *Register of Youth Orchestras* and the bulletin *Full Orchestra* with news of youth orchestras, courses, future events, repertoire, foreign travel. It can provide information on editions and publishers, ideas for concert programmes, exchange of platforms within the UK,

foreign travel and is always happy to deal with enquiries about youth music whether from members, the public, or individual young musicians.

National Children's Orchestra
157 Craddocks Avenue, Ashtead, Surrey KT21 1NU [0372 276857]. Vivienne Price, music teacher, organizer and conductor of youth orchestra, in 1978 achieved her ambition of providing talented 7–13-year-olds with the opportunity of playing together in a full symphony orchestra. HRH the Princess of Wales became Patron in 1982 and her visit to see what goes on, how it works is of course fully recorded. She was presented with a quarter-size violin for Prince William, not just handed over but played by a young violinist. The idea is of course making music together, stretching capabilities, to take back to school or youth orchestras, but also more than that.

Mainstream is the 8-day residential Easter course which has been held in Eastbourne, Skegness, Hereford, York, Sussex, Manchester, Berkshire, culminating in public concerts. Newish are the 5-day summer courses in Edinburgh, also with concerts. Think of some 6 hours' rehearsal times, learning many new pieces, giving every child the chance to use his/her instrument. But add in lots of indoor/outdoor activities which can be informal music-making but also theatre visits, treasure hunts, outings, playing games, rounders, football, swimming, socializing with same age group, similarly music-addicted.

Auditions are held in major cities all over the country in October. Children play 2 pieces of their own choice, and sight-read. Selection is on a competitive basis.

But let's think in age levels. It's a wide range. Older (!) string players could be reaching grades 7–8, but younger ones should not be deterred since age is taken into account. Flautists, clarinettists, trumpeters, need to be at least grade 6.

Younger ones could be in the Training Orchestra, playing as a group, moving into the next level. Now 4 orchestras, Main (under-14s), Second (under-13s), Third (under-12s), full symphony orchestras and training, strings only (under-11s). Other specialist courses are held for percussionists, woodwind and brass players. You pay, of course, for residential events.

But for music-oriented families, it's very much worth keeping in touch with what is happening next. NCO application form sets out information wanted (examinations, schools), gives dates of current courses, lots more. It's a charity so SAE please.

The National Children's Wind Orchestra of Great Britain The Bourne, 20 Salisbury Avenue, Harpenden, Herts AL5 2QG [05827 60014]. Formed by David and Gillian Johnston, realizing the enormous development in the standard of wind-playing at the 10-plus age range. So this is bringing children together, meeting those from other parts of the country, sharing a common interest. So for woodwind, brass, saxophone, double bass, percussion players, grades 6 to 8 though those still studying for grade 6 may also apply, ages 10–15, to form annual Wind Orchestra of around 85 players. These are selected by auditions in October/November in, say, Belfast, Cambridge, Coventry, Edinburgh, London, Manchester, Worcester, York. Actual residential course held at Easter at Oakham School, Leics., the repertoire chosen with a 'symphonic outlook', 2 concerts given during period, one chamber music, the other a finale for the entire ensemble. Facilities also include the indoor swimming pool, squash courts, sports hall.

Christmas lectures

A number of institutes, colleges and societies organize events for children during the Christmas school holidays. Sometimes free, sometimes charges; mostly tickets needed; would always recommend booking, keeping in touch, knowing about what's coming up, since they are very popular, can be oversubscribed.

The Historical Association 59a Kennington Park Road, London SE11 4JH [071-735 3901]. Lectures held at the Museum of London. On life as a child in Victorian times; life in Roman London (plus the Ermine Street Guard); Vikings (plus men in Viking costume); the London Blitz and wartime London life. For 8s–13s.

Manchester Medical Society John Rylands University Library, Oxford Road, Manchester M13 9PP [061-273 6048]. 'Madmen and Geniuses', discussing the popular notion that you have to be mad to be a genius; 'Heart Surgery – What It Is and How It Developed'. 15s–18s but no strict adherence to age limit.

Registrar's Office The University, 6 Kensington Terrace, Newcastle-upon-Tyne NE1 7RU

[091-222 6000]. 'Water, Earth and Us', where it comes from, what it costs, pollution; 'Measuring the Earth', how the Greeks and Romans did it, modern methods, to satellites, by photography. For 10s–16s. Also Easter lectures, could be on artworks. SAE please.

Richmond Scientific Society 22 Denbigh Gardens, Richmond, Surrey TW10 6EL [081-940 5941]. 'Motion – the Constant Challenge', human, natural and man-made, motor cars, space rockets, etc; 'Wind Power: Britain's Best Renewable Energy Option'. For 12s–16s. Started in Christmas holidays but moved to termtime, November, at request of teachers. Held at Richmond-upon-Thames College, Egerton Road, Twickenham.

Royal Aeronautical Society 4 Hamilton Place, London W1V OBQ [071-499 3515]. Could be such as 'To Fly By Night', about night vision systems, so talks, videos, equipment, including robot called Piros. Can be termtime, about the military and civil avionics industry for 14s–18s considering a career in the aerospace industry.

Royal College of Obstetricians and Gynaecologists 27 Sussex Place, Regent's Park, London NW1 4RG [071-262 5425]. Such as 'The Miracle of Human Conception' with modern scientific applications on aiding such a development, told through talks, slides, films, for

12s–18s, or 'Dangerous Journeys', how each of us managed to be born, for 14s–18s. Held in early December.

Royal College of Surgeons of England 35–43 Lincoln's Inn Fields, London WC2A 3PN [071-405 3474]. Such as 'The Romance of Surgery: Operations on the Heart', 'You Too Can Save a Life – Now!', 'The Sixth-Former and Medicine', 'Stories from Skeletons', 'Cavities, Cancer and Caring: Some Challenges of Contemporary Dental Surgery', 'This is no Humbug – the Early History of Anaesthesia'. For 12s–18s. Tours of the Hunterian Museum have a minimum age of 14, preference given to 16s–18s, parents requested to give way.

Royal Institute of British Architects 66 Portland Place, London W1N 4AD [071-580 5533]. Could be practical demonstrations on how buildings work and how architects design them, 14s–18s; workshops preparing a brief and drawings for a new Docklands building, 14s–17s; designing a life-size space for a person, animal or object, 8s–13s. Also held at Easter.

Royal Institution 21 Albemarle Street, London W1X 4BS [071-409 2992]. Groupings of talks, say courses, or single lectures, for 10s–17s, always stimulating, unexpected, lively, shown on TV. Such titles as 'Atoms for Enquiring Minds: a Circus of Experiments', 'Common Sense', 'Machines in Motion', covering movement on the ground, in the air. The lectures are open to non-members. The RI also has a junior associate membership subscription for 11s–18s offering information on what's going on, discounts, annual visits, summer holidays, to places of interest.

Royal Society of Arts John Adam Street, Adelphi, London WC2N 6EZ [071-930 5115]. Could be a lecture, 'Stagecoach to Supertrain' or 'An Afternoon of Magic', 'The Secrets of Being a Clown', say, for 8s–18s, and followed by tea and cakes, not unusual in the Christmas lectures scene. Also at Easter.

Sport

A case of going and asking, at local level. If there is a riding school around, facilities, tuition for youngsters can be taken for granted; but the local tennis club could have specifically reserved court times for juniors and summer holiday tuition; football teams, competing in local leagues, may often only exist because of the dedication of organizing parents and the sympathy of sports clubs who lend their fields for practice.

I have listed first around a handful of centres which cater for children especially during the school holidays as examples. They may not be near you. Why not go and ask your local swimming pool, sports centre, what they offer children on the basis of 'if not, why not'? Look under Round up for the cities, districts, publishing what's on for children in the holidays and generally including sporting activities. Summer Camps for children (pages 336–40) tend to offer the option of 'multi-activities', the chance to taste a variety of sports, and most useful, too, when you consider the cost of appropriately equipping a child for a sport that may turn out to be a 9-day wonder. The individual centres I have listed also offer the chance to try before you buy, since the equipment is usually provided.

But there may be a strong inclination towards a talent for one particular sport. I asked Governing Bodies of Sport what they offer the young and report where appropriate.

Note: indication of age suitability is usual but never assume this means the child alone. Always check.

London

Leisure Services, London Borough of Greenwich 147 Powis Street, Woolwich, London SE18 6JL [081-854 0055]. A wide-ranging programme of activities for young people including play, sports, arts and entertainment. All-year-round activities are expanded during school holiday periods and encouragement is given to local voluntary groups to create their own programmes. An extensive activities magazine is available free each summer.

Westminster Children's Sports Centre Crompton Street, London W2 [071-724 0038]. **The only one in the country designed entirely for children**, meaning all the equipment is for their height and age instead of the usual for adults. The hall, equivalent in size to 5 badminton courts, offers 5s–12s tuition in all kinds of ball games, also badminton, judo, gymnastics, trampolining, mini-hockey, much more, in 10-week courses. Parents have to register their children on first visit, providing a contact in case of emergency. There is a regular family session Wednesday when parents are welcome, also school holiday programmes. Very much a community facility and the community has great pride in it. The centre was opened in 1984 and was achieved through the pioneering work of the Westminster Play Association [147 Church Street, London W2 1NA, phone 071-258 3817], a charity which manages it. It was financed with national and local government support aid from charities and commercial companies. It is built on what was derelict land near Paddington Green and the structure itself, 'light-weight', looks from the outside like a green bubble and has been compared with a stretched igloo and an inflated maggot. Not a lot of use if you live in another part of London, let alone the other side of the country. But it is an example of what can be achieved.

Regions

Centre for Sport and Physical Recreation Lancaster University, Lancaster LA1 4YW [0524 65201 ext 4000]. Unusual in being open to the public. School holiday Fun Days with a wide range of sports including swimming, aeroball, football, gymnastics and trampolining. Coaching and supervision by centre staff. Places limited, book in advance. Also after-school and Saturday classes including judo, tennis, short tennis. Midday parent and child swimming.

The Dome Doncaster Leisure Park, Bawtry Road, Doncaster DN4 7FD [0302 370888]. 'Kids' Club' for 5s–10s, £4.50 a year: quarterly newsletter, badges, stickers, pens, Saturday morning free admission to swimming pools and skating-rinks if accompanied by admission-paying adult, monthly Saturday Club Party with games, films, songs, stories, competitions.

Indoor Recreation Dept Cabot House, Deanery Road, Bristol BS1 5TZ [0272 223519]. A source of information but simpler to check with your nearest centre. Look for *year-round* sessions, family sessions, pre-school, a wide variety of sports (trampolining, badminton, short tennis, 5-a-side, roller skating, gymnastics, squash, more), school holidaytime events and activities, say 8s–14s.

Robin Cousins Sports Centre West Town Road, Avonmouth, Bristol [0272 823514].

Easton Leisure Centre Thrissel Street, Easton, Bristol [0272 558840].

Horfield Sports Centre Crow Lane, Henbury, Bristol [0272 521650].

Kingsdown Sports Centre Portland Street, Kingsdown, Bristol [0272 426582].

Whitchurch Sports Centre Banfield, Whitchurch, Bristol [0272 838505].

Lee Valley Regional Park Authority See page 106 Essex, for addresses, phone numbers. Picketts Lock Leisure Centre; Lea Bridge Riding School; Eastway Sports Centre. School holidaytime activities/courses.

Leisure Centre College Road, Oswestry, Shropshire SY11 2SA [0691 659349]. Summer and Easter holiday activities for 5s upwards including most racket sports, team games (including bulldog, pirates, etc.) roller-skating, coaching courses and tournaments. Swimming pool activities including games, fun races. Children are cared for during set session times. At all times a wide variety of courses, sessions on a regular basis.

National Sports Centre for Wales Sophia Gardens, Cardiff CF1 9SW [0222 397571]. Holidaytime courses, activities for school children, say 6s–17s, grouped according to appropriate ability, age. Could be archery, association football, badminton, fencing, short tennis, netball, small-bore shooting, squash, all kinds of different swimming achievements, table tennis, trampolining. But also get hold of the publications on year-round courses by the Sports Council for Wales, same address. Courses for children in such as archery, association football, badminton, dancing, fencing, judo, squash, swimming, short tennis, trampolining, more. The swimming side includes mother and baby classes, mother and toddler classes but also, recruiting guinea pigs, between 6 and 12, to help in the training of teachers. Very much worth while keeping in touch, finding out what's going on either specifically for children or for families, including residential activities. Summertime Festival of Outdoor Sport offers 'come and try it' sessions for all ages.

Governing bodies of sport

Amateur Fencing Association
88 Perham Road, West
Kensington, London W14 9SP
[071-385 7442]. One of the
oldest of sports and even
possible in wheelchairs, as in the
Paraplegic Games. Leaflets
(SAE): *Children's Guide*, about the
swords, equipment, clothes,
language and warning about not
fencing without qualified
supervision and correct
equipment; *Fencing – A Modern
Sport*, about achievement awards,
coaching schemes, quarterly
journal, competitions, insurance,
organizing clubs, classes. Your
nearest club: ask AFA. Fencing in
schools: Mr Len Harris, 25
Ravensworth Road, London
NW10 5NP [081-969 9924].

Amateur Swimming Association
Secretary: D.A. Reeves, Harold
Fern House, Derby Square,
Loughborough LE11 0AL [0509
230431]. Books by mail order:
*The ASA Guide to Better Swimming,
Anyone Can Swim* (including
children and those with
disabilities), *Swimming For All,
Swimming Games and Activities,
Teach Your Child to Swim, Water
Activities for Parents and Babies,
The Teaching of Swimming* (for
teachers). Also *Swim All the Way
with the ASA*, the awards scheme.
Swim For Your Life is the
consultative committee's report
on the teaching of swimming by
schools.

**British Amateur Rugby League
Association** West Yorkshire
House, 4 New North Parade,
Huddersfield HD1 5JP [0484
544131]. An extraordinarily
comprehensive annual record in
BARLA's *Official Handbook*
(about the size of a small brick):
games, results, personalities
(international); Youth Player of
the Year; rules; the national
coaching scheme with coaches'
names and addresses; member
clubs, with contact addresses,
junior and youth leagues.
Welcome to Rugby League, £1
(comic style), explains the game
at mini-league level with
illustrations, of young players,
aimed at under-10s, with codes of
conduct for players,
coach/parent/teacher,
spectators, referees and officials.
The English Schools Rugby League,
competition rules, qualified
referees, the Secretary's Report
on developments in schools.

The British Horse Society British
Equestrian Centre, Stoneleigh,
Kenilworth, Warwickshire
CV8 2LR [0203 696697]. BHS's
Want to go Riding? should be
closely read before a child even
goes near a horse/pony and well
before buying one. BHS Welfare
Dept knows about ponies cast
aside when the novelty wears off.
Leaflets: *The Cost of Keeping a First
Horse or Pony* (time and
commitment as well as money);
*Buying, Leasing or Borrowing
Horses*; *Careers with Horses, What
and Where*; and *Riding Holidays*.
Riding tests at approved riding
establishments. Pony Club,
owning or having access to a
pony, for under-21s, over 370

branches in the UK, show jumping, competitions, mounted games, fun: Membership Secretary, The Pony Club, BEC. SAEs welcomed. Annual *Where to Ride* is a solid, comprehensive guide to over 550 inspected and approved riding establishments throughout the British Isles, riding holidays, buying your mount, career opportunities, more, £3.95 from book stores or adding £1.05 from BHS Approvals Dept, BEC.

British Judo Association 9 Islington High Street, London N1 9LQ [071-833 4424]. A qualified coach is most important. Clubs registered with the association provide them and an up-to-date list of such clubs in your district can be obtained from the association. Age: not under-8s who have their own. 'Mon' grades for 8s–15s (Mon meaning gate and there are 18 gates through which a junior can pass). However, there is the Kai scheme for under-8s, who can study simple actions and refereeing terms and then demonstrate them, earning certificates and badges. BJA can supply badges of all kinds and a list of suppliers of suits and mats. For schools (and affiliated to the BJA) the British Schools Judo Association (General Secretary, Simon Hicks), 21 Finborough Road, Tooting, London SW17 9HY. Composed largely of school teachers and they organize school tournaments around the country throughout the year. BJA-approved Easter and

summer camps in Scotland for juniors (and seniors). Information: Club Sportif, 36 Ellen's Glen Loan, Edinburgh EH17 7QN [031-666 2355].

British Orienteering Federation Riversdale, Dale Road North, Darley Dale, Matlock, Derbyshire DE4 2HX [0629 734042]. Has been called 'the thought sport'. Involves navigation between given points on foot, walking, jogging or running, with the aid of a specially drawn map and compass. National awards scheme for all ages, even 10 or younger. 2 informative leaflets *Discover a Hidden Local Leisure Activity* and *Getting Started into Orienteering* are illustrated with participating youngsters who enjoy the outdoor sport, attractive locations, challenge of decisions. Events usually held Sunday mornings or summer weekday evenings. Find your local club: SAE 9in x 6in marked 'GI Pack' (general information pack) to BOF. Membership includes under-18s and family. Courses, instructional films, holidays. Information sheet, leaflet *Orienteering* for schools and a teachers' Open Learning Course.

English Ski Council Area Library Building, The Precinct, Halesowen, West Midlands B63 4AJ [021-501 2314]. Run by skiers, for skiers. Leaflets on: *Ski Racing*; *Freestyle Skiing* (clubs' addresses); *Nordic Skiing* (equipment, centres, holidays); *Grass Skiing*; *Dry Ski Slope List*.

Award scheme. *The Ski-Way Code*, video for leaders/organizers and pupils. *Ski Course Organizer Handbook* £5, principally for teachers taking parties of young people on skiing trips.

English Table Tennis Association Queensbury House, Havelock Road, Hastings, East Sussex TN34 1HF [0424 722525]. Would you believe this sport has had names like Gossima and Whiff-Whaff and Ping-Pong? ETTA is campaigning to increase the participation and opportunities for women and girls and produces a bright and glossy poster of a sparkling schoolgirl in action and a leaflet *Women and Girls in Table Tennis*. In more general terms they advise contacting a local club and having a go, any problems phone them; they have a leaflet describing the sport, equipment, suppliers, a separate Competitions Dept (categories include under-11s) and Dunlop Skills Award Scheme. The English Schools' Table Tennis Association, Mr C. Henry, Hon General Secretary, Engelberg, Badger Lane, Woolley Moor, Derby DE5 6FG [0246 590164 home, or 413145 school] also organizes team and individual championships for children under 11, 12, 16 and 19 at the local, county, regional, national and international level.

The Football Association 16 Lancaster Gate, London W2 3LW [071-402 7151]. Did you know that in England in the Middle Ages 'A wild and brutal kind of game was played in which whole towns or villages took part, the object being to drive a ball from one district to another by fair means or foul'? No, neither did I until I read the *History of the FA*, formed in 1863 and establishing official rules. FA publications: *Playing the Game*, the young footballer's guide to behaviour like not jumping all over each other when your team scores; *Football As a Career*. All FA-approved courses are organized by the local County Football Associations; the office can give you the appropriate address. 'Soccer Star' scheme, courses, awards, a book and a video on how to acquire the essential soccer skills. 'Soccer Star Funweeks', FA's officially recognized holiday courses, with instruction from qualified coaches, games, competitions, for 6s–16s, Easter holidays onwards, at over 250 venues, and residential courses at Chester, Doncaster, Lilleshall, in August. All 'Soccer Star' information from 22-24A The Broadway, Darkes Lane, Potters Bar, Herts EN6 2HH [0707 50057].

The Grand National Archery Society 7th Street, National Agricultural Centre, Stoneleigh, Kenilworth CV8 2LG [0203 696631]. Requirements: a preparedness for self-discipline. Attitudes: serious or mature behaviour as a ballistic sport *but* this does not preclude enjoyment in any way. Cost: do not buy equipment before attending a club. Adequate equipment can be under £70. Age 9 upwards but some younger are accommodated. Nearest location: SAE to office; over 1000 clubs Shetlands to Channel Islands. Duke of Edinburgh Awards and the society's own performance badges. Coaching: most GNAS clubs or through them. The society also runs residential coaching courses for the more advanced. Approved holidaytime opportunities: (a) being a member of GNAS club (b) PGL Young Adventure (see page 340) have instructors the society has taught and examined. Association for Archery in Schools, Secretary Mr C. Fletcher-Campbell, Bloxham School, Bloxham, Banbury, Oxon OX15 4PE.

The Lawn Tennis Association
The Queen's Club, West Kensington, London W14 9EG [071-385 2366]. Soundest way to learn is through the teaching of a LTA-qualified coach; lists in the LTA *Handbook*. There are about 2500 tennis clubs in Great Britain, usually offering junior coach programmes. New: LTA Trust Star Club Programme for 8s–16s to encourage youngsters to take up the game in places open to all, like publicly owned tennis courts; by 1990 there were 200 3-Star Clubs (organized nationally and subsidized by the LTA Trust) and 600 Star Centres (organized by local authorities and the County LTA) offering opportunities to 22,500 children. Wherever you play, join the LTA and get your free Rating, a number referring to standard of play in order to play in tournaments, matched against opponents of the same standard. Leaflets and booklets: *Star Club Programme*; *Short Tennis* (played with foam balls and plastic rackets) for the very young, say 5s upwards; *Tennis Awards*; *A Career in Coaching*; *Everyone for Tennis*; *Parents are Important Too* (dos and don'ts like post-mortems, a stream of instructions, making a child fearful of failure); *Tennis in London* (where, events, tournaments); *British Schools Lawn Tennis Association Yearbook*; *Rover Junior Tennis Initiative*, scholarships for highly motivated under-14s of proven performance. Residential tennis courses for 12s–16s who already play regularly: LTA Office, Bisham Abbey, nr Marlow, Bucks [0628 483084].

National Skating Association of Great Britain Ltd 15–27 Gee Street, London EC1V 3RE [071-253 3824]. Represents the interests of all skaters in Britain, ice and roller, excluding hockey. Under-16 membership group. If you have not found out by local enquiries, Association can tell you your nearest rink in the UK. New National Award Scheme, launched 1990, badges and certificates, all standards, beginners to experts, all ages, basic, Figure, Free, Dance, Speed skating. Most rinks have instructors, or alternatively contact the British Ice Teachers'

Association, (Miss L. James, Hon Secretary), 30 Onslow Avenue, Richmond, Surrey TW10 6QB, who may also offer advice on career prospects. SAE please.

Squash Rackets Association
Westpoint, 33–34 Warple Way, Acton, London W3 0RQ [081-746 1616]. Can supply enquirers with a list of coaches and clubs in your county and a basic 1-sheet explanation of the game, scoring, service, strokes, tactics, rules. *Starting Squash* video aimed at encouraging 8s–10s to start the game; 7 minutes long and costing £6 from SRA including postage. Junior Skills Award, red, bronze, silver, gold star, tested by any qualified leader, teacher or coach. Information on courses for would-be coaches, needing to be 17 plus.

More information on sports

The Sports Council's Regional Offices Contact the Information officer.

Yorkshire and Humberside, Coronet House, Queen Street, Leeds LS1 4PW [0532 436443].

East Midlands, Grove House, Bridgford Road, West Bridgford, Nottingham NG2 6AP [0602 821887].

Northern Region, Aykley Heads, Durham DH1 5UU [091-384 9595].

Eastern Region, 26 Bromham Road, Bedford MK40 2QP [0234 45222].

North-West, Astley House, Quay Street, Manchester M3 4AE [061-834 0338].

West Midlands, Metropolitan House, 1 Hagley Road, Five Ways, Birmingham B16 8TT [021-456 3444].

Greater London and South-East, PO Box 480, Crystal Palace National Sports Centre, Ledrington Road, London SE19 2BQ [081-778 8600].

Southern Region, 51A Church Street, Caversham, Reading, Berks [0734 483311].

South-Western Region, Ashlands House, Ashlands, Crewkerne, Somerset TA18 7LQ [0460 73491].

The Scottish Sports Council, Caledonia House, South Gyle, Edinburgh EH12 9DQ [031-317 7200].

The Sports Council for Wales, National Sports Centre, Sophia Gardens, Cardiff CF1 9SW [0222 397571].

The Sports Council for Northern Ireland, House of Sport, Upper Malone Road, Belfast BT9 5LA [0232 381222].

Books and libraries

Public libraries are a major source of information on what's on locally, and they're especially useful in school holidays – look for posters, leaflets. Children's sections may offer more than the (never-to-be-denigrated) chance to borrow books; over a wide age range there are such as story times and sundry activities, book-connected; some areas pour resources into attracting children through various ingenious ways towards the immense life-long satisfaction of book reading.

Then there is book *buying*. Your well-read child will be holding on to the cream on bookshelves for rereading into adulthood, parenthood.

Over the last 20 years we have had a revolution in children's literature, and I mean literature, in some instances far superior to what has been published for adults.

Fortunately there is guidance for parents, grandparents, wanting to buy a book as a present. There are always classics at the back of the mind like the Pooh stories, *Wind in the Willows*, Rev Awdry's railway stories, but today's parents are faced with lots of new characters, TV-expanded, new titles, new publishers, in the bookshop, or on the rack in the local multi-purpose shop.

If your school has a book club, selling books, that is one way through the jungle of what is published.

This section has been arranged alphabetically by name.

Books For Your Children
34 Harborne Road, Edgbaston,
Birmingham B15 3AA [021-454
5453/4344]. Launched in the
mid sixties by Anne Wood,
secondary schoolteacher, who
found herself going to parents'
meetings, saying, all right, of
course build in all the things we
know raise healthy children, but
what about the rest,
imagination, reading.

Since then she has founded
the Federation of Children's
Book Groups, see below, edited
Yorkshire TV's *The Book Tower*
and acquired many awards. Her
independent production
company Ragdoll Productions
(UK) Ltd, which specializes in
children's programmes, now
owns *Books For Your Children*.
Ragdoll has produced *POB* for
Channel 4, *Story Time* for BBC
Education, *Playbox* and *The
Magic Mirror* for ITV, *BOOM!* for
Channel 4, *Rosie and Jim* for
ITV. Anne is also a founding
member of British Action for
Children's Television (see
page 313). The campaigning
goes on.

Thrice-yearly publication,
specially useful for reading pre-
summer hols, all kinds of
interests, or pre-Christmas when
looking for presents, for what
has been published over the
year, mostly written by those
who have themselves tried books
on children, seen the reaction,
so lots of involvement, how they
have found things. Basically an
informed way through the
wealth of publications for the
young. Wide age range.

Children's Book Foundation
Book House, 45 East Hill,
London SW18 2QZ [081-870
9055]. The children's division of
the educational charity Book
Trust (formerly National Book
League). Children's reference
library, consisting of every
children's book published
during the previous 2 years,
open to the public
Monday–Friday 9 a.m. – 5 p.m.
Also information on current
children's literature, posters,
bookmarks, stickers, useful for
Book Weeks, etc. Authorbank
service provides information on
most children's writers and
illustrators (children are author-
led, want to read every book, say,
by Ahlbergs) and a guide to
authors, poets, illustrators, story-
tellers willing to visit schools,
participate in book events – free
to members.

**Community Leisure Services
Dept (Libraries)** Dunsterville
House, Manchester Road,
Rochdale OL11 3RB [0706
47474]. Check your local library
for details, and *Holiday
Happenings* leaflet. Story-telling
sessions for up to 9s, followed by
a simple craft activity;
'Eggsperiment' creating a
character from the outline of an
egg shape using crayons, pencil,
paint, collage; Design a Book
Jacket; 'Pumpkin Pie', an hour-
long musical entertainment for
4s–8s; *Christmas Choice*, an annual
magazine with games, puzzles,
quizzes; kite- and puppet-
making, clowns, competitions.
All free.

Federation of Children's Book Groups (address can change, so check back to *Books For Your Children*). Parent-oriented association growing from Anne Wood's specific enthusiasm about feeding imagination as well as vitamins into children. It's a charity, independent of *Books For Your Children*. There are grassroots groups with story-telling, children's activities, hospital reading, playgroup visits, involvement with local libraries, school, backing for local bookshop (if you have one), any of these dependent on what parents put in.

Humberside Libraries and Arts Unit Central Library, Albion Street, Hull HU1 3TF [0482 224040]. Pick up the leaflets in your local library. Story times in the libraries but also in the parks, and in summer there's one story time with a difference, being the 'Teddy Bears' Picnic' with teddies and a session of stories, songs, rhymes. Then the 'Pied Piper' is a brightly painted, red, orange, yellow, mobile library touring rural parts with story-telling and book-choosing. In the libraries too, craft sessions (origami, Indian crafts, puppet-making, print and paint), Punch and Judy shows, chess, films. Mad Hatters' Tea Party, quizzes, competitions. All free.

Puffin Book Club 27 Wrights Lane, London W8 5TZ [071-938 2200]. Developed from the Puffin Club, launched by Puffin editor Kaye Webb in 1967 to encourage the life-long joys of reading for pleasure and coinciding with a golden age in children's literature which made previous generations, with only a few children's classics, look positively deprived. Coincided too with the arrival of reasonably priced children's paperbacks. You enrolled by post, paying a subscription, 5 old shillings, and received by mail the quarterly *Puffin Post*. Personally encouraged by Kaye to contribute, this was largely written by children, comments on books, poems, drawings. There was the password 'sniffup spotera', 'Puffins are tops', spoken backwards.

As part of the Puffin Books 50th birthday celebrations around 160 of the Puffin Club founder members had a Grand Reunion. They were 30-somethings and included lecturers, bookshop owners, librarians, teachers, playwrights, poets, journalists, several working in major publishing houses, but also 2 doctors and at least 1 engineer, surely confirming the relationship between prolific reading for pleasure and intellectual achievement.

The Puffin Book Club functions through schools: Fledgling for up to 6 years, Flight 6–9 years, and Post for 9s–13s, each with their own magazine containing stories, quizzes, competitions, puzzles, poems and readers' own jokes, drawings, contributions. Each member also gets glossy colourful leaflets depicting books available which can even be bought by saving stamps. The club has 12,000 member schools reaching over 1 million children. Teachers' Notes cover parental involvement in children's reading skills and information on such as the annual autumn Children's Book Week.

Scholastic Book Clubs, Scholastic Publications, FREEPOST CV 1034, Westfield Road, Southam, Leamington Spa, Warwickshire CV33 0BR. Run through schools. Grouped in 4 age levels: See-Saw up to 6, Lucky 7s–9s, Chip 9s–12s and Scene for 12 plus. Books at discounted prices. Each child receives *Club News,* with a description and illustrated front cover of books on offer, with symbols indicating reading levels, and can take part in competitions and quizzes. Teacher-Organizer receives teachers' notes, free books for school library. Parents are involved in choosing books from *Club News,* or indeed in encouraging a school to start such a club.

Toy libraries

It's such a simple idea, surprising nobody thought of it before,'
I chatted. 'Ah,' (I'm not quoting, it's just from memory) said
Her Majesty Queen Elizabeth the Queen Mother, 'the best
ideas are like that.' She had done her homework, was briefed.
There we were, in our best, having practised bows, curtsies, for
the presentation, but once facing Her Majesty it was a friendly,
relevant chat. The occasion was the official opening of the
extension to Toynbee Hall including various facilities for the
handicapped, also the then-office of the Toy Libraries
Association. I was honoured to be a co-opted member of TLA's
national council, co-opted as a parent and as a journalist, a
long-time writer about toys.

Not trying to drop names but just to emphasize that this is
essentially a simple idea. You borrow books from public
libraries, records, videos; why not toys? Well, so far only a very
few public libraries also offer toys. It can come.

The concept of borrowing/lending toys came from Jill
Norris, mother of 2 handicapped sons, who, among friends
and neighbours, was lending round and borrowing all kinds of
playthings, big like slides, medium, say things on wheels to sit
on, small, well, you name it.

It was too good an idea to confine and in 1967 Jill organized
a toy library in an Enfield church hall, for handicapped
children because they cannot wander around and get all the
many experiences of able children, so they need things
provided, many and various.

The secondary aspect not to be ignored, was that parents
came in, discovered they were not alone, talked about their
problems together, comforting, or shall we call it sanity.

From that beginning (I said it was a simple idea) and Jill's
founding the Toy Libraries Association in 1972 to provide
support, training courses on how to start, run a library, choose,
clean, present toys, came the current national movement
which has spread internationally. It could be considered as a
gift from the handicapped to able children, especially those
not normally considered 'handicapped' yet who are socially
handicapped by lack of space, poor housing conditions. TLA
became the National Toy Libraries Association.

Toy libraries are as varied today as the groups they serve. They may be run by parents, they may be open to all children and stock special toys for special children. They can be run by the Red Cross, Barnardo's, Save the Children, National Childminding Association, MENCAP. They can be in hospitals serving in-patients as well as out-patients, in community centres, in church halls, in schools, in children's book libraries, even mobile for inner cities or isolated communities.

In 1983 the association joined with **Active** and adopted the overall title **Play Matters**. Active brings together disabled people, their relatives, designers, technicians and DIY experts to produce aids for communication, leisure and play to suit individual needs. Worksheets give clear instructions for making up these one-off items. Many Active groups are particularly interested in the application of computer technology in meeting the needs of the disabled.

But back to toy libraries. Early on a panel of specialists in childcare and play needs started assessing toys to be tested by that vital consumer, the child. Assessments include play value, safety, durability, children's and parents' reactions, value for money, versatility, design and packaging, clarity of manufacturers' instructions. The information was once just for toy library organizers.

Now *What Toy* published annually mid October, available from WH Smith, Menzies, other major newsagents for around the cost of a die-cast toy, gives fully illustrated information on around 600 tested toys, games and playthings, the only impartial guide. They are old favourites or new that year, categorized into convenient sections, with loads of advice on what is appropriate at different ages, the kind of action/enjoyment, plus a Play Development Guide from birth to 5 years. *What Toy* also available direct (cheque/postal order) from CT Publications, Mantle House, Broomhill Road, London SW18 4JQ. Check current price at Play Matters, 68 Churchway, London NW1 1LT [071-387 9592].

Play space

'Go and play' is a common parental request. Question is: where? Hardly in the street with neighbouring children since vehicles not only dominate the road but cars are parked on pavements. Parks can mean people you would not want your children to meet alone. The wild plot down the road is now a grandparents' memory; after all, any gardens with frontage have been sold off, built on. Gardens are not only smaller but also more carefully tended to keep up the tone of the neighbourhood; any family prepared to allow child activities in the garden (which, note, they usually devise for themselves) can be sure that the children will not lack friends. Oddly enough the country child may be not that much more privileged than the city child. The country child can be isolated, surrounded by agricultural land, with fast-running vehicles passing the front of the home. The city child in a block of flats is excluded by notices, 'No ball games', over the bit of ornamental grass, or a play area which parents discount since they are too far up to see what is going on.

New town planning recognized modern conditions; for instance, in Peterborough provisions were made for children through the age range, like doorstep play areas, kickabout areas, junior play areas, adventure playgrounds, lots more including centres for arts and crafts, leisure-time happenings. There was a lot of forward thinking in the New Towns, but most of us live in districts that develop haphazardly.

In 1970 I wrote a series for the *Guardian* listing holiday schemes for children that I knew about with the idea of attracting information about more, which happened. The series was presented in campaigning style under the title 'Holiday Action'. It put together, for the first time, a national picture of the scattered organized activities that existed. I wrote a leaflet on 'how to' with contacts for those roused to get something going themselves.

The pioneers were mostly church groups or mothers who had started modestly among friends, hiring a local hall, and expanded because of demand. Art, drama, making things, games, sports, featured according to available adult skills. One

mother, Wendy Whitehead, even set up HOLS, standing for
Help Organize Local Schemes, a self-help exchange of
information and experience, by post.

But the mothers were battling against society's apathy. Their
problems included isolation, grants, premises. In the *Guardian*
the following year I pinpointed the need for a national centre
keeping registers of existing schemes, potential ones,
volunteers, providing guidance, literature and creating a bank
of information.

Offers to service one came from major organizations.
Ultimately 'Holiday Action Co-operative' was serviced by the
National Playing Fields Association. Its title explains its role but
the children's section, headed by Drummond Abernethy,
veteran children's champion, had long advised, supported all
kinds of community-based, year-round, child-oriented
enterprises, even with priming grants.

NPFA organized a HAC conference, the first time the
pioneers got together to talk shop. A working party was
formed, but we got entangled in the probability that a new
national organization would compete with NPFA for funds. My
main memory of the second HAC conference, since I was in
the chair, is of Ed Berman of Inter-Action advancing towards
me through the big conference hall declaiming 'We must tear
open the belly of the NPFA, become the Trojan Horse, and
take it over', meaning instead of setting up another
organization. We went home wondering what would happen
next.

Next was Trevor Huddleston, Bishop of Stepney, appealing
in *The Times* for adequate play space after 2 East End boys
drowned in the local canal. NPFA reacted, a group was formed
(many from the now-defunct HAC) and an independent body,
Fair Play for Children, was launched in 1973 with a $2^1/_2$-year
priming grant from the Voluntary Services Unit of the Home
Office. FPC had an office, a staff which never exceeded $4^1/_2$,
and a management committee elected from the membership
which rose to about 750, ranging from national organizations
to community-based play schemes, with no subscription in case
anybody, however small, be excluded. It was swiftly swamped
but somehow never overwhelmed by requests for aid,
information; it managed to publish *Make Waste Space Play Space*;

Danger on the Playground, about safety problems in fixed-equipment playgrounds; *Why Lock Up Our Schools*, meaning out of school hours when the facilities, equipment could still be used, ironically today government policy. FPC tottered on only through dedication. But the dedication, and the cause, was getting through to MPs, stirred by NPFA's director. It also helped that Ed Berman was at the time special adviser on inner cities to Michael Heseltine at the Department of the Environment. So over 200 MPs signed an 'early day motion' in 1982, which led to parliamentary debate and government acceptance, for the first time, of responsibility for children's play, expressed in the Association for Children's Play and Recreation, under the Department of the Environment, with a Minister Responsible for Children's Play and a grant of £700,000 a year, channelled through the Sports Council.

What went wrong? Even at the euphoric launching of what became more familiarly known as 'Play Board', criticisms were voiced about none of the £2 million over 3 years going to those actually working with children, financing the grassroots. These continued as the staff of around 30 in offices in Birmingham, London and the regions sought to find out just what was going on nationally and where and by whom. Internal dissension did not help. The wonderfully dedicated campaigners for children's right to enjoy space for play would no doubt add other elements. Finally the Department, fed up with the hot chestnut, proposed that Play Board should merge with the Sports Council. The directors and staff voted instead to go into voluntary liquidation, in 1987.

The Sports Council, the channel for the grant, understandably took its time, conferring widely with local authority and voluntary organizations, before agreeing to be a 'host', with a broadly based Management Committee for the new National Children's Play and Recreation Unit operating under its umbrella. The unit's role is clear: 'To bring together all those agencies responsible for delivering services to children, so that jointly a course may be set to improve the range and standards of what is currently available, and a much greater recognition of the significance of play in the healthy development of children may be achieved.'

National Children's Play and Recreation Unit 359–361 Euston Road, London NW1 3AL [071-383 5455]. Set up in 1988. Speaking up for children and a vital component of their growing up – play, which is how they develop skills, physical, social and intellectual. Closely involved in any legislation affecting children. Funds exciting, *innovative*, adding to knowledge, projects (examples, a guide on 'green' play; a street play scheme encouraging parents in a multi-cultural neighbourhood to pass down childhood games to local children). Has 3 Demonstration Projects. Working on a programme to revolutionize training for the half-million adults working with children. Has produced safety guidelines to encourage play providers to look at where children play and consider safety in its widest sense.

Sponsored the first Playday in August 1988 for over 50,000 children in 27 London boroughs, since when the idea has spread nationally. Aim: to raise public awareness of the crucial role of play in the development of children.

Houses the National Play Information Centre. Database created by Play Board (see Introduction), 4000 books, journals, articles, reports, videos to be watched or borrowed, on play and playground design, safety aspects, games, activities, education, training, play and child development. Open to the public Monday–Friday 10 a.m. – 4 p.m. If you cannot visit (and people come even from other countries to tap this extraordinary bank of knowledge about play) write to or ring the Information Officer.

London Adventure Playground Association 279 Whitechapel Road, London E1 1BY [071-377 0314]. Publishes and sells a range of educational and informational leaflets, books and videos concerning various aspects of adventure playgrounds and their management. Examples: *Adventure Play, the Theory and Philosophy, Constitutions, LAPA Trainee Scheme, Playground Location List* (where members located), *Child Sexual Assault* (self-help pack for dealing with this issue), *Recruitment.*

National Federation of City Farms Avon Environmental Centre, Junction Road, Brislington, Bristol BS4 3JP [0272 719109]. If you have no garden you will not have rabbits, guinea pigs, to tend, care for. If you have a small city garden you are unlikely to have chickens and their products, like previous generations, around and taken for granted, which is why little ones today can be frightened at the sight of a pecking chicken. Inter-Action set up a city farm late seventies in Kentish Town, London. Prince Charles appeared in the film (televized) which promoted the idea, which has spread nationally. The federation, established in 1980, has the experience of many years of successful advice and training for community projects in urban areas. 'City' can mean tower blocks, factories, whizzing traffic, on the edges of what was a bit of derelict land till someone in the community saw the possibilities of setting up a small-scale working farm, so children can discover that eggs don't just come from boxes in supermarkets, how piglets feed from the opulent sow, the caring, grooming of ponies, add the presence of goats, ducks, geese, sheep, depending on the kind of space. Emphasis is on participation, helping, which could be feeding, cleaning out, or otherwise just enjoying the farm down the road instead of 'in the country'. Sometimes demonstrations, say of milking, shearing, sometimes community gardens or workshops. So choice is of a casual visit or getting involved. Details of your nearest city farm from the Federation, *SAE please.*

Pre-School Playgroups Association (PPA) 61-63 King's Cross Road, London WC1X 9LL [071-833 0991]. Launched by Belle Tutaev's letter to the *Guardian* in 1961 when she was collecting names for a petition to the Education Minister on behalf of the Nursery School Campaign and suggested that meantime mothers could start their own. Provision of state nursery education has not increased that much over decades. If you have a playgroup (could be called play

school) in your district it's most likely to be part of this parents' self-help organization (not part of the Welfare State as many assume, though supported by national government and local authority grants), now an established part of British family life. Safe opportunities to play help to develop skills and add to knowledge. For the under-5s play and learning are one and the same. This is the philosophy which goes through all PPA playgroup activities. As children grow and develop they will use play opportunities in new ways both at home and in playgroup. These come about through books and stories, sand and water, music, outdoor and junk play. There is much much more in the way of activities, but add the vital factor of socializing, learning about other people of the same age and incidentally making friends, who may well be alongside and familiar, in the great adventure of going to 'big' school. Parents, if they want, help with laces, buckles, buttons, paint mixing, story-reading (incidentally discovering other people's children behave much like yours), or serving on committees, local or right up to national level. Lots of literature on 'how to' and courses to attend to find out more about children.

Playgroups are valued not only by parents, but by educationalists, social workers, health visitors. PPA playgroups are attended by more than 50% of 3- and 4-year-olds. In England alone there are 14,000 with some 600,000 children attending. More than 800 offer extended hours or full daycare facilities. Apart from the mainstream, meeting for less than 4 hours a day, there are Opportunity playgroups for children with disabilities and learning difficulties, drop-in centres for families needing extra support, hospital playschemes for sick children, Armed Forces playgroups for service families.

Add Mother and Toddler Groups. A lot started, as did playgroups, in people's homes. The playgroup movement has given heavy backing to this concept, literally meaning that the parent is present too. But this can be a lifeline, space for a little one to charge about or socialize with others same age while bashing shapes out of dough, and mothers, between 'There, there', and 'Let's try this', even manage to communicate.

PPA's Daycare Consultancy, for employers and others making provision for under-5s, offers help with assessing the childcare needs of the workforce; feasibility studies and recommended options; partnership with PPA and daycare playgroups; development and support for work-based daycare; published guidelines for good practice and quality daycare.

Under 5 magazine, about living with young children, published under licence from PPA, is available on news-stands.

PPA sister organizations:
Northern Ireland (NIPPA) 11 Wellington Park, Belfast BT9 6DJ [0232 662825]; Scotland (SPPA) 14 Elliott Place, Glasgow G3 8EP [041-221 4148]; Wales (Wales PPA) Resource Centre, 150 Commercial Road, Newport, Gwent NP9 2GW [0633 67712].

So you're working

There is little state support for childcare when both parents are working outside the home or when one is carrying the load. In fact the UK is around the bottom of the league of European countries when it comes to consideration, support, provision of high-standard facilities for the children of working mothers. An abundance of state day nurseries were found to be possible in World War II when it was a case of Your Country Needs You, to do the work of the men who had been marched off to war. Afterwards the attitude was – back to the kitchen. Since then there have been only minor surges of provision such as during the seventies' teacher shortage when some nurseries were set up if a proportion of the children's mothers were teachers. Around the end of the eighties/beginning of the nineties, you could hardly open a newspaper without reading about the 'demographic' changes, a shortage of school-leavers, and the gap in the workforce that would have to be filled by women, which brought to the fore yet again the lack of childcare provision.

This time the government made encouraging noises, encouraging employers, local authorities, voluntary organizations, to get together as set out in the 1989 Ministerial Group of Women's Issues plan to promote childcare so that mothers can go back to work but with no financial input.

You might have got the impression reading newspapers in 1989–90 that the country was breaking out in a rash of nurseries set up by desperate employers unless you read cold facts like the Workplace Nurseries Campaign's report that we still had around 100, as before, and mostly in the public sector, like hospitals who realized their pregnant nurses would return to work if good childcare was provided, or colleges – teachers again. (WNC has changed its name to Working for Childcare.)

There was however a lot of interest. The long-running Fleet Street Nursery (with the media, newspapers and TV taking most of the places) had a rush of phone enquiries from employers of all kinds who got the straight facts on just what was involved so they would grasp that it was far more than just utilizing some otherwise-unused office space; long and careful planning was needed.

There have been advances. Luncheon Vouchers Ltd initiated Childcare Vouchers, working in the same way. Allied Dunbar started a network of childminders in Swindon. The Midland Bank opened the first of its unique-for-a-bank chain of nurseries in September 1989 in Sheffield, subsidized, with places for 46 children between 6 months and 5 years and with provision also for school holidays and after-school care, which parents find as difficult to organize as full-time care for the younger ones.

A government circular to schools encouraging them to start after-school clubs again lacked financial backing. The Kids' Clubs Network (see page 301), the only national organization promoting over-5s childcare compiled *A Patchwork of Provision* in 1990 reporting that there were only about 300 out-of-school clubs in the UK with places for 8500 during termtime and for 11,500 in the summer holidays. It described the report as 'a damning indictment of the lack of school-age childcare and the lack of a government strategy to tackle the childcare crisis'.

Day camps are a relatively new idea. Children attend weekdays in school holidays, generally Easter and summer, for a programme of many indoor and outdoor activities. Wide age range from nursery school age (see pages 336–40).

Alternatively there are residential holidays for unaccompanied children. See also pages 329–35.

Daycare Trust Wesley House, 4 Wild Court, London WC2B 5AU [071-405 5617]. Provides free information for parents and offers a range of information services for employers, policy-makers, trades unions and anyone concerned about childcare services. Offers a consultancy service for those planning or running daycare services, publishes a guide to employers thinking about staff childcare needs, a survey of those who have done so, a booklet on the architectural design of nurseries and creative use of space. Also *Daycare for Kids: A Parents' Survival Guide,* a book on where and how to find good-quality childcare. *Childcare Links: Information for Childcare – The Start-Up Guide* is about developing a national network of local computerized banks for parents seeking up-to-date information on daycare availability. Campaigning arm: National Childcare Campaign working for quality daycare affordable by all parents, equally accessible to all, flexible and diverse, and recognition from policy-makers and employers that it will need money and positive planning to make this happen. DT and NCC quarterly newsletter on current issues. Publications list available, SAE welcomed.

Gingerbread 35 Wellington Street, London WC2E [071-240 0953]. Founded 1970 by a lone mother living in London who wanted to bring lone parents together to help each other. Support organization for one-parent families and for those professionals working with one-parent families. Managed nationally/locally by lone parents. 300 local self-help groups offer lone parents the opportunity to find support and friendship from other lone parents, the chance to develop skills and grow in confidence. There are now more than 20 advice centres and 15 childcare facilities in the England/Wales network. Some groups organize crèches and holiday events for families.

The national office advice service operates from 2–5 p.m. weekdays providing specialist information and publications. Gingerbread actively campaigns on all issues affecting lone parents and their children, for example with the pamphlet *One-Parent Families and Childcare,* about Britain's 1 million lone parents, nine-tenths of them women, caring for $1\frac{1}{2}$ million children. While the right not to work must be preserved, most who wished to as an escape from poverty and isolation cannot, simply because there is no one to look after their children. Childcare costs are not recognized when a lone parent works and claims Income Support, other benefits; flexible working hours, job sharing, workplace nurseries, are limited; childminding can be too expensive. Gingerbread wants childcare provided nationally for all working parents, and its costs subsidized, and sets out standards.

Kids' Clubs Network 279–81 Whitechapel Road, London E1 1BY [071-247 3009]. Previously National Out of School Alliance, formed 1981 by people mostly meeting through International Year of the Child (1979), concerned about latch-key and other children in out-of-school hours, when early research revealed that at least 300,000 5s–10s were left alone during summer holidays, that 225,000 5s–10s and 300,000 11s–15s were left alone after school each day. A 1990 report *Patchwork of Provision* was a damning indictment of the on-going lack of school-age childcare and the lack of a government strategy to tackle the childcare crisis. Clubs are unevenly distributed around the country with more than a third in Greater London. Many *counties* have none. It found that there are 538 primary schoolchildren for every place in a club; Wales has a far worse ratio. Over half the clubs have a waiting list. Almost half the clubs said over 40% of the parents were single parents.

There is a widespread assumption that once the youngest child starts school a mother is free to work outside the home. Hollow laugh from mothers. Kids' Clubs is the only national organization promoting over-5s out-of-school childcare.

The Network supports, encourages, community-based and local authority provision through advice, training, research, information. High-quality care and enjoyable creative play are the key elements in a club which will collect children from school if it is held on other premises (as most are), give them a meal, keep a register and see them home safely. Publications: *Up, Up & Away*, DIY guide to setting up a kids' club; *Guidelines of Good Practice for Out of School Care Schemes*; *Childcare for School Age Children: an Employers' and Employees' Guide*. KCN maintains a UK Directory of Clubs for parents, schools, employers, local authorities, etc.

National Childminding Association 8 Masons Hill, Bromley, Kent BR2 9EY [081-464 6164]. Set up in 1977 by childminders, parents, childcare workers. Aims to improve status, conditions, standards of childminding by providing advice, information, support services. Some 45,000 members, within that membership over 1000 affiliated groups. Childminding is the largest form of full daycare for the under-5s, but minders can well be caring for school-age children after school or in the school holidays.

Childminding – In Business! Ltd Consultants in childminding services, 8 Masons Hill, Bromley, Kent BR2 9EY [081-460 5427] the NCA's response to increasing demands made upon it by employers researching childcare provisions. Aims to ensure that when employers offer supported childcare to their employees they insist upon quality and that they consider childminding as a valid cost-effective option. Childminders working through the consultancy abide by a Quality Charter. The first UK Childminding Network was launched December 1990, in Swindon for Allied Dunbar covering training childminders, matching parents and children with suitable minders, toy and equipment libraries, support and back-up for emergency cover. Information Packs: ask for prices: *Maternity Leavers' Pack* (containing Childcare Checklist about types of childcare available), *Parents Guide to Childminding, Guidelines on Childminders' Pay and Conditions, Sample Childminding Contract and Record Form;* these can be bought separately or in other variations, plus *Looking for a Childminder?* and *Employer Starter Pack.* Send for *Free Information Pack.*

Pre-School Playgroups Association See page 296.

Working for Childcare 77 Holloway Road, London N7 8JZ [071-700 0281]. Formerly known as the Workplace Nurseries Campaign. Its report on the provision of workplace childcare in 1989 *Workplace Nurseries – Who Cares?* punctured the media euphoria of the time with the findings that, of around 100 workplace nurseries in the UK, the majority were in the public sector, hospitals – since around 30,000 nurses were leaving the profession per year, local authorities – as part of their equal opportunities stand, and colleges – for students as well as staff. Around 20 were in the commercial sector though some employers were facing up to the loss of trained personnel by taking action, the Midland Bank being an example. The authors detected little urgency, some hesitancy, perhaps to do with a deeper underlying reluctance based on traditional ideas about the role of women. That was written when their phone was occupied by requests from employers, parents and trade unions wanting to know what they could do about childcare provision and the postbag with requests for their information guides and letters from mothers and expectant mothers suddenly discovering there was nowhere to leave their children while they went out to work.

Its campaigning arm works closely with trades unions, other childcare organizations, community groups and parents, campaigning for quality childcare for working parents. Members receive a monthly newsletter, plus details of reports, conferences and campaigning activities. Its report *A Working Choice For Parents 1991* (£10 including p and p) found that as few as 230 workplace nurseries operate in the UK with 55% sited in London and the south-east; many companies had gone for cheaper options which do not increase provision; we are near the bottom of the European childcare league, and going down.

Its Childcare Consultancy Service's clients include names like Midland Bank, Eagle Star and more than a dozen local authorities. *A Practical Guide to Workplace Nurseries* covers all aspects of non-parental childcare, minders, nurseries, after-school schemes, vouchers, as well as workplace nurseries' management, staffing, legislation, good practice. When the workplace nurseries tax was abolished in the 1990 budget (a campaigners' victory) *After the Nursery Tax* explained the complexities of employer-sponsored childcare.

Working Mothers Association 248 Lavender Hill, London SW11 [071-228 3757]. Set up in 1985 to provide information and support to working parents with childcare needs. Its *Working Mother's Handbook*, a practical guide to finding the right childcare for parents, has sold in thousands.

Its *Working Mother's Charter* (free with SAE) was set down for the reasons already explained in my introduction and under Kids' Club Network and Gingerbread. It covers childcare services and planning, day nurseries state and workplace; childcare in the home (interestingly including support for nannies, au pairs, as well as childminders with such as group play facilities, assistance with special needs children); nursery education (not to be confused with all-day nurseries and needing to be supplemented with after-school-hours provision); employment rights (time off for clinics, maternity leave, consideration on return to work); the cost of childcare to be taken into account in claims for income support (see under Gingerbread) and before assessment of income tax; child benefit should be raised significantly.

The Employer's Guide to Childcare was launched at the Confederation of British Industry and produced because of the demographic time-bomb, the shortage of school leavers, and increasing enquiries from employers. It covers many of the points in its *Charter*, changing work patterns like flexitime, job-sharing, working from home, and childcare provision, with options like workplace nurseries, salaried childminders, childcare allowances, support for out-of-school schemes.

Working Mothers' Groups: local, autonomous, provide support, information about local childcare, may organize weekend playgroups, put childcarers in touch with one another, collective efforts may improve local provision.

Specially for the handicapped

I would never claim that there were enough leisure opportunities for the disabled any more than I would for able children. But there may be more chances than you imagined.

Join a relevant organization; almost all of them were formed originally by involved parents. They will know of what is open either from the home base or as holidays to families or for group bookings. Examples are **Play Matters, Toy Libraries Association** (pages 290–1), **Association for All Speech-Impaired Children** (page 306), **Handicapped Adventure Playground Association** (page 306), **Riding for the Disabled** (page 308), **Spastics Society** (page 310), **Royal Society for Mentally Handicapped Children and Adults** (page 309), **National Deaf Children's Society** (page 307). Add also organizations like **Pre-School Playgroups** (page 296), **Guides/Scouts** (pages 333–4), **Boys/Girls Brigade** (page 333).

Modern leisure complexes and the new museums cater for wheelchairs and older ones have built ramps which also help those transporting small able children in pushchairs, so here there has been a mutual benefit.

From the responses to my questions to the national attractions for **Part one: Family outings,** I got the strong impression of much more practical action and plans to do even better.

But ring beforehand to check whether suitable for a family visit, always for a group, to find out what is possible and so avoid disappointment about physical access.

Regard the 'people with disabilities' symbol only as a guide to partial access (in ancient buildings) or unlimited access and toilet facilities and all kinds of techniques to aid the visually or aurally handicapped.

Then, among the museums and art galleries, London's **Natural History Museum** (page 84) has organized special exhibitions for blind and partially sighted children who enjoy, discover, through feeling, skin, fur, teeth of exhibits. **The British Museum** (page 90) for groups, arranged beforehand, has put exhibits into a separate room so they can be touched, handled. The **Dinosaur Museum**, Dorchester (page 44) has year-round attractions for the blind or partially sighted who can feel the textures of dinosaurs (were they hot, cold, smooth?).

The **Museum of Antiquities**, Newcastle (page 188) has occasional special days for children with handicaps or learning difficulties. The **Aberdeen Art Gallery** (page 208) has weekly drama groups for the handicapped. London's **Museum of the Moving Image** (page 83) as well as access has induction loops, a leaflet for visitors with special needs and some workshops. **Haggs Castle**, Glasgow (page 197) arranges events for mentally handicapped children in groups. **Dobwalls Theme Park**, Cornwall (page 24) has a special wheelchair path to the foot of 'a mountain', Braille pad introductions to each 'room' and blind visitors can feel the exhibits such as the fur of a hare, smell a garden or woodland. **Alexandra Palace** (page 80) has workshops for the disabled. Activity Days at **Capel Manor**, Enfield (page 104) include those designed for children with special needs. **Jonah's Journey**, Aberdeen (page 208) provides, where possible, activity sheets for the mentally handicapped.

Among the theatres, London's **Polka Children's Theatre** (page 255) organizes workshops for children with various handicaps. London's **Unicorn Theatre** (page 256) is a focus for theatre for and by the deaf. The National Deaf Children's Society has held its annual Festival of Mime there. Many staff learn sign language. There are drama workshops for 4s–8s, deaf and hearing so as to provide understanding, communication between the two. The **Little Angel Marionette Theatre**, London (page 252) arranges workshop facilities for those working with the handicapped. The **London Bubble** and the **Tricycle Theatre** have induction loops and some signed performances (pages 252 and 256). Manchester's **Contact Theatre** (page 259) has wheelchair places, toilets, easy access seats for ambulant disabled and an assisted hearing facility. There are others. But the **Kinderland** fun play and activity park in Scarborough (page 168) is unusual, maybe unique, in providing play equipment for the disabled.

Association For All Speech-Impaired Children 347 Central Markets, Smithfield, London EC1A 9NH [071-236 3632/6487]. Concerned with understanding of, care for, development and education of children who have developmental speech and/or language impairments. AFASIC organizes 'Activity Weeks' where such children can have the same kind of adventure holidays as other children. Idea evolved by chairwoman Elizabeth Browning who knew that with her own son such fun was possible, with adult aid. Incidentally, raising funds for the project, she jumped with the Red Devils and broke her pelvis! On these weeks each child has a 'link', a young adult volunteer (who has been on a training session) as friend and companion. Activities are led by qualified instructors. Age grouping around 6s–9s, 8s–14s, 14s–18s, 18 plus. Activities can include caving, canoeing, climbing, games, music, arts/crafts, pony-trekking, swimming, sailing, excursions, walking.

British Sports Association for the Disabled The Mary Glen Haig Suite, 34 Osnaburgh Street, London NW1 3ND [071-383 7277]. Participation in sport is the objective and this is the co-ordinating body of sport for people with disabilities. Hundreds of Disabled Sports Clubs are affiliated. It organizes sporting events, offers advice to local groups wanting to form new sports clubs, endeavours to secure improved facilities by government and local authorities particularly aiming to help young disabled people to participate in sport and to keep it up after leaving school. Leaflets available giving some idea of what there is, what's possible, so much more than you might imagine, with information on regional contacts, recreational facilities, specialist books, and other resources.

Disabled Living Foundation 380–384 Harrow Road, London W9 2HU [071-289 6111]. Publications include *Clothing for the Handicapped Child, Footwear and Footcare for Disabled Children, Access to Music for the Physically Handicapped Schoolchild and School Leaver, The Garden and the Handicapped Child, Play Helps: Toys and Activities for Handicapped Children, Toys and Play for the Handicapped Child.*

Handicapped Adventure Playground Association Fulham Palace, Bishop's Avenue, London SW6 6EA [071-731 1435]. Established 1966 under the inspiration of Lady Allen of Hurtwood, by 1984 had built and equipped 5 adventure playgrounds for handicapped children and young people in London. Each is staffed by experienced play leaders who work to ensure each child has a choice of activities to enjoy at its own pace. These adventures through play into new physical and mental activities can give the joy of achievement, however small.

HAPA runs 5 adventure playgrounds for children and young people with disabilities and special educational needs. The playgrounds are in the London boroughs of Wandsworth, Lambeth, Kensington and Chelsea, Islington and Hammersmith and Fulham. They provide play sessions to over 50 special schools and organize play schemes during the holidays and on Saturdays for local disabled children. This wonderful idea has spread well beyond London. HAPA's National Information Service offers advice and information to individuals and organizations interested in play for children with disabilities and special educational needs and to groups setting up similar playgrounds in the UK and abroad. The HAPA journal features articles on play and disability with news from the playgrounds and conferences.

Holiday Care Service 2 Old Bank Chambers, Station Road, Horley, Surrey RH6 9HW [0293 774535]. This national charity is the UK's central source of holiday information for people whose age, disability, or other personal or family circumstances make it difficult for them to find a holiday. Individuals, their family or friends can telephone or write explaining their requirements, the type of holiday they are looking for and where they would like to go. The service will then provide detailed information, free of charge, on holidays in the UK and abroad that meet their needs, and enquirers can then make their own reservations direct. Runs **Holiday Helpers** which matches a volunteer to act as a helper on holiday.

Invalid Children's Aid Nationwide Allen Graham House, 198 City Road, London EC1V 2PH [071-608 2462]. Concerned with understanding of, care for, development and education of young children with speech and language disorders/learning difficulties I CAN runs 3 residential schools for children aged 5–16 with learning difficulties. 1 residential school for children with chronic asthma and eczema and a college of further education for the disabled. It also runs the Keith Grove Project' (life and social skills training) for the disabled. I CAN publishes a wide range of reading/drawing sets, along with books for teachers, people involved with speech and language disorders and a quarterly newsletter. It offers advice and help wherever possible to parents and guardians.

National Deaf Children's Society 45 Hereford Road, London W2 5AH [071-229 9272]. Only national charity working for all deaf children, their parents and carers. Work includes useful free publications, local support from 140 family self-help groups, advice on education and advocacy for appeals, counselling and advice on health and welfare, advocacy for state benefit claimants, briefings for MPs and peers on issues relevant to deaf children, training for families, volunteers and professionals, grants to families in need for equipment, holidays, respite care and essential household items, loans of otherwise expensive equipment, such as radio hearing aids for children to try out, a quarterly magazine about deaf children, a special group for young deafened people. Publications include books on mathematics, reading, a chart on the fingerspelling alphabet, car stickers 'Mind! that child may be deaf'.

National Trust 36 Queen Anne's Gate, London SW1H 9AS [071-222 9251]. Publishes annual free *Information for Visitors with Disabilities* with detailed information on facilities at the Trust's properties like access for wheelchair-users and less able walkers including powered vehicles at properties, refreshments, toilet amenities, adapted holiday cottages, features for the visually and hearing-impaired. Booklet available to anyone but should be used with the annual *Handbook*, free to NT members which gives opening details and is available from NT properties or shops or by post price £4.95 from the NT, Dept KB, address above.

Riding for the Disabled Association Avenue 'R', National Agricultural Centre, Kenilworth, Warwickshire CV8 2LY [0203 696510]. A child who may not be able to walk and is normally confined to a wheelchair can ride a pony, discover new possibilities, capabilities. A 4-legged friend can also aid the mentally handicapped. You have to see this idea in action to see the fun and laughter, new achievements, wider horizons. Take it as said they need more voluntary helpers, in all sorts of ways.

The charity is expanding providing riding for over 25,000 disabled adults and children through the 702 member groups, mostly in country areas but wanting to put more such facilities into cities and large urban areas. HRH The Princess Royal has given RDA invaluable support, by being patron and therefore getting RDA mentioned in the press, and also by attending groups' happenings, talking to the children, presenting awards for events.

RDA also arranges riding holidays for those who ride with the groups and also through its 18 regions; holidays which have included a theatre visit, swimming, expeditions, picnics.

The Royal Association for Disability and Rehabilitation (RADAR) 25 Mortimer Street, London W1N 8AB [071-637 5400]. Publishes *Holidays in the British Isles – A Guide for Disabled People*, an annual comprehensive guide including where unaccompanied disabled children can take holidays, £4.50 by mail order including postage from RADAR or at main branches of WH Smith. Also, 'Holiday Accommodation for Children and Young People' factsheet, 55p including postage and packing. Other publications: county, town, city, access guides in the UK, about places of interest, restaurants, shops, accommodation, cinemas, theatres, public conveniences accessible to wheelchair-users, some free, some for a fee, specify area; *Travel with British Rail*, a guide for disabled people, £4.50 including p and p. Write for free publication list, SAE welcomed.

Royal National Institute for the Blind 224 Great Portland Street, London W1N 6AA [071-388 1266]. RNIB Leisure Service aims to meet leisure needs among visually handicapped people by providing information and advice on all activities and pursuits. The service produces publications, for example *Leisure for All – Opportunities for Visually Handicapped People* and provides financial help to individuals in specific activity areas. It also supports projects initiated by other agencies as well as organizing seminars and conferences to draw attention to particular topics or activity areas in need of further development.

Royal Society for Mentally Handicapped Children and Adults (MENCAP) 123 Golden Lane, London EC1Y 0RT [071-454 0454]. Founded by parents in 1946. Now has 500 local societies. Information available on education and many other kinds of provision. Over 500 Gateway Clubs nationally offer local getting together with others, including the non-handicapped, with parties, events, various sports opportunities including an award scheme. MENCAP publishes the solid *Holiday Accommodation Guide*, £3 including postage/packing, with detailed national information on accommodation where mentally handicapped are welcome, either unaccompanied, with families, or in groups, and covering full catering, self-catering, holiday and activity centre and specialist accommodation. It includes advice on where to find out more elsewhere. **MENCAP Holiday Services** 119 Drake Street, Rochdale, Lancashire, arranges a programme of unaccompanied holidays through the UK for mentally handicapped children whose needs are not normally catered for, and over a wide range of handicap. Details available, SAE appreciated.

Spastics Society 12 Park Crescent, London W1N 4EQ [071-636 5020]. Founded 1952 by parents, now has around 200 local groups and 60 national schools and centres to cater for needs at different ages. It runs Churchtown Farm Field Studies Centre in Cornwall, which is specially designed for disabled people, so that they can participate in adventure activities such as sailing, canoeing, fishing, abseiling, to widen horizons. Features include heated swimming pool, games room, an adjoining farm. The SS also has a sports section.

Round up

A lucky dip

Campus Fletcherscombe, Diptford, Totnes, Devon TQ9 7NQ [054 882 388]. A novel family holiday for people who love the arts, have children and enjoy camping. Annual festival of contemporary theatre, music and dance, workshops, discussion groups and outdoor activities for both children and parents. The small company provides a beautiful camp site, in Devon, culture and entertainment, helpful staff to babysit, toilets and showers for village-size plots, breakfasts delivered. Supervised Children's Area for 3s–6s. A theatre for older children and adventure playground. You take tent or caravan but no dogs, and pay for a site plus fees per person. 10 days late July – early August.

Cheddar Showcaves Cheddar Gorge, Somerset BS27 3QF [0934 742343]. Hard, dirty, but a real adventure, a caving expedition led by an Adventure Caving Leader. Your journey begins at the 'Black Cat' in Gough's Cave, a quarter of a mile inside one of Europe's finest showcaves – an easy climb to Mushroom Chamber, crawl into Sand Chamber, lifeline down a 40-ft steel ladder into Boulder Chamber, climb up to the Far Rift, emerge through April Fool's Squeeze, clip on to a wire traverse, crawl across the top of Boulder Chamber and over the Bottomless Pit, returning, through Sand Chamber, to the public Showcave. Minimum age 12 years. Pre-booking advisable.

Inter-Action, HMS *President* (1918), Victoria Embankment, London EC4Y 0HJ [071-583 2652]. Involved in problem-solving work of an educational or community-development nature. It takes on specific challenges and tries to develop practical projects and techniques which can be widely disseminated and used by others throughout the country. Free tour of this World War I submarine destroyer 2 hours from 4 p.m. Friday; creative family weekends (poetry, theatre, singing, desktop publishing, Lego), always check first by phone. Schools, children's clubs, playgroups can book Prof Dogg's Troupe for songs, games, activities or Captain James Cook (in 18th-century uniform) telling stories of explorations. Schools can book Starlab, portable planetarium. Among publications: books/cassettes *New Game Songs* and *Healthy Learning Activities*, songs to sing, games to play, activities and projects to do, to develop children's social skills and understanding.

Midlands Arts Centre Cannon Hill Park, Birmingham B12 9QH

[021-440 3838]. So much: Cannon Hill Puppet Theatre, resident year-round professional company; cinema which pays attention to children; Midlands Arts Jazz Centre, big bands, audition. Then year-round classes, workshops, tuition, at weekends or after school, say 5s upwards, in appropriate groupings; ballet, informal or creative dance, tap; art, that is painting, printing, collage, drawing, sculpture; music, like piano, flute, recorders, classical guitar, clarinets, various levels, but add in steel band, also Suzuki violin, even for pre-schoolers, and needing parental involvement in home practice, getting suitable instrument and getting on to waiting list; pottery workshops (under-12s need to be adult-accompanied).

Splendid school holiday programme. In summer could include a 'Fun Week' with kite-making, face-painting, pony rides, train rides, steel band workshops, drama workshops, street-dance competitions, children's shows, and other jollifications. But very much worth thinking forward and getting hold of the specific different school holiday programme, and booking. Films, child-oriented of course, and generally something new in the Puppet Theatre, like *Pinocchio* set in a traditional British seaside resort. A wide range of courses, like all kinds of dancing; making pictures move, puppets, comic strips, creating a table-top circus, monsters, underwater creatures;

making jewellery from feathers, shells, pebbles, beads; music, a fine mix of those who have played with others and those who are starting; pottery, think of anything to make, caterpillars, gargoyles, crocodiles, clowns, fruit and veg, your pet, your gran, a castle, an historic figure; making things from textiles, ribbons, calico and lace, like puppets, purses, mice, kites, patchwork, tapestry. Add sports tuition and expeditions exploring some particular theme. Enquire for costs.

Science Projects Turnham Green Terrace Mews, Chiswick, London W4 1QU [081-994 3996]. 'Discovery Dome', mobile in large yellow tents, where you can explore the world of science through hands-on exhibits. Examples: multiple mirrors, mirror drawing, make music without a keyboard, build a bridge solid enough to walk on, suspend a ball on a jet of air, speak into a phone which plays back your voice (uncanny). Find it at festivals, major complexes like Quarry Bank Mill, Styal. One permanent: Dome of Discovery, Glasgow (page 198). 'Schoolworks', mobile inter-active science exhibitions which travel to schools, one on light and one on sound.

Permanent hands-on science centres are listed under locations: for example, Launch Pad, Science Museum London; Exploratory, Bristol; Techniquest, Cardiff; Xperiment, Manchester's Science and Industry Museum, and more.

SPLASH Police HQ, PO Box 188, Bristol BS99 7BH. Began as an inner-city scheme in 1986, devised by a Police Community Involvement Team to provide worthwhile activities during the school summer holidays, so reducing nuisance crime which can occur through boredom, and encourage police involvement with young people. Now extended over the whole Greater Bristol area and into Somerset. In 1990 3709 youngsters registered. For 10s–15s who join and get a membership card which gives bus discounts. Free annual *Splash* magazine sets out everything you would want to know, what is on, when, where, how to book tickets. Obtainable from schools, youth clubs, libraries and (something different you must admit) police stations. The action-packed programme includes loads of sports, workshops (modelling, puppets, drama) films, discos, excursions to places like Wookey Hole, Longleat. Supervised by police in their own time, or parents, volunteers always welcomed. A wonderful and, as far as I know, unique scheme in which other police forces are showing interest. So full praise to the Bristol police team that launched it and keep it going.

Organizations

Association of Railway Preservation Societies 42 North Street, Oundle. Publishes annual *Guide to Steam Trains* in the British Isles with details of 129 railway attractions.

British Action for Children's TV (BAC TV) 21 Stephen Street, London W1P 1PL [071-255 1444]. A national organization which believes that TV is a great asset in children's lives, when used appropriately. It believes that what is appropriate for children is different from what serves the interests of adults. Aims to represent the interests of children to the authorities responsible for broadcasting policy and practice, and to the general public. An alliance of TV users who, in co-operation with TV producers, are seeking to maintain and enhance the range of TV programmes available to younger views, that is people from birth to the end of statutory schooling.

Seeks: to create a nationwide network of all those interested in children and TV, particularly parents and children; to establish mutually co-operative and informing relationships with TV companies and programme-makers; to collect information about children's needs and activities in relation to TV and to initiate research into these needs and activities; to represent these needs and views to national and international agencies and individuals, public and private, who are responsible for TV programmes received in Britain; to encourage education about TV and the wider dissemination of research and writing about children and TV; to support and promote a diversity of choice in TV for children which is at least equal to that available to adults; to seek representation on public bodies concerned with the relationship between children and TV; to identify and encourage programmes which do serve the interests of children and meet their needs for entertainment and information in creative and stimulating ways – perhaps by initiating a Children's Television Award.

BAC TV aims to undertake these activities through a variety of means: conferences, workshops, symposia, research projects, publications and its own awards. These will involve parents, children, the TV industry, educators, politicians and other interested groups and individuals. Founded in 1989, it campaigned against the possibility that, under the Broadcasting Bill, minority programming, which includes children, could be squeezed out; in 1990 the government announced that it was making children's programmes, along with religious programmes, a requirement within the new contracts.

Steering group members take part in meetings organized by groups such as the Pre-School Playgroups Association, National Childbirth Trust, Children's Book Circle, Mothers' Union. Two 1990 BAC TV events: a celebration of the work of Children's ITV, in an event where a panel of young people talked about their likes and dislikes as regards children's programmes; a seminar exploring the question 'Growing Too Fast?', whether children's exposure to the world as represented on TV might either help to develop their moral awareness or might present them with experiences for which they were not ready.

Members of the co-ordinating Steering Group are almost all themselves parents keen to promote a positive use of TV as a resource for children and to safeguard the variety and quality of programmes available for children. They also represent a range of interests and involvement in TV including children's programme-makers, pre-school playgroup organizing, education and media research. It is working on a pack of materials *Living with TV: a Parent's Guide* intended to provide ideas, activities and information about viewing which can be used both by parents with their children and as a basis for groups of interested people to discuss children and TV. Members receive newsletters to keep them informed about developments and activities. Enquiries: in writing please, since there is only limited part-time office staff.

Countryside Commission John Dower House, Crescent Place, Cheltenham, Glos GL50 3RA [0242 521381]. Neither owns nor manages but cares about all types of countryside, mountains and moorlands, intensively farmed lowlands, coastlines and the run-down edges of towns and cities. An advisory and promotional body working to achieve the collaboration and understanding of all concerned. Publications: the free *Country Code Bookmark*, *Task Force Trees Action Park* (encouraging community groups to care for trees and woodlands); *Out in the Country* (where you can go and what you can do); *Country Code Poster*, full colour version and black and white 'outline' versions for colouring in. Catalogue of publications includes videos for hire or purchase. All publications from Countryside Commission Publications, Printworks Lane, Levenshulme, Manchester ML9 3JP [061-224 2825].

The Duke of Edinburgh's Award Madeira Walk, Windsor, Berks SL4 1EU [0753 810753]. A programme of leisure-time activities challenging all young people between 14 and 25, able-bodied or disabled, to serve others, acquire new skills, experience adventure and make new friends. Not competitive, you aim to achieve an Award, Bronze for over-14s, Silver for over-15s and Gold (requiring a residential project) for over-16s, by progressing in 4 sections: Service (community service, first aid, conservation are only examples), Expeditions (plan, train for and undertake a journey on foot, cycle, boat), Skills (over 200, maybe improving on an interest or trying something new), Physical

Recreation (orienteering, dancing, yoga, the list is long). The residential project for the Gold has taken participants to the French Alps, the Rift Valley, a Mombasa orphanage, the Highlands. More than 2 million have taken part since the Duke founded it in 1956; now operates worldwide. Take part through schools, youth clubs, Scouts, Guides, Boys' Brigade, or your nearest Award Officer (enquire at local Council's Education or Youth Dept or address from HQ above) will put you in touch with an 'Operating Authority' which provides a Record Book. Patron HRH The Duke of Edinburgh. HRH The Prince Edward, a Gold Award holder, is chairman of the Special Projects Group which promotes the scheme (he travels widely meeting young people) and fund-raises to support the scheme in inner city, rural areas and overseas in Africa and the Caribbean.

English Heritage Keysign House, 429 Oxford Street, London W1R 2HD [Events 071-973 3457, membership 071-973 3400]. Secures the preservation of the country's architectural and archaeological heritage and promotes the public's enjoyment and knowledge of this through the management of more than 350 historic properties in its care. Annual free events diary *Bringing History Alive* gives details of dressing up, re-enactments, music, dancing, entertainment, drama, sometimes of warlike activities, at different periods of history, Romans, Normans, medieval, Napoleonic, at castles, stately homes, where, when, how much, mostly free to members. *Family Discovery Packs*, practical activities to help understanding of the site and its history including activity cards, a fill-it-in-yourself wall chart and suggestions for nearby attractions to visit, with map. For sale on sites like Audley End, Battle Abbey, Rievaulx Abbey, Totnes, Tintagel and Kenilworth Castles. More planned. Mail order from Education Dept, EH. KEEP, the junior section, has its own supplement in the quarterly magazine.

Forestry Commission Public Information Division, 231 Corstorphine Road, Edinburgh EH2 7AT [031-334 0303]. Protects all manner of wildlife in 46 forest nature reserves which also include lakes, sand dunes, bogs, moors. Also cares for environmental interests in 340 Sites of Special Scientific Interest and in forest parks. Publications: *Forest Visitor Information*, listing information centres and including a map and who to contact to find out more about any area you plan to visit; *Forest Nature Reserves*, map, locations and what flora, fauna, to spot; *Forest Parks*, with Visitor Centres, camp sites, holiday cabins and opportunities for specialist wildlife study and a variety of sports like walking, riding, orienteering; single-topic booklets like *Larch, Sitka Spruce, Forests for Birds*; *The Forest*

Adventure, teachers' resource pack for 8s–14s; free quarterly magazine *Forest Life*; and, for children, *Welcome to my Forest* (20p), large-size glossy magazine-style with David Bellamy taking a walk, so facts, lots of pictures, illustrations about flowers, creepy crawlies, trees and their uses.

Groundwork Foundation
Bennetts Court, 6 Bennetts Hill, Birmingham B2 5ST [021-236 8565]. About the environment, especially dereliction and wasteland around our towns and cities, and working together, industry, public authorities, voluntary groups, individuals, the community, to make this a green and pleasant land, and appreciated as such. Now 26 local Groundwork operations, expected to double in 3 years. Family involvement: contact your nearest office, through national office above, maybe to help on projects like stone wall-building, litter-picking, footpath restoration, pond cleaning up, creating wildflower meadows, or to find a new appreciation of your surroundings. The network organizes an attractive variety of events: any number of walks to see birdlife, wildflowers, wildlife, tours around ancient buildings, old workings, boat trips to places of historical and natural interest, beachcombing, visits to such as farms or boat yards, often activity days with an introduction to a sport. You could be surprised at your local group's activities; the Macclesfield and Vale Royal

Groundwork Trust operates 3 cycle hire centres weekends Easter–October and daily in the school summer holidays.

MENSA Foundation for Gifted Children Mensa House, St John's Square, Wolverhampton WV2 4AH [0902 772771]. Its approach: children of very high mental ability are found at all levels in all communities; intelligence testing has become unfashionable in schools so that potentially able children are not recognized and when they are spotted teachers are often unable to provide suitably challenging education. Aim: to seek out and offer practical help to families with children of high intellectual ability. Parents are offered a professional testing service and a certificate is provided so that parents and teachers are informed. Children who reach the right level are offered Mensa membership. In some cases the foundation can suggest alternative schools or enrichment classes. Under the 'Mentor Scheme' parents needing help to guide their children's education are offered an individual counselling service, a mentor, or personal tutor who can spend time with a child. Plans include a network of 'Magnet' schools for outstandingly intelligent and studious children, the first opened in 1991, and approved schools with specialist provision to be known as Mensa Foundation Schools. The Junior Summer School and Camp, first held in 1990, will become an annual event. Local groups, already over 50, organize Saturday Clubs and other get-togethers. Plans for pen pals and exchange visits both internationally. Junior Special Interest Group has its own magazine *Pigasus*. Publications: *Educating The Intelligent Child* and several books of games and puzzles.

The National Association for Gifted Children Park Campus, Boughton Green Road, Northampton NN2 7AL [0604 792300]. The association which helps to develop gifts and talents in children. Pioneered the concept of bringing together the exceptionally talented, meaning right across the board, not only the academic, to stretch themselves by meeting, mixing, with others of the same calibre. A seed which has spread, influenced thinking, through the educational system.

Saturday Clubs are run by parents, all over the country in various kinds of premises like schools, community centres. Age range from pre-school upwards, and drawing in all the family, since membership of NAGC is a family one. There are around 40 branches nationally and many run Saturday Clubs.

Kinds of activities, for example: paper, how it's made, even cooking with rice paper; 'Roman Invasion', children acting as Roman soldiers and making a mosaic floor and water clock; 'Young Person's Guide to the

Orchestra', examining instruments, judging children's own home-made musical instruments, also professional musical entertainment with children participating; a talk on 'Dragons and Monsters', but also practical and safe electrical work, and a fancy dress party. That's just one club. Another mentions cooking and chemistry, typewriting and computing, fencing and board games, woodwork and pottery, members taking along their own computers, swords, etc. Or what about one that found premises with a computer room, full of computers, plus essential kitchen for refreshments, but with talks from 'Spaceflight' to 'Cat Care', plus a playgroup, a Christmas party, summer holiday outings? Young members, called Explorers, help to organize and produce magazines in some of the branches. There are 2 regular publications of the association, *Gossip Column*, in which children's work also sometimes features, and *Looking to their Future*, for parents, academics and libraries. NAGC publishes some specialist books on gifted and high-ability children, of which *Help with Bright Children* is the most widely appreciated by parents. There is a free counselling service for gifted and high-ability children who are facing difficulties. Discussion groups for parents are run along with the Explorers' groups. Information pack available (large SAE please), about how to identify a gifted child, why they need help, the NAGC services.

The Potential Trust 7 Bateman Street, Headington, Oxford OX3 7BG [0865 750360]. Aims to help children with special needs arising from a high degree of unfulfilled potential in whatever areas – intellectual, practical, aesthetic, creative, social, personal . . .

The Trust, under the name of Questors, has for many years been involved with a wide variety of residential Quest Weeks, mostly for the 7–15 age range. Many of these have been organized and run by the Trust team themselves, but they also publicize those run by others where they feel they can genuinely recommend both content and pastoral care. The Trust also offers information on exciting non-residential activities available to Questors, such as hands-on experience centres for science and technology.

The Trust's current Questor's publications are *Quest Ions.* A quest is a search. An ion is a charged particle, a radical, going . . . somewhere. A quest ion is a charged notion, a beginning from which you set off on a quest for questions and quest ions of your own making.

Everything the Trust offers to Questors is intended to be an open-ended beginning from which Questors can set off on individual quests of their own.

No entry qualification or membership fee is necessary for a child to become a Questor.

National Association for the Welfare of Children in Hospital Argyle House, 29–31 Euston Road, London NW1 2SD [071-833 2041]. Founded in 1961, supports the emotional needs of children of all ages, including adolescents, either admitted to hospital or (3 million a year) going through the Accident and Emergency Departments. The crux, of course, is being separated as little as possible from parents. So from NAWCH came the difference between being parted from a screaming child, frightened by the unfamiliar, or dropping in, with other parents, through the day, sitting around, reading stories, playing games (you can see I've been through it), nothing to do with rigid visiting hours. Staying overnight is much more common now, particularly with very young children, but that battle is not won!

NAWCH lobbies MPs, hospital administrators, tries to persuade hospitals of the importance of the parental role and of the need for specially trained staff who understand children's needs. NAWCH runs an information/advisory service consulted by professionals all over the world.

Some 70 branches supplying services in their locality, like counselling, driving parents to hospital, running crèches for siblings while they visit, providing night-clothes/tooth-brushes for those staying unexpectedly overnight, lots of other back-up; supporting hospital playschemes meaning since minimum time may be spent in bed (and if you are confined you *can* be suitably entertained), there should be plenty of activities on tap, all kinds. These vital play opportunities included during the long waits in Outpatient Departments, even some distractions provided in the Accident/Emergency Departments.

Branches also raise large sums for parent accommodation and facilities locally as well as for play equipment and play areas. Publications: *Parents' Pack*, designed to help parents and their children prepare for hospital – includes a parents' handbook, comic, colouring sheet and reading list; *Sammy Goes to Hospital*, comic using real colour photographs to prepare children for a stay in hospital; *When I Went to Hospital*, a colourful comic for children. SAE please for price list, order form.

National Gardens Scheme Hatchlands Park, East Clandon, Guildford, Surrey GU4 7RT [0483 211535]. Around 2500 private gardens, mostly not normally open to the public, where, what, when open, charges, are listed in the annual publication *Gardens of England and Wales*, better known as the 'Yellow Book' available from large bookshops £2.50 or from NGS plus postage and packaging. Adult gardening addicts will find enchanting places to visit from a tiny London patio to great sweeping lawns, lakes, and anything in between. Studying the 'Yellow Book' you could be surprised by the attractions specifically for children. Beneficiaries include nurses in need, National Trust gardens of special historic interest, training of Macmillan Nurses in the care of the terminally ill, and other national and local charities.

National Trust 36 Queen Anne's Gate, London SW1H 9AS [071-222 9251]. 16 regional offices. Look up in your local phone book. In the late seventies I joined a group of NT members for a weekend at Sudbury Hall, Sudbury, Derby, to learn about upstairs from Lord Vernon, whose family had owned the property, and downstairs from family servants and from doing it yourself the hard way. Great fun. The youngest was under 5 and had a go at what it would have been like to sweep a very wide chimney. Children dressed up, well, so did some adults. That was a rare one-off but it illuminates the slant towards the family that is developing, demonstrated in children's rates for concerts, but also events like fun runs, Punch and Judy shows, farm walks, presentations by the Young National Trust Theatre, more discovery sheets, guides, aimed at the young, available at NT properties, experiments like 'Field Days' for young members; 'Family Days', a course on country houses for parents with a

linked activity course for children. Then there is *Young National Trust,* a magazine for younger members, colouring sheets, quizzes, etc. Add Acorn Camps, week-long residential work camps on National Trust properties in spring and summer months, for 16s upwards. *The Family Handbook* (£3.50 from bookshops) is a solid paperback about properties judged to interest families. It picks out what to look for among the often bewildering abundance, adding details like: Lyme Park's ghost and chairs covered with material from the cloak Charles I wore at his execution, the Cage once a lock-up for poachers; at Dyrham Park a trick picture giving the illusion of another corridor; Wenlock Edge once a barrier reef; the grave of a man buried upside down at Box Hill so come the resurrection and the world turned upside down he would be the right way up. Just some examples. Worth joining, lots going on.

National Women's Register 9 Bank Plain, Norwich, Norfolk NR2 4SL [0603 765392]. Formerly National Housewives' Register. A mother's helpline though many groups hold children's parties, say at Christmas, picnics in school summer holidays and, as mothers become friends, children can have a wider circle of friends beyond school/street, and when mothers childmind for each other (and that can be after school or for a day) children have someone to play with. As one member told me, 'My two think it's a black day when there's no one to play with.' But the national, now international network, founded 1960 so that mothers who had to haul up their roots, leave friends behind, move house according to husband's job, could quickly find kindred spirits in the new location, hardly seemed particularly relevant to children though sanity for mothers is an indirect effect. Then a member told me in 1984 about how her family, because of husband's job, had to move halfway across the country just as the summer school holidays started. She explored the locality with son. He was accepted into an informal football game. But would he find his way back to the new home? Another participant offered to guide him back. Seeing the logo already displayed in the window, he declared, 'My mum goes to their meetings.' His mother was soon on the phone and literally next day newly arrived mother and small daughter, as well as son, were part of the usual school holiday socializing.

My book on the first 20 years, *The Lively-minded Woman* (Heinemann), is available in public libraries.

Royal Society for Nature Conservation – The Wildlife Trusts Partnership The Green, Witham Park, Waterside South, Lincoln LN5 7JR [0522 544400]. WATCH is the junior wing, for under-18s, sponsored by the Partnership and by the *Sunday Times*. For details send SAE. 47 local Wildlife Trusts and 50 Urban Wildlife Groups provide local bases. WATCH is about the environment, town and country. Recent projects have included an award-winning investigation into acid rain; ladybird, bumblebee and dragonfly surveys and a study of low-level ozone in towns. Over 800 local WATCH groups with study days, excursions, activities for members. Magazine *Watchword* 3 times a year pre-main school holidays including members' contributions plus quizzes, competitions. Add nature guides for family expeditions, project packs or, for group-thinking adults, information sheets, group leaders' pack. Add, too, family camps and adventure holidays for families or for unaccompanied 11s upwards, arranged with Youth Hostels Association.

Society of Young Mathematicians 5 Tower Road, Orpington, Kent BR6 0SG [0689 830380]. 'If you enjoy patterns and puzzles, paradox and proof . . . ', or in other words enjoy maths, SYMS is for under-18s. Launched in March 1991 it had 1200 members within 5 months. Around 800 attended the first annual SYMS Maths Fair. Membership, £5 a year, enrolment £1, brings termly copies of *SYMmetry*, the newsletter (articles, news, puzzles, calculator hints, book reviews, games, competitions) and of *Plus* a mathematical magazine and *Mathematical Pie*, both produced by the Mathematical Association. A network of local contacts and SYMS clubs is being set up and a penfriend scheme is planned. Adults can become a 'Friend of SYMS' (£10 minimum sub) receiving the same mailings, reports on progress, events, and news of maths activities for youngsters.

Young Archaeologists Club
Clifford Chambers, 4 Clifford Street, York YO1 1RD [0904 611944]. National club for 9s–18s wanting to know more about prehistoric monuments, Roman villas, castles, fascinated by archaeologists' work. Members' magazine gives news of recent discoveries, information about monuments, museums to explore, chances to work on excavations, go on field study holidays (11s upwards) in different parts of the country, or take part in activity days also in various parts of the country, or enter the annual Young Archaeologists of the Year award. Worth checking local

branches through schools, museums, who may arrange activities like site visits, fieldwork. Parents can help to get branches going. New: National Archaeologists' Day, in August, countrywide. Events of interest to all the family like site tours, handling and identifying artefacts, craft demonstrations, making mosaics, trying prehistoric pot-firing, levelling and surveying, competitions.

Young Ornithologists Club The Lodge, Sandy, Bedfordshire SG19 2DL. National club for up to 18s, members mostly 9s–14s, to encourage an interest in birds and wildlife among young people. Lively colour magazine *Bird Life* contains illustrations, articles by experts and members, quizzes, jokes, projects, competitions, information about 1-day events in various locations, holiday courses; annual competition for Young Ornithologists of the Year. Worth checking local branches through schools. Parents can help to get branches going.

Resources

Over the last few years there has been a considerable, and most welcome, expansion in the number of cities, towns, districts, gathering together and publicizing information about school holiday activities. You may find this in the local newspapers or in a booklet produced by Amenity, Leisure or Recreation Departments and to be found in libraries, sports centres, museums, schools.

Guardian Look for my What's On For Children' in the school holidays, nationally, published in the *Guardian* at least 10 days before the start of the major holidays, Easter, summer, Christmas.

Kidsline A personal service, so there are people at the other end when you ring [071-222 8070], weekdays, 9 a.m. to 4 p.m. in holidays, including half-terms, and 4–6 p.m. termtimes. With an astonishing battery of information they can answer straight questions about the nearest play-scheme, jazz club, disco, specific sports facilities, or how to get started in a new sport, interest, but are also accustomed to the less defined requirement and can offer ideas on what's on, exhibitions, films, shows, festivals, museum projects, all kinds of sports, or planning family outings, with all kinds of possibilities; area, say 30-mile radius of Central London.

Edinburgh The title could be *School's Out, Summer Splash, Xmas Extra, Eggciting,* for the Easter, summer and Christmas booklet about puppet shows, sports, museum workshops, story-telling, a variety of activities in the libraries, many free events. Find it in libraries, sports centres. Produced by the Department of Recreation, 17 Waterloo Place, Edinburgh EH1 3BG [031-557 1265].

Leicester Link Look for the July issue of the free monthly that goes into every home for information about play schemes, sports centres, activities in the parks.

Things to Do in Milton Keynes Wide age range, including pre-school, published Easter and summer holidays. Distributed through schools, information centres, otherwise PO Box 113, Civic Offices, 1 Saxon Gate East, Milton Keynes MK9 3HYN [0908 691691]. Tells of happenings in libraries, story-telling, craft workshops, bookworm clubs; any number of sports, opportunities, swimming, trampolining, golf, athletics, badminton, cycling, football, canoeing, rowing, sailing, tennis, squash, gymnastics, more; lots about play-schemes with many and varied programmes (arts, crafts, sports), about play parks, playgrounds, leisure centres, happenings in community workshops, in a country park, in a summer music camp, dates, information about shows indoors and outdoors.

Amenities Summertime, by City of Norwich Amenities Division, 15 Chapel Field, East Norwich NR32 1RN [22233]. About 'Tiddlers' Splashdown', meaning under-5s, or swimming lessons for 5s–12s, or coaching, different ages, in badminton, football, hockey, tennis, etc.; information about holiday play-schemes; shows, like Punch and Judy, and other sorts of fun and games, concerts, happenings for children.

Part three: Going it alone

Day camps

Here is such a good idea that I wonder nobody thought of it before. Well I didn't. It came from the United States. The basic idea is to offer children loads of physical and mental activities during the school holidays, for a fee. I always had a clutch of children, including my own, in the garden, the house, partly occupied with activities devised by me, some devised by them. Yes of course I met the 'I'm bored' groan. That's absolutely normal. But then I work in the house, as a freelance journalist, am around, can be moaned at.

So if I emphasize the day camps coming to the aid of working mothers, I am talking about where else, if you are away from the house and are prepared to pay the fees, you can find not only daytime care but lots of fun, interests, activities, outings, all the sort of things that become the memories of school holidays, and what you think/feel they should have.

But for women *not* working outside the home, and having to organize holidaytime outings (zoo, swim, stately home) or the interest of attendance at a local holidaytime play-scheme, then a week at a day camp can add an extra dimension.

For the children there is the advantage of a great variety of facilities indoors and outdoors on site. The camps are often held in large boarding schools which means not only equipment but space, and for a town child it's a country experience, grass, trees. Then, because they travel to the camp in the morning and come back home at night (not a case of parents taking off on their own holiday), they do not have to face the adjustment of a residential stay, which is why some camps can cater for under-5s who, like the school-age campers, may be collected and returned to specific points by coach, or otherwise travel privately. And there is the companionship of children their own age.

I visited the first day camp, Camp Beaumont, held in a

school near Windsor in summer 1981, doubting whether parents would produce the weekly fees. I was wrong. The pioneers, Stuart and Catherine Wiley (he experienced in the travel business, she experienced in family city-life when even a Hyde Park picnic with the children could be spoilt by marauding children) had to reassess for increased numbers even before the camp opened.

Children were organized into groups, colour-coded, under a monitor, usually a student, or for under-5s, someone with the appropriate experience. Over 30 different activities were offered and fitted into each child's chosen programme. So I saw children trailing off into the woods to find out what grew, why; sailing, windsurfing, canoeing; swimming with tuition; a drama group working away under sheltering trees; children off on ponies; some were gathering to go off on an outing; others making their way to a small farm enclosure to see how animals are cared for and to help make huts, cages. You will have gathered that it was a fine day and almost everybody was outdoors, so the chances for playing indoor games, like table tennis, or trying painting (among various handicrafts), were left for the time being. About the only children indoors were in the computer camp.

We foregathered for the midday meal (I had often been offered sweeties by children before then!) and I noticed then, and frequently through the day, how quickly children became buddies, in fact it was sitting around having a jaw that sometimes meant they missed their next programme bit and had to be reconnected by staff into their colour-coded group. I liked that, the 'Where do you live?', 'Where do *you* live?', 'Where's that?' Or 2 boys on land after windsurfing: 'Have you done that before?' 'No.' 'You were pretty good.' Sorry, I'm a reporter, I *do* eavesdrop!

So, an interesting new development. There may be a day camp in your district for your children. Worth checking, plus what's offered and costs.

I have listed here those running only non-residential activities. See pages 329–35 for both day and residential activities.

Lee Valley Leisure Park Myddelton House, Bulls Cross, Enfield, Middx EN2 9HG [0992 700766]. 5s–14s in appropriate programmes. Held in various locations within the park. Activities include many sports, film-making, computer games, arts, crafts, face-painting. Sporting Excellence courses. 1-day 'taster'. Collects and delivers over a considerable area.

St Albans Leisure Ltd Watling House, Dunstable Road, Redbourn, Herts AL3 7RG [0582 794023]. 6s–16s in appropriate programmes. Held in 2 local sports centres but also excursions. Activities include many sports, drama, pottery, photography, cookery, dance. Also a single full or half-day Tuesdays and Thursdays. Collects and delivers over a considerable area.

The following are members or associate members of the British Activity Holiday Association (see page 338).

Camp Aldenham Aldenham School, Elstree, Herts WD6 3AJ [0923 857553]. 3s–16s. Easter: multi-activity and special-interest courses in various sports, video-making, computing, summer over 50 activities and specialist soccer coaching camp.

Champion Day Camps Plas yn Llanfair TH, nr Abergele, Clwyd LL22 8RT [0745 84 318]. 3s–15s with special programmes for teenagers. Multi-activities based in Merseyside.

Genesis Leisure Ltd 213 Belsize Avenue, Woodston, Peterborough, Cambs PE2 9HY [0733 555 152]. 4s–14s. Multi-activity, horse riding, dry skiing. Day camps at Farnham, Bath, Warwick and Bristol.

Kingfisher Activity Centres Ltd 3 Crewe Curve, Berkhamsted, Herts HP4 1SE [0442 870649]. 3s–13s. Multi-activities in two Hertfordshire centres in Berkhamsted and Harpenden. Summer. Collects and delivers.

Leisure Leaders 48 Winchcombe Drive, Blackpole, Worcester WR4 9XA [0905 58068]. 5s–14s. Over 30 activities with many sports, art, motorbikes. In Worcestershire and Gloucestershire.

Multibase Day Camps 154 Heath Road, Twickenham TW1 4BN [081-744 2083]. 3s–14s. Half-terms as well as Easter and summer. Wide range of sports, performing and creative arts, computers. Centres: Twickenham, Richmond and Kingston-upon-Thames. Collects and delivers.

The Sport and Hobby Camp 25 Hammond Court, College Lawn, Cheltenham, Glos GLC53 7AF [0242 261 770]. 4s–11s. Sports, games, arts and crafts, drama. School locations in Malvern, Cheltenham, Pershore, Tewkesbury and Droitwich. Summer.

Wroxall Abbey Enterprises Ltd Wroxall Abbey School, Warwick CV35 7NB [0926 59866]. 4s–12s. Various sports, computing, pottery, pony rides, in Victorian mansion. Summer. Contact Course Director: Mrs D Harrison, 10 Queens Road, Kenilworth.

Staying away from home

To go on holiday alone, without a parent, is an adventure in itself, so it is understandable that so many such opportunities are described as 'adventure holidays', though really referring to chances to try out all kinds of different sports. My own children didn't want to know, taking the attitude 'You only want to get rid of us for a week' (as though that had *ever* crossed my mind!); not that the thought of rejection made any difference to their later travel across continents.

I think going alone is a great idea, first, of course, because the holiday is age-based, relating to the child, rather than the mix and match to be hoped for in the usual family holiday; I'd say lovely to have both.

The 'adventurer' then is offered a programme of varied or specific activities and entertainments, but also the new experience of living away from the familiar family framework and with other children from other parts of the country, some with different accents, different habits, maybe currently eating only certain foods (what mothers know as 'going through a phase'), but friendships are quickly made, everybody is in the same boat. It's a junior version of what happens in the early weeks at university, with adjustment, illumination about people other than relatives, neighbours, a lot of discovering far beyond the interests and activities offered.

Some centres offer escorted travel for youngsters.

Check in the brochures whether special clothing (most likely to be casual, and waterproof, maybe boots) should be taken or any particular equipment is needed – usually it's provided, but could be a musical instrument, a riding hat, a sleeping-bag, a torch, or even a tin opener should be taken along.

Opportunities are many and various in style. Do not assume your children will be cared for, supervised, **all the time**. Read the literature you have asked for carefully. If in doubt, ask.

Costs? Wide-ranging, since the opportunities extend from some organizations taking tents and own food to children staying in specialist sports centres or major educational complexes.

I emphasize about reading the brochures, literature. They should tell you just the style, taste, of the enterprise. Also the number catered for; can be many but if divided into small groups there is much the same familiarity as a class within a school.

Decisions, decisions, among the wide choice. No problem if there are definite addictions, otherwise what about tasting new, different activities? Where? Something nearby for the younger ones? Otherwise, if your children know the Lakes or Norfolk or Merseyside, from family holidays what about some degree of finding out about Cornwall, Devon, Sussex, also vice versa, of course, and referring to all round Britain.

If you cannot brace yourselves for the parting, and then feel guilty about depriving your children of such fun, take a look at *Time to Learn* (£2.50: National Institute of Adult Continuing Education, 19B De Montford Street, Leicester LE1 7GE, 0533 551451). About summer schools for adults but includes a number which provide separate and appropriate programmes for accompanying children. Examples Lancaster University, Millfield School.

Traditional

School journeys can provide a comforting introduction into this new experience, being among classmates and known teachers, but many children go off alone even before the school-journey age. Similarly, going camping with Scouts, Guides, Girls' or Boys' Brigade means a new experience in various ways but with the reassuring base of known companions, even parents or grandparents, running and/or supporting the expedition.

I am indebted to the Girls' Brigade's National Training Officer for an insight into the *receiving* end of going it alone (see also page 333):

'The child's background and environment help some children more than others, but it is impossible to generalize. There are children from secure stable backgrounds who do cope well away from home, but equally there are those who haven't a clue about what they should wear or how to perform a simple task, and in a number of cases it's not because the parents always do it for the youngster.

'Some young children have been to camp, glad to get away from the responsibility of coping with siblings, getting them washed, dressed, fed and looked after while a parent is at work – some are excellent little mothers and use their skills at camp to help other girls.

'Children from unsettled or broken homes are often insecure (but not always) and homesickness can be a problem, but so it is for the secure child. We very rarely have to resort to getting the child back home and get over the problem by letting the child help with some "special" duty, e.g. helping "cook" to perform her task. Being a one-to-one situation this sort of relationship helps the child to cope and to come to terms with the problem. A little cuddle also helps a great deal.

'Some children find it almost impossible to accept a disciplined way of life and camp does not prove the right place for them to be. These sort of problems usually indicate behavioural difficulties and sometimes these are sorted out at camp.

'There are children who get very upset at leaving a parent for a spell and will not show this. Sometimes they react by having an almost "imaginary" illness, or are spiteful, steal money and/or possessions from others, eat far more than they need at meals and especially sweets and show greediness in all sorts of ways.

'Children often find washing at camp difficult and will try and go unwashed. Whether this has anything to do with the child's background, laziness or some lack of privacy, the officer in charge will resolve the problem.

'Most children reflect their homes and parents in all sorts of ways and at camp this can mean good standards of behaviour, cleanliness and help to others, but can also mean the opposite when we see bad table manners and have words added to our vocabulary.'

Worth looking at the Girls' Brigade standards when you are sending your children off alone.

On the child side (or is it the parent's side?), I have twice (over a decade) known of boys who had to be collected from camps and brought home. Children do react in different ways. As to washing, I liked the explanation given by a brother and sister who had been camping but were tardy about taking baths when they got home because the dirt reminded them of the marvellous time they had had at the Forest School Camps! But then mothers are not surprised when boys, particularly, return with their clothes in the same clean condition as when packed for departure.

The Boys' Brigade 1 Galena Road, Hammersmith, London W6 0LT [081-741 4001]. But find your local company through school, library, CABs. 8s–11s can go to permanent camps, in buildings, so sleeping in bunks rather than on groundsheets, but at weekends they can try the traditional tented camps available for the 11s plus. The weekend allowance is by way of an introduction for future camping. The original purpose of BB camping was to give city and town dwellers an introduction to the countryside and to an outdoor life that for them at the time was quite unknown. Camps are run by officers and helpers, nowadays supported by older boys of the Brigade. Some have lady helpers taking charge of catering and cooking but many are run by officers entirely. Lots of activities of the sporting and adventurous nature, games, potted sports, cross-country running, exploration, also visits to local places of interest. Add 'light-weight' camping for the experienced 14 plus. For the uninformed, as I was, this means a tent you can swiftly erect yourself, even in a gale, and take down when you move on. It will pack on to your back, but it's just for sleeping, you cannot stand up in it. This is allied to the Duke of Edinburgh's Award, meaning you fend for yourself in a personal test. It all adds up to adventure at different age levels.

The Girls' Brigade Girls' Brigade House, Foxhall Road, Didcot, Oxon OX11 7BQ [0235 510425]. Find local group through grapevine, library, etc. 8s upwards go to camp, run by someone at least 20 years old, holding a GB Camping Certificate, signifying training. Camps can be in schools, various halls, conference centres, boats, providing catering or self-catering. From 11 is usually the age for Canvas Camps, which range from running water, showers, flush loos, to an empty field with a waterpipe and all facilities, including chemical toilets, tents, cooking, to be loaned, hired or bought. Case of learning 'how to' without mechanized appliances. Activities can include nature trails, walking, tracking, orienteering; any number of sports, expeditions to castles, museums, trips by steam train, coach, boat. Otherwise competitions, games, camp fire activities. Strict ratio of adults to children and, in joint camps (girls and boys) ratio of women maintained. Two companies for the disabled (in schools for their particular disability) otherwise the disabled are integrated into the normal company and go to camp with their friends.

Girl Guides Association 17–19 Buckingham Palace Road, London SW1W 0PT [071-834 6242]. But you would find your local group on the school grapevine, or through the library or CABs. A Brownie (7s–10s) can go on a Pack Holiday, that is with other Brownies from her Pack, staying in a building that could be a school, church hall, and in beds. Duties like helping lay table, prepare vegetables, etc. Otherwise games, fun. Adults in charge will hold a GGA licence, after training, or look after catering, or first aid; add assisting Guides, also volunteering parents. Parents are asked to attend parents' meetings but otherwise to check on clothes, pocket money, visiting, letter-writing, and reassuring daughter for the adventure ahead.

Guide camps 10s–15s do mean camping, collecting wood, fetching water, caring for own tents. Otherwise games, nature study, expeditions, camp fire activities (devising fancy dress, from what?). Guider in charge has gained GGA licence, assistants will care for catering, first aid. Add those qualified to superintend swimming, pony-trekking, canoeing, etc. Write letters, provide a SAE or card, for daughter to post.

Leaflets for parents on both age groups published by GGA.

Scout Association Baden-Powell House, Queen's Gate, London SW7 5JS [071-584 7030]. But you would check your local group through school grapevine, library, CABs, even get on to the waiting list, to join. Cub scouts (8s–10^1/2s) can go on Pack Holidays (suitable accommodation) or camps under canvas, expecting some

chores. Programme emphasis on outdoor and adventurous activities. Leader has undertaken training (I spent a day at Gilwell Park, the SA Training Centre, near London, and was astonished by the variety of skills being acquired by those attending, all voluntary, of course).

Scouts (10^1/2–15^1/2) operate in a gang of friends called the Patrol. Their activities may be indoor or outdoor but Patrol Camps are encouraged. The Scout Leader has the responsibility for the Scouts, knowing where they intend to go and what activities they wish to undertake and that safeguards have been taken into account. However, Patrol Camps take place without an adult. The Scout Leader checks the expedition is properly planned and worked through, that there is necessary training for activities they wish to undertake, or that they are going to a place where suitable instruction given.

Recommend same points as under Girl Guides Association: writing letters to younger ones, providing stamped methods of correspondence for older ones.

Field Studies Council Preston Montford, Montford Bridge, Shrewsbury SY4 1HW [0734 850674]. Examples of kind of week-long courses for unaccompanied children, 12s upwards, during summer holidays, with staff in charge. At Dale Fort Field Centre, Dale, Haverfordwest, Dyfed: introducing young people to the natural history of the Pembrokeshire Coast National Park, concentrating on looking at flowers, birds, mammals, seashore life and including a visit to Skomer Island to see breeding sea-birds and seals. At Montford Bridge: a course for the young enthusiast covering mammal-trapping, badger-watching, pond-dipping, bird-watching, some botanizing and searching for fossils and minerals. Entertainments like slide shows etc. in the evenings. Accommodation shared bedrooms.

Forest School Camps New enquiries secretary, c/o 110 Burbage Road, London SE24 9HD [071-242 7566]. Long-established charity with more or less all-year-round camping, each camp becoming a community. Easter and summer camps suggested for first introduction, even from 6½ years (and including those with disabilities). Children learn how to camp, put up a tent, make fires, cook food, keep dry. Events can include swimming, exploring, country dancing, walks, camp fires, games. Camps, say from 8s upwards, can include exploring waterways, kiln- and oven-building, rope-work like hammocks, bridges, swings, making rafts, lots of walking. Read the brochure carefully to understand the philosophy.

Youth Hostels Association Trevelyan House, 8 St Stephens Hill, St Albans, Hertfordshire AL1 2DY [0727 55215]. Object: 'To help all, especially young people of limited means, to a greater knowledge, love and care of the countryside, particularly by providing hostels or other simple accommodation for them in their travels, and thus to promote their health, rest and education.' Members, even 12s upwards, can use hostels on their own. Also families of course. Accommodation in hostels, increasingly modernized, where young are expected to make own bed (why not?) but read up on what they need to take along. Recommend getting handbooks, scope extraordinary.

'**Great Escapes**' [0727 45047], wide choice of activities, sailing, windsurfing, pony-trekking, archery, orienteering, hillwalking, mountain biking, etc. Easter, summer, winter. 12s–15s, also up to 18s, and families. Participating non-members get a year's free YHA membership, members a free membership renewal. (BAHA member see page 338).

Two Youth Hostels in Wales specifically designed for the handicapped. Facilities elsewhere vary so best to check. *YHA of Northern Ireland, 56 Badbury Place, Belfast BT7 1RU [0232 224733]; Irish Youth Hostel Association, 39 Mountjoy Square, Dublin [0001 745734]; Scottish Youth Hostels Association, 7 Glebe Crescent, Stirling FK8 2JA. Different areas offer different activities, interests.*

Activity holidays

The American custom of sending the children on holiday alone to 'summer camp' is now taking hold here in what can be fairly classed as the first generation since previous chances in that direction like Forest Camps and the, now sadly closed-down, Colony Holidays. Yet we have not adapted their term, not necessarily because there are also Easter opportunities. Here they are more likely to be called 'adventure' or 'activity' holidays because constant action is laid on.

The choice of activities is wide with just about every suitable land and water sport and many forms of art and drama. There are centres or programmes concentrating on, say, tennis or riding for those wanting to polish skills but 'multi-activity' is the widely used term in this business meaning providing tasters according to choice. This is good value because children have a go at something they fancy and probably get it out of their system with all gear provided instead of being kitted out by parents at considerable expense for what turns out to be only a 9-day wonder.

Locations are likely to be the independent boarding schools with their already built-in facilities for the young, indoors like sleeping and eating, outdoors for letting off steam. Children are divided into groups with their own leaders, young adults known by their Christian names, to look after them. Beamont and PGL are the firms offering a wide spread of such places though PGL also owns many of its centres. Some schools run their own holidaytime projects; Millfield becomes a 'Village of Education' in the summer.

Then there is another group, enterprises which function all year, generally on their own premises, catering for termtime school groups, so again they have the facilities and staff for the school holidaytime programme.

8s–13s are the main core for this useful experience of living away from home in a community and adjusting to children from other parts of the country, even other countries. A large school can take 1000 a week including teenagers, all in groups according to age. One 6- or 7-year-old can take to it like a duck to water, another 8–9-year-old might not. You will know your

own child. In uncertainty or maybe with a first-timer consider a
family-style atmosphere like Mill on the Brue.

It is hard to conceive that anybody can set up an adventure
or activity holiday scheme. There is no protective legislation.
Holiday organizers have told me of people ringing up to 'pick
their brains' with the attitude that it 'could be fun' to run
something 'for the kiddies'. Laudably the industry founded the
'British Activity Holiday Association', literally self-policing (see
page 338). The centres I have listed are members. I have
picked out some examples. This is not the full membership.

**British Activity Holiday
Association** Norton Terrace,
Llandrindod Wells, Powys LD1
6AE [0597 823902]. 'The only
legislation we had to worry about
was paying VAT on our takings. If
we had wanted to open dog
kennels it would have taken 18
months, so much legislation.' Bill
Higginson, ex-public-school
cricket coach, recalling when he
and his wife Liz started activity
holidays for youngsters some 18
years ago. 'Anybody can put an
advert in the paper saying "Send
your children to us and they will
have a wonderful time." They
could have a criminal record, be
child molesters. Responsible
people in the holiday business
think this situation is
horrendous.'

In January 1986 a Consumer's
Association *Which* report on 12
centres came to disturbing
conclusions on hazards and poor
practices and recommended
government action. In February
1986, with Bill as the catalyst,
activity-holiday organizers
formed BAHA. Founder
members spent a lot of time in a
fruitless attempt to get
government action. So they
proceeded with self-policing and
incidentally self-financing since
efforts for sponsorship were also
fruitless.

The Sports Council chaired its
steering group which drafted a
Constitution and Code of
Practice, the latter being
endorsed by the Office of Fair
Trading. BAHA has set up a
system of inspection of
members' centres. It is probably
unique in functioning for both
its members and for the
consumer. Guidelines are
provided to parents on the
selection of suitable holiday
arrangements and the
association provides an
Arbitration and Consumer
Advice Service.

Pack, £3, contains Consumer
Guide with region-by-region
index and thumbnail sketches of
activities offered by each centre,
printed sheet listing centres
offering particular activities
requested, i.e. football coaching,
tennis, English as a Foreign
Language courses, day camp
operators, and an update on
members. Over a quarter of
enquiries come from abroad.
Some examples of members and
associate members. Residential
only unless 'day' specified.

Action Holidays Ltd Windrush,
Bexton Lane, Knutsford,
Cheshire WA16 9BP [0565
654775]. Multi-activities, day and
residential, in Cheshire,
Hampshire and Surrey. For
3s–15s. Summer.

Anglian Sports Promotions
28 Everington's Lane, Skegness,
Lincs [0754 610288]. Coaching
in soccer, hockey, golf, athletics,
swimming, tennis, archery. At
Kimbolton School. 8s–16s.
Summer.

Ardmore Adventure Ltd 11–15
High Street, Marlow, Bucks
SL7 1AU [0628 890060].
Multi-activities in 20 centres, day
and residential. 6s–16s.

Beaumanor Hall Adventure Holidays Beaumanor Hall, Woodhouse, nr Loughborough LE12 8TX [0509 890119]. Multi-activities, some under canvas. 10s–16s. Summer.

Camp Beaumont 9 West Street, Godmanchester, Cambs PE18 8HG [0480 456123]. Multi-activities, also specialist camps like riding, computers, stage and screen, English language. Day: Wimbledon, Ascot, Leatherhead, Orpington, Brentwood, with collection and delivery. Residential, mostly independent boarding schools, Norfolk, Clwyd, Staffordshire, Devon. 3s–17s, with 3s–5s a separate group and 13s–17s Teen Camp.

Escapade Activity Holidays 7 Birch Lea Close, Bury, Lancs BL9 9RZ [061-764 1684]. Multi-activities, day (3s–14s), residential (6s–18s). Stanmore, London, and Derbyshire. Easter and summer.

Experience UK Ltd Poolside Manor, Lyndhurst Gardens, Finchley, London N3 1TD [081-349 1444]. Multi-activities, day (3s–13s), residential (6s–16s). Various locations.

Freetime Camps 149–151 Goldsworth Road, Woking, Surrey GU21 1LS [0483 740242]. Multi-activities, also specialist tennis, windsurfing and golf camps. Multi-activity day and residential in Surrey and Hampshire. 4s–16s. Easter and summer.

Heart of Wales Riding Holidays Tyddu, Dolau, Llandrindod Wells, Powys LD1 5TB [0597 87 884]. Lessons in basic riding, dressage, cross-country, show-jumping. Trekking in Radnor Hills. 8s–16s.

Isca Children's Holidays Bonnaford, Brentor, Tavistock, West Devon PL19 0LX [0822 810514]. Activity and riding holidays. Royal School, Bath, summer, in Devon Easter. 7s–15s.

Kids Klub The Hall, Great Finborough, nr Stowmarket, Suffolk 1P14 3EF [0449 675907]. Activities include camping, golf, arts, crafts, abseiling, English language tuition. 5s–16s. Easter and summer.

Kudos Activity Holidays Ltd 25 Plants Hollow, Brierley Hill, West Midlands DY5 2BZ. Multi-activities, day and residential, in 5 centres around the Midlands. 3s–16s.

Merlin Activity and Adventure Holidays Freepost, 120 Allerton Road, Liverpool L18 2DG [051-734 2477]. Canoeing, windsurfing, sailing, abseiling, orienteering, in Llanberis, North Wales. Day and residential. 6–18.

Mill on the Brue Activity Centre Trendle Farm, Bruton, Somerset BA10 0BA [0749 812307]. Based on 2 old farmhouses surrounded by 80 acres of fields, woods. Over 30 activities to taste, climbing, abseiling, canoeing, grass skiing, assault courses, pony riding, video-making, orienteering, problem-solving, camping. 8s–14s. Easter, summer and autumn holidays. Day and residential. Separate 'Mendip Challenge' for 14s–17s.

Millfield Village of Education Street, Somerset BA16 0YD [0458 45823]. Quantities of sports, computers, dance, drama, board games, arts, crafts in multi-activity programme. 8s upwards. Summer. Family holidays.

PGL Young Adventure Ltd Alton Court, Penyard Lane, Ross-on-Wye, Herefordshire HR9 5NR [0989 768 768]. Probably the oldest established and the largest. Multi-activity including abseiling, orienteering, pony riding, motor sports. Also specialist holidays, motor sports, golf, tennis, riding, stage, video, nature watch, English language, and, unusual, a week on a working farm, sleeping under canvas. Wide range of different styles of locations. Day camps also in all the multi-activity centres with the chance of a couple of days taking pot luck on what is going on. 3s–18s with the littlest having their own groupings and adventures. Also holidays in Europe and America. Family holidays.

Prime Leisure The Old Mill, Mill Street, Wantage, Oxfordshire

OX12 9AB [0235 770261]. Multi-activities in different locations in southern England. Day (non-residential) Easter and summer, 4s–14s, residential in summer 8s–16s.

Sports Experience 12a Merton Parade, London SW19 3NT [081-543 4207]. Sports but also computers, drama, video film-making in 12 centres in south-east England and a Welsh adventure centre. Day and residential. 5s–17s.

Trekkas Ltd 26 Heathgate, Hertford Heath, Herts SG13 7PR [0992 586 858]. Adventure and sports holidays. Residential camping and a specialist tennis coaching course at Haileybury College, Hertford. Non-residential activities in Hertford, Hitchin and Sevenoaks. 4s–15s. Summer.

Young Leisure Activity Holidays Ltd Rock Park Centre, Llandrindod Wells, Powys LD1 6AE [0597 822021]. Run by the Higginson family, see under BAHA. Activities include canoeing, windsurfing, sailing, abseiling, orienteering, pottery, swimming, assault course, raft-building, overnight camping, excursions. English language tuition. Also daytime, non-residential, 1 day or several. 7s–16s.

Names and Places Index

Subject Index